JAPAN'S NEW SECURITY PARTNERSHIPS

Manchester University Press

Japan's new security partnerships
Beyond the security alliance

EDITED BY WILHELM VOSSE AND
PAUL MIDFORD

Manchester University Press

Copyright © Manchester University Press 2018

While copyright in the volume as a whole is vested in Manchester University Press, copyright in individual chapters belongs to their respective authors, and no chapter may be reproduced wholly or in part without the express permission in writing of both author and publisher.

Published by Manchester University Press
Altrincham Street, Manchester M1 7JA
www.manchesteruniversitypress.co.uk

British Library Cataloguing-in-Publication Data
A catalogue record for this book is available from the British Library

ISBN 978 1 5261 2312 1 hardback
ISBN 978 1 5261 5176 6 paperback

First published 2018

The publisher has no responsibility for the persistence or accuracy of URLs for any external or third-party internet websites referred to in this book, and does not guarantee that any content on such websites is, or will remain, accurate or appropriate.

Book cover design by Wilhelm Vosse. Copyright of the photo granted by Ministry of Defense of Japan. It shows a Japanese MSDF and a Royal Australian Navy vessel at the KAKADU 2016 multinational maritime joint exercise, hosted by the Royal Australian Navy from 12–24 September 2016 in and around Darwin, Australia. Ministry of Defense of Japan. 2016. Japan Defence Focus, Issue 81 (October), p. 5, at: http://www.mod.go.jp/e/jdf/sp/no81/sp_topics.html.

Typeset by Deanta Global Publishing Services

CONTENTS

List of figures—vii
List of tables—viii
Notes on contributors—ix
List of abbreviations—xiv

Introduction *Wilhelm Vosse and Paul Midford*	1

Part I: Japan–Australia security partnership

1 The Australian perspective on the security partnership with Japan *Thomas S. Wilkins*	19
2 The Japanese perspective on the security partnership with Australia *Yusuke Ishihara*	36

Part II: Japan–India security partnership

3 The Indian perspective on the security partnership with Japan *Madhuchanda Ghosh*	57
4 The Japanese perspective on the security partnership with India *Satoru Nagao*	73

Part III: Japan–Southeast Asia security partnership

5 Japan's multilateral security cooperation with East Asia *Paul Midford*	89
6 The East Asia perspective on the security partnership with Japan *Stephen R. Nagy*	112
7 The Philippine perspective on the security partnership with Japan *Renato Cruz De Castro*	130
8 The Vietnamese perspective on the security partnership with Japan *Swee Lean Collin Koh*	149
9 The Japanese perspective on the security partnership with Vietnam *Bjørn Elias Mikalsen Grønning*	173

Part IV: Japan–Europe security partnership

10 The Japanese perspective on the security partnership with the EU *Akiko Fukushima*	187
11 The European perspective on the security partnership with Japan *Axel Berkofsky*	203

Contents

12 EU–Japan security partnership in practice: The counter-piracy
    mission off the coast of Somalia   *Wilhelm Vosse*   219

Conclusion   *Wilhelm Vosse and Paul Midford*   236

Appendix—244
Index—246

LIST OF FIGURES

4.1	China's naval activities around Japan	74
4.2	Influential area of empires in the sub-continent	79

LIST OF TABLES

I.1	Level of security integration (as of 2017)	7
4.1	The list of India's military operations	83
6.1	Balance of power strategy as an outcome of the interaction of economic dependency and threat perception	116
6.2	Country categorisation regarding economic dependency v. threat perception	116
8.1	Visits to Vietnam by JMSDF and JCG	159
12.1	EU NAVFOR–MSDF encounters in 2015 and 2016	224
12.2	EU NAVFOR–MSDF exercises and training between 2014 and 2016	225
C.1	Trade dependency with Japan (2015–2016)	238
C.2	Trade dependency with China (2015–2016)	239

NOTES ON CONTRIBUTORS

Axel Berkofsky is a senior lecturer at the University of Pavia, Italy, and a senior associate research fellow at the Milan-based Istituto per gli Studi di Politica Internazionale (ISPI). He is also an Executive Committee board member at the Stockholm-based European Japan Advanced Research Network (EJARN) and research affiliate at the EU Centre for Japanese Studies at the Stockholm School of Economics. Previously, he was senior policy analyst and associate policy analyst at the European Policy Centre (EPC) and research fellow at the European Institute for Asian Studies (EIAS), both in Brussels, and also lectured and taught at numerous think-tanks, research institutes and universities in Europe and Asia. His research interests are Japanese and Chinese foreign and security policies, Chinese history, Cold War history, Asian security and EU–Asia relations. He has authored two and edited four books and has widely published articles and essays in academic journals, as well as newspapers and magazines. Recent publications include *A Pacifist Constitution for an Armed Empire* (FrancoAngeli, Milan 2012), *Understanding China* (co-edited with Silvio Beretta and Lihong Zhang, Springer 2017), and 'ASEM and the Security Agenda: Talking the Talk but also Walking the Walk?' in Gaens and Khandekar (eds.) *Inter-Regional Relations and the Asia–Europe Meeting (ASEM)* (Palgrave 2017).

Renato Cruz De Castro is a professor in the International Studies Department, De La Salle University, Manila, and holds the Charles Lui Chi Keung Professorial Chair in China Studies. He recently held visiting research positions at the Japan Institute of International Affairs (JIIA) and the East-West Center in Washington DC as the U.S.–ASEAN Fulbright Initiative Researcher. In 2009, he was the US State Department ASEAN Research Fellow from the Philippines and was based in the Political Science Department of Arizona State University. He taught international relations and security studies at the National Defense College and the Foreign Service Institute (Philippines), is a member of the Board of Trustees of the Albert Del Rosario Institute for Strategic and International Studies (ADR Institute), and was a consultant in the National Security Council of the Philippines during the Aquino administration. He earned his PhD from the Government and International Studies Department of the University of South Carolina, and is an alumnus of the Daniel Inouye Asia-Pacific Center for Security Studies in Hawaii, US. He has written over ninety articles on international relations and security.

Akiko Fukushima is a professor in the School of Global Studies and Collaboration, Aoyama Gakuin University. She holds a PhD from Osaka University and an MA from the Paul H. Nitze School of Advanced International

Notes on contributors

Studies (SAIS), Johns Hopkins University. She is also a non-resident fellow of the Lowy Institute, Australia. In the past, she held positions as adjunct professor at Keio University Law School, Director of Policy Studies at the National Institute for Research Advancement (NIRA), senior fellow at the Japan Foundation and a visiting scholar of CSIS, US. She also served on Japanese government, committees including the Advisory Council on National Security and Defense Capabilities and the Advisory Council of Ministry of Foreign Affairs. Her publications include 'Multilateralism Recalibrated' in *Postwar Japan* (CSIS, 2017), 'Global Merits of Alliance: A Japanese Perspective' in *The US–Japan Security Alliance* (Palgrave, 2011), *Conflict and Cultural Diplomacy* (Keio University Press, 2012), 'Japan's Perspective on Asian Regionalism' in *Asia's New Multilateralism* (Columbia University Press, 2009), 'Human Security and Global Governance' in *Security Politics in the Asia-Pacific* (Cambridge University Press, 2009) and *Japanese Foreign Policy: The Emerging Logic of Multilateralism* (Palgrave Macmillan, 1999).

Madhuchanda Ghosh is an assistant professor in the Department of Political Science at the Presidency University, Kolkata, India. She received her PhD in India–Japan Relations from the Jadavpur University, Kolkata. Her research interest is foreign policy studies pertaining to India, the US, Japan and China. She conducted extended research in Japan and has been the recipient of Japan Foundation fellowships in 2011 and 2014. In 2014, she was a Visiting Japan Foundation Scholar at Rikkyo University, Tokyo, and in 2006, visiting researcher at the Graduate School of Political Science and Economics, Waseda University, Tokyo, as a Tokyo Foundations SYLFF fellow. She is the editor of three books, of which the latest is *USA's Policy towards China, India and Japan* (Atlantic Publishers, 2013). Other publications include 'India's Economic Dynamism and India–Japan Relations' in *An Introduction to Contemporary India–Japan Relations* (University of Tokyo Press, 2017) and 'India and Japan's Growing Synergy: From a Political to a Strategic Focus' (*Asian Survey* 48:2, 2008).

Bjørn Elias Mikalsen Grønning is Centre for Asian Security Studies Research Fellow at the Norwegian Institute for Defence Studies. He holds a doctoral degree in Political Science from the Norwegian University of Science and Technology with a dissertation examining Japan's security policy response to the contemporary power shift in China's favour. He has served as a trainee at the Royal Norwegian Embassy in Tokyo, as a visiting research fellow at Keio University and as a specially appointed researcher at Osaka University. The topics of his publications include Japan's security, defence and alliance policy, missile defence and maritime security. He is the author of 'Japan's Shifting Military Priorities: Counterbalancing China's Rise' (*Asian Security*, 2014) and co-author of 'Protecting the Status Quo: Japan's Response to the Rise of China' in Ross and Tunsjo (eds.) *Strategic Adjustment and the Rise of China: Power and Politics in East Asia* (Cornell University Press, 2017).

Notes on contributors

Yusuke Ishihara is a research fellow at the National Institute for Defense Studies (NIDS) of the Ministry of Defense, Japan. His expertise is Japanese foreign policy in the Asia-Pacific region. In 2014 to 2015, he served as a deputy director at International Policy Division, Bureau of Defense Policy, where he handled Japan's security engagement with ASEAN and regional multilateral institutions in Asia. His publications include 'Japan–Australia Defense Cooperation in the Asia Pacific Region' in *ANU–NIDS Joint Research: Beyond Hub and Spokes* (Tokyo: NIDS), March 2014, pp. 93–122, and *Japan–Australia Security Relations and the Rise of China*, UNISCI Discussion Papers, No. 32, May 2013, pp. 81–98. He is also the author of the Australia chapter in the recent series of *East Asian Strategic Review* (EASR), and NIDS annual report on security affairs in Asia and beyond.

Swee Lean Collin Koh is a research fellow at the Maritime Security Programme, the Institute of Defence and Strategic Studies, which is a constituent unit of the S. Rajaratnam School of International Studies, based in Nanyang Technological University, Singapore. He has research interests in naval affairs in the Indo-Pacific, focusing on Southeast Asia. Collin has published several op-eds, policy and academic journal articles, as well as chapters for edited volumes covering his research areas. His most recent publications include: *In for the Long Haul: Sustaining the INDOMALPHI Trilateral Maritime and Air Patrols in the Sulu/Celebes Seas* (Naval Forces, 2017); 'Reasons for Optimism? China, Japan and Unilateral Naval Restraint in the East China Sea', in Alan Chong (ed.), *International Security in the Asia-Pacific: Transcending ASEAN towards Transitional Polycentrism* (2017); and *Incident Prevention and Mitigation in the Asia Pacific Littorals: Framing, Expanding, and Adding to CUES*, co-written with Graham Ong-Webb and Bernard Miranda in the RSIS Working Papers series (2017). Collin has also taught on Singapore Armed Forces professional military education and training courses. Besides research and teaching, he also contributes his perspectives to various local and international media outlets, and participates in activities with geopolitical risks consultancies.

Paul Midford is a professor, and director of the Japan Program, at the Norwegian University of Science and Technology (NTNU) in Trondheim. Midford received his PhD in Political Science from Columbia University in 2001. His research interests include Japanese foreign and defence policies, the impact of public opinion on policy, renewable energy and energy security, and East Asian security and multilateralism. He has published over two dozen book chapters, has co-edited seven books, and has published articles in *International Organization, International Studies Quarterly, Security Studies, Pacific Review, Asian Survey, Japan Forum* and *International Relations of the Asia-Pacific*. Midford is the author of *Rethinking Japanese Public Opinion and Security: From Pacifism to Realism?* (Stanford University Press, 2011), the co-editor of *The Japanese Ground Self-Defense Force: Search for Legitimacy* (Palgrave, 2017), and *New Directions in Japan's Security: Non-U.S.*

Notes on contributors

Centric Evolution (Routledge, 2020), and author of *Overcoming Isolationism: Japan's Leadership in East Asian Security Multilateralism* (Stanford University Press, 2020).

Satoru Nagao is a research fellow at the Institute for Future Engineering (strategy, defence policy), a visiting research fellow at the Research Institute for Oriental Cultures at Gakushuin University, and a research fellow at the Japan Forum for Strategic Studies. He is also a senior fellow at the Institute of National Security Studies Sri Lanka, a senior research fellow of the Indian Military Review, a research fellow at the Security and Strategy Research Institute for Japan, and a lecturer at Aoyama Gakuin University (Tokyo) and Komazawa University. He was awarded his PhD by Gakushuin University in 2011. His recent publications include 'The Role of Japan–India–Sri Lanka Maritime Security Cooperation in the Trump Era' (*Maritime Affairs: Journal of the National Maritime Foundation of India*, 2017), 'The Importance of a Japan–India Amphibious Aircraft Deal' (*The Diplomat*, 2016), and *The Japan-India-Australia Alliance as Key Agreement in the Indo-Pacific* (ISPSW Publication, 375, 2015).

Stephen R. Nagy is a senior associate professor in the Department of Politics and International Studies at the International Christian University. Previously he was an assistant professor at the Department of Japanese Studies at the Chinese University of Hong Kong from December 2009 to January 2014. He obtained his PhD from Waseda University, Japan in International Relations in 2008. He has published widely in peer-reviewed international journals such as *China Perspectives*, *East Asia*, the *Journal of Asian Politics and History* and the *International Studies Review* on trade, nationalism and China–Japan relations. He has also published in think-tanks and commercial outlets such as the *China Economic Quarterly* and the *World Commerce Review* on trade and political risk. His most recent funded research project is 'Sino-Japanese Relations in the Wake of the 2012 Territorial Disputes: Investigating Changes in Japanese Business' Trade and Investment Strategy in China'. Currently, he is conducting a research project entitled 'Perceptions and Drivers of Chinese View on Japanese and US Foreign Policy in the Region'.

Wilhelm Vosse is Professor of Political Science and International Relations at the International Christian University (ICU) in Tokyo, Japan, where he also served as director of the Social Science Research Institute (SSRI). He has held positions at the University of Hanover, Germany, and Keio University, Tokyo, and visiting research positions at the University of Warwick, University of Oxford and Harvard University. His research interests include Japanese foreign and security policy, and the domestic discourse on defence issues. Current research projects deal with Japan's new security partnerships, maritime piracy, and cyberspace and international relations. Recent publications include 'Learning Multilateral Military and Political Cooperation in the Counter-Piracy Missions'

(*The Pacific Review*, 2017), 'Heightened Threat Perception and the Future of Japan's Anti Militarism' in Vosse, Drifte and Blechinger-Talcott (eds.) *Governing Insecurity in Japan. The Domestic Discourse and Policy Response* (Routledge, 2014), and 'Comparing Japanese, Australian and European Responses to "Out-of-Area" Security Challenges' in Tow and Kersten (eds.) *Bilateral Perspectives on Regional Security. Australia, Japan, and the Asia-Pacific Region* (Palgrave Macmillan, 2012). He is also the co-editor of five books, of which the most recent are *Governing Insecurity in Japan: The Domestic Discourse and Policy Response* (Routledge, 2014), and *New Directions in Japan's Security: Non-U.S. Centric Evolution* (Routledge, 2020).

Thomas S. Wilkins is a senior lecturer in the Department of Government and International Relations at the University of Sydney. He specialises in Asia-Pacific regional security issues, including alliances/alignment, Australia–Japan relations and middle powers. He received his doctorate from the University of Birmingham in the UK (with one year spent at Johns Hopkins University as exchange student) and conducted post-doctoral work at the University of San Francisco and East-West Center, Honolulu. He has since been a Japan Foundation and Japanese Society for the Promotion of Sciences fellowship recipient at the University of Tokyo, totalling two years, and is a visiting associate professor at the University of Hong Kong. He has published in journals such as *Review of International Studies*, *International Relations of the Asia Pacific*, *Pacific Review*, *Australian Journal of International Affairs*, *Asia Policy* and *Asian Security*.

LIST OF ABBREVIATIONS

ACSA	Acquisition and Cross-Servicing Agreement
ADIZ	Air Defence Identification Zone
AIIB	Asian Infrastructure Investment Bank
APT	ASEAN+3
ARF	ASEAN Regional Forum
ASDF	Japanese Air Self-Defense Force
ASEAN	Association of Southeast Asian Nations
CCG	China Coast Guard
CMS	China Maritime Surveillance
ECS	East China Sea
EEAS	European External Action Service
FLEC	Fisheries Law Enforcement Command
HA/DR	Humanitarian Assistance/Disaster Relief
ISA	Information Sharing Agreement
JAEPA	Japan–Australia Economic Partnership Agreement
JCG	Japanese Coast Guard
JSDF	Japanese Self-Defense Force
Kantei	The Prime Minister of Japan and His Cabinet
MOD	Ministry of Defense of Japan
MOFA	Ministry of Foreign Affairs of Japan
MSDF	Japanese Maritime Self-Defense Force
NDPG	National Defense Program Guidelines (of Japan)
NSS	National Security Strategy (of Japan)
PN	Philippine navy
ReCAAP	Agreement on Combating Piracy and Armed Robbery against Ships in Asia
SCS	South China Sea
SDF	Japanese Self-Defense Forces
UNPKO	United Nations Peacekeeping Operation
VCG	Vietnam Coast Guard
VFA	Visiting Forces Agreement
VPN	Vietnam People's Navy

Introduction

Wilhelm Vosse and Paul Midford

THE SECURITY ENVIRONMENT in East Asia is in the process of fundamental change. Core factors are the rise of China as a superpower and its assertive security policy, the North Korean nuclear weapons and ballistic missile programme, and territorial conflicts in the East and South China Seas, as well as maritime and energy security. While the US has been the sole security provider for Japan since 1952, beginning with the end of the Cold War and particularly after the US wars in Iraq and Afghanistan, the Japanese government has become increasingly concerned about the US commitment to protect Japanese territorial interests (abandonment). On the other hand, American pressure on Japan to deploy the Self-Defense Forces (SDF) to Iraq and join the so-called 'coalition of the willing' in 2004 increased the fear of entrapment.

As one response to these concerns, over the last two decades, Japan has begun to broaden and deepen its security cooperation not only with countries in East Asia, but also with Australia, India, the EU and some of its member states. During Shinzō Abe's second term as prime minister (since 2012), these security partnerships have been further intensified and now include military cooperation, the exchange and joint acquisition of military hardware, joint military exercises and capacity building.

The main purpose of this volume is to analyse these new security ties and look at them from both sides: the Japanese as well as the partner country. While most recent books on Japanese security policy focus exclusively on the Japanese perspective, its alliance relationship with the US, the debate in Japan, positions of Japanese government leaders, and to some degree the public discourse, such as the still strong support for anti-militarist values among the Japanese public and some political parties, this book argues that Japanese security policy is also influenced by the blossoming cooperation with, and the specific demands and interests of, these new partner countries.

During the Cold War, Japan essentially pursued an isolationist security strategy, eschewing security ties with every other country save one, the US. However, with the end of the Cold War, Japan began moving away from security isolationism and towards security engagement with a broadening range of partners. Tokyo began security dialogues with the Soviet Union/Russia, China and South Korea. As discussed in Midford's chapter, Japan, on the cusp of the Cold War's end in 1991, abandoned its opposition to regional security multilateralism and proposed a regional multilateral security dialogue, an important antecedent to the establishment of the Association of Southeast Asian Nations (ASEAN) Regional Forum (ARF) in 1993. Participation in the ARF allowed Japan to discuss security with a wide variety of countries and engage in limited forms of security cooperation, such as devising confidence-building measures (CBMs) and holding joint disaster relief exercises. This in turn encouraged Japanese leadership to promote multilateral maritime security cooperation, specifically through proposing the Regional Cooperation Agreement on Combating Piracy and Armed Robbery against Ships in Asia (ReCAAP), soon after the turn of the century. At the global level, the end of the Cold War saw Japan beginning to send the SDF overseas for the first time to participate in UN peacekeeping operations in Asia, Africa and the Middle East, which allowed Japan and the SDF to begin building concrete and direct cooperation with countries and militaries other than the US and its military.

A new stage in Japan's post-Cold War shift towards broad security engagement was reached soon after the turn of the century, when Japan began building new security partnerships. The first one was with Australia, the second with India. By 2011, Japan was also beginning to build nascent security partnerships with the Philippines and Vietnam.

Diversifying security ties and recent security policy

The emergence of this wide-ranging security engagement during the first two decades following the end of the Cold War was reflected in recent Japanese innovations in defence policy, specifically the establishment of a new National Security Council (December 2013), a new defence concept known as the Dynamic Joint Defense Force, an increase of defence spending since 2014, and the increasingly force-focused and assertive defence policy announced in the then National Defense Program Guidelines for 2014 and beyond and the Five-year Defense Program for 2014 through 2018, both decided in December 2013. The June 2014 Cabinet decision to reinterpret the Japanese constitution to allow the exercise of the right of collective self-defence can also be seen in this light (Cabinet of Japan, 2014).

The National Security Strategy (NSS), which also was promulgated in December 2013, defines the central objectives of Japan's security policy. The three main objectives are to (1) strengthen Japan's deterrence, and (2) improve the 'security environment of the Asia-Pacific region' as well as the (3) global security environment. It aims to achieve this not only by 'strengthening the Japan–U.S. Alliance', but also by enhancing 'cooperative relationships between Japan and its partners inside and outside the Asia-Pacific region, and promoting practical security cooperation'. The NSS specifically mentions that Japan wants to strengthen its 'diplomacy and security cooperation with Japan's Partners for

Introduction

Peace and Stability, such as Australia, the countries of ASEAN, and India, as well as the Republic of Korea'.[1] Australia is considered an 'important regional partner that shares not only universal values but also strategic interests with Japan', which is why Japan aims to 'strengthen its strategic partnership' by cooperating on regional issues in the Asia-Pacific and on 'peace and stability in the international community'. India is considered an important strategic and global partner because of its geopolitical significance as a country at the 'center of sea lanes of communication'. For similar geo-strategic reasons related to sea-lane security, Japan also considers several ASEAN member states to be critical partners. The NSS specifically mentions their significance for responding to China's expansion in the South China Sea.

In this context, Japan considers deepening security cooperation with the EU and its member states, such as the UK, France, Germany, Italy, Spain and Poland, as useful, not only because it shares their 'universal values of freedom, democracy, respect for fundamental human rights and the rule of law, and principles such as market economy' (National Security Council of Japan, 2013), but also because of their 'capacity to develop norms in major international frameworks' (National Security Council of Japan, 2013).

Apart from the EU, the NSS also mentions the intention to further deepen Japan's security ties with the North Atlantic Treaty Organization (NATO) and the Organisation for Security and Co-operation in Europe (OSCE).

The National Defense Program Guidelines (NDPG) for FY 2014 and beyond, which were also promulgated in December 2013, has a whole section on the active promotion of security cooperation (section 4). As both are partners of the US, Australia is seen as sharing Japan's security interests, which is why Japan intends to deepen security cooperation with Canberra through joint training to improve interoperability. India is mentioned as an important security partner in maritime security, which is why joint training and exercises will be the focus of mid-term military-to-military cooperation. Cooperation with countries in the Asia-Pacific region had so far mostly been in non-traditional security. However, the 2014 NDPG indicates that Japan wants to further deepen its security cooperation in the region through multilateral frameworks such as the ARF, the ASEAN Defense Ministers' Meeting-Plus (ADMM Plus) and the East Asia Summit (EAS). This may involve joint military training and exercises, and multi-layered defence cooperation and exchange in a wide range of security areas, from humanitarian assistance/disaster relief (HA/DR) to maritime and cyber security, and capacity building.

Cooperation with the EU and some of its member states is to be intensified not just on the diplomatic level, but also through increased military-to-military cooperation and exchanges and through the joint development and acquisition of military equipment and technology. The NDPG specifically mentions 'cooperation between the defense and foreign affairs authorities' and the possible dispatch of the SDF, if SDF units can be accepted by the partner country.

The International Peace Support Bill, which was part of the package of security legislation passed in 2015, created a permanent legal framework for support activities for 'armed forces of foreign countries collectively addressing the situation which threatens the international peace and security'. It reflects the drive for deeper and broader military and security cooperation by the Japanese government and the SDF with governments and military forces of partner countries such as the EU, but also, currently and more importantly, with Australia and India, and with Asian countries other than China that have territorial claims in the South China Sea. The Australian and Indian governments, also the EU Commission as well as the UK and German governments, publicly embraced Japan's so-called 'proactive contribution to peace' policy and Tokyo's willingness to become a more prominent actor in times of crisis.

Overall, the set of major security policy documents issued at the end of 2013 includes provisions and expectations to further deepen and broaden Japan's security cooperation, not just with its core security guarantor, the US, but also with the countries and regional organisations analysed in this volume, specifically Australia, India and several countries in East Asia, as well as the EU, the ARF, and NATO.

The concept of security partnerships

The concept 'security partnership' has been widely used in the post-Cold War period, but since about the mid-2000s 'security partnership' has become especially common when describing the security relationship between Japan and two countries in particular: Australia (Sahashi, 2013; Satake and Ishihara, 2012; Terada, 2010; Walton, 2008, 2012) and India (Brewster, 2010; Paul, 2012). Over the last five years, the term has also been used more frequently to describe the security angle of the relationship between Japan and ASEAN (di Floristella, 2015),[2] and the EU (Gilson, 2016; Tsuruoka, 2015) and NATO. In Japan's security relations with the EU, NATO or the ARF, the term 'regional security partnership' is frequently used to indicate a form of security arrangement in a region that deals with specific security threats but is usually based on formal security agreements, international organisations, peace and stability pacts, and confidence-building measures (Atina, 2007).

The term 'security partnership' or 'strategic partnership' has frequently been used in agreements between NATO or the EU and third countries they collaborate with. In some of these cases, the term 'security partnership' is far more loosely applied; some authors use it to describe alliance systems such as NATO (Hamilton, 2014) or even for the US–Japan Alliance (Ikenberry and Inoguchi, 2013). One obvious reason why the Japanese government prefers the term 'security partnership' over 'security treaty', just as it prefers 'economic partnership agreement' to 'free-trade agreement', is that it sounds less committed

Introduction

and more neutral, and, at least until the Cabinet reinterpretation of Article 9 of the Constitution in 2014, did not include any connotation of collective self-defence (see also Tsuruoka, 2016).

Security partnerships in this volume

The use of the term 'security partnership' in this volume is closely based on a definition developed by Wilkins (2011, 2012). Wilkins defines 'strategic partnership' as 'structured collaboration between states (or other actors) to take joint advantage of economic opportunities, or to respond to security challenges more effectively than could be achieved in isolation' (Wilkins, 2011: 363). The key characteristics of such partnerships are that (1) they are 'built around a general (security) purpose' and not for 'deterring or combating a hostile state', (2) they are primarily 'goal-driven' rather than 'threat-driven' alignments, (3) they tend to be informal in nature and entail low commitment costs, (4) they allow states to pursue multidimensional bilateral, regional and global issue agendas and diverse domestic goals without compromising freedom of action, (5) they are less rigid and provocative instruments, and (6) due to the term's inception in the business world, economic exchange (or 'economic security' issues) appear foremost among their 'functional areas' of cooperation. They are, therefore, 'a type of security alignment well-fitted to challenging non-traditional security threats, not provoking great power rivalry, while retaining an ability to "hedge" against it' (Wilkins, 2012: 214–215).

While Wilkins developed this definition with a focus on the Japan–Australia security partnership, this broad and pragmatic definition describes perfectly the core ideas and reality of the security partnerships analysed in this volume.

Core questions raised in this volume are:

1. What is the current state of these bilateral relationships?
2. How have Japan's security relations evolved since the end of the Cold War?
3. How are these security partnerships discussed domestically?
4. Are there opposing or critical views among the main political parties in participating countries regarding these partnerships?
5. To what extent do the main security concerns and threat perceptions in Japan and the individual partner countries converge or diverge, and what explains this degree of convergence/divergence?

This volume's core hypotheses about Japan's security partnerships are:

1. Increasingly closer diplomatic dialogue and military-to-military exchange will increase trust and mutual understanding of the partners' security concerns.

2. While the original rationale for closer security cooperation might have been non-traditional security issues, consistent cooperation can lead to closer cooperation in traditional security issues.
3. Closer security cooperation with non-US partners can give Japan (and these partners) more leverage in security negotiations with the US and encourage a more independent foreign and security policy.

Given this specific definition of 'security partnership', this volume takes a closer look at Japan's security ties with Australia, India, the Philippines, Vietnam and the Southeast Asia region more generally, as well as with the EU and to some extent some of its member states, specifically the UK[3] and France.

The reason why these country and regional pairs were chosen is that all of them have already established either deep security ties, from annual security consultative meetings and cross-servicing agreements to defence equipment and technology agreements, at the deeper end of the spectrum, or some cooperation in non-traditional security and economic partnership agreements, at the other. Table I.1 provides a general overview of the depth of security cooperation between all of the pairs included in this volume. The Republic of Korea, which could otherwise be included as an almost natural security partner of Japan, given their shared concern about North Korea, is included in this table to illustrate how underdeveloped security and even economic cooperation are. Most cooperation takes place in the context of the trilateral security cooperation with the US, and to a limited extent in UN peacekeeping operations, such as in South Sudan, or the counter-piracy mission off the coast of Somalia.

Security partnerships not in this volume

Some of Japan's new security engagements and potential security partnerships are not examined by this book. First, security engagements that are primarily confidence-building in nature are not examined. Japan's security engagements with China and Russia are the prime examples of this type of engagement. Japan has engaged both countries with a variety of exchanges, including military cadet exchanges, Track One and Two security dialogues, exchanges between military units and non-combat exercises.

Japan's security engagement with Russia is especially notable, as it features Japan's only two-plus-two dialogue (i.e. a dialogue between the foreign and defence ministers of Japan with the foreign and defence ministers of the partner nation) with a partner that is not allied with or leaning towards the US. Japan's engagement with Russia would seem to have the potential to blossom into a security partnership, perhaps comparable to Japan's partnership with India. However, given Japan's present level of deep dependence on the US for its security and the continuing Russian–US confrontation over Ukraine, allegations

Introduction

Table I.1 Level of security integration (as of 2017)

	Security consultative meetings (two-plus-two)	Cross-Servicing Agreement (ACSA)	Defense Equipment and Technology Transfer Agreement	Trilateral security dialogue (with the US)	Joint Declaration on Security Cooperation	Joint military exercises	Non-traditional security cooperation[i]	Economic Partnership Agreement (EPA)
Japan–Australia	YES[ii]	YES[iii]	YES[iv]	YES	YES	YES	YES[v]	YES
Japan–India	YES		YES[vi]	YES[vii]	YES	YES	YES[viii]	YES
Japan–ASEAN							YES[ix]	YES
Japan–Philippines			YES[x]		YES		YES[xi]	YES
Japan–Vietnam								YES
Japan–EU					YES[xii]	YES	YES	YES[xiii]
Japan–UK	YES	YES[xiv]	YES[xv]			YES	YES	
Japan–France			YES[xvi]					
Not included in this volume								
Japan–Russia	YES							
Japan–ROK				YES			YES[xvii]	

[i]This includes the cybersecurity dialogue and anti-terrorism cooperation, etc.
[ii]Since 2008.
[iii]Signed in 2010 and entered into force in 2013. Renewed in 2017.
[iv]Signed in July 2014 and entered into force in December 2014.
[v]For example, Information Security Agreement (2012).
[vi]Signed in December 2015.
[vii]Japan–US–India, and Japan–Australia–India (since 2017).
[viii]For example, Japan–India Joint Working Group on Counter-Terrorism (since 2010), Japan–India Cybersecurity Dialogue (since 2012).
[ix]For example, ASEAN–Japan Cybercrime Dialogue (since 2014).
[x]Signed in February 2016, and entered into force in April 2016.
[xi]Japan and the Philippines held a joint naval exercise in the South China Sea on 12 May 2015.
[xii]The EU–Japan SPA, which is in its final stages of negotiations in early 2018, can be considered equivalent to a Joint Declaration on Security Cooperation.
[xiii]Agreed in July 2017. Final version publicized in December 2017.
[xiv]Signed in January 2017.
[xv]Signed and entered into force in July 2013.
[xvi]Signed in March 2015.
[xvii]For example, the Japan–Republic of Korea (ROK) Counter-Terrorism Consultations (since 2002). Additionally, trilateral dialogues such as the Japan–US–ROK Experts Meeting on Cybersecurity of Critical Infrastructure (since 2016) and the Trilateral Cyber Policy Consultation among Japan, the People's Republic of China and the ROK (since 2014). Also, Japan–China–ROK Counter-Terrorism Consultations (since 2011).

of Russian meddling in the 2016 US election, and other bilateral tensions, it remains very difficult for Japan to significantly upgrade its security partnership with Russia, despite interest on both sides. The unresolved bilateral territorial dispute between the two countries also remains an obstacle.

In the case of China, the emergence of deep mutual suspicion since the late 1980s, driven by diverging historical memories of the Sino-Japanese War and Japanese imperialism in China, differences over ideology and human rights, and a regional competition for influence, make significant bilateral security cooperation beyond confidence building difficult. Indeed, even confidence-building measures have often proven difficult to implement in view of the deep mutual suspicion and competition for power.[4]

Another country that would seem logical to include in this volume is South Korea, a '*de facto* ally' of Japan by virtue of their mutual ally, the US (Cha, 1999). Nonetheless, South Korea is not included, because security engagement between the two countries has hardly progressed much beyond the confidence-building level achieved in Japan's security engagements with Russia and China. As with China, deep suspicion, especially on the South Korean side towards Japan, stemming from diverging historical memories of Japan's colonisation of the Korean peninsula, has made security cooperation, including even the sharing of classified information, difficult to achieve. Public opinion polls in South Korea have regularly shown that more Koreans view Japan than China as a military threat, and Seoul's defence elites have rejected offers of security assistance from Japan, even in the event of a crisis (Midford, 2010). Korean suspicion of Japan has thus far prevented a meaningful security partnership like those examined in this book from developing.

The views from both sides

Debate about the benefits and the future trajectory of the revised security components of these relationships occurs in Japan and all of its security partners, since the cost-benefit calculations and risk assessments made to justify closer security ties are potentially diverging. The cases introduced here demonstrate the different level and depth of some of these partnerships. In some cases, security cooperation involves regular so-called two-plus-two security dialogues of the respective foreign and defence ministers, or the exchange of intelligence. In other cases, security cooperation involves joint development, the acquisition or sale of weapons systems, joint military exercises, support for improving defence capacities, or the monitoring and control of territorial waters.

For this reason, this book is organised into pairs of chapters written by experts analysing the respective views of Japan and each of its most important new security partners: Australia, India, the Philippines, Vietnam, East Asia more broadly and the EU. All chapters analyse the current state and future trajectory of these security partnerships and their significance for security alignments over the next decade.

Part I looks at *Japan–Australia* security relations. The significance, specific structure, and actual and potential challenges are analysed first from the Australian and then from the Japanese perspective.

Australia and Japan were both part of the US security architecture in the Asia-Pacific during the Cold War as two spokes in the American 'hub and spoke' regional alliance system and have, therefore, even been referred to as a 'quasi-alliance' (see also Cha, 1999). Over the last decade, however, the security ties between them have deepened substantially, and recent Australian governments have described it as a true bilateral strategic partnership. Thomas S. Wilkins analyses the multi-faceted relationship with Tokyo, which he considers a foreign policy triumph for Australia. He demonstrates how the two countries have strengthened their bilateral security relationship to a significant degree independently of the US, and have developed a 'strategic partnership' or a new form of 'security alignment' (Wilkins, 2011), in which the two regional powers align more closely with each other in some form of coalition, a concept that does not easily fit into traditional alliance paradigms.

Yusuke Ishihara looks at bilateral security ties from a Japanese perspective. For Japan, trust towards Australia has begun to deepen during the years of bi- and multilateral cooperation on non-traditional security issues such as peacekeeping operations (PKO) and HA/DR. It was important in this regard that Australian forces were central in protecting the Japanese *Ground Self-Defense Force* (GSDF) during their deployment to Samawah (Southern Iraq) in 2006. What Ishihara calls the second evolution of Japan–Australia security relations began to take shape with the Joint Declaration on Security Cooperation (2007) signed by Prime Minister Abe during his first term in office. After returning to the premiership for the second time in December 2012, Abe continued to further deepen these special ties to include traditional security cooperation. Ishihara analyses the deeper reasons for this second evolution of Japan–Australia security ties. He argues that the deepening strategic convergence of Japan's and Australia's regional policies towards a more assertive direction is a response to the perceived challenges posed by the rise of China, as well as their shared views on the rules-based international order and the US role in the Asia-Pacific region. Ishihara then argues that this 'alignment' of Japanese and Australian security views has led to a deepening of their diplomatic relationship in principle. However, although both Tokyo and Canberra have a strong trade dependency on China while sharing concerns regarding China's growing regional influence, their respective responses do sometimes differ, which is the reason for the so-called China gap. Ishihara argues this China gap is evolving, as the regional security dynamics as well as bilateral relations have become more strained in recent years.

Part II looks at *Japan–India* security relations from both Indian and Japanese perspectives. From the Indian perspective, Madhuchanda Ghosh argues that given India's long-held position as the leader of the non-alignment movement, the turnaround of India–Japan security relations has been quite remarkable. The relationship now ranges from the sale of amphibious aircraft and civilian nuclear cooperation to Japan becoming a permanent member in India's Malabar naval exercise. She identifies shared core strategic interests in the area of energy security, the security of sea lanes of communication (SLOCs) in the Indian Ocean region and ameliorating the power disequilibrium in Asia. She argues that India's growing economic power has made New Delhi an increasingly important regional and global player, and building security partnerships with major powers in the region and throughout the world is a major tool for realising the country's potential on both regional and global stages. Japan has begun to build an increasingly significant relationship with India since 2000, when then Prime Minister Mori declared that Japan and India were now global partners. Since then Japan has become one of India's most trusted partners in the region and an essential part of India's so-called 'Look East' and 'Act East' foreign policy doctrine. Ghosh analyses the different steps and India's incentives to further deepen its security ties with Japan based on public records as well as personal interviews with some of the major Indian and Japanese actors over the years.

From the Japanese perspective, Satoru Nagao also stresses the importance of deepening dialogue between foreign and defence ministers and Japan's now regular participation in naval exercises in the last few years, which Nagao considers to be remarkable. For Japan, the main rationale is geo-strategic, namely, the changing US–China balance. Japan is no longer certain that the US will continue to balance against China and support Japan's interests in the region, which makes India a central ally, initially for burden sharing with the US in the Indian Ocean, for protecting SLOCs, and eventually for collaborating with Japan to support South China Sea littoral countries. For Japan, the fact that India is a democracy and shares Japan's values, that it does not challenge the status quo in South Asia and exercises strategic restraint, and that it has a long history of cooperation in international institutions with Japan facilitate trust building between the two countries.

Part III looks at *Japan–East Asia* security relations and includes five chapters that analyse Japan's security initiatives towards East Asia, the rationale for closer security cooperation from Japanese and Southeast Asian perspectives, recent developments in Japan's security partnerships with the Philippines, and two chapters analysing Japan–Vietnam relations from Vietnamese and Japanese perspectives.

In Chapter 5, Paul Midford analyses Japan's initiatives towards regional security multilateralism in East Asia since the end of the Cold War. He argues that Japan promoted multilateral security forums through initiatives such as the

Introduction

Nakayama proposal, the Hashimoto Doctrine and its promotion of Northeast Asian Cooperation (NEA 3), as well as initiatives in response to specific security challenges such as maritime piracy in East Asia. Midford argues that these were significant because Japan often acted independently of the US and set up institutions that sometimes did not include US participation. The core reasons for this policy were to reassure Japan's neighbours that Tokyo would not become a threat to their security again, to hedge against potential US abandonment and, ironically, to help keep the US engaged in the region.

In Chapter 6, Stephen R. Nagy analyses Japan's Southeast Asian security partnerships from a Southeast Asian perspective. Japan had begun to re-enter East Asia through trade and economic development (official development assistance (ODA)) initiatives in the 1970s and 1980s. As a still growing industrial economy that nonetheless lacked most of the necessary natural and energy resources, Japan's infrastructure and industrial investment in many countries of the region, in combination with official development programmes, furthered economic growth and prosperity in many East Asian countries as well as Japan – a mutually beneficial relationship that largely remained unsecuritised. Beginning with the launch of the second Abe administration in late 2012, Japan has started to include security components in a number of bilateral relations with countries in the region. However, the countries in Southeast Asia are not uniform. Therefore, Nagy distinguishes among Southeast Asian countries according to their level of economic dependence on China and their threat perception vis-à-vis China, and divides them into two groups, which he calls 'peripheral-core' countries, such as the Philippines, Indonesia, Vietnam, Malaysia, Brunei, Singapore and Thailand, which have more favourable views on security cooperation with Japan, and 'core-peripheral' countries, like Cambodia and Laos, which see them more critically. This, in turn, determines their rationale for why and how to engage with Japan, and shapes Southeast Asian perspectives of Japanese–Southeast Asian security partnerships. This chapter asks how the Japan–China security rivalry, Japan's trade, and its advocacy for civil and human rights affect Southeast Asian countries' evaluations of Japan's security partnerships.

In Chapter 7, Renato Cruz De Castro analyses the security ties of one of the peripheral-core countries studied in Chapter 6 by taking a closer look at the Philippines' perspective on its deepening security ties with Japan. The chapter examines the external and domestic forces behind their increased security cooperation and explores the status of this security partnership. It argues that China's maritime expansion in East Asia negatively affected both Japan and the Philippines, which in turn led to a deepening of their security partnership. The chapter predicts that despite recent changes in the Philippine government, Manila has a strong interest in further deepening the security partnership with Japan.

Chapters 8 and 9 analyse security ties between Japan and Vietnam. In Chapter 8, Swee Lean Collin Koh looks at these ties from the Vietnamese perspective. As is the case with the Philippines, the Chinese maritime expansion and territorial claims in the South China Sea are also an important motivation for Vietnam to deepen security ties with Japan. This chapter examines how Vietnam has dealt with post-Cold War and contemporary maritime security challenges and discusses Japan's role in developing their bilateral maritime security partnership, before assessing the future trajectory of the Vietnam–Japan security partnership. In Chapter 9, Bjørn Grønning then looks at the same relationship from the Japanese perspective and shows that the relationship grew from a security talk shop until 2011, when relations began to grow markedly towards substantial cooperation, especially on maritime security, and today are on the verge of becoming militarily significant. He argues that Japan's incentive to develop this partnership is primarily to assist and induce Vietnam's continued resistance against the rise of Chinese maritime power. The recent changes in Japan's domestic security legislation (see earlier) potentially open new opportunities to further broaden and deepen bilateral maritime security cooperation, because they legally enable Japan to assist Vietnam militarily in some respects.

Part IV looks at *Japan–Europe* security relations and includes three chapters, one from a European and one from a Japanese perspective, and one chapter that introduces ongoing long-term military cooperation involving Japan's Maritime Self-Defense Force (MSDF) and European Union Naval Forces (EUNAVFOR), namely, the counter-piracy mission off the coast of Somalia. Since their initiation in 1991, EU–Japan relations have often suffered from a gap between ambitious plans for closer cooperation in a wide field of policy areas, including non-traditional security challenges, and the depth of their actual cooperation, especially in the area of international security.

In Chapter 10, Axel Berkofsky recognises this gap but focuses on the most ambitious plan to revive or substantially deepen their security ties; namely, the negotiations for a Strategic Partnership Agreement (SPA), potentially the 'big bang' of EU–Japan cooperation. Short of having the final version of the actual agreement, the chapter asks what kind of agreement we can most likely expect based on their security cooperation, including Japan's contribution to recent EU Common Security and Defence Policy (CSDP) missions, EU–Japan cooperation on banning anti-personnel mines and limiting the illicit trade in small arms, and the significance of defence cooperation by France and the UK with Japan. Finally, this chapter also assesses the impact that differing assessments of China's role in international affairs by the EU and Japan might have on current and future security cooperation. Overall, Berkofsky's expectations are moderate. He does not think that the SPA will be the 'big bang' of EU–Japan regional and global security cooperation, but believes it will provide an institutional framework for future cooperation. Nonetheless, even such an institutional framework will

Introduction

probably not provide military security for Japan against Chinese expansion. In Chapter 11, Akiko Fukushima looks at the EU–Japan security partnership from the Japanese perspective. While recognising its shortcomings, including the expectations gap between the EU and Japan, which has frequently been problematised (as in Chapter 10), Fukushima emphasises the significance of the recent changes in Japanese security policy, such as the 2013 NSS, as evidence that Japan does consider the EU and NATO as important security partners in order to 'ensure a peaceful and prosperous international community', and wants to enhance these relationships. The chapter analyses the domestic debate and government initiatives, as well as Japan's expectations for the above-mentioned SPA, and the enablers and inhibitors of closer security ties. Fukushima argues that while Japan–Europe security cooperation has so far excluded hard security, the changing international security environment and a narrowing perceptions gap should allow deeper cooperation in non-traditional security fields, because Japan would benefit from the European experience of forging consensus in shaping international rules and norms.

In the final chapter, Wilhelm Vosse introduces a practical case of EU–Japan out-of-area security cooperation, and the first example of operational security cooperation, namely the counter-piracy mission off the coast of Somalia. This went beyond standard security diplomacy to include military-to-military cooperation in the field. This chapter introduces the main reasons and different stages of involvement of the Japanese government, the MSDF and the Japan Coast Guard (JCG) in the Somalia counter-piracy mission. It then analyses the extent to which this mission provided opportunities for closer EU–Japan security cooperation, and what significance this case has for future EU–Japan security cooperation more broadly. Vosse argues that this mission, with the complexities of multilateral security coordination and operational cooperation between European and Japanese forces, provided an ideal learning opportunity for Japanese government representatives and SDF personnel. In the end, it was also an exercise in deepening trust and understanding. The latter is an important condition for furthering the above-mentioned SPA negotiations. During these negotiations, the counter-piracy mission has frequently been mentioned as a prime example of successful EU–Japan security cooperation. While it is unlikely that the EU–Japan security partnership and the upcoming SPA will substantially increase the EU's role in the national defence of Japan, missions like this lead to increased EU–Japan coordination in regional and global bodies, and a better coordinated joint response to security challenges from third countries.

NOTES

1 This volume does not include security relations with the Republic of Korea, as these are still in their infancy and have been severely retarded by disagreements about the

sovereignty of a disputed island (Takeshima/Dokdo) and other historical memory issues such as the comfort women controversy. While Japan and the ROK have been negotiating an economic partnership agreement since 2011, which could include closer cooperation on security issues concerning North Korea, it does not look likely in 2017 that this partnership will be concluded soon.
2   di Floristella (2015) described some of the ties between ASEAN members states as 'regional security partnership' (*The ASEAN Regional Security Partnership*).
3   At the time of writing this volume, the UK was still a member of the EU. However, after triggering Article 50 of the EU Treaty in March 2017, the UK is destined to leave the EU in March 2019. Nevertheless, in 2017, the UK government has frequently expressed its intention and willingness to continue its security ties with the EU.
4   For an overview of security cooperation and confidence-building measures between Japan and China, see Akiyama and Shu (2011).

REFERENCES

Akiyama, M. and Shu, H. (eds), 2011. *Nicchū anzen hoshō bōei kōryū no rekishi, genjō, tenbō* [History, Current Situation and Prospects of Japan-China Security and Defense Exchanges] (Tokyo: Akishobō).

Atina, F., 2007. 'The European Security Partnership: A Comparative Analysis', in Foradori, P. and Rosa, P. (eds), *Managing a Multilevel Foreign Policy: The EU in International Affairs* (Lanham, MD: Lexington Books), pp. 87–110.

Brewster, D., 2010. 'The India–Japan Security Relationship: An Enduring Security Partnership?', *Asian Security*, 6(2): 95–120.

Cha, V., 1999. *Alignment despite Antagonism: The United States–Korea–Japan Security Triangle* (Stanford: Stanford University Press).

di Floristella, A. P., 2015. *The ASEAN Regional Security Partnership* (Houndmills, Basingstoke: Palgrave Macmillan).

Gilson, J., 2016. 'The Strategic Partnership Agreement between the EU and Japan: The Pitfalls of Path Dependency?', *Journal of European Integration*, 38(7): 791–806.

Hamilton, D., 2014. 'The Transatlantic Pivot', in Roy, S., Cooper, D. and Murphy, B. M. (eds), *Transatlantic Relations and Modern Diplomacy: An Interdisciplinary Examination* (New York: Routledge), p. 81f.

Ikenberry, J. and Inoguchi, T. (eds), 2013. *Reinventing the Alliance: US – Japan Security Partnership in an Era of Change* (New York: Palgrave Macmillan).

Midford, P., 2010. 'Historical Memory versus Democratic Reassurance: The Security Relationship between Japan and South Korea', in Söderberg, M. (ed.), *Changing Power Relations in Northeast Asia: Implications for Japan–South Korea Relations* (London: Routledge), ch. 5.

National Security Council of Japan, 2013. 'National Security Strategy', 17 December, at: japan.kantei.go.jp/96_abe/documents/2013/__icsFiles/afieldfile/2013/12/18/NSS.pdf (accessed 19 April 2016).

Paul, J. M., 2012. 'India–Japan Security Cooperation: A New Era of Partnership in Asia', *Maritime Affairs: Journal of the National Maritime Foundation of India*, 8(1): 31–50.

Sahashi, R., 2013. 'Security Partnerships in Japan's Asia Strategy Creating Order, Building Capacity and Sharing Burden', IFRI Center for Asian Studies, *Asie.Visions*, 61 (February): 1–23.

Satake, T. and Ishihara, Y., 2012. 'America's Rebalance to Asia and Its Implications for Japan–US–Australia Security Cooperation', *Asia-Pacific Review*, 19(2): 6–25.

Introduction

Terada, T., 2010. 'Evolution of the Australia–Japan Security Partnership: Towards a Softer Triangle Alliance with the United States?', IFRI Center for Asian Studies, *Asie. Vision*, 35 (October): 1–29.

Tsuruoka, M., 2015. 'Japan–Europe Relations: Toward a Full Political and Security Partnership', in Tatsumi, Y. (ed.), *Japan's Global Diplomacy: Views from the Next Generation* (The Henry L. Stimson Center), pp. 43–53.

Tsuruoka, M., 2016. 'Ōshū ni okeru dōmei, shūdan bōei, shūdantekijieiken — aratana kyōi e no natō EU ni yoru taiō' [Alliances, Collective Defence and the Right of Collective Self-Defence in Europe: NATO and EU responses to New Threats], *Kokusai anzen hoshou* [*The Journal of International Security*], 44(1): 64–82.

Walton, D., 2008. 'Australia and Japan: Towards a New Security Partnership?', *Japanese Studies*, 28(1): 73–86.

Walton, D., 2012. 'Australia and Japan: Toward a Full Security Partnership?', in Struett, M. J., Carlson, J. D. and Nance, M. T. (eds), *Maritime Piracy and the Construction of Global Governance* (Routledge), pp. 149–173.

Wilkins, T. S., 2011. '"Alignment", not "Alliance" – the Shifting Paradigm of International Security Cooperation: Toward a Conceptual Taxonomy of Alignment', *Review of International Studies*, 38(1): 53–76.

Wilkins, T. S., 2012. 'Japan-Australia Security Relations: Building a Real Strategic Partnership?', in Tow, W. T. and Kersten, R. (eds), *Bilateral Perspectives on Regional Security* (Basingstoke: Palgrave Macmillan), pp. 111–127.

Part I

Japan–Australia security partnership

1

The Australian perspective on the security partnership with Japan

Thomas S. Wilkins

Introduction

During the Cold War period Japan and Australia were sometimes referred to as the northern and southern 'anchors' of the American alliance system in the Asia-Pacific. These two important 'spokes' in the so-called American 'hub-and-spoke' regional alliance system therefore found themselves in a condition of indirect alignment – or, to use Victor Cha's term, 'quasi-alliance' (Cha, 1999). This implies that while the two countries participated in no direct defence relationship, by dint of their separate military alliance treaties they were on a parallel security course throughout this period, united in common resistance to the threat posed by the Soviet Union. Theoretically, this description could still be applied to the current Australia–Japan relationship, and indeed, it has been labelled as such by some official Japanese sources (though in this case I suspect they mean 'almost-an-alliance' rather than a parallel relationship with a third party (Garnaut, 2014)). But this does not capture much more than a reductionist notion of how the bilateral relationship fits into the broader US alliance presence in Asia, and ignores the far-reaching developments occurring between the two states as they work to build a true bilateral strategic partnership.

The pace and extent of Australia's broad security cooperation with Japan is somewhat remarkable when one recalls the suspicion and bitter enmity towards Japan held by Australians in the wake of World War II. However, the combination of the US Cold War alliance system and the re-emergence of an important trading, then political/diplomatic, relationship, from the 1957 Commerce Agreement (Parliament of Australia, 2000) through the 1976 NARA (Nippon–Australia Relations Act) treaty, has assisted in building a strong track record of interaction between the countries (Department of Foreign Affairs and Trade, 1976; Rix, 1999). Then, the post-Cold War and post-9/11 period saw cooperation between the countries in areas such as peacekeeping and counterterrorism reach new heights. Over the past two decades, Australia has added a robust security dimension to its relationship with Japan, with the result that 'Japan–Australia security ties are now stronger than ever' (Satake, 2015). The construction of a positive and now multifaceted relationship with Tokyo represents a foreign policy triumph for Australia, perhaps only rivalled by its linkages to the US or the UK.

The purpose of this chapter is threefold. First, in accordance with the theme of this volume, it will examine the overall relationship between Canberra and Tokyo from a distinctly Australian perspective. Second, it will disaggregate Australia–Japan bilateral relations from the simplistic 'allies of the US' context ('quasi-alliance') to demonstrate how the two countries have developed a hugely strengthened bilateral security relationship to a significant degree independently of the US context (if not of US influence). Their so-called 'strategic partnership' is a new form of security alignment that does not neatly fit the traditional alliance pradigm (Wilkins, 2011). Third, it will consider the wider contexts within which the bilateral strategic partnership exists, firstly by restoring its place in the overall American-led San Francisco (alliance) system, including trilateral cooperation, and secondly by considering an alternative non-US context in which the two powers align more closely with other regional states in some form of coalition. The approach of this chapter is thematic; it ranges across a number of key questions and issues that frame the improved state of Australian ties with Japan in recent years. The chapter does not dwell extensively upon outlining the historical background or bureaucratic structure of the strategic partnership, which the author and others have documented extensively elsewhere (e.g. Walton, 2007).

A new 'special' strategic partnership

In 2014, in one of two joint annual leadership summits that have become a feature of Australia–Japan ties, Prime Ministers Shinzō Abe and Tony Abbott announced that a 'new special relationship had been born' (Placek, 2014). The term 'special relationship' has usually been reserved only for the closest of 'allies' – such as the UK and the US, or the US and Israel – which imbues such proclamations with a serious degree of political capital. Though the term 'ally' has been used by politicians, analysts and commentators rather unguardedly, it is important to note that despite all of the unprecedented developments in the political, diplomatic, security/defence and economic spheres, no direct mutual defence pact (alliance) exists or is likely to appear in the near future between Canberra and Tokyo (Wilkins, 2015). As we will see, on the Australian side this has been an issue of contentious debate over the past few years.

Nevertheless, since the official founding of the strategic partnership in 2005, Australia has invested major diplomatic effort into following through on its declared policy to build a deeper and more comprehensive bilateral relationship with Tokyo. Standout developments include the groundbreaking Joint

Declaration on Security Cooperation (JDSC) in 2007 that committed the parties to enhanced collaboration on a range of traditional and non-traditional security issues (Ministry of Foreign Affairs of Japan, 2007). The subsequent ACSA (Acquisition and Cross-Serving) and ISA (Information Sharing) agreements lent substance to this declaration to operationalise joint activities (Ministry of Foreign Affairs of Japan, 2010; 2012). The Agreement on Defence Cooperation (Department of Defence Australia, 2014) – including the sharing of military technology – was likewise put into operation by the creation of a (unique) Japan–Australia Defence Cooperation Office at the Ministry of Defence (MOD), 'to keep up with the unprecedented pace of activity in Japan' (Lang, 2015: 6). Lastly, not to neglect the economic pillar, which appears to be fundamental to such strategic partnerships, Canberra signed the long-awaited free trade agreement (FTA) (called the Japan–Australia Economic Partnership Agreement (JAEPA)) in 2014, seeking to enhance mutual trading benefits (Department of Foreign Affairs and Trade, 2014). These and a number of more minor related initiatives (looked at later in the chapter) have demonstrated Australian commitment to its strategic partnership with Japan as a major diplomatic objective. These headlining developments are set against a steady accretion of institutional interconnections throughout all levels of the hierarchy (for example two-plus-two Foreign and Defence Minister's Meetings, now entering their seventh iteration) across a broadening range of joint 'issue areas' (Wilkins, 2010).

Strategic interests

Australia has consistently stressed both its common (strategic) interests and its shared values with Japan as drivers for closer ties. The fifth two-plus-two meeting agreed to 'elevate the strategic partnership between Australia and Japan to a new special relationship based on common values and interests including democracy, human rights, the rule of law, open markets and free trade' (Minister for Foreign Affairs, 2014). Indeed, the interests/values declaration has now become de rigueur for (Western) states justifying their security cooperation, especially within the US alliance framework. Often, 'interests' are subsumed or conflated with 'values' in political rhetoric, or otherwise stated nebulously – for example, Abe has noted joint 'strategic interests in peace, stability and prosperity' (Ministry of Foreign Affairs of Japan, 2014). Actual specifics on strategic/security cooperation are diffused throughout statements/documents and must be parsed together here to form a coherent and composite analysis.

In terms of common interests with Japan, the emphasis here is on coordinating their mutual position as status quo powers in an international system experiencing (disruptive) change. On a global level, Australia seeks to work closely with Japan in major diplomatic forums such as the G20 and the UN, where it has been an assiduous supporter of a permanent seat on the

UN Security Council for Tokyo. Accordingly, 'Australia and Japan consulted closely during Australia's term as a non-permanent member of the Security Council in 2013–14' (Department of Foreign Affairs and Trade, 2016b). Australia and Japan have also jointly led efforts towards disarmament through this channel, such as the Evans–Kawaguchi UN Commission and the Non-Proliferation and Disarmament Initiative; (Evans and Kawaguchi, 2009). Australia has also participated in several peacekeeping missions alongside Japan, for example in Cambodia, East Timor and currently South Sudan (UNMISS).

Australia's 'internationalist' strain of foreign policy places priority on maintaining a stable and rules-based security order. This is especially evident at the regional level, where both countries have depended upon and benefitted from the American hegemonic presence in the Asia-Pacific. Neither wishes to see rising powers such as China revise the regional order, which has worked so well for them in both security and economic terms since the 1950s. In addition to this underlying balance of power approach to order is their shared enthusiasm for multilateral approaches to regional security. Collaboration in appropriate regional forums such as the East Asia Summit (EAS), Asia-Pacific Economic Cooperation (APEC) and the Association of Southeast Asian Nations (ASEAN) Regional Forum (ARF), for example, is a key aspect of the bilateral relationship. Both countries were instrumental in the establishment of APEC and the ARF, and Canberra has received unswerving support from Japan in its efforts to 'integrate' into the Asian region. In return, Australia has been a strong supporter of Japan's reforms aimed towards a 'proactive contribution to international peace'. Foreign Minister Julie Bishop claimed that 'Australia fully supports reforms that increase Japan's role in our shared interests in regional and international peace and security' (Bishop, 2015). An enhanced international role for Japan, including the ability to contribute to 'collective self-defence', is seen by Australia as a welcome and beneficial move towards 'normalisation'. Moreover, by bolstering Japan's diplomatic space, it 'reassures' a Japan that might feel increasingly isolated and threatened in what it identifies as 'an increasingly severe security environment' – assailed from all sides by territorial disputes and incursions by its neighbours (Ministry of Defense of Japan, 2016). Thus, according to Yusuke Ishihara, 'In Australia's view, this reassurance function helps prevent an extensive Sino-Japanese rivalry from emerging and disrupting the regional order' (Ishihara, 2013: 92).

As well as their joint investment in building a stable regional security architecture, Australia has specifically worked in accord with Japan to fend off disruptions to regional norms, such as Chinese challenges to freedom of navigation in the South China Sea and the attempt to extend an Air Defence Identification Zone (ADIZ) over the area. At their July 2014 summit, Prime

Ministers Abbott and Abe declared that '[t]hey opposed any unilateral attempt to alter the status quo in the East and South China Seas by the use of force or coercion' (Ministry of Foreign Affairs of Japan, 2014).

In relation to this issue, Canberra coordinates defence engagement and capacity-building efforts with Southeast Asian states (such as the Philippines) with Tokyo. Australia has received similar support in its own 'near abroad' through the coordination of official development assistance (ODA) with Japan among the Pacific Island Countries (PICS) (through the 2011 Memorandum of Understanding on International Development Cooperation) (Department of Foreign Affairs and Trade, 2011). Also on a regional plane, their close cooperation on non-proliferation and disarmament extends to a mutual interest in the denuclearisation of the Korean peninsula, through efforts to persuade the Democratic People's Republic of Korea (DPRK) to divest itself of its nuclear weapons programme. Taken together with the agreements described earlier, these amount to what might be dubbed a 'Japan–Australia security consensus' (Ishihara, 2014: 121).

While the evidence and ability to cooperate across this array of shared interests/issue areas are found across several agencies and in the contents of a large number of joint documents/statements, it is perhaps the seminal JDSC that best expresses how wider security cooperation will be operationalised. The Department of Foreign Affairs and Trade (DFAT) calls it 'a foundation for wide-ranging cooperation on security issues between Australia and Japan, including in law enforcement; border security; counterterrorism; disarmament and counter-proliferation of weapons of mass destruction; maritime and aviation security; peace operations and humanitarian relief operations' (Department of Foreign Affairs and Trade, 2016b).

In other words, it creates the basis for broad bilateral security cooperation in both the 'traditional' and 'non-traditional' spheres. Examples of this practical cooperation in action include the HA/DR (Humanitarian Assistance/Disaster Relief) provided by Australia in the wake of the 3.11 'triple disaster' under Operation Pacific Assist, and their joint efforts in SAR (Search And Rescue) for the missing Malaysian airliner MH370. Operationalizing JDSC activities naturally requires an enhancement of military-to-military cooperation.

Normative umbrella

Concomitantly, Australian alignment with Japan is reinforced (and sometimes justified) in terms of shared values. DFAT proclaims that '[t]he relationship is underpinned by a shared commitment to democracy, human rights and the rule of law' (Department of Foreign Affairs and Trade, 2016b). Whether security alignments are actually driven by 'values' is questionable (and would be rejected in standard realist/structural explanations) (Wilkins, 2007). This is revealed through Abe's proposals for an 'arc of democracies' or 'democratic security diamond' (with the latter in particular alluding to its real purpose through the inclusion of the term 'security'). Yet there is some evidence in the same accounts that 'ideology' and 'domestic similarities' make for smoother alignments/alliances, and this would certainly apply to Australia and Japan (as it does with the US) (Kegley and Raymond, 1990; Risse-Kappen, 1995). A common refrain heard from official and other sources is that the countries are 'natural partners' (Downer, 1997). On the basis of liberal democratic traditions, principles of 'free trade' and commitment to human rights, Australia shares with Japan certain behavioural 'norms' that create mutual understanding and facilitate cooperation. John Lee points out that 'both countries share very similar political systems and moral world views to each other, unlike China' (Lee, 2014).

Part of this has to do with issues of 'trust'. Some data show that high levels of trust have been accumulated between the Australians and the Japanese, and the evidence of forthright cooperation and wide interaction bears witness to this. As a result, it may be appropriate to characterise Australia and Japan as inhabiting a bilateral condition of 'security community' – they enjoy mutual expectations of peaceful relations and no longer seriously plan for war against one another (Nautilus Institute, 2011; Weeks, 2011). This is particularly notable in a region where Japan is persistently held accountable for its misdeeds during World War II, foreclosing close cooperation with the People's Republic of China (PRC) and the two Koreas, and restricting Tokyo's space for foreign policy manoeuvre. It is clear from discussion with Australian (and American) interlocutors that while historical issues continue to permeate the policies of some countries in the Asian region, this factor is not present to any noticeable degree in the case of relations between Canberra and Tokyo.[1] Indeed, Australia has appeared largely satisfied with Prime Minister Abe's speech in Parliament expressing regret for events that occurred during the Pacific War (and Prime Minister Abbott even went as far as to praise the bravery of Japanese submariners in return). Peter Mauch notes, 'Australian receptivity to a forward-looking bilateral relationship, as opposed to a rancorous relationship defined by deep divisions over memories of Japan's imperial past' (Mauch, 2014: 2). On the contrary, Canberra, like Washington, has supported Japan's tentative steps towards 'normalisation' of its international status and security role, a posture that has been strongly welcomed by the government of Japan.[2]

There is no doubt that even if shared values/trust are not the principal reasons for the closer alignment, they certainly actuate it and reinforce it, making certain 'sensitive' activities in the security/defence/intelligence sphere realistic options. As part of the 'diffuse reciprocity' that has begun to characterise the relationship, ASIS (the Australian Secret Intelligence Service) has provided training for Japanese intelligence services (Maley, 2015). Such cooperation will likely advance as Japan works to tighten up on the frequency of intelligence 'leaks' (Williams, 2010).

Military and defence integration

Building upon the joint operational experience gained in working with the Japanese Ground Self-Defense Force (GSDF) in southern Iraq in 2006, Australia has continued to deepen its military-to-military relations with Japan. This has involved regularised joint exercises since 2009, such as the *Nichi-Go* Trident maritime exercises, as well as air and special operations joint exercises. The loosening of Japanese prohibitions on 'collective self-defence' potentially allows more productive cooperation with Australia on peacekeeping or other military operations. As a result of Japan's loosening of its arms export limitations, Australia is primed to benefit from the transfer of high-end defence technology. However, after a controversial competitive evaluation process, Canberra eventually rejected Japan's bid for the SEA 1000 Future Submarine Programme. After awarding the tender to the French manufacturer DCNS, the Australian government has been faced with the challenge of how to delicately handle this major setback in bilateral relations (see Gady, 2016). With the submarine procurement perhaps seen as rather over-ambitious at the time by many in Canberra, this setback does not preclude future defence technology collaboration, particularly on more modest proposals.

Economic ties (trade and investment)

Australia enjoys a very healthy trading and investment relationship with Japan, with a high degree of complementarity between them. Though, like all countries in the Asia-Pacific region, China takes precedence in terms of sheer economic weight (accounting for c. A$150 billion of Australia's two-way trade against c. A$70 billion for Japan), the country remains the second most important overall partner for Australia (and the second largest export market, enjoying a substantial trade surplus). Japan has been a long-term and trusted trading partner since the boom days of the 1970s–1990s, its apogee reflected in the NARA treaty of 1976, though the flow has plateaued over recent years (Drysdale, 2006). Given the significance of Japan as an export destination and investor, Australia has a strong stake in the success of 'Abenomics', with Prime Minister Abbott giving his endorsement to this plan during the 2014 leadership summit. Another of Abbott's achievements was to get a rapid resolution of the ongoing FTA negotiations in 2014 with the signing of the *Japan–Australia Economic Partnership Agreement* (JAEPA), which entered into force in 2015. A Joint Statement in 2014 asserted: 'The JAEPA will underpin the expansion of bilateral trade and investment for decades to come, taking bilateral economic relations to a new level' (Ministry of Foreign Affairs of Japan, 2014). Moreover, Japan is the fourth largest investor in Australia (c. A$199.6 billion) in 2015 after the US and the UK, and has not faced the same suspicions as China when seeking major investments in strategic industries or infrastructure (Department of Foreign Affairs and Trade, 2016a). Indeed, Japan's investment in major infrastructure projects in Australia, such as the Ichthys project near Darwin, is expected to assist the country in being the world's largest producer of Liquid Natural Gas (LNG) in the coming years.

People-to-people ties

As part of the prioritisation of the special relationship, Australia has renewed its former interest in building upon the strong civil connections that were begun in the 1980s–1990s with the establishment of 'sister city' relationships (e.g. Sydney–Nagoya, 1980) (City of Sydney, 2016). There is a suite of relevant civil organisations dedicated to furthering either general or specific aspects of Australia's relations with Japan. These include, for example, in no particular order, the Australia-Japan Foundation (in DFAT, and related Australia–Japan Conference/Australia–Japan Dialogue), the National Federation of Australia–Japan Societies, the Australia Japan Business Co-operation Committee, the Japanese Studies Association of Australia and the Australia–Japan Research Centre (at the Australian National University (ANU)). Increased attention is being given to people-to-people ties through programmes like the Japan Exchange and Teaching Programme (JET), the Japan External Trade Organization (JETRO), the New Colombo Plan (Department of Foreign Affairs and Trade, 2016c) and the (study-abroad) *tobitate* programme (Department of Education and Training, 2014). Finally, tangible bilateral institutional linkages between universities are emerging (e.g. Meiji-University of Western Sydney (UWS)). People-to-people (track III or IV) ties should not be exaggerated in this case, but evidence from similar strategic partnerships, for example Russia–China, shows that leaders pay attention to the development of reciprocally friendly contacts with states that are key diplomatic partners in order to generate and buttress grass-roots support for relevant policies.

Incentives/disincentives for Canberra

Continuing to deepen security relations with Japan (and enhance the overall relationship) offers appealing incentives for Australia. First, as the world's third largest economic power, with formidable technological expertise and highly convergent diplomatic/security interests, Japan's friendship is an immensely powerful asset for 'middle power' Australia. That Tokyo has assiduously pursued closer ties with Australia cannot be seen as other than an immensely valuable opportunity, according to mainstream opinion. Japan's proactive pursuit of 'like-minded' partners has redounded to Australia's benefit, with Tokyo acceding to favourable FTAs and opening the way for major defence-technological cooperation (though the failed submarine deal mentioned earlier has set this back considerably, at the time of writing). There are few likely candidate states that could replicate these benefits for Australia, and it should be noted that despite the strong economic plank of the Australia–PRC relationship (frequently given inordinate emphasis among commentators), broader cooperation is extremely limited when measured against common strategic interests and shared values.

Political support in Australia

The strategic partnership relationship was initiated (1995) and pushed forward energetically (2007) under the Coalition (Liberal) leadership of Prime Minister John Howard. Though the Labour government of Kevin Rudd failed to exhibit the obvious warmth towards Japan of the previous government – his personal expertise naturally inclining him towards China – the momentum built up under Howard continued unabated nonetheless. When Julia Gillard took over as prime minister, she enjoyed an excellent relationship with Tokyo on account of the generous support provided under Pacific Assist and her visit to disaster-stricken areas in Tohoku ('koala diplomacy'). As indicated in the introduction, Coalition Prime Minister Tony Abbott took the relationship to new heights to create the 'special strategic partnership', energised by his warm relations with like-minded conservative Prime Minister Shinzō Abe. Indeed, he appeared to get carried away with his enthusiasm for Japan, proclaiming it the 'best friend' and 'ally' of Australia (and controversially praising Japanese World War II submariners). The abrupt displacement of Abbott and his replacement with Malcolm Turnbull in July 2015 may have interrupted the momentum built up under Abbott, though it remains too early to forecast at this time, Turnbull is widely held to be more 'nuanced' as well as more 'pro-Chinese'. This may not matter, as the strategic partnership is now firmly embedded into Australian foreign policy and has thus acquired a bureaucratic/institutional momentum of its own. Moreover, as a diplomatic priority, it enjoys bipartisan support in Australia (as well as Japan). Peter Jennings confirms that 'growing military ties with Tokyo aren't accidental but the result of careful and bipartisan policy development over recent years' (Jennings, 2012: 12). The strategic partnership therefore has firm support in Australia, and the next two-plus-two meeting is expected to work on 'enhancing training and exercises, increased personnel exchanges, deepening cooperation on humanitarian assistance and disaster relief, maritime security, peacekeeping, capacity building and enhanced trilateral security cooperation' (Minister for Foreign Affairs, 2014).

This is not to say that the bilateral relationship is entirely without disagreement or friction. There are two prominent issues of discord at this time. The first is confined to a specific issue: Japanese whaling activities in waters of the Southern Ocean (a portion of which are claimed by Australia as territorial waters). Australia took Japan to the International Court of Justice over breaches of international law regarding its illegal harvesting of whales in the name of 'research'. Australia won the case, and Japan has been forced to desist from these activities. However, recent news suggests that Japan is actively seeking ways to challenge or circumvent the ban, and this has become an emotive issue between environmental protectionists, on the one side, and Japanese nationalists, on the other (the irony being that Japan actually fails to consume most of the meat it argues is such a distinctive part of its national cuisine). However, acrimony between the two countries has largely been confined to this narrow issue, and many officials on both sides have insisted that it will not interfere with the overall relationship. At the level of high politics, this is probably accurate, however, if an unfortunate incident of some kind occurred in the Southern Ocean, this could quite easy inflame Australian public opinion into broader anti-Japanese sentiment.

The second, and perhaps more consequential, cleavage between Australia and Japan can be dubbed the 'China gap'. Ishihara has identified a 'significant divergence between Japan and Australia in both policy and perception vis-à-vis China' (Ishihara, 2014: 94). More specifically, Australia, though sharing general concern with Japan and the US about Chinese provocations in the East China and South China seas, for example, does not feel strongly threatened by the rise of Chinese military power per se due to its geographic distance and the absence of territorial and historical disputes. On this basis, a number of scholars and analysts have articulated their opposition to the increasing security cooperation – and especially the promulgation of a full military alliance – with Japan (discussed at length by the author elsewhere) (Wilkins, 2015, 2016). Hugh White in particular has publicly argued that Australia needs to 'hit the pause button' and to 'think twice' about further solidifying its new strategic partnership with Japan. He is joined by other academics and commentators who share the view that under no circumstances should Beijing be provoked and that Canberra should (correctly) not 'take sides' over the Senkakus/Diaoyu issue (Jaivin, 2014). In this reading, any form of defence alliance or axis of democracies creates unacceptable risks for Australia. Raoul Heinrichs adds that '[n]either would serve Australia's interests. Both are thinly veiled attempts at edging Australia into a more confrontational posture towards China' (Heinrichs, 2013).

This view, though vociferously expressed, has yet to gain serious purchase in mainstream academic or policy circles in Australia (or elsewhere). There is little evidence that this perspective has influenced government policy, especially under Abbott, but it may potentially gain a more sympathetic hearing under the new prime minister, Turnbull. The failure of such arguments to gain more traction is at least partially accounted for when the bilateral strategic partnership is placed into two different contexts.

The wider contexts

Up to this point, this chapter has sought, as much as is feasible, to keep its analysis of relations between Australia and Japan confined to the purely bilateral context. However, the reality is that no strategic partnership is created to operate in an exclusively bilateral vacuum. It is now worth examining, first, how Australia's enhanced security alignment with Japan fits into the context of the overall US alliance system, of which both form an integral part. Second, it is possible to consider that the bilateral context could operate in an alternate and possibly emerging context of 'middle power concert' in which the US factor no longer takes precedence.

It is rather complicated to entirely disaggregate the bilateral Australia–Japan security alignment from the context of the American alliance system in the Asia-Pacific for two intertwined reasons. The first aspect is the continuance of their Cold War status as 'quasi-allies', as noted earlier. Australia and Japan remain indirectly (or 'passively') aligned through their formal defence treaties of 1951 with a third party (the US). But the scale of increased bilateral security ties raises the question of whether these serve as the building blocks of an 'alliance' in all but name; an alliance with a small 'a' (Dobell, 2014). The second aspect is the appearance of direct trilateral security cooperation between all three allies, mainly through the mechanism of the Trilateral Strategic Dialogue (TSD) process, begun in 2006. Thus, Ishihara recognises that '[t]he most important item on the agenda of Japan–Australia cooperation in the Asia-Pacific is the further strengthening of the trilateral defence collaboration with the United States' (Ishihara, 2014: 110). For reasons noted earlier, the commitment of Australia and Japan to the American alliance system is deepening as they seek to preserve American pre-eminence and the San Francisco system of regional order that Washington upholds (along with other treaty allies). As Ishihara attests, 'One of the factors underlying the advancement of the Japan–US–Australia trilateral cooperation in the Asia-Pacific is a shared objective to assist US rebalancing towards the Asia-Pacific' (Ishihara, 2014: 111). Other attempts to 'network' existing American allies and partners, such as 'trilateralization' between the US, Japan and Korea, and the effort to add India to the TSD to form a 'quadrilateral' (Abe's 'democratic security diamond'), have met with considerably less success. Such allegiance is reflected on a broader scale by their participation in the American-led Trans-Pacific Partnership (TPP), which seeks to consolidate the economies of Washington's main allies, partners and clients into a coherent trading bloc (potentially vis-à-vis Chinese/ASEAN-led attempts to build economic architecture, such as the AIIB (Asian Infrastructure Investment Bank) and RCEP (Regional Comprehensive Economic Partnership)) (though at the time of writing the TPP appeared to have been discarded by the US, leaving Canberra and Tokyo scrambling to either salvage or remake the TPP minus Washington).

As a result of these two factors – the failure of the Australian and Japanese 'spokes' to dissolve their individual treaty alliances with the US upon the expiry of the Soviet threat (against which they were primarily designed), in accord with traditional alliance theory, and their proactive attempts to consolidate and strengthen the trilateral 'core' of a recalibrated US alliance network – commentators have been led to speak of a 'virtual alliance' (or 'JANZUS') emerging between the three powers (Wilkins, 2007). Washington's encouragement of its allies to connect or 'network' the spokes is a gambit to reinforce the existing alliance system by getting its allies to contribute more to its overall maintenance and compensate for the leader's relative decline in overmatching power. Numerous trilateral (as well as multilateral) military exercises have occurred between the three countries since 2009, the most recent being Pacific Bond (2012) and Cope North Guam (2013). Graeme Dobell identifies that 'Australia and Japan are becoming allies, without a formal when-the-shooting-starts-bilateral-alliance, because of the trilateral that expresses their alliances with the US' (Dobell, 2014). An examination of the convergence of the military procurement and defence postures (new amphibious/submarine capabilities) of Australia and Japan in relation to overall American strategy (and 'Air-Sea Battle' doctrine) supplies further evidence to substantiate this contention. Of course, a bona fide alliance, according to international relations theory, is predicated upon a common danger or mutual threat. While the TSD and other joint statements highlight non-traditional security challenges and upholding 'peace and prosperity' in the region, most observers – including the Chinese themselves – have discerned the real (potential) target: the PRC. This accounts for some of the former critique, with White arguing: 'Our enthusiasm for an alliance with Japan, like our agreement to host US Marines in Darwin, clearly put us in the US–Japan camp, supporting what is in effect a policy of containing China' (White, 2012: 4). Thus, the important point is that the bilateral Australia–Japan security alignment, perhaps seemingly innocuous at first glance, takes on a more robust and, to some, dangerous aspect when considered explicitly within the context of the US alliance system as a whole and the TSD in particular.

On the other hand, looked at from an alternative perspective, Australia's new strategic partnership with Japan could independently be viewed as a nascent attempt between two important secondary powers to 'hedge' against possible (negative) future outcomes in the regional security order, should their attempt to reinforce existing US pre-eminence fail and the San Francisco system that they currently rely upon crumble. This could occur through natural decline or active Chinese pressure. Analysts such as David Lang indicate that China is 'working to push the US out of the region by eroding US military primacy and power and raising the cost of intervention, leaving an "Asia for Asians"' (Lang, 2015). This could happen through the gradual (or sudden) withdrawal of American power and influence in the region, whereby China becomes the new regional hegemon – a circumstance that both countries seek to avoid. Or, it could eventuate by some form of grand bargain whereby the US and the PRC come to an arrangement to share power and create a new bipolar order, in which the significant secondary powers such as Australia and Japan would be sidelined. As such, the Australian strategic partnership with Japan – two countries that share a strong track record in forging and upholding new forms of regional security architecture – could provide the nucleus of a form of so-called 'middle power concert' (or 'coalition'), according to some commentators (Medcalf and Mohan, 2014). Obvious additions to this concert would be India, South Korea and Indonesia (all countries sometimes labelled as 'middle powers') or, indeed, ASEAN as a whole.[3] A recent example of a new effort in middle power cooperation is a trilateral between Australia, Japan and India. Lang notes that

> there's a growing alignment of interests, values and concerns among Australia, Japan and India. All share an interest in preserving a peaceful and stable regional order and avoiding a Pax Sinica. All value democracy, freedom and the rule of law. And all are concerned by China's military build-up, defiance of international law and norms, and increasingly assertive attempts to unilaterally force a shift in the regional status quo. (Lang, 2015)

Notably, all these three countries have bilateral 'strategic partnership' relationships with one another (Australia–Japan/Australia–India/Japan–India). The thickening network of connections between these countries indicates that such possibilities are being contemplated, even if the time is not yet deemed ripe for more overt action. Prudent statecraft dictates a contingency plan against both the withdrawal of the US and the possibility that China's rise does not turn out to be 'peaceful'.

Conclusions

Since the development of the 'strategic partnership' mechanism of security cooperation is a relatively new development in terms of security alignment and most markedly fails to conform to well-entrenched notions of 'alliance', analysts have struggled to grapple with its purpose and implications. Though such partnerships have proliferated widely since the first (genuine) example of the Sino-Russian partnership in 1996, we still lack an effective means of classifying and conceptualising them. The Australian strategic partnership with Japan entails peculiar difficulties, since it inhabits multiple contexts (and embodies multiple purposes) at the same time, thus confounding straightforward analyses. The *a priori* existence of 'quasi-alliance' status through independent defence treaties with the US and the emergence of dedicated trilateral security cooperation blur the boundaries of the constituent parts of the bilateral strategic partnership, as well as obfuscating its true nature and purpose. Malcolm Cook offers a neat way to bridge its multifaceted nature by referring to Australia and Japan as 'aligned allies'; that is, aligned through strategic partnership as allies of the US (Cook, 2015).

In conclusion, the strategic partnership/special relationship with Japan serves Australian national interests when perceived from three different (but not necessarily mutually exclusive) angles. First, Australian alignment with Japan is an enhancement of direct security ties with a longer-term partner, which yields multiple benefits. Second, such cooperation assists Australia (and Japan) in reinforcing its alliance relationship with the US, and the 'hub and spoke' system as a whole, upon which its ultimate security rests. Third, from an alternative perspective, the strategic partnership may serve as the nucleus of a wider coalition/concert of medium powers as a 'hedge' against future scenarios involving US strategic withdrawal, Chinese hegemony, or 'G2' power-sharing.

Notes

1 Interestingly, South Korean organizations tried to orchestrate the erection of a 'comfort women' statue in a predominantly Korean neighbourhood of Strathfield near Sydney. The citizens voted down the proposal.
2 Some in Australia have been critical of this direction; see Morris-Suzuki, Chapman and Stevens (2014).
3 This chapter acknowledges the problematic nature of applying the term 'middle power' to such a diverse set of states, especially in the case of Japan. The term is, however, widely used as shorthand, and its full permutations can be examined in Bruce and O'Neil (2014).

References

Bishop, J., 2015. 'Australia Welcomes Japan's Security Reforms', 19 September, at: http://foreignminister.gov.au/releases/Pages/2015/jb_mr_150919.aspx.
Bruce, G. and O'Neil, A. (eds), 2014. *Middle Powers and the Rise of China* (Washington, DC: Georgetown University Press).
Cha, V., 1999. *Alignment despite Antagonism: The United States-Korea-Japan Security Triangle* (Stanford: Stanford University Press).
City of Sydney, 2016. 'Sister Cities', at: www.cityofsydney.nsw.gov.au/learn/about-sydney/sister-cities.

Cook, M., 2015. 'Aligned Allies: The Australia-Japan Strategic Partnership' (Speech at the Lowy Institute), 19 February, at: www.lowyinstitute.org/news-and-media/audio/aligned-allies-australia-japan-strategic-partnership.

Department of Defence Australia, 2014. 'Defence Minister David Johnston Hails Defence Science and Technology Accord with Japan', 8 July, at: www.minister.defence.gov.au/minister/david-johnston/media-releases/minister-defence-defence-minister-david-johnston-hails.

Department of Education and Training, 2014. 'Strengthening University Partnerships Australia-Japan', at: internationaleducation.gov.au/News/Latest-News/Pages/Article-Strengthening-university-partnerships-Australia-Japan.aspx.

Department of Foreign Affairs and Trade, 1976. 'Basic Treaty of Friendship and Co-operation between Australia and Japan', 16 June, at: http://dfat.gov.au/geo/japan/pages/basic-treaty-of-friendship-and-co-operation-between-australia-and-japan.aspx.

Department of Foreign Affairs and Trade, 2011. 'Memorandum of Understanding (MOU) on International Development Cooperation between Australia and Japan', 12 December, at: dfat.gov.au/geo/japan/Pages/memorandum-of-understanding-mou-on-international-development-cooperation-between-australia-and-japan.aspx.

Department of Foreign Affairs and Trade, 2014. 'Agreement between Australia and Japan for an Economic Partnership', 8 July, at: http://dfat.gov.au/trade/agreements/jaepa/official-documents/Pages/official-documents.aspx.

Department of Foreign Affairs and Trade, 2016a. International Investment Australia 2015 (Canberra: Statistics Section, Department of Foreign Affairs and Trade).

Department of Foreign Affairs and Trade, 2016b. 'Japan Country Brief', at: http://dfat.gov.au/geo/japan/pages/japan-country-brief.aspx.

Department of Foreign Affairs and Trade. 2016c. 'New Colombo Plan', at: dfat.gov.au/people-to-people/new-colombo-plan/Pages/new-colombo-plan.aspx (accessed 30 June 2017).

Dobell, G., 2014. 'Japan as Small "a" Ally', *The Strategist*, 22 September.

Downer, A., 1997. '"Natural Partners" – Australia and Japan: Past, Present and Future' (Address by The Hon Alexander Downer, Minister for Foreign Affairs, to the 20th Australia Japan Relations Symposium, Canberra, 26 May).

Drysdale, P., 2006. 'Did the NARA Treaty Make a Difference?', *Australian Journal of International Affairs*, 60(4): 490–505.

Evans, G. and Kawaguchi, Y., 2009. *Eliminating Nuclear Threats: A Practical Agenda for Global Policymakers, Report of the International Commission on Nuclear Non-proliferation and Disarmament* (Canberra: International Commission on Nuclear Non-proliferation and Disarmament).

Gady, F.-S., 2016. 'Why Japan Lost the Bid to Build Australia's New Subs', *The Diplomat*, 27 April, at: http://thediplomat.com/2016/04/why-japan-lost-the-bid-to-build-australias-new-subs/.

Garnaut, J., 2014, 'Ties with Japan Amount to a Quasi-alliance, Says Tokyo' *The Age*, 27 October, p. 7.

Heinrichs, R., 2013. 'PM Stumbling around the International Stage', *Sydney Morning Herald*, 6 November.

Ishihara, Y., 2013. 'Japan-Australia Security Relations and the Rise of China: Pursuing the "Bilateral-Plus" Approaches', UNISCI Discussion Papers: 81–98.

Ishihara, Y., 2014. 'Japan-Australia Defence Cooperation in the Asia-Pacific Region', in Tow, W. and Yoshizaki, T. (eds), *Beyond the Hub and Spokes: Australia-Japan Security*

Cooperation, ANU-NIDS Joint Research Project No. 10 (Tokyo: The National Institute for Defense Studies), pp. 93–122.

Jaivin, L., 2014. 'Japan, China, Senkaku, Diaoyu: Why Is Australia Taking Sides in the East China Sea?', *Monthly*, February.

Jennings, P., 2012. 'Defending Stronger Ties with Japan', *The Australian*, 14 December, p. 12.

Kegley, C. and Raymond, G., 1990. *When Trust Breaks Down: Alliance Norms and World Politics* (Columbia, SC: University of South Carolina Press).

Lang, D., 2015. 'The Not-Quite-Quadrilateral: Australia, Japan and India', *Strategic Insights*, 92(July): 1–14.

Lee, J., 2014. 'Why Australia's Relationship with Japan Infuriates China', *Business Spectator*, 10 September.

Maley, P., 2015. 'Spies Like Us: ASIS Training Japanese', *The Australian*, 21 March.

Mauch, P., 2014. 'Abe's Recent Visit to Australia: Building Domestic Consensus behind a Strategy of Containing China?', *China Policy Institute Policy Paper*, 1: 1–9.

Medcalf, R. and Mohan, C. R., 2014. 'Responding to Indo-Pacific rivalry: Australia, India and Middle Power Coalitions', *Lowy Institute Analysis*, 8 August 2014, at: www.lowyinstitute.org/publications/responding-indo-pacific-rivalry-australia-india-and-middle-power-coalitions.

Minister for Foreign Affairs, 2014. '5th Japan-Australia 2+2 Foreign and Defence Ministerial Consultations', 12 June, at: http://foreignminister.gov.au/releases/Pages/2014/jb_mr_140612a.aspx.

Ministry of Defense of Japan, 2016. *Defense of Japan 2016* (Tokyo: Ministry of Defense).

Ministry of Foreign Affairs of Japan, 2007. 'Japan-Australia Joint Declaration on Security Cooperation', 13 March, at: http://www.mofa.go.jp/region/asia-paci/australia/joint0703.html.

Ministry of Foreign Affairs of Japan, 2010. 'Agreement between the Government of Japan and the Government of Australia concerning Reciprocal Provision of Supplies And Services between the Self-Defence Forces of Japan and the Australian Defence Force', 19 May, at: www.mofa.go.jp/region/asia-paci/australia/pdfs/agree1005.pdf.

Ministry of Foreign Affairs of Japan, 2012. 'Signing of the Japan-Australia Information Security Agreement (ISA)', 17 May, at: www.mofa.go.jp/announce/announce/2012/5/0517_01.html.

Ministry of Foreign Affairs of Japan, 2014. 'Prime Minister Abbott and Prime Minister Abe Joint Statement: Special Strategic Partnership for the 21st Century', 8 July, at: www.mofa.go.jp/files/000044543.pdf.

Morris-Suzuki, T., Chapman, D. and Stevens, C., 2014. 'Australia-Japan Relations: An Alternative Future', *Inside Story*, 15 July.

Nautilus Institute, 2011. 'Australia-Japan: Towards a Sustainable Security Community' (Public forum, International House, Tokyo, 12 November).

Parliament of Australia, 2000. 'Agreement on Commerce between Australia and Japan, 1957', in *Japan's Economy and Implications for Australia* (Canberra: Parliament House), pp. 257–270.

Placek, K., 2014. 'Australia and Japan's "Special Relationship": Abe's Visit Looks Set to Bolster Bilateral Ties on Both the Economic and Defence Fronts', *The Diplomat*, 9 July.

Risse-Kappen, T., 1995. *Cooperation among Democracies: The European Influence on U.S. Foreign Policy* (Princeton, NJ: Princeton University Press).

Rix, A., 1999. *The Australia-Japan Political Alignment: 1952 to the Present, Routledge Studies in the Modern History of Asia* (London: Routledge).

Satake, T., 2015. 'Why a Strong Japan–Australia Relationship Matters', *East Asia Forum*, at: www.eastasiaforum.org/2015/06/02/why-a-strong-japan-australia-relationship-matters/.

Walton, D., 2007. 'Australia and Japan: Challenges and Opportunities', in *Trading on Alliance Security: Australia in World Affairs 2001–2005* (Oxford: Oxford University Press 2007), pp. 72–88.

Weeks, D., 2011. 'An East Asian Security Community: Japan, Australia and Resources as "Security"', *Australian Journal of International Affairs*, 65(1): 61–80.

White, H., 2012. 'An Australian-Japan Alliance?', in *The Centre of Gravity Series*, No. 4 (Canberra: Strategic & Defence Studies Centre ANU College of Asia & the Pacific).

Wilkins, T. S., 2007. 'Towards a "Trilateral Alliance?" Understanding the Role of Expediency and Values in American–Japanese–Australian Relations', *Asian Security*, 3(3): 251–278.

Wilkins, T. S., 2010. 'Japan's Alliance Diversification: A Comparative Analysis of the Indian and Australian Strategic Partnerships', *International Relations of the Asia-Pacific*, 11(1): 115–155.

Wilkins, T. S., 2011. '"Alignment", not "Alliance" – the Shifting Paradigm of International Security Cooperation: Toward a Conceptual Taxonomy of Alignment', *Review of International Studies*, 38(1): 53–76.

Wilkins, T. S., 2015. 'From Strategic Partnership to Strategic Alliance? Australia-Japan Security Ties and the Asia-Pacific', *Asia Policy*, 20: 81–111.

Wilkins, T. S., 2016. 'The Japan Choice: Reconsidering the Risks and Opportunities of the "Special Relationship" for Australia', *International Relations of the Asia-Pacific*, 16(3): 477–520.

Williams, B. 2010. 'The Challenges of Intelligence Oversight in a Normalising Japan', in Baldino, D. (ed.), *Democratic Oversight of Intelligence Services* (Annandale, NSW: The Federation Press), pp. 161–186.

2

The Japanese perspective on the security partnership with Australia

Yusuke Ishihara

Introduction

THIS CHAPTER ARGUES that what can be called the second evolution is taking shape in the bilateral relationship between Tokyo and Canberra, especially in the security-defence field. In retrospect, during the years since the Joint Declaration on Security Cooperation in March 2007, the two countries were going through the period of the first evolution, in which the bilateral cooperation focused on non-traditional security issues such as peacekeeping operations (PKO) and humanitarian assistance/disaster relief (HA/DR). By contrast, the key trend that has been emerging over the past few years, particularly since the inauguration of the second Shinzō Abe government in December 2012, is that Japan and Australia are going beyond the first evolution and developing bilateral cooperation in more traditional security fields. This is what this chapter calls the second evolution of Japan–Australia security ties.

Even though, to the disappointment of experts and officials in many quarters of both countries, Japan was not chosen as the primary partner for Australia's Future Submarine Fleet programme, the second evolution is by no means dead. As this chapter will analyse, other key items of more traditional security cooperation are being actively planned and implemented.

The analysis in this chapter is threefold. Its first section sheds light on the deepening strategic convergence between the two countries' regional policies. As China's challenge vis-à-vis regional security has been turning in more assertive directions, the two countries are finding each other's policies in a closer synthesis, as Tokyo and Canberra have closely aligned, if not identical, views on the rules-based order and the US role in the Asia-Pacific region.

The second section analyses the second evolution of the bilateral relations, explaining why the aforementioned alignment of Japanese and Australian security views is closely related to developments in the Japan–Australia relationship.

Finally, the last section discusses the so-called China gap issues. Despite the aforementioned increasing convergence, the residual differences between the two countries' perceptions and policies vis-à-vis China remain as real and potential limits and, if mismanaged, could even become sources of friction and division between Japan and Australia. This section also highlights that the China gap issues have been evolving as the regional security dynamics as well as bilateral relations have changed over recent years.

Abe's security diplomacy in Asia

Particularly since the inauguration of the Abe government in December 2012, Japan's regional diplomacy has been rapidly deepening in ways that enhance Tokyo's security ties with a number of regional partners. Indeed, Japan's active regional diplomacy itself is not news, given that Tokyo has been promoting its relationships with regional partners for decades. A key new trend is that Japan is increasingly willing to inject security items onto the cooperation agenda with countries in the Asia-Pacific and beyond. As the Abe government continues its efforts to change some of the long-standing policies and principles that shaped Japan's security strategy for decades, a number of new security tools have become available for Japan's Asian diplomacy. Defence equipment cooperation, deeper and wider exercise activities, expanded capacity-building programmes, high-level and multi-layered strategic dialogues with 10 Southeast Asian countries, India, Mongolia, Australia, New Zealand, France and the UK have been rapidly expanded to a level that few expected a decade ago.

Needless to say, the key, if not the only, driving force of Japan's increasingly active security diplomacy in the Asia-Pacific region is the assertive turn of China's rise. In 2008, Chinese law enforcement ships began to enter both the contiguous zone and the territorial waters around the Senkaku/Diaoyu Islands, while the People's Liberation Army Navy and Air Force have been stepping up their activities around Japan, including some risky activities such as the direction of fire control radar upon Japanese vessels and aircraft (Ministry of Foreign Affairs of Japan, 2016). The yearly number of scrambles conducted by the Air Self-Defense Force has risen rapidly over recent years.[1] In Japan's perception, China's expansive behaviour is not only a direct risk to Japanese sovereign interests but also part of China's broader challenge to regional order in at least two regards, namely, the rules-based order and the US leading role in Asia.

First, the ways in which China is attempting to challenge Japanese security interests, in Tokyo's perception, constitute direct challenges to international rules and principles. Even though China appears to have, at least so far, avoided provoking deliberate escalations into an outright military conflict, its relentless employment of coercive force to challenge the status quo does contradict the principle of peaceful resolutions of conflict. Likewise, imposing rules upon flight above the high seas fundamentally risks undermining the freedom of overflight. The coercive and risky conduct of Chinese law enforcement vessels and the

People's Liberation Army in the high seas are considered in many quarters of Tokyo and beyond to endanger the free use of the open seas, legally recognised in the *United Nations Convention on the Law of the Sea* (UNCLOS).

When put in this broad perspective, it is no surprise that Japan is also expressing its concerns about China's behaviour in the South China Sea, where Beijing has been using more escalatory tools such as land reclamation activities and positioning some military units on those artificial islands. In his keynote address to the annual Shangri-La Dialogue in 2014, Prime Minister Shinzō Abe emphasised the three key principles for the maritime rules-based order: (1) no claim without legitimate basis in international rules; (2) no coercion; and (3) peaceful settlement for any disputes. Thus, Japan implicitly emphasises these principles as a clear common stake in the context of both the South and East China Seas (Abe, 2014).

This is the strategic context in which Japan's new security diplomacy in Asia is designed to contribute to promoting the rules-based order. One of the key foci is Southeast Asia, where Japan is working to forge a more capable and more integrated Association of Southeast Asian Nations (ASEAN). Japan's capacity-building assistance activities in Southeast Asia, including its projects to support legal knowledge development and the building of medical and other skills in the maritime security area, contribute to the improvement of capability on the part of individual ASEAN countries (Onodera, 2014). Japan's renewed engagement with ASEAN aims to support further integration of ASEAN through a number of ways. For example, by holding the equipment exhibition for ASEAN countries in February 2014 and September 2014, Japan sought new opportunities to take a more direct role in the military build-up of Southeast Asian countries. As the co-chairing country, along with Lao PDR, Japan plays a leading role in the experts' working group (EWG) on HA/DR under the ASEAN Defense Ministers' Meeting (ADMM) Plus framework, which is one of Japan's key policies in its support for ASEAN integration (Chair of the Tokyo Defense Forum, 2015). The EWG on HA/DR is a channel through which Japan could directly offer support for ASEAN defence integration, which plans to establish an ASEAN Militaries Ready Group so that ASEAN can more readily respond to regional disasters under the doctrine of One ASEAN, One Response (Chairman of the 26th ASEAN Summit, 2015). Even though this cooperation is strictly limited to the HA/DR area at the time of writing, this may turn out to be only a stepping stone for the future integration of ASEAN defence organisations to eventually expand into other areas.

The second aspect of Tokyo's view on China's broader challenge concerns its long-term efforts to erode the US role in Asia. To begin with, China's activities in the East China Sea appear to be testing the credibility of the US–Japan alliance and the role of the US in the Asia-Pacific region. Simply put, when and if Japan and the US respond to Chinese provocations differently, that may appear to be a window of opportunity for Beijing to drive a wedge between Tokyo and Washington (Sevastopulo, 2014). In this context, the record of US behaviour over recent years largely underscores the strength, not the weakness, of the US–Japan alliance. On his trip to Japan in 2014, President Barack Obama unequivocally stated that the Senkaku Islands are covered by Article Five of the US–Japan security treaty, while the new Defense Cooperation Guidelines announced after the Security Consultative Committee, or the US–Japan two-plus-two, in May 2015 offer a blueprint for more seamless alliance cooperation and coordination and politically underscore that the defence of Japan remains a core mission for the alliance (Aoki, 2014).

China's challenge to the alliance appears to be a part of China's broader challenge to the US role in Asia. At the 2014 Conference on Interaction and Confidence Building Measures in Asia (CICA), Chinese President Xi Jinping declared China's intention to promote a new Asian security architecture, emphasising the importance of a controversial dictum: Asian problems should be solved by Asian countries themselves (Tiezzi, 2014). This exclusive Asia vision sharply contradicts Japan's long-standing policy of promoting an open and inclusive Asia where the US key roles are firmly anchored. In this context, Japan and China are competing to promote differing visions, not only in the East China Sea but also in Asian institutional architecture. Again, another rationale for Japan's support for ASEAN integrity is ASEAN's role in developing an open multilateral architecture that welcomes the active participation of the US in a number of regional multilateral forums, such as the East Asia Summit (EAS).

On balance, however, it would be misleading to suggest that the Abe government's security diplomacy was so far progressing without challenges. Instead, the past few years have seen some limits and setbacks in the process of boosting Japan's security activities and ties with its regional partners. The most recent example in this regard was the 2015 ADMM Plus meeting, which could not achieve an agreement among the participating countries about the words of the Joint Declaration (JD) (Mahadzir, 2015). As China, Japan and the US competed to promote their own views in the drafting process of the JD, ASEAN countries collectively made the decision to cancel the release of the JD on this occasion. Needless to say, the issue was whether and how the declaration should treat the South China Sea and the rules of the sea.

In fact, the increasing competition between China, Japan and the US in ASEAN-centred multilateralism poses not only a challenge to ASEAN but also a difficult issue for Japan's regional diplomacy. On the one hand, precisely because Japanese policymakers are well aware that ASEAN does not want to invite tension and conflict among external powers into its multilateral endeavours, Japan's struggle vis-à-vis China may be harmful to Japan's efforts to build its image as a constructive partner for ASEAN's integrity and centrality. On the other hand, it is also difficult for Japan to stay silent and avoid counter-moving against China's diplomatic efforts to play down important issues such as the instability in the South China Sea and the maritime rules. Indeed, finding a way out of those two competing logics is a key policy challenge for Japan's security diplomacy in Asia.

Synergy with the coalition governments

Japan has been actively pursuing its new security diplomacy in Asia at a time when Australia's recognition of China as a security challenge is also growing sharper. Australia's perception of China as a security concern started deepening particularly under the Tony Abbott government during the period from September 2013 to September 2015. In the joint statement after the foreign minister-led Trilateral Strategic Dialogue between Japan, Australia and the US in October 2013, the Abbott government agreed to include sharp words of opposition to any unilateral attempt to change the status quo by force in the East China Sea (Department of Foreign Affairs and Trade (Australia), 2013). One month later, the Abbott government issued a strong statement immediately after China's announcement of the establishment of a so-called Air Defence Identification Zone over the East China Sea. The statement criticised China's step as a unilateral and coercive attempt to challenge the status quo (Bishop, 2013). In the same line of logic, the Abbott government also stepped up its criticism of China's assertive moves in the South China Sea in a number of unequivocal ways, including jointly calling for an end to land reclamation activities in the joint statement following the Japan–Australia–US trilateral defence ministerial meeting in May 2015.

The Abbott government's motivation for its move to stand closer to the US and Japan in expressing concerns about China's actions was deeply rooted in its commitment to the rules-based order as well as its alliance relationship with the US. When in opposition, Abbott emphasised the concept of the Anglosphere, a community led once by the UK and now by the US, comprised of those two countries, Australia, New Zealand and Canada. He declared that a large part of modern history was written in English, highlighting the special roles played by the Anglosphere community (Abbott, 2009). What Abbot stressed as the binding element in this community was not only shared linguistic characteristics but values such as freedom, democracy and human rights. With such a strong and, indeed, personal identity of seeing Australia as a part of the Anglosphere, it was no surprise that the Abbott government brought Australia closer to the US and its key Pacific ally Japan in addressing the security risks posed by the assertive rise of China.

Sharing the strong commitment to the rules-based order as well as the recognition of the key role of the common ally in the Asia-Pacific, the two countries' perspectives on China's challenges became more closely aligned than ever. This is one of the primary factors that encouraged the political and personal ties that rapidly developed between the two countries and, indeed, the two leaders. Prime Minister Abbot became the first foreign leader to attend Japan's National Security Council, while Prime Minister Abe also participated in Australia's National Security Committee of the Cabinet and was given a historic opportunity to address the Australian parliament for the first time as Japanese prime minister. Such close ties between Canberra and Tokyo were also given some symbolic nicknames, such as 'New Special Relationship' in reference to the US–UK Special Relationship declared by British Prime Minister Winston Churchill, while Prime Minister Abbot called Japan Australia's best friend in Asia, and Japanese policymakers started designating Australia as Japan's 'quasi-ally', a new terminology widely used in the policy circle in Tokyo (Ishihara, 2015a).

This was the context in which the Japanese policy community received sudden news in September 2015 that Abbott had been toppled by the new Prime Minister Malcolm Turnbull. Particularly in the initial aftermath of the leadership change, there was some concern in many quarters of Tokyo about the future prospects for the bilateral relationship. One Japanese newspaper noted that Australia might possibly tilt towards China and adjust the balance between its bilateral relations with Beijing and Tokyo under the new Turnbull government (Takahashi, 2015). In fact, some of the earlier remarks by Turnbull further fuelled these concerns. For example, when he was communication minister in the Abbott Cabinet, Turnbull stressed at length that Australia and China had fought together against Japan World War II (Turnbull, 2014). Also, media reports from Australia even mentioned Turnbull's 'pivot' to China (McDonald, 2015).

In retrospect, it has become clear that these early concerns about the Turnbull government were largely premature and in many ways misplaced. For one thing, the Turnbull government often appears to use critical language vis-à-vis China's challenges. Prime Minister Turnbull mentioned that China was pushing the envelope in the South China Sea and that Beijing's policies over recent years were 'counterproductive', given that they only encouraged regional countries to further welcome the role of the US, which China has been working hard to compete with (Greene, 2015). The joint statement of the October 2015 US–Australia two-plus-two or AUSMIN, the first such meeting after the inauguration of the Turnbull government, went so far as to refer to the Chinese president and his public statement that China did not intend to militarise the features in the Spratly Islands, and even asked China to follow through (Department of Foreign Affairs and Trade (Australia), 2015). When the US navy conducted Freedom of Navigation Operations within 12 nautical miles of the disputed land features in the South China Sea, first in October 2015 and again in January 2016, Defence Minister Marise Payne released a statement that publicly underscored Australia's position of support for the rules-based order and the US efforts in this context (Wroe, 2016).

Most importantly, the Turnbull government's security concerns about China's rise have been channelled into its defence strategy, outlined in the 2016 Defence White Paper. Careful comparison between the Turnbull government's White Paper and its successors helps illuminate the rise of the China factor in Australia's defence thinking (Department of Defence (Australia), 2016: 67–82). The conceptual basis of the previous three White Papers had been formed largely in the so-called 'concentric circles' (White, 2006: 34–40). The 'concentric circles' idea is basically a geography-based hierarchy of priorities in which the direct defence of Australia is considered as Australia's primary interest, the immediate neighbourhood comprised of the South Pacific, Timor-Leste and Papua New Guinea as the second, the Asia-Pacific or Indo-Pacific region with a special emphasis on Southeast Asia as the third, and finally global security as the fourth.

At first sight, the 2016 White Paper may appear similar in its way of using geography as a key measure in conceptualising Australia's thinking on its strategic interests and objectives. Indeed, what the 2016 Defence White Paper calls the Strategic Defence Interests are conceived as three layers of 'a secure, resilient Australia', 'a secure near region, encompassing maritime South East Asia and the South Pacific' and 'a stable Indo-Pacific region and a rules-based global order'. While these new Strategic Defence Interests clearly embody key conceptual continuities from the previous concentric circles configuration, one significant discontinuity is that all the defence objectives that contribute to these three Strategic Defence Interests are now treated as factors in force building, whereas in the previous idea of concentric circles, the defence of Australia and of the immediate neighbourhood alone were treated as the force structure determinants. The factors that encouraged this evolution of Australia's defence thinking include the importance of maritime Southeast Asia, the rules-based order, important trade routes and the changing power dynamics, all of which are closely related to the rise of China, even though the White Paper unsurprisingly avoids directly mentioning the C word (Schreer, 2016). Many aspects of the thinking implicitly or explicitly expressed in the current White Paper are in close synthesis with the aforementioned policy lines of Japan's security diplomacy in the Asia-Pacific region. In other words, the two countries' views and policies towards regional issues, including the rise of China, have become increasingly aligned over recent years (Satake, 2015b).

Second evolution of Japan–Australia defence cooperation

The new level of strategic convergence between Japan and Australia has been encouraging the further evolution of the already strong bilateral relationship, most visibly in the defence field. The truth is that, particularly since the landmark Joint Declaration on Security Cooperation between Tokyo and Canberra in March 2007, Australia has been increasingly perceived in the Japanese policy circle as Tokyo's second closest security partner. For a long time, the Japanese government has consistently expressed the view that the *de facto* focus of bilateral security cooperation was on the so-called non-traditional security issues. In fact, for many years, the annual Japanese defence White Paper noted: 'as responsible countries in the Asia-Pacific region, Japan and Australia are strengthening mutual cooperation focused primarily on non-traditional security areas such as humanitarian assistance and disaster relief activities' (Ministry of Defense of Japan, 2013: 233). There is an impressive record of close cooperation between the Australian Defence Force (ADF) and the Self-Defense Forces (SDF) in HADR and PKO; we have witnessed their operational collaborations on the ground, for example, in the wake of the March 11 Triple Disaster in Japan in 2011 and the Philippines Typhoon Haiyan disaster in 2013, and in the on-going UNPKO Mission for the newly independent South Sudan. For a long time, non-traditional security has been a flagship area of Japan–Australia cooperation.

Importantly, the long-standing focus on non-traditional security issues in Japan–Australia cooperation was a carefully chosen pathway for the two countries to navigate the development of their closer relationship through a complex set of strategic factors. For one thing, the non-traditional security area was useful for encouraging Japan to build security ties with countries other than the US, as Tokyo was not yet ready to cooperate on any agenda beyond practical activities such as HA/DR and PKO. It was also a useful way for Tokyo and Canberra to demonstrate their strategic willingness to cooperate with Washington in ways that did not necessarily impose too heavy a burden on the shoulders of Japan and Australia. On top of those considerations, the most important factor had to do with China. While Japan and Australia clearly have the motivation to demonstrate the strategic ties among the US and its allies to the regional audience, including those in Beijing, which some policy officials of both sides considered as 'a democratic counter-balance' against China, Tokyo and Canberra were also cautious enough to make sure that the increasing networking of what used to be called the 'hub and spokes' would not be perceived as too provocative a move against Chinese interests. In fact, focusing on the non-traditional security issues was often given as a reason why China should be reassured about the growing Japan–Australia relations and, for that matter, the trilateral cooperation with the US (Minister for Foreign Affairs and Trade (Australia), 2010).

This long-standing characterisation of Japan–Australia bilateral cooperation as a partnership focusing on the non-traditional security areas is, however, rapidly moving into history, as the scope of bilateral cooperation has started expanding over the last few years. Japan's perception of Australia has changed accordingly; the aforementioned Japanese defence White Paper dropped the long-used term 'non-traditional security' as a focus of the bilateral cooperation since 2014 (Ministry of Defense of Japan, 2014: 279). In fact, Japan and

Australia are now closely either cooperating or exploring at least the following two items of rather traditional security cooperation.

The first item is the two countries' respective and coordinated involvement in the South China Sea. In May 2015, Defence Minister Nakatani suggested in the press conference that deterrence vis-à-vis China's activities in the South China Sea is a subject for the trilateral discussions between Japan, Australia and the US at a trilateral coordination mechanism called the Security and Defense Cooperation Forum (SDCF) (Ministry of Defense of Japan, 2015). In fact, Japan and Australia are becoming close partners in contributing to the rules-based order in maritime Southeast Asia, including the South China Sea, through the following two sets of efforts.

First, as the joint statement following the second trilateral summit in November 2014 emphasised, Japan and Australia, along with their ally the US, have been having close discussions to coordinate their respective capacity-building assistance efforts in the maritime security area (Ministry of Foreign Affairs of Japan, 2014). Given that a huge disparity between the capabilities of China and the other Southeast Asian countries creates a window of opportunity for challengers against the status quo, it is self-evident why Japan, Australia and other countries are interested in providing capacity-building assistance to the Philippines, Vietnam and others.

To name a few examples, Tokyo has agreed to offer patrol boats to Vietnam and the Philippines, while, based on the treaty for the transferring of defence equipment signed in February 2016, Japan is reportedly considering the possibility of offering its retired TC-70 aircraft to the Philippines, which will contribute to enhancing Manila's maritime patrolling activities (*Nikkei Shimbun*, 2015). Australia has been a long-standing partner in capacity-building assistance towards the Philippines, which, in Australia's policy terminology, is called the Defence Cooperation Programme. Australia has offered two landing ships to the Philippines and plans to sell three more in the future while cooperating with Japan and the US in assisting the management of the 'National Coast Guard Watch System,' the Philippines' inter-agency coordination mechanism for maritime patrolling and monitoring (Australian Embassy in the Philippines, 2011).

The other set of activities that both countries are conducting in the South China Sea is the deployment of SDF/ADF for a range of missions, including joint training, port calls and surveillance operations. Australia conducts a regular intelligence, surveillance and reconnaissance (ISR) operation called Operation Gateway, in which ADF units, including AP-3Cs using RMAF Butterworth airbase in Malaysia, conduct ISR activities in the Indian Ocean and South China Sea (Department of Defence (Australia), 2015b). ADF has started joining the US–Philippines bilateral exercise, Balikatan, in recent years (Department of Defence (Australia), 2015a). Likewise, Japan sent observers to Balikatan as well as a US–Philippine amphibious exercise, Phiblex, while Tokyo also started holding bilateral naval exercises with Manila, including the surface ship exercise in May 2015 as well as the disaster relief exercise in June 2015, when Philippine officers got on board a Japanese P-3C surveillance aircraft flying over the South China Sea (Ministry of Defense of Japan, 2015).

Japanese Defence Minister Nakatani explains that these activities conducted by SDF and other partners in South China Sea may somewhat discourage the attempts to challenge the status quo. Indeed, none of these activities means Japanese and Australian military commitment to the defence of the Philippines, and nothing guarantees the two countries' operational support for the US–Philippines alliance should a crisis happen in the South China Sea. Yet the explicit and continued demonstration of joint military activities, including frequent joint trainings in contested waters, might make it difficult for Beijing to simply rule out some extreme conflict scenarios in which China would face countries beyond the US and Southeast Asian states (Ishihara, 2015b).

The second item of future cooperation is the application of Japan's new Legislation for Peace and Security, which passed the Diet in September 2015. This is another emerging item on the table between Tokyo and Canberra, which may change the scope of the two countries' operational cooperation in the future. The new legislation introduced roughly three major areas of Self-Defense Forces activities: the limited exercise of the UN chapter right of collective self-defence, the upgraded version of what used be called 'situation in areas surrounding Japan' (SIASJ), and the international peace operations supported by the revised PKO law as well as the newly installed international peace support law. One remarkable feature that can be observed throughout the legislation is that the US is no longer the only potential partner in those legally defined situations where the SDF may operate. Explaining this at the Diet deliberations, Defence Minister Nakatani referred to Australia a few times as a potential partner in those contexts on 12 June 2015 in the National Diet (National Diet of Japan, 2015). Indeed, the introduction of the new legal foundation that allows Japan to consider operationally collaborating with international partners other than the US never automatically presupposes that Japan is ready to actively cooperate with them in those situations. These legally conceived possibilities remain hypothetical unless close discussions and joint planning have been conducted between Tokyo and Canberra as to when, how and why SDF and ADF should be prepared to operationally cooperate based on the new legislation. In this sense, it may be a little premature to have further discussions on the implications of the new Legislation for Peace and Security for Japan–Australia relations. What is at least remarkable and, indeed, unprecedented, however, is that the government does not hesitate to mention Australia explicitly as a potential partner for operational scenarios beyond PKO and HA/DR.

If such new operational planning is to be pursued, it will likely change the nature of the bilateral and trilateral exercises in due course. Currently, the Japanese government cannot conduct any specific-scenario-based exercise with Australia, on the assumption that there is no war-fighting situation in which Japan and Australia will cooperate operationally. The application of the new legislation, if it happens, will change this very assumption and require SDF and ADF to conduct the exercises in such a way as to prepare operational readiness for bilateral cooperation in planned situations. Such potential changes of the nature of the exercise may increase the weight of the messages that these joint exercises send out to the region. This topic only appears more important considering that Japan and Australia are now negotiating a new treaty that will facilitate reciprocal access to each other's sovereign territories and encouraging Australia to participate in the US–Japan alliance exercise, and vice versa.

The second evolution of the bilateral relationship that is encouraging the two countries to go beyond non-traditional security or newly cooperate on issues of a more traditional security nature is related to the China factor in two ways. First, the end of the almost exclusive focus on non-traditional security suggests that the two countries' attitude to the risk of self-fulfilling prophecy has been evolving, though not disappearing, over the past years. This should not be a surprise for anyone who follows Asian security, given that China has started showing a more assertive face to the region, and the notion of the so-called charm offensive strategy is increasingly out of touch with reality. Second, some of the items on which Japan and Australia are now seeking to cooperate closely are clearly directed towards security challenges associated with China. In particular, the coordinated capacity-building assistance and increasing operational activities in the South China Sea are clearly designed to promote stability and the rules-based order in maritime Southeast Asia, where China has been expanding rapidly to create a new normal in its favour.

Evolving 'China gap'

The China gap is a key long-standing issue facing Japan–Australia relations (Ishihara, 2014: 113–120; Satake, 2015a: 24–25). While the rise of China is clearly playing a key role in promoting the second evolution of Japan–Australia defence cooperation, the China factor also appears to continue to constrain the bilateral relationship. Among a number of issues caused by the China gap between Tokyo and Canberra, one long-standing problem is the so-called reassurance gap.

The classic episode of this reassurance gap appeared in the 2006–2007 period, when Japan was proposing the idea of a quadrilateral framework between Japan, Australia, the US and India in the hope of promoting closer cooperation among the democracies at the time of China's historic rise. In fact, those four countries held a separate meeting on the sidelines of the ASEAN Regional Forum (ARF) Senior Officials' Meeting (SOM) in Manila, May 2007, while Japan and Australia participated in the India–US Malabar exercise in the Indian Ocean (United States Navy, 2007). Even though the John Howard government shared the long-term concerns about the rise of China and understood the importance of close ties among these democratic countries, Canberra was also paying more cautious attention to China's perceptions and reactions. Symptomatic of this was Defence Minister Brendan Nelson's statement after the bilateral meeting with his counterpart in Beijing that Australia tried to 'reassure' China about the quadrilateral moves and guaranteed that it did not intend to establish any formal framework (Chellaney, 2007).

Likewise, in the process of the fourth two-plus-two meeting in September 2012, Australia appeared again particularly sensitive about China's perception of Japan–Australia relations. Foreign Minister Bob Carr intended to play down the two-plus-two at a time when the bilateral tensions between Beijing and Tokyo were rising due to the increasing activities of Chinese law enforcement ships in the East China Sea and the Japanese government's policy of purchasing most of the Senkaku Islands in that very month. The Defence Cooperation Agreement, a treaty that was being discussed on the bilateral tracks at that time, was not mentioned in the outcome statement, partly because of the aforementioned concern about China's perception. In his memoirs, Carr emphasised that it was important for Australia to behave carefully so that Japan–Australia relations did not appear to be a containment effort (Carr, 2014: 157–158). Clearly, the issue of reassurance made Australia more cautious in building ties with Japan.

In fact, the potential assurance gap is not just a challenge for Japan's security partners, including Australia, but a difficult question for Japan as well. This is precisely because the solution for addressing this problem is far from easy to find, let alone to implement. For the sake of building closer ties with the partner countries, or more specifically Australia in this chapter's context, it might be wise for Japan to simply work harder to reassure China by refraining from taking steps which China may perceive as provocative. The logic is that such reassurance efforts by Japan vis-à-vis China may also contribute to reassuring its security partners. The risky side of this approach, however, is that it might give Beijing the impression that China has a veto on ways of cooperation among the US allies. This would be counterproductive to Japan's policy aim of showing China the strategic solidarity of Japan and its regional partners. As this chapter has already discussed, the two countries' answer to this strategic question used to be a deliberate focus on non-traditional security. Now that the scope of bilateral cooperation has started going beyond the narrow confines of non-traditional security cooperation, there may no longer be such a straightforward answer to this question.

What makes this issue even more complex is that reassurance is no longer the only aspect of the China gap between Japan and Australia. In fact, the Japan–Australia relationship is increasingly facing two other types of China gap as it goes through its second evolution. First, one emerging issue can be termed an 'engagement gap'. Obviously, there are qualitative and quantitative differences in terms of the two countries' engagement with China. On the one hand, under the banner of Comprehensive Strategic Partnership, China and Australia have been deepening their multi-layered relationship, including defence ties (Ministry of Foreign Affairs of the People's Republic of China, 2014). Based on the 2014 bilateral defence engagement action plan, the ADF and the People's Liberation Army (PLA) regularly conduct joint exercises, such as the live fire and manoeuvre exercise in the South China Sea, as well as the Kowari survival training involving Australia, China and the US, and the HA/DR exercise Cooperation Spirit with the participation of New Zealand (Department of Defence (Australia), 2014).

On the other hand, China and Japan have not yet fully normalised and stabilised their defence contacts. Indeed, it might be misleading to imply that Japan does not take the engagement as seriously as before. The reality is that Japan aims to revitalise its engagement with China, albeit to a very small extent so far. For example, when the SDF participated in the Khan Quest exercise in Mongolia, despite the media reports that Japan's move to get closer to Mongolia is part of Japan's effort to counter-balance against China, the fact is that the deployed SDF officers and the PLA participants did get involved in the joint training and communicated closely with each other (Ground Staff (Japan), 2015). Furthermore, Japanese civil-military teachers took an active part in the 2015 ARF DiREx, co-hosted by Malaysia and China. Japan engages with China in the security-defence field (Ministry of Foreign Affairs of Japan, 2015).

These small signs of increasing engagement, however, have not so far cleared the way for more fundamental items on the bilateral table to substantially progress. While the defence dialogue for the key bilateral agenda of installing a maritime and air communication mechanism was resumed in January 2015 after the Abe–Xi summit in November 2014, the two countries have not reached a final agreement on this issue, reportedly because Tokyo and Beijing hold different views as to the geographical area of application for a new mechanism (Hiraga, 2016). There are no formal defence ministerial visits to each other, let alone bilateral exercises. In this sense, Japan and Australia are at sharply different stages in developing engagement with China.

The most recent episode that sheds light on the engagement gap was the politics regarding the Asian Infrastructure Investment Bank (AIIB). To come straight to the point, while Japan and the US have chosen not to participate in its establishment, Australia has become a founding member of AIIB. Even though AIIB is essentially an organisation for international cooperation in the economic-financial field, the issue of whether and how to approach this new China-led organisation was clearly discussed in much broader contexts. According to Paul Kelly, the Abbott government, who initially appeared reluctant to join the AIIB and later changed their policy, continued to deliberate on this issue in the National Security Committee of the Cabinet (NSC) (Kelly, 2014). Given the mandate of the NSC, it is clear that the Abbott government treated Australia's participation in AIIB as a broader policy issue than just an economic-financial one.

One hint regarding the policy thinking of the current Australian government on this issue is a series of speeches delivered by Foreign Minister Bishop in October and November 2015 (Bishop, 2015). She emphasised the importance of willingly accepting larger roles of emerging powers and, when legitimate, modifying the international institutions to this very end. In this sense, it is possible that Canberra sees the gap between Japan and the US, on the one hand, and Australia, on the other, in terms of accepting China's greater role on the international scene.

Lastly, another potential China gap that may become a real issue between Australia and Japan over the coming months and years is the possibility of expectation gaps. Illustrative of this risk is the aforementioned 2016 Defence White Paper. In emphasising the importance of maritime security, the rules-based order and the role of the US, the White Paper clearly raised the status of maritime Southeast Asia as a priority subregion for Australia's defence planning. In this context, the document asserts that Australia needs to make an 'effective' contribution and to have capabilities to conduct independent operations in Southeast Asia. By contrast, the White Paper appears more reserved in describing Australia's role in North Asia, as it explicitly notes that Australia's capacity to influence the strategic affairs of this subregion is limited. In comparison, Japan's view of its own roles is clearly conceived in the reverse order. Needless to say, security in North Asia, a subregion normally called Northeast Asia in Japanese policy discussions, is not a regional issue for Japan but largely directly concerns Japan's national defence and sovereignty. Indeed, it is too early to see how these differing priority settings will affect the ways the two countries will cooperate in the future. At a time when Australia is on track towards expanding its operational activities in and around Japan, perhaps it is becoming more important for the two countries to clarify what they should and should not expect from each other.

Conclusion

This chapter argues that Japan–Australia security and defence ties are undergoing the second evolution of bilateral cooperation. After years of deliberate focus on non-traditional security cooperation, Tokyo and Canberra are now taking steps to expand their cooperation into more traditional security fields. The fact that the two sides are actively considering the coordination of their efforts in the South China Sea, potential submarine cooperation and possibly the application of the new Legislation for Peace and Security is simply remarkable, given that the non-traditional security focus was a carefully chosen pathway for reasons that included the management of the self-fulfilling prophecy risk in relation to China. The two countries' increasing concerns over China's challenges to the rules-based order and the US role in the Asia-Pacific are providing a foundation for the on-going second evolution of Japan–Australia relations, particularly in the defence field.

Perhaps this chapter's analysis of the Japan–Australia second evolution is little more than tentative and preliminary, given that discussions are still going on between the two governments, while some of the key items still remain potential areas of cooperation. In fact, there is no guarantee that Japan–Australia cooperation in each new field of traditional security implications will progress smoothly into the future. For example, no one can be certain about how the China gap issues, which the third section of this chapter discussed in depth, may impact the ways that the bilateral and trilateral cooperation develop in the future. In this sense, this chapter should be taken as the first step in the continuing analytical efforts on the on-going evolution of Japan–Australia security ties for the months and years to come.

Note

1   For example, among the 567 scrambles by the Air Self-Defense Force in the period from the first to the third quarter of FY 2015, approximately 66 per cent were conducted in response to Chinese activities. See Joint Staff (2016).

References

Abbott, T., 2009. *Battlelines* (Melbourne: Melbourne University Press).
Abe, S., 2014. 'Keynote Address at the 13th Shangri-La Dialogue', 30 May, at: www.mofa.go.jp/fp/nsp/page18e_000087.html (accessed 1 February 2017).
Aoki, M., 2014. 'Obama Assures Abe on Senkakus', *The Japan Times*, 24 April.
Australian Embassy in the Philippines, 2011. 'MR120314 – Australia, Philippines ink the 2012–2017 Development Cooperation Strategy', at: http://philippines.embassy.gov.au/mnla/medrel120314.html (accessed 10 October 2017).
Bishop, J., 2013. 'China's Announcement of an Air-Defence Identification Zone over the East China Sea', Media release, Minister for Foreign Affairs, 26 November.
Bishop, J., 2015. 'Address to Centre for Strategic and International Studies', Speech, Minister for Foreign Affairs, 14 October.
Carr, B., 2014. *Diary of a Foreign Minister* (Sydney: New South Press).
Chair of the Tokyo Defense Forum, 2015. 'Summary by the Chair', The 19th Tokyo Defence Forum (TDF), 4–5 March, at: www.mod.go.jp/j/approach/exchange/dialogue/tdf/pdf/19th_en_summary.pdf (accessed 30 March 2016).

Chairman of the 26th ASEAN Summit, 2015. 'Chairman's Statement of the 26th ASEAN Summit Kualalumpur and Langkawi: "Our People, Our Community, Our Vision"', 26–27 April, at: www.miti.gov.my/miti/resources/Chairman_Statement_26th_ASEAN_Summit.pdf (accessed 30 March 2016).
Chellaney, B., 2007. '"Quad Initiative": An Inharmonious Concert of Democracies', *Japan Times*, 19 July.
Department of Defence (Australia), 2014. 'Lieutenant General Wang Guanzhong visits Australia for the 16th Australia-China Defence Strategic Dialogue', 15 January, at: https://news.defence.gov.au/media/media-releases/lieutenant-general-wang-guanzhong-visits-australia-16th-australia-china-defence (accessed 30 March 2016).
Department of Defence (Australia), 2015a. 'Balikatan', at: www.defence.gov.au/exercises/balikatan (accessed 30 March 2016).
Department of Defence (Australia), 2015b. 'Operation Gateway', at: www.defence.gov.au/operations/SouthChinaSeaIndianOcean (accessed 30 March 2016).
Department of Defence (Australia), 2016. *2016 Defence White Paper* (Canberra: Department of Defence).
Department of Foreign Affairs and Trade (Australia), 2013. 'Joint Statement: Trilateral Strategic Dialogue', 4 October, at: http://foreignminister.gov.au/releases/Pages/2013/jb_mr_131004.aspx?ministerid=4 (accessed 30 March 2016).
Department of Foreign Affairs and Trade (Australia), 2015. 'Joint Statement AUSMIN 2015', 13 October, at: https://foreignminister.gov.au/releases/Pages/2015/jb_mr_151013a.aspx (accessed 30 March 2016).
Greene, A., 2015. 'Defence Minister Payne Backs Turnbull over China Comments', *ABC News*, 22 September.
Ground Staff (Japan), 2015. 'Khan Quest 15, a Multilateral Joint Training', News Release, Ground Staff (Takokukankyodokunrenkankuesuto15nitsuite), 4 June, at: www.mod.go.jp/gsdf/news/press/2015/pdf/20150604.pdf (accessed 30 March 2016).
Hiraga, K., 2016. 'Tainaka gunji kiki kanri (shinrai jōsei) mekanizumu no genjō — Nichibei no shiten kara — (sono 1)' [The Current Situation of Military Crisis Management (Confidence Building) Mechanism vis-à-vis China: From the Viewpoint of Japan and the United States – (Part 1)], 11 July, at: www.mod.go.jp/msdf/navcol/SSG/topics-column/039.html (accessed 1 March 2018).
Ishihara, Y., 2014. 'Japan-Australia Defence Cooperation in the Asia-Pacific Region', in: Tow, W. and Yoshizaki, T. (eds), *Beyond the Hub and Spokes*, NIDS Joint Research Series, No.10 (Tokyo: NIDS), pp. 113–120.
Ishihara, Y., 2015a. 'Japan-Australia "New Special Relationship"', NIDS Commentary, No. 44, 4 April.
Ishihara, Y., 2015b. 'The Japanese POV: Japan-US-Australian Trilateralism', National Commentaries, ASEAN Forum, 18 December.
Joint Staff, 2016. 'Press Release: Statistics on Scrambles through the Third Quarter of FY2015', 22 January, at: www.mod.go.jp/js/Press/press2016/press_pdf/p20160122_02.pdf (accessed 30 March 2016).
Kelly, P., 2014. 'Strategy Fears Sank China Deal', *The Australian*, 31 October.
Mahadzir, D., 2015. 'ASEAN Defence Chiefs Meeting Ends without Joint Statement due to South China Sea Row', *HIS Jane's Defence Weekly*, 3 November.
McDonald, H., 2015. 'Turnbull's Foreign Policy Likely to Pivot to China', *ABC News*, 16 September.
Ministry of Defense of Japan, 2013. *Defence White Paper 2013* (Tokyo: Ministry of Defence Japan).

Ministry of Defense of Japan, 2014. *Defence White Paper 2014* (Tokyo: Ministry of Defence Japan).
Ministry of Defense of Japan, 2015. 'Outlook of Ministerial Press Conference', Press Release, 30 May.
Ministry of Foreign Affairs of Japan, 2014. 'Australia-Japan-United States Trilateral Leaders Meeting Joint Media Release', 16 November, at: www.mofa.go.jp/files/000059829.pdf (accessed 30 March 2016).
Ministry of Foreign Affairs of Japan, 2015. 'Outcome of the 4th ARF DiREx (Dai 4 kai ARF saigai kyuen jitsu doenshu (DiREx2015) (Kekka))', 8 June, at: www.mofa.go.jp/mofaj/fp/nsp/page25_000054.html (accessed 30 March 2016).
Ministry of Foreign Affairs of Japan, 2016. 'Trends in Chinese Government and Other Vessels in the Waters Surrounding the Senkaku Islands, and Japan's Response: Records of Intrusions of Chinese Government and Other Vessels into Japan's Territorial Sea', 2 November, at: www.mofa.go.jp/files/000170838.pdf (accessed 30 March 2016).
Ministry of Foreign Affairs of the People's Republic of China, 2014. 'Xi Jinping Hold Talks with Prime Minister Tony Abbott of Australia Deciding Unanimously to Establish China-Australia Comprehensive Strategic Partnership and Announcing the Substantive Completion of the China-Australia FTA Negotiation', 17 November.
Minister for Foreign Affairs and Trade (Australia), 2010. 'Joint Foreign and Defence Ministers' Meeting in 2010. Joint Foreign and Defence Ministers' Press Conference', Iikura House, Tokyo, Transcript, Minister for Foreign Affairs and Trade, 19 May.
National Diet of Japan, 2015. 'Transcript of the Special Committee on the Legislation for Peace and Stability of Japan and International Society' (Japanese), 189th Diet Session, 12 June, at: www.shugiin.go.jp/internet/itdb_kaigiroku.nsf/html/kaigiroku/029818920150612009.htm (accessed 30 March 2016).
Nikkei Shimbun, 2015. 'Major Shipbuilding Company JMU to Build Ten Patrol Boats for the Philippines with ODA' [Zosenote no JMU, Firipin mukejunshisen 10 sekijuchu, ODA de], *Nikkei Shimbun*, 4 June.
Onodera, I., 2014. 'Speech at the 13th Shangri-La Dialogue: Advancing Military-to-Military Cooperation', 30 May.
Satake, T., 2015a. 'Japan-Australia Relations: Toward Regional Order-Building', in Tatsumi, Y. (ed.), *Japan's Global Diplomacy* (Washington DC: The Stimson Center).
Satake, T., 2015b. 'Why a Strong Japan-Australia Relationship Matters', *East Asia Forum*, 2 June.
Schreer, B., 2016. 'The 2016 Defence White Paper, China and East Asia: The End of an Illusion', *The ASPI Strategist*, 25 February.
Sevastopulo, D., 2014. 'US Says China "Acting Professionally" in Air Defence Zone', *The Financial Times*, 5 February.
Takahashi, K., 2015. 'Ōsutoraria shushō, koyō akka de kōtai Nihon no sensuikan juchū ni eikyō mo' [Australian Prime Minister, Worsening Employment also Affects the Japanese Submarine Bid], *The Nikkei*, 15 September.
Tiezzi, S., 2014. 'At CICA, Xi Calls for New Regional Security Architecture', *The Diplomat*, 22 May.
Turnbull, M., 2014. 'Address at NAB Australia-China Business Week', Speech (Minister for Communications), 5 September.

United States Navy, 2007. 'Exercise Malabar 07–2 Kicks Off', 7 September, at: www.navy.mil/submit/display.asp?story_id=31691 (accessed 30 March 2016).

White, H., 2006. *Beyond the Defence of Australia: Finding a New Balance in Australian Strategic Policy* (Sydney: Lowy Institute for International Policy), pp. 34–40.

Wroe, D., 2016. 'Australia Knew of US Patrol of South China Sea', *The Sydney Morning Herald*, 31 January.

Part II

Japan–India security partnership

3

The Indian perspective on the security partnership with Japan

Madhuchanda Ghosh

IN THE EMERGING geopolitical scenario in Asia, India and Japan are moving closer. For decades, the two states could not develop the bilateral relationship, which remained low profile because of their different approaches towards international politics during the Cold War era. The post-Cold War structural changes in the Asia-Pacific region have provided India and Japan with much more strategic manoeuvrability as compared with the Cold War period. The Asia-Pacific region, as Kurt Campbell argues, is on the cusp of major changes in its strategic environment, which is marked by unprecedented developments (Campbell, 2000: 128). The region is in a dramatic state of flux, as is evident from the rise of new power centres and changing power equations as well as the formation of new strategic partnerships and military arrangements. Greater cooperation among the major regional powers, including India and Japan, is imperative for ameliorating concerns about the uncertainties arising from the fluid post-Cold War Asia-Pacific regional scenario. This chapter argues that the structural changes in the Asia-Pacific geostrategic environment are impelling India and Japan to move closer together, from merely maintaining political ties to having a deeper security partnership.

Introduction

In the changing and complex Asia-Pacific geopolitical landscape, few relationships among the major powers have undergone such a remarkable turnaround as that between India and Japan. Japan's defence deal with India on the sale of the amphibious aircraft US-2, the India–Japan civilian nuclear cooperation agreement and Japan becoming a permanent member in the *Malabar* exercise are some of the unprecedented developments that have transformed the low-intensity Indo-Japanese relationship into one of the fastest-growing bilateral relations. In the emerging security architecture in Asia, a growing synergy from a political to a strategic focus could be noted in India–Japan relations, given that both countries share core strategic interests, whether over their heavy dependence on West Asian oil, the safety of the sea lanes in the Indian Ocean region or the growing power disequilibrium in Asia.

Japan appears to be moving from a 'trading state' of the Cold War era to a 'normal state' in the post-Cold War period, with growing political and military potentiality, as is evident from the Abe government's endeavour to restore Japan's position as a 'normal' country by receding from its pacifist constitutional orientation. India is being viewed as a major 'swing state' in the global geopolitical landscape and one of the key players in the regional balance of power configuration. India's strategic weight in the global and regional politics is rapidly growing with its emergence as an economic powerhouse of the world. The rise of India and China is one of the major factors shaping the Asia-Pacific strategic environment. Though the US remains the predominant power in the region, balancing tendencies are already taking place. The primacy of the US is increasingly challenged by a rising China. Strengthening Sino-Russian bonhomie along strategic lines appears to be a balancing strategy of China to counter the American preponderance of power and influence in the region. Asian major powers, including India and Japan, share a common concern with the ensuing regional imbalance of power.

India is developing its strategic profile by forging strategic links with the major powers in the region and throughout the world and expanding its naval influence beyond the Indian Ocean. The then prime minister, Manmohan Singh, suggested an expansive definition of India's strategic frontier as he reportedly stated: 'our strategic footprint covers the region bounded by the Horn of Africa, West Asia ... South-east Asia and beyond, to the far reaches of the Indian Ocean. Awareness of this reality should inform and animate our strategic thinking and defence planning' (Singh, 2004). Japan's changing perception of India's growing profile at the regional and international level has been markedly evident since the August 2000 visit to India of Japanese Prime Minister Mori Yoshiro. Mori prepared the ground for treating India as an important partner of Japan by declaring that 'Japan and India are global partners.'

In the post-Cold War era, the parameters of India's foreign policy are undergoing major changes as the country strives for a larger regional and global role for itself. Forging a strategic partnership with the US, the quest for a permanent seat on the UN Security Council, rapprochement with China and Pakistan, and aspirations for a 'blue water' navy are all indicators of a major shift in India's foreign policy approach. India's growing strategic interests in Asia are particularly reflected in the following statement made by the former national security adviser, Menon:

> If Asia is our theatre, South Asia is our home. And the situation in South Asia is still fraught. If our partners in our region so desire we would work with them to provide and enhance security in the subcontinent, the Asian landmass and the Indian Ocean

littoral. India as a society and nation has by and large made wise choices in the past on matters relating to the use of force, showing strategic restraint and realism. We have contributed force to internationally legitimate uses such as UN peacekeeping, while limiting its domestic deployment. Today, we are in a position to make a greater contribution to global public goods in areas such as maritime security. (Menon, 2011)

In the emerging global scenario there is little doubt that the US, China, Japan, India, Russia and a few other core states will continue to assert their leading roles in international politics. It is likely that in the evolution of such a power structure the six powers would tend to balance each other through a cluster of like-minded states. While realists refer to India as an 'emerging power' (Cohen, 2001), 'a regional power' (Rajamohan, 1998) and 'an Asian power' (Cohen, 2001), the notions of 'assertive civilian power' (Katzenstein, 1996: 205) and 'normal state' (Green, 2001: 32) are frequently contrasted with Japan. The former idea connotes a state that employs civilian policy instruments with the objective of affecting the course of non-military world events (Drifte, 1996). The idea of a 'normal state' depicts a 'great power' (Waltz, 1993). Japan has been viewed as a great economic power, a 'global economic power' (Johnson, 1994: 260), but a relatively minor military one. The term 'major power', which is often used by scholars like Kuriyama working on Japan's foreign policy, refers to the impact that Japan's behaviour has on the international environment. Analyses on Japan by scholars like Reinhard Drifte reflect some structural thinking:

> The mere anticipation of any Japanese action can prevent other players from pursuing their national interests if they are seen as conflicting with Japan's. Japan's structural power may not yet be the same as that of the US but its relative and even ideological/ cultural power has grown considerably and is affecting perceptions, alternatives and players, irrespective of their geographical or cultural distance from Japan. Japan now matters so much that it does not actually have to do something in order to effect an outcome which is beneficial to its national interest. (Drifte, 1996: 162)

The foundation for a strong India–Japan partnership has been laid by the sustained engagement and concerted efforts of the leadership of the two states, who have made critical contributions to bolstering the bilateral ties since the early 2000s. Mori opined that he envisioned India's rise as a global power in the 21st century, compelling him to make the historic declaration of an India–Japan global partnership.[1] Japan, for the first time, used the term 'global partnership' in reference to a nation other than the US, which demonstrated the Mori government's drive to increase Japan's diplomatic options. It is also an important indicator of the assertive foreign policy approach that Japan is exhibiting in the post-Cold War international situation. Over the past decade, former Indian Prime Minister Manmohan Singh, along with Japanese prime ministers starting with Junichiro Koizumi, have revitalised the bilateral relationship.

Since the forging of the global partnership, the leadership of the two states has continued to seek close ties and endeavoured to give the bilateral relations a strategic orientation. For example, the 2006 joint statement focused on transforming the bilateral relationship into a strategic partnership, the 2007 joint statement sought to provide a roadmap for building enduring strategic relations, while the joint statement signed by Prime Minister Abe and the Indian premier Narendra Modi in 2014 elevated it to a special strategic and global partnership. Abe's visit to India in 2015 was yet another milestone in the deepening of the bilateral strategic relations as the two leaders issued the Japan–India Vision 2025 Special Strategic and Global Partnership (Ministry of Foreign Affairs of Japan, 2015).

The strategic rationale behind India's bolstering relations with Japan is reflected in its endeavour to engage with Japan in two areas of its core national interests, economic and security, and to cope with a rising China. As an analyst noted more than a decade ago, '[i]n the emerging Asia, the two non-Western democracies, India and Japan, look like natural allies as China drives them closer together' (Chellaney, 2006: 221). In the economic domain, the Indian leadership perceives Japan, which is a global industrial powerhouse, as a key partner in India's economic development. Pressure is mounting on the Modi government to emphasise the acceleration of infrastructural development, which is imperative for sustaining high growth in the economy over the next fifteen years. Japan has agreed to deepen cooperation with India in upgrading its infrastructure and strengthening its manufacturing base. Japan has committed billions of dollars to India's infrastructural upgrade. Tokyo is investing heavily in the freight and industrial corridors linking Delhi and Mumbai. The Delhi–Mumbai freight corridor will be the largest industrial corridor in India, connecting industrial complexes and harbours in six states from Delhi to India's industrial capital, Mumbai. Japan is extending financial assistance for more metro railway projects modelled on the successful Delhi Metro and high-speed railway (Shinkansen) systems. In his visit to India in September 2017, Prime Minister Abe inaugurated the high-speed railway project, which is scheduled to be completed by 2022. Japan has committed to provide 81 per cent of the funding for the US$16.9 billion project through a 50-year loan at 0.1 per cent annual interest. In Tokyo, a Japanese foreign ministry official reportedly stated, 'We would like to support "Make in India" as much as possible', referring to Modi's signature policy to lure investors in manufacturing (Wilkes and Takenaka, 2017).

Along with India's economic interests, its security interests have played a vital role in shaping its foreign policy calculus vis-à-vis Japan. In this context, it needs to be noted that energy security is a particularly critical challenge for India, considering its mounting energy needs and limited availability of conventional sources of energy. A veritable roadblock to accelerating the pace of India's economic development is the shortage of power to meet its growing energy demands. India is in urgent need of a clean source of energy that will arrest environmental degradation. The India–Japan civilian nuclear agreement, concluded in 2016, will help India combat climate change through the consumption of clean energy. Japan's energy cooperation with India, therefore, specifically the civil nuclear cooperation, constitutes a core pillar of the growing strategic partnership between the two countries.

Enhancing military capabilities is another long-term security interest of India, besides energy security, which has been a factor in India's strategic thinking vis-à-vis Japan. This is reflected in New Delhi's bid to strengthen its defence ties with Tokyo. For instance, in the 2014 Tokyo Declaration, India pledged with Japan to 'upgrade and strengthen' their partnership in defence by regularising joint maritime exercises and collaborating on military technology. The two premiers declared, 'We intend to give a new thrust and direction to our defence cooperation, including collaboration in defence technology and equipment, given our shared interest in peace and stability and maritime security' (Ministry of Foreign Affairs of Japan, 2014). This indicates the degree of importance that the two leaders have attached to the expanding India–Japan defence cooperation. The Abe government's decision to sell the US-2 amphibian aircraft to India is likely to give a major boost to the bilateral defence cooperation. However, one veritable impediment to India's procurement of the US-2 aircraft was that India is not a signatory to the Wassenaar Arrangement, a multilateral export control regime governing transfers of conventional arms and dual-use goods and technologies, or other international frameworks for arms trade control. To overcome this hurdle and to facilitate the sale of US-2 to India, two agreements were concluded during the December 2015 visit of Prime Minister Abe to India: the 'Agreement concerning the Transfer of the Defence Equipment and Technology' and the 'Agreement concerning Security Measures for the Protection of Classified Military Information'.

India's bid to forge defence ties with Japan was first evident from the landmark visit to Japan by the Indian Defence Minister George Fernandes of the last National Democratic Alliance government in 2000. It was the first ever visit by an Indian defence minister. Thus, a defence component was added to their bilateral agenda for the first time, as the two sides agreed to initiate a security dialogue. Japan's initiative to open a high-level strategic dialogue with India was evident from the 2005 visit to India of Prime Minister Koizumi Junichiro, when the two sides decided to 'reinforce strategic focus' in their bilateral relations (Ministry of Foreign Affairs of Japan, 2005). Under the Manmohan Singh government, the May 2006 visit of the Indian Defence Minister Mr Pranab Mukherjee to Japan was also a major milestone in the evolution of India–Japan security partnership, as it unfolded a new chapter in the growing bilateral defence ties. For the first time, the two states decided to hold meetings of their defence ministers at regular intervals. The visit marked a significant step towards achieving the goal of reinforcing the 'strategic focus' in bilateral relations as the defence chiefs of India and Japan identified the 'mechanisms of implementation' for realising that goal.

The joint statement of the two defence chiefs is perhaps the most comprehensive declaration of intent ever issued by the two states to forge a cooperative strategic partnership (Ministry of External Affairs of India, 2006). This is because the two sides announced a series of measures to step up defence cooperation, including regular comprehensive security dialogue and meetings between the defence ministers. A high frequency of official visits of top-ranking leaders and policymakers could be noted from the annual prime ministerial meetings, strategic dialogue and comprehensive security dialogue of the two states. Such a high frequency of reciprocal visits by the leadership of India and Japan indicates their desire to consolidate and expand bilaterally their security cooperation. As India expands its strategic outreach in the Asia-Pacific, its evolving politico-strategic ties with Japan will be of critical importance.

In this context, it is important to note that one of the significant factors that have influenced Japan to perceive India as a like-minded partner in Asia is the growing proximity between the US and India. The warming up of Indo-US ties, especially since the late 1990s, has helped India gain a growing importance in Japan's Asia policy. As the Obama administration endeavoured to deepen its engagement with the regional allies and partners through its policy of rebalance towards Asia, Washington perceived its relations with India as central to maintaining long-term stability in Asia. The US has been encouraging India and Japan to come closer as it endeavours to maintain the strategic balance in Asia. In the 'Common Strategic Objectives' earmarked in the 'Joint Statement of the US–Japan Security Consultative Committee 2011', both the US and Japan welcomed 'India as a strong and enduring Asia-Pacific partner' (Ministry of Foreign Affairs of Japan, 2011). In the light of the changing, complex regional security dynamics in the Asia-Pacific, the Japan–US military alliance is being redefined on the basis of a broad security agenda: the prevention of nuclear and missile proliferation by North Korea, combating international terrorism and ensuring the freedom of the vital sea lines of communications in the Asia-Pacific.

Pointing to the US factor in India–Japan relations, like his predecessor, the Japanese premier Mori, Abe also maintained that the evolving relations among the US, India and Japan are of crucial importance in the context of the emerging regional security environment.[2] Of all the Japanese premiers, Shinzō Abe has been the most enthusiastic about giving a strategic orientation in the bilateral relations. During his maiden visit to India in his first term as prime minister in 2006–2007, Abe emphasised the 'confluence of the two seas', the Pacific and the Indian Oceans – anticipating Hillary Clinton's idea of the 'Indo-Pacific' – which indicated Japan's strong intent to deepen its maritime security cooperation with India. In Abe's view, India–Japan security cooperation would act as a stabilising force in the Indo-Pacific, particularly in the light of the growing power disequilibrium in Asia.[3]

Converging interests in the area of maritime security

The strategic interests of India and Japan seem to converge on the issue of maritime security. The issue of a stable maritime order figures very prominently in the security dialogue between India and Japan. This is because the economies of the two states are heavily dependent on sea-based transport and the supply of oil from the Persian Gulf. Securing the energy supply routes in the Indian Ocean region is, therefore, a core strategic interest of both India and Japan.

India's geography imparts a unique strategic location to India in the economically strategic waterways in the Indian Ocean region, and therefore, Indian political elites, as well as several British scholars, have viewed India's predominance in the Indian Ocean as virtually inevitable. As the Indian diplomat-historian K. M. Panikkar argued, 'to other countries the Indian Ocean could only be one of the important oceanic areas, but to India it is a vital sea because its lifelines are concentrated in that area, its freedom is dependent on the freedom of that coastal surface' (Panikkar, 1945: 45).

India sits astride two 'choke points' for global oil supplies – the Strait of Malacca to its east and the Strait of Hormuz to its west. Approximately one-third of international trade and half of the world's oil pass through these sea lanes. The Strait of Malacca, which is the main passage between the Indian Ocean and the South China Sea, is the vital lifeline for Japan's international trade. Over 80 per cent of Japan's oil cargo from the Persian Gulf is transported through the Malacca Strait. India's strategic location in the Indian Ocean region is one of the factors that propelled Japan to engage with India in the area of maritime security.

In this context, it needs to be noted that the Indian navy has assumed critical significance in the domain of anti-piracy operations in the Indian Ocean region. Many Japanese ships have been a target of attacks by the pirates. In a swift and planned operation on 16 November 1999, the Indian coast guard and navy rescued the Japanese vessel MV *Alondra Rainbow*, which had been hijacked in the South China Sea by pirates. It is important to consider the ramifications of the Indian navy's rescuing the Japanese ship. The incident gave an indication to the world, including Japan, that the Indian navy is a stabilising force in the rapidly deteriorating security environment in the Indian Ocean region. The significance of this incident also lies in the fact that it played a catalytic role in the opening of the security dialogue between the two states.

Since the initiation of the bilateral security dialogue, India and Japan have been engaged in maritime security cooperation, which encompasses anti-piracy operations and security of the sea lanes of communication (SLOCs). Pointing to such cooperation between the two states, Yoriko Kawaguchi, the then

Japanese foreign minister, during her visit to India in 2003, stated: 'Cooperative maintenance of the security of maritime traffic in the sea lanes that stretch across the Indian Ocean and the Strait of Malacca are among the security and defence issues which deserve our increased attention. Both countries share common interests and concerns regarding these issues' (Kawaguchi, 2003). The Indian defence establishment seems to be increasingly focusing on how to conduct effective naval diplomacy, which is exhibited by the Indian navy's growing engagement with the naval powers in the Indo-Pacific region. In this context, it is worth noting Ken Booth's idea of what constitutes 'effective naval diplomacy':

> When used effectively, naval diplomacy in its various guises can reassure, strengthen, symbolize a growing relationship or commitment, establish rights and interests in near or distant regions, impress onlookers with the country's technical competence or diplomatic skill, restrain allies or adversaries, bolster the strength and confidence of allies and associates or third parties, encourage or dissuade states in relation to particular policies, signal intentions or expectations, create uncertainty when necessary, neutralise the naval diplomacy of adversaries, complicate the problems and planning of adversaries and their associates, deter inimical actions, foreclose the options of competing states, reduce the confidence of selected targets, cause loss of faith in the associates of one's adversaries, discourage opponents, create a different politico-military environment and set of expectations, increase the level of profitable interaction with near or distant countries, gain access to new countries, maintain or improve access with existing associates, and create a degree of dependency and so the possibility for manipulation. In short effectively employed naval diplomacy can be used (usually incrementally) to maintain or increase a country's political influence over allies, associates and third parties. (Booth, 1977: 47)

Booth also highlights the pitfalls of naval diplomacy, as he contends: 'If naval diplomacy is badly managed or misperceived by relevant onlookers, or even if it is skilfully managed but none the less perceived in a perverse manner, it can result in the opposite of all these effects' (Booth, 1977: 47). Perhaps the most significant development in India's naval diplomacy vis-à-vis Japan is that what had been limited to coastguard-to-coastguard exercises, consequent to the May 2006 bilateral defence agreement, was elevated to the level of joint naval cooperation. Japan's interest in deepening its defence cooperation with India is evident from the flurry of visits to India by the chiefs of the Japanese defence establishment. Since the institutionalisation of a security dialogue between the two states, there have been three levels of defence cooperation: annual comprehensive security dialogue, service-to-service exchanges and military-to-military talks, and joint naval exercises. This indicates the comfort level in the strategic relationship between India and Japan.

Prime Minister Modi has given a new focus to bolstering India's naval defence. A strong indication in this regard is that soon after assuming power,

Modi commissioned INS *Kolkata*, which is an advanced version, but significantly more versatile, of Indian naval ships such as the INS *Delhi*, INS *Mysore* and INS *Mumbai*. At the commissioning ceremony, Modi pointed out that the INS *Kolkata*, which is entirely built in India, symbolises India's self-reliance. INS *Kolkata* will add considerable teeth to India's maritime warfare capabilities, with all-round capabilities against enemy submarines, surface warships, anti-ship missiles and fighter aircraft. Modi's emphasis on strengthening India's naval capabilities could be noted from his stress on the Indian navy's role in the area of maritime security, thereby drawing attention to the 'inextricable connection between maritime power and India's national growth story' and 'the Indian navy's potential to inspire confidence among those involved in maritime trade'.

US–India–Japan strategic convergence on maritime security

A convergence of Modi's Act East policy, Obama's rebalance to Asia, and Abe's renewed focus on freedom of navigation could be perceived in the expanding trilateral strategic cooperation, as indicated in the upgrading of the US–Japan–India trilateral dialogue to the level of foreign ministers. The mutual strategic interests of the three states were clearly revealed in the joint statement of the inaugural US–India–Japan trilateral foreign ministerial meet in Washington in September 2015. While the Indian External Affairs Minister Swaraj emphasised the importance of the 'sea lanes of communication in the region' as 'the lifeline of India's trade and commercial externalities', the US Secretary of State John Kerry described East Asia as 'a place of challenge for some issues of security', and the Japanese Foreign Minister Kishida Fumio depicted the Indian and the Pacific oceans as 'oceans of freedom and prosperity'(Kerry, 2015).The foreign ministers 'underscored the importance of international law and peaceful settlement of disputes; freedom of navigation and overflight and unimpeded lawful commerce, including in the South China Sea', which symbolised the strong focus of these maritime nations on the deteriorating maritime security environment in the Indo-Pacific region (US Department of State, 2015).

The Tokyo Declaration also gave a new fillip to the trilateral security engagement when India and Japan agreed not only to upgrade the 'two-plus-two' security talks and increase working-level talks on defence equipment and technology cooperation, but also to hold regular maritime exercises, attaching importance to 'continued participation' of Japan in the Malabar[4] exercises (Ministry of Foreign Affairs of Japan, 2014). Japan last participated in the Malabar drills in 2007, 2009 and 2014. It needs to be noted that Japan's participation in all these Malabar exercises was in the capacity of an invited observer. In this regard, the October 2015 Malabar exercise marks a major turning point in the naval cooperation between the three states with Japan's inclusion as a permanent participant (Miller, 2015).

From 14 to 19 October 2015, the three navies participated in the Malabar drills near the Chennai coast in the Indian Ocean region. Malabar was a series of complex and high-end war-fighting exercises conducted to advance mutual security. It encompassed a wide range of naval drills, including air defence collaboration, anti-submarine warfare and surface drills conducted by the naval warships. The three navies rehearsed scenarios for destroying hostile submarines, surface warships and aircraft (United States Navy, 2015). India's decision to include Japan as a permanent member in the Malabar exercises, traditionally a bilateral India–US exercise, signifies the importance which the Modi government attaches to Japan as its security partner. It also reveals that Japan has assumed a key importance in Modi's Act East policy.

Non-proliferation: A common strategic interest

Apart from the issue of maritime security, non-proliferation constitutes an important area of mutual strategic interest of India and Japan, as is evident from the various joint statements and joint declarations. India's impeccable track record as a non-proliferator seems to have prompted Japan to engage in a cooperation with India in the area of non-proliferation. In this regard, perhaps the most important consensus that has emerged in the high-level deliberations between India and Japan is that the two states have decided to work as partners against the proliferation of weapons of mass destruction (WMDs). Tokyo and New Delhi have confirmed their cooperation in implementing vigilant export control (Ministry of Foreign Affairs of Japan, 2001).

It is pertinent to note in this context that the issue of nuclear proliferation in the Korean peninsula is an area of common security concern for India and Japan. Perhaps one of the most volatile flashpoints in the Asia-Pacific in the 21st century is the Korean peninsula. Pyongyang's provocative acts have only heightened Japan's security concerns, North Korean missile tests in the Sea of Japan could be perceived as a serious problem from the standpoint of Japan's national security. With regard to nuclear proliferation in the Korean peninsula, it is important to mention that unless the problem of clandestine proliferation is tackled, the region is not going to reap a dividend of peace simply from the dismantling of North Korea's nuclear weapons programme. India and Japan have underscored the grave security challenge posed by the problem of clandestine proliferation (Ministry of Foreign Affairs of Japan, 2006).

What needs to be seriously taken note of is that the problem of proliferation of WMDs stretches from the east to the west of Asia, as is evident from the nuclear nexus between North Korea, Iran and Pakistan. Pakistan's quid pro quo relations with North Korea on the issue of proliferation have been a cause of anxiety for the Indian defence establishment over the years (Sharma, 2002) According to analyses by missile experts, Pakistan's missile Ghauri I is nothing but North Korea's No Dong-1 missile (Ramachandran, 2002). The Rumsfeld Commission Report of 1998 has only heightened India's worries about this nexus, since Pakistan's clandestine role in transferring nuclear technology under AQ Khan for developing North Korea's nuclear programme is well documented (Commission to Assess the Ballistic Missile Threat to the United States, 1998).

Terrorism: An issue of common concern

The issue of terrorism figures prominently in the joint statements of India and Japan as an area of common concern. In the post-9/11 and 7/7 scenario, the larger and more horrifying implications of terrorism have become apparent. Both India and Japan are located in a security environment that is plagued by burgeoning terrorist networks and terrorist activities. As a victim of terrorism, India continues to be one of the worst-hit countries in the world, suffering from countless terrorist incidents. Pakistan remains the safe haven for at least five State Department-designated terrorist groups: Al Qaeda, HizbulMujahadeen, Harkut-ul-Mujahadeen, Jaish-e-Muhammed and Lashkar-e-Taiba. The series of terrorist attacks in Mumbai in 2008, which killed countless innocent civilians, once again reveals how the people in India have to cope with daily doses of mindless violence.

Japan has also experienced terrorism in the brutal killings of Japanese citizens by the Islamic State of Iraq and Syria (ISIS). This violence perpetrated against Japanese nationals is a new security challenge for Japan. India is more experienced in this sphere, and therefore, a good counter-terrorism partner for Japan. New Delhi has now offered training and related support to Tokyo's newly established terrorism-focused intelligence collection unit. A next step may be intelligence-sharing on the critical issue of terrorist financing. Moreover, the sarin gas attack in the Tokyo subway in 1995 cannot be brushed aside as an isolated act of terrorism, given that terrorist networks in Japan's vicinity, especially in some of the countries in Southeast Asia, such as Thailand and Indonesia, are burgeoning.

China's expanding military influence: Security implications for Japan and India

The rapidly growing military power of China has security implications for Japan and India. Both the states have reasons to be concerned about China's growing emphasis on naval power projection capabilities and ballistic missiles. For instance, Beijing's naval ambitions in the East China Sea region and in the Indian Ocean region have caused anxiety in Japan and India. In the East China Sea, while Beijing claims jurisdiction over the entire continental shelf, Japan considers the median line as the boundary of its exclusive economic zone.

Moreover, both the states are engaged in a maritime territorial dispute over the Senkaku/Diaoyu Islands and have competing interests in the three oil and gas fields in the East China Sea. With the surge in tension over the maritime disputes, the East and South China Sea regions are emerging as global flashpoints as China locks horns with its neighbours, including Vietnam, the Philippines, Brunei, Malaysia and Taiwan, over the control of the three sets of islands and rocks in the South China Sea – the Spratly Islands, the Scarborough Shoal and the Paracel – and with Japan over competing claims to the Senkaku/Diaoyu islands in the East China Sea.

As India deepens its economic and strategic engagement with Japan and the Association of Southeast Asian Nations (ASEAN) states, the ensuing tensions in the East and South China Seas impinge on India's economic and strategic interests in the region. India's concern over the issue of regional maritime security and the growing military assertiveness of China was reflected in the speech of the Indian premier Narendra Modi during his maiden visit to Japan as India's prime minister in 2014. Lambasting the expansionism of yesteryear, Modi expressed the view that it was not a viable model for Asia. In a veiled reference to China, Prime Minister Modi reportedly stated, 'We have to decide if we want to have "vikasvaad" (development) or "vistarvaad" (expansionism) which leads to disintegration. Those who follow the path of Buddha and have faith on "vikasvaad", they develop. But we see, those having ideas of the 18th century, engage in encroachments and enter seas (of others)' (*Times of India*, 2014). In the 2015 and 2016 joint statements, India and Japan voiced serious concern over the developments in the South China Sea region and stressed the importance of resolving the disputes by peaceful means, in accordance with the principles of international law, including the *United Nations Convention on the Law of the Sea* (UNCLOS). In a similar vein, in the 2017 joint statement issued during the visit of Prime Minister Abe to India, the two premiers laid emphasis on the issue of freedom of navigation for ensuring a 'Free, Open and Prosperous Indo-Pacific' (Ministry of External Affairs of India, 2017). The 2017 visit of Prime Minister Abe to India holds a special significance, since it marked a decade of the Japanese premier's celebrated speech at the Indian Parliament – 'Confluence of the Two Seas'.

As India and Japan deepen maritime security cooperation in the Indo-Pacific, China's growing naval influence in the Indian Ocean region is being monitored closely by the two states. China's endeavour to secure the SLOCs along the Indian Ocean is evident from its 'string of pearls' policy (Gertz, 2005). Beijing's 'string of pearls' policy of setting up military and naval facilities in India's immediate neighbourhood, especially in Myanmar, Pakistan, Sri Lanka and Bangladesh, has been a cause of apprehension to the Indian defence ministry. Thus, Beijing is focusing on acquiring naval facilities along the crucial choke points in the Indian Ocean to enhance its strategic presence in the region.

China's string of pearls strategy and the expanding influence of the Chinese navy in the Indian Ocean, including submarines docking in Sri Lanka in 2014 and again in Karachi in May 2016, are likely to cause serious security worries for the Modi administration. These developments have propelled New Delhi to accelerate the modernisation of the Indian naval forces. For rapid naval modernisation, the Modi government is increasingly seeking cooperation from the US and Japan. For example, New Delhi has sought technology share from the US for India's next aircraft carrier and is exploring the possibility of working with Japan in building submarines.

India–Japan relations are set to reach a new high as the leadership of the two states focuses on expanding cooperation in the defence, security and economic domains. However, the leaders of the opposition in both states have been critical regarding different issue areas in which the two states are deepening their engagement. For instance, opposition parties in India, including the Congress as well as political allies of the federal government like the Shiv Sena, have critically viewed India's engaging with Japan in the bullet train project and maintained that the bullet train is being introduced at the cost of the cash-strapped and broken-down local rail network (*Telegraph*, 2017). While in India the leaders of the opposition are critical vis-à-vis India–Japan cooperation on the issue of the bullet train project, sharp criticism has been levelled in Japan at the bilateral civilian nuclear cooperation, given that there are contrasting perceptions on the issue of domestic nuclearisation. India is the first non-member of the Nuclear Non-Proliferation Treaty (NPT) to have signed a civilian nuclear agreement with Japan in 2016 after six years of wrangling and intense negotiations. Japan, a signatory of the NPT, vociferously advocates the non-proliferation regime as a step towards the abolition of nuclear weapons. In contrast, India views the NPT as discriminatory, preventing the 'have nots' from acquiring this technology, and argues that the original nuclear powers that support the NPT have not succeeded in fulfilling the obligation spelt out in Article VI of the treaty, which specifies a time-bound elimination of nuclear weapons. Though there are such divergences in India–Japan relations, the public opinion in India, as a survey demonstrated, viewed the growing partnership between the two states favourably. Eighty per cent of respondents perceived the current state of Japan–India relations as being either 'very friendly' or 'friendly', while 95 per cent of survey participants responded positively when asked whether Japan is a reliable friend of India (Hosoya, 2016).

Conclusion

A number of trends will determine the future pattern of India–Japan relations and the scope of their security cooperation. First, to maintain the strategic balance in the Indo-Pacific region, the US would encourage India and Japan to further step up and expand bilateral strategic engagement in the region. Second, India and Japan have high stakes in the regional stability in western Asia. In the coming years, the two states could deepen and expand the scope of their strategic cooperation to western Asia for ensuring energy security and regional stability. Third, both the states value the freedom of the high seas for their economic prosperity. Given the deteriorating maritime security environment in the region, India and Japan are likely to intensify their ongoing maritime security cooperation. Fourth, both the states have an interest in maintaining the power equilibrium in Asia. While it is too early to suggest that India and Japan's security cooperation is aimed at any third country, a convergence of Indian and Japanese security interests could be perceived in keeping a wary eye on the growing imbalance of power in the emerging complex regional geostrategic scenario. Given Prime Minister Abe's strong admiration for India, his bonhomie with Modi and his urge to bolster the India–Japan strategic and global partnership, India–Japan security engagement is likely to undergo a major transformation. The extent to which the Indo-Japanese security ties are transformed will have a decisive impact on the political and military balance of power in Asia.

Notes

1   Author's interview with Mori Yoshiro (former prime minister of Japan), Tokyo, 22 June 2006.
2   Author's research interview with Shinzō Abe, the then former prime minister of Japan, Tokyo, 21 October 2011.
3   Ibid.
4   The Malabar exercise, which initially began as a bilateral naval exercise between the US and India back in 1992, has at times been expanded to include other partners as well. Japan, Australia and Singapore participated in the Malabar exercise hosted by India in 2007, but after a strong reaction from China against the inclusion of Japan and Australia, the exercises became largely bilateral thereafter, although Japan did participate in 2009 and 2014.

References

Booth, K., 1977. *Navies and Foreign Policy* (London: Croom Helm Ltd).
Campbell, M. K., 2000. 'Energizing the U.S.-Japan Security Partnership', *Washington Quarterly* (autumn): 128.
Chellaney, B., 2006. *Asian Juggernaut: The Rise of China, India and Japan* (New Delhi: Harper Collins Publishers India).
Cohen, S. P., 2001. *India: Emerging Power* (New Delhi: Oxford University Press).
Commission to Assess the Ballistic Missile Threat to the United States, 1998. 'Report of the Commission to Assess the Ballistic Missile Threat to the United States: Executive Summary, Pursuant to Public Law 201 104th Congress', 15 July, at: https://fas.org/irp/threat/missile/rumsfeld/index.html (accessed 28 October 2017).

Drifte, R., 1996. *Japan's Foreign Policy in the 1990s: From Economic Superpower to What Power?* (London: Macmillan Press).
Gertz, B., 2005. 'China Builds Up Strategic Sea Lanes', *Washington Times*, 18 January.
Green, M., 2001. *Japan's Reluctant Realism: Foreign Policy Challenges in an Era of Uncertain Power* (New York: Palgrave).
Hosoya, Y., 2016. 'The Evolution of India-Japan Strategic Partnership: A Japanese Perspective', *ICRIER*, 14 March.
Johnson, C. A., 1994. *Japan: Who Governs? The Rise of the Developmental State* (New York and London: W.W. Norton).
Katzenstein, P. J., 1996. *Cultural Norms and National Security: Police and Military in Postwar Japan* (Ithaca, NY and London: Cornell University Press).
Kawaguchi, Y., 2003. Speech at the Federation of Indian Chamber of Commerce and Industry, 8 January, at: www.mofa.go.jp/region/asia-paci/fmv0301/india.html (accessed 1 October 2015).
Kerry, J., 2015. 'Remarks with Indian External Affairs Minister Sushma Swaraj and Japanese Minister Fumio Kishida', Palace Hotel, New York City, 29 September, at: https://2009-2017.state.gov/secretary/remarks/2015/09/247485.htm (accessed 5 October 2015).
Menon, S. S., 2011. 'Address at the Cariappa Memorial Lecture on "The Role of Militaries in International Relations"', 5 October, at: www.mea.gov.in/in-focus-article.htm?412/Address+by+NSA+at+the+Cariappa+Memorial+Lecture+on+The+Role+of+Militaries+in+International+Relations (accessed 9 February 2016).
Miller, B. J., 2015. 'Japan Makes Three: India, U.S. Trilateralize Malabar Drills', *World Politics Review*, 11 August, at: worldpoliticsreview.com/articles/16427/japan-makes-three-india-u-s-trilateralize-malabar-naval-drills (accessed 10 October 2015).
Ministry of External Affairs of India, 2006. 'Joint Statement, Visit of Mr. Pranab Mukherjee, Minister of Defence to Japan', 25 May, at: http://mea.gov.in/bilateral-documents.htm?dtl/6159/Joint+Statement+Visit+of+Mr+Pranab+Mukherjee+Minister+of+Defence+to+Japan (accessed 5 December 2015).
Ministry of External Affairs of India, 2017. 'Toward a Free, Open and Prosperous Indo-Pacific', at: www.mea.gov.in/bilateral-documents.htm?dtl/28946/IndiaJapan+Joint+Statement+during+visit+of+Prime+Minister+of+Japan+to+India+September+14+2017 (accessed 15 September 2017).
Ministry of Foreign Affairs of Japan, 2001. 'Japan-India Joint Declaration', Tokyo, 10 December, at: www.mofa.go.jp/region/asia-paci/india/joint0112.html (accessed 10 August 2015).
Ministry of Foreign Affairs of Japan, 2005. 'Japan-India Partnership in a New Asian Era: Strategic Orientation of Japan-India Global Partnership', at: www.mofa.go.jp/region/asia-paci/india/partner0504.html (accessed 15 September 2015).
Ministry of Foreign Affairs of Japan, 2006. 'Joint Statement towards Japan-India Strategic and Global Partnership', Tokyo, 15 December, at: www.mofa.go.jp/region/asia-paci/india/pdfs/joint0612.pdf (accessed 20 October 2015).
Ministry of Foreign Affairs of Japan, 2011. 'Joint Statement of the Security Consultative Committee Toward a Deeper and Broader U.S.-Japan Alliance: Building on 50 Years of Partnership, June 21, 2011 by Secretary of State Clinton Secretary of Defense Gates Minister for Foreign Affairs Matsumoto Minister of Defense Kitazawa', at: www.mofa.go.jp/region/n-america/us/security/pdfs/joint1106_01.pdf (accessed on 2 February 2018).

Ministry of Foreign Affairs of Japan, 2014. 'Tokyo Declaration for India-Japan Special Strategic and Global Partnership', 1 September, at: www.mofa.go.jp/files/000050532.pdf (accessed 10 December 2015).

Ministry of Foreign Affairs of Japan, 2015. 'Japan and India Vision 2025 Special Strategic and Global Partnership: Working Together for Peace and Prosperity of the Indo-Pacific Region and the World', at: www.mofa.go.jp/s_sa/sw/in/page3e_000432.html (accessed 1 November 2016).

Panikkar, K. M., 1945. *India and the Indian Ocean: An Essay on the Influence of Sea Power on Indian History* (London: George Allen & Unwin).

Rajamohan, C., 1998. 'India and Nuclear Weapons', *International Politics and Society*, 4, at: http://library.fes.de/pdf-files/ipg/ipg-1998-4/artmohan.pdf.

Ramachandran, R., 2002. 'Missile Match', *Frontline*, 19:12, June, at: www.frontline.in/static/html/fl1912/19120180.htm (accessed 21 August 2015).

Sharma, R., 2002. 'Pak-N.Korea N-Nexus Threat to Global Security, USA Told', *Tribune*, 5 December.

Singh, M., 2004. 'PM's Address at the Combined Commanders' Conference', 24 October, at: http://archivepmo.nic.in/drmanmohansingh/speech-details.php?nodeid=32 (accessed 10 March 2015).

Telegraph, 2017. 'Indian Bullet Train Met with Criticism as Modi Celebrates with the Japanese PM', at: www.telegraph.co.uk/news/2017/09/14/indian-bullet-train-met-criticism-modi-celebrates-japanese-pm (accessed 18 September 2017).

Times of India, 2014. 'Modi Takes "Swipe" at China, Deplores "Expansionist" Tendency of Some Nations', *Times of India*, 2 September.

United States Navy, 2015. 'Trilateral Air Defense Exercise Launches Malabar 2015', 17 October, at: www.navy.mil/submit/display.asp?story_id=9158 (accessed 7 October 2015).

US Department of State, 2015. 'Inaugural U.S.-India-Japan Trilateral Ministerial', 29 September, at: www.mofa.go.jp/s_sa/sw/page4e_000325.html (accessed 5 October 2015).

Waltz, K. N., 1993. 'The Emerging Structure of International Politics', *International Security*, 18(2): 44–79.

Wilkes, T. and Takenaka, K., 2017. 'Japan PM Abe to Launch $ 17-Billion Indian Bullet Train Project as Ties Deepen', *Reuters*, 12 September 2017, at: https://in.reuters.com/article/india-japan-bullettrain-modi-abe/japan-pm-abe-to-launch-17-billion-indian-bullet-train-project-as-ties-deepen-idINKCN1BN15T (accessed 15 September 2017).

4

The Japanese perspective on the security partnership with India

Satoru Nagao

Introduction

WHEN WE THINK about Japan–India security relations as they stand today, it must not be forgotten that Japan is located far from India. It takes about 10 hours to fly from Tokyo to New Delhi. The database of Japan's Ministry of Foreign Affairs points out that about 9,000 Japanese lived in India in 2016, while about 422,000 Japanese lived in the US; about 128,000 Japanese lived in China and about 19,000 Japanese lived in Indonesia (Ministry of Foreign Affairs of Japan, 2016). These factors that create distance between Japan and India have also been a geographical reason for fewer security relations between the two countries.

However, since the 2000s, Japan–India security cooperation has intensified quite significantly. Japan and India began their Japan–India–US foreign minister-level trilateral dialogue, the Japan–India–Australia vice-ministerial-level trilateral dialogue and the vice-ministerial-level foreign and defence two-plus-two bilateral dialogue. Since 2012, Japan has participated in the Indian Ocean Naval Symposium (IONS), and the two countries began joint naval exercises as an annual bilateral exercise called the Japan–India Maritime Exercise (JIMEX). The India–US Malabar exercises have included Japan as a regular member since 2016. It is important to bear in mind that Japan has not entered into this kind of deep security relationship with any other countries except the US and Australia. This makes the military ties between Japan and India quite remarkable. Therefore, this chapter will analyse why Japan has sought such security cooperation with India, and asks three questions. First, to what degree have changes in the security environment influenced Japan's decision? Second, what can Japan–India cooperation do to maintain a military balance? Third, why does Japan believe that India is a responsible great power?

Japan–India security partnership

The security environment around Japan

Japan–India relations have advanced since the 2000s, when the perception of China as a threat began to increase. Therefore, China is certainly a decisive factor when assessing Japan–India security cooperation. While China's rise has had both positive and negative ramifications for Japan, the negative aspects had a more significant influence and will, therefore, be analysed first.

China has been expanding its military activities around Japan and countries around the South China Sea. For example, in the East China Sea, a Chinese nuclear attack submarine violated the territorial seas of Japan in 2004. Since 2008, China has also started naval exercises on the Pacific side of Japan. The area of these naval exercises has been expanding from the first island chain to the second island chain, which forms the defence line of China (Figure 4.1). As well as these naval activities, the Chinese air force has also been expanding its activities. Incidents of scrambles of aircraft against Chinese aircraft increased from 96 in FY2010 to 571 in FY2015 (Ministry of Defense of Japan, 2016: part III, 15).

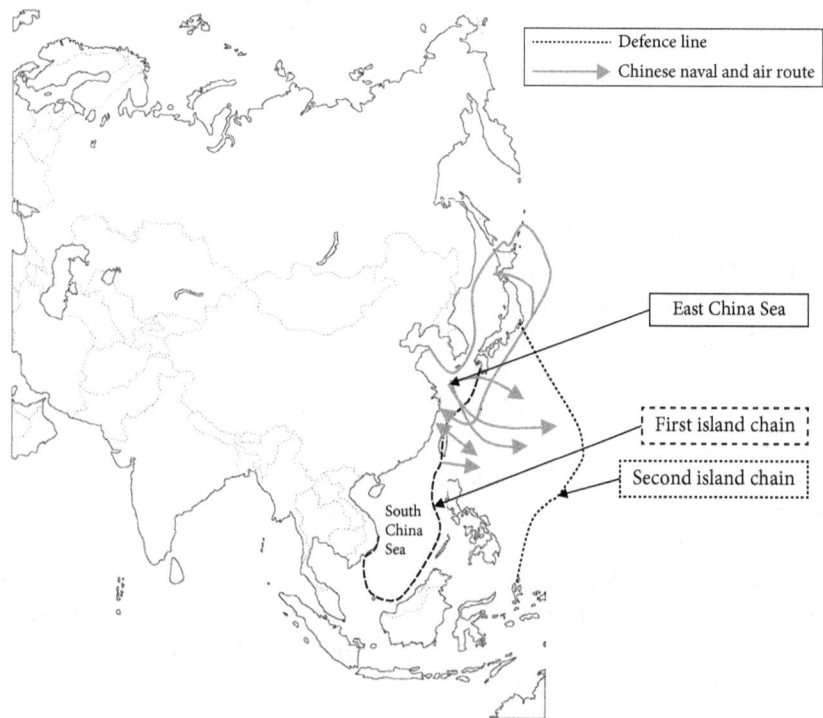

Figure 4.1 China's naval activities around Japan.
Source: Chapter author.

From the Japanese perspective, the South China Sea situation is an important factor. Although the Permanent Court of Arbitration rejected China's ownership claim of 90 per cent of the South China Sea in 2016, China is ignoring the verdict and building three new airports on its seven artificial islands in the South China Sea (Singh and Yamamoto, 2015). These facts indicate that China will deploy ballistic missile submarines under the protection of fighter jets launched from these artificial islands and then exclude all foreign ships and airplanes that might identify its submarines (Yoshida, 2012). A report written by Japanese Prime Minister Shinzō Abe pointed out that 'if Japan were to yield, the South China Sea would become even more fortified' (Abe, 2012).

It seems that the tendency of China's maritime expansion has been based on military balance, if history is any guide. For example, when France withdrew from Vietnam in the 1950s, China occupied half of the Paracel Islands. China occupied the other half of the Paracel Islands in 1974 immediately after the Vietnam War ended and the US withdrew from the region. After the Soviet Union withdrew from Vietnam, China attacked the Spratly Islands controlled by Vietnam in 1988. Along similar lines, after the US withdrew from the Philippines, China occupied Mischief Reef, which was claimed by both the Philippines and Vietnam (Ministry of Defense of Japan, 2015).

As background to the current situation, the military balance between the US and China has also changed after the Cold War. The US has acquired only 13 submarines, while China has acquired at least 42 submarines between 2000 and 2015. Vice Admiral Joseph Mulloy, deputy chief of Naval Operations for Capabilities and Resources of the US Navy, reported that China had more diesel-powered and nuclear-powered submarines than the US in February 2015 (Reuters, 2015). As a result, China has been expanding its military activities. Therefore, a need exists for us to maintain a military balance with China despite its military budget being larger than that of Japan.

Despite the negative ramifications discussed in the preceding paragraphs, the positive aspect of China's rise should not be overlooked, because we are facing not only a statist quest for power but also non-state security threats and other global challenges. Although countries around the Indo-Pacific have been experiencing increased economic development, there are still other challenges, such as piracy, smuggling, terrorism, failed states and so on. Thus, Japan sees China's efforts to deal with Islamic extremism in Central Asia, the Middle East and Africa, anti-piracy measures in the coast of Somalia, and so on in a positive light. Japan has already negotiated with China on how to keep peace and order in Afghanistan. Japan has also cooperated with China in anti-piracy measures.

In addition, pressing concerns such as rising sea level, climate challenges and so on will trigger novel security problems in the near future. By 2015, millions of refugees from the Middle East, Africa, Central Asia and other areas had come to Europe. Such an influx of refugees caused by the sea level rise will affect world politics sooner rather than later by changing the economic and environmental conditions of the region. If China shares the responsibility for these global problems, China's rise will also have a positive impact.

However, what remains of concern is China's irresponsible behaviour. In 2014, China sent submarines towards the Indian Ocean on the pretext of anti-piracy measures, although submarines are not an effective weapon to deal with piracy. If China shows such an irresponsible attitude to global issues, countries around China, including Japan, will not be able to see China's rise in a positive light.

The most central reason for the rising significance of new security partnerships for Japan is the speed of China's military modernisation. While, on a positive note, China's rise could be integral in dealing with pressing problems, China needs to construct a responsible image, and the surrounding countries need to persuade China to work on it. Here, it is argued, there are two effective strategies. First, maintaining the military balance is the topmost priority to prevent military conflict. Second, great powers around China, including Japan, must demonstrate to China that responsible behaviour will have mutually beneficial outcomes for all concerned, rather than having a forceful attitude. Therefore, in view of both the positive and negative sides of China's rise, cooperation between a proactive Japan and a rising India will be the deciding factor. The following presents an analysis of two related questions: (1) what Japan–India cooperation can do to maintain military balance and (2) why Japan believes India to be a responsible great power.

What is the role of Japan–India cooperation in maintaining the military balance?

What could be the role of Japan–India strategic cooperation in this regard? There are three areas in particular where Japan–India cooperation can help maintain the military balance with China and avoid the worst-case scenario: (1) the linkage of the Indo-China border area and the East China Sea, (2) the increase of Indian military influence leading to better burden sharing in the Indian Ocean, and (3) Japan–India collaboration to support countries around the South China Sea.

The linkage of the Indo-China border area and the East China Sea

In the Indo-China border area, it is known that the military balance is changing, because Chinese military infrastructural modernisation (such as roads, airports and so on to deploy armed forces) is very fast. Within 48 hours, Chinese armed forces can be ready for battle in the border area, whereas India needs one week for preparation, as there are not enough roads on the Indian side (Tiwary, 2013). This means that India could find itself in a dangerous situation, facing Chinese forces more than three times bigger in the border area (Pandit, 2012; Singh, 2013).

Japanese perspective on India partnership

Along with such rapid military modernisation, the area of Chinese military activities, too, has been widening. Since 2011, India has recorded more than 400 incursions every year. The frequency of Chinese air force activities has increased in the Tibet region (Matheswaran, 2015). In addition, China is deploying troops in Pakistan-administered Kashmir. Thus, nowadays, Japan and India are sharing a similar problem. And because of their geographical location, located on opposite sides of China, Japan–India cooperation can rectify their respective numerical inferiority. For example, if India cooperates with Japan, India will not need to deal with all the Chinese fighters at once, because China is likely to keep some of its fighters in its east side against Japan, and vice versa.

Therefore, under the Japan–India strategic cooperation, using high-end military infrastructural development know-how, Japan is willing to support India's efforts to modernise India's defence in the Indo-China border area (Jacob, 2016). Since 2014, Japan has decided to invest in India's strategic road project in the northeast region of India (Singh, 2014). By using this road, the Indian army can deploy more forces and supplies to the border area. This road building project is just a beginning. Because the Japanese government will ease regulations that restrict Japan's official development assistance from supporting military-related infrastructural projects, further substantial support from Japan's side may be expected for India's strategic projects, such as construction of roads, tunnels, airports and helipads of strategic importance.

Increase of Indian military influence and burden sharing in the Indian Ocean

China has started to increase its military activities in the Indian Ocean. Because China is concerned about its total dependence on the sea line of communications from the Middle East to China through the Strait of Malacca, it has tried to make an alternative route via Middle East–Pakistan–China and/or Middle East–Myanmar–China, and so on, through the Indian Ocean. Since the mid-2000s, China's military activities in the Indian Ocean have been expanding. In 2012, at least 22 contacts were recorded with vessels suspected to be Chinese nuclear attack submarines patrolling in the Indian Ocean. On 3 December 2013, the Foreign Affairs Office of China's Ministry of Defence informed India's military attaché in Beijing about the two-month deployment of their nuclear submarines (Anon, 2014). In 2014, at least two Chinese submarines and one submarine support-ship docked at a port in Sri Lanka. The activities of these submarines indicate that the area of influence of China in the Indian Ocean is going to expand, because these Chinese submarines can potentially attack India's nuclear ballistic missile submarines and sea line of communications.

In addition, China also exports weapons to countries around India. A submarine, especially, has an important role and effect in India's strategy. Pakistan decided to import eight Chinese submarines for its navy in 2015. Bangladesh imported two submarines from China in 2016. Logically, then, the Indian navy will need to have enough ships to keep a regular watch over the location and purpose of other countries' submarines. This means that these submarines will, to a great extent, regulate India's naval activities. In addition, the possibility that India's hostile neighbour, Pakistan, may also wish to possess nuclear submarines in its constant effort to counter India's rising power in the region must not be overlooked. Further, because Pakistan does not have the technology, there is again a reasonable possibility that China will support such 'indigenous' nuclear submarines to counter India.

China's strategic weakness is, however, that it does not have a naval port in the region. Therefore, under the 'String of Pearls Strategy', China is investing in the development of many ports, such as Gwadar in Pakistan, Hambantota in Sri Lanka, Chittagong in Bangladesh and Kyaukpyu in Myanmar in the Indian Ocean. If the Chinese navy uses civil-purpose ports as naval supply bases, China could successfully tackle its weakness of not having a naval port in the Indian Ocean.

Why has China's assertiveness heightened in the Indian Ocean lately? The changing US–China military balance could have affected the situation. The US influence in the Indian Ocean region increased in the 1970s. The US dispatched aircraft carrier battle groups several times in order to respond to conflicts within the region, such as the third Indo-Pakistan War, the Gulf War, Operation Enduring Freedom after 9/11, and the Iraq War. The US used the island of Diego Garcia as a hub to deploy military power. Thus, the US continues to be the most powerful presence within the region. However, because US naval power has been declining, China has been increasing naval activities in the Indian Ocean as it has in the East China Sea and South China Sea. Thus, we need to find an alternative country to fill a potential power vacuum in this region.

There is a high possibility that, in the near future, India will be the most influential sea power to fill the power vacuum in the Indian Ocean region. There are six reasons that Alfred Thayer Mahan (1890), who analysed why Britain had been a sea power, pointed out. He listed six core factors: 1) 'Geographical Position', 2) 'Physical Conformation (which is national environment, especially, the length of coast lines, existence of natural ports etc)', 3) 'Extent of Territory (This is the situation whether enough military power to defend coastal line or not)', 4) 'Size of Population (for working at sea)', 5) 'Character of the People' and 6) 'Character of the Government' (Mahan, 1890).

Taking these factors into account, India has an advantageous 'geographical position' because the Indian sub-continent is separated from the Eurasian continent by high mountains. This advantage has historically proven significant. Only three empires dominated most of the sub-continent in Indian history: the Maurya Empire, the Mughal Empire and the British Raj. The territories of

Japanese perspective on India partnership

these three empires were very similar, and all their territories are based on the mountain range (Figure 4.2). Thus, the Indian sub-continent is one kind of 'island'. And India can concentrate on its naval forces only if it possesses the necessary will.

In addition, the history of the Cholas indicates another geographical advantage for India. Representatives of the Chola Empire, which was located in southern India, made an expedition to Southeast Asia in the 11th century. The sphere of its influence had expanded along the entire coastal area off the Bay of Bengal. This historical fact is another prominent example of India's geographical advantage. Since India is located at the northern centre of the Indian Ocean, it is able to access not only Southeast Asia but also all sides of the Indian Ocean, including the Middle East and East Africa.

India has 'physical conformation' because it has 7,517 (only 6,100 of which is mainland) km of coastline and many natural ports. And the fact that the Indian navy is the only strong power of a coastal country of the Indian Ocean region means that India has enough 'Extent of Territory'. Presently, India is acquiring more than 100 warships. And by 2030, India is planning to increase its number of warships from 139 to 212 (Subramanian, 2016; *Times of India,*

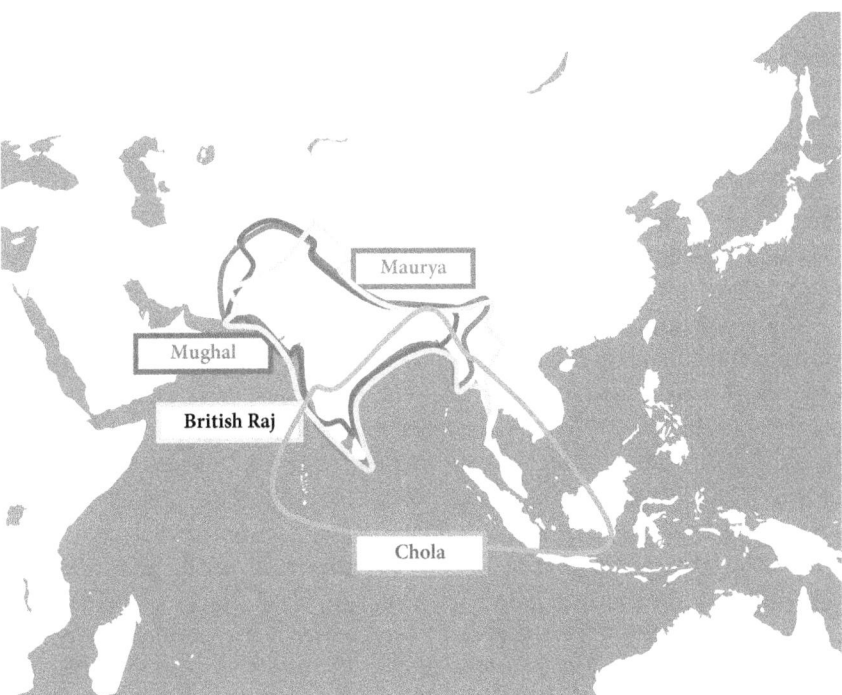

Figure 4.2 Influential area of empires in the sub-continent.
Source: Nagao, 2012: 99–109.

2013). There is a possibility that India will possess three aircraft carrier battle groups and six nuclear submarines by 2030.

India has the fifth or sixth largest number of seafarers, about 55,000 sailors employed around the world. Thus, India also satisfies the condition of 'number of population' working at sea. Based on the history of the Chola Empire, there is also a possibility that the 'character of the people' in India could be sea power oriented. And finally, taking these two characteristics and the 'character of government' into account, the Indian government is interested in expanding its sea power. The 2012 'Nonalignment 2.0: A Foreign and Strategic Policy for India in the Twenty First Century' report, based on the discussions of many former national security advisers of India, states that 'presently, Indian military power has a continental orientation. Emerging as a maritime power should thus be India's strategic objective' (Khilnani et al., 2012). And India's navy has increased its share of the defence budget from 12.7 per cent in 1990 to 15.8 per cent in 2015 (Ministry of Defence of India, 2016).

Thus, according to Mahan's theory, India has sufficient potential to become a sea power, and thereby an influential country in the Indian Ocean region. If India has the required will and develops sufficient capabilities, cooperation with India could contribute a lot to Japan. This is because Japan and its ally, the US, will be able to release themselves from the heavy burden of safeguarding security in the Indian Ocean and will be able to deploy more military force in the East China Sea and West China Sea to maintain the military balance in Asia.

If India becomes a sea power, what could be the contribution of Japan–India defence cooperation in the Indian Ocean? First, India can use Japan's technology to strengthen India's naval power. For example, as in the Indo-China border area, Japan is also planning to assist India's airport project in the Andaman Nicobar Islands. If India could strengthen these bases, it would be relatively easy to project power in the Malacca Strait.

Japan will also contribute to India's shipbuilding capabilities to build warships, including aircraft carriers and submarines. Japan already possesses sophisticated helicopter carriers, cruisers, destroyers, frigates, conventional submarines and so on. At present, India wants to get not only arms but also the capacity to build under the 'Make in India' policy. In this case, shipbuilding cooperation between Japan and India would be an important initiative.

Beyond shipbuilding, arms trade will be another important part of Japan–India strategic cooperation. Currently, Japan and India are in negotiations regarding the trading of US-2 rescue planes (Nagao, 2016). This rescue plane can land on the sea and take off from the sea. Despite rescue being the main purpose of the plane, it can also be used for marking the country's presence. For example, if India deploys this plane for rescuing people or for disaster management in other countries, it will be perceived as a marker of India's will to extend tangible support to those in need and thus mark India's presence. Their image of India will improve, and India can expand its influence in these countries. From Japan's perspective, this plane could be a very useful political tool for India.

Hence, the US-2 is just the beginning of arms trade between the two countries. Japan has a considerable number of such sophisticated technologies and know-how. For example, to protect India's aircraft carriers, India needs to deal with China's anti-ship ballistic missiles, which can attack India's aircraft carriers. This means that India needs a sea-based missile defence system. Now, under the Japan–US joint development of a sea-based missile defence system, Japan is developing some of the most important parts of this system. If so, Japan and India, along with the US, can cooperate in the missile defence sector. And because missile defence systems are closely related to space technologies, there is a possibility that Japan–India–US cooperation in the missile defence sector will develop into space defence cooperation as well.

Mine sweeping is also an important tool for India to deal with Chinese submarines, because submarines can set up sea mines. Japan has good know-how and equipment to deal with sea mines. Because of World War II, Japan needs to sweep these sea mines more than 65 years after the war. In 1950, the Japanese coast guard joined the Korean War to sweep sea mines. And after the first Gulf War in 1991, Japan deployed mine sweepers to the Persian Gulf. If India needs to deal with sea mines set up by China's submarines, Japan and India can jointly detect them under the Japan–India strategic cooperation. Therefore, to deal with China's naval activities in the Indian Ocean, Japan–India strategic cooperation could be very effective and useful.

In addition, even when we think about developing infrastructure in countries around India, Japan–India cooperation is useful there too. In the countries around India, China has invested heavily in building infrastructure and expanded its influence. If India does not possess enough budget and technology, China will increase its influence in the Indian Ocean region and harm the 'great power image' of India. Thus, cooperation is a useful method to rectify India's individual numerical inferiority. If India's knowledge of South Asia and Japan's budget and technology could be coupled, India's influence would strengthen.

Japan–India collaboration to support countries around the South China Sea

Because China's military power is far bigger than that of other countries, the countries around the South China Sea need to amalgamate their leadership as one integrated power and beef up their military power with a trustworthy partner to provide coastal countries with military support. By now, India has already started to support armed forces in Southeast Asia as a part of 'Look East Policy' and its updated version 'Act East Policy'. India has trained the crew of aircraft carriers in Thailand, submarine crews and fighter pilots in Vietnam, and pilots and the land crew of fighter airplanes in Malaysia. Further, India has agreed to train the pilots and provide maintenance to the fighter airplanes in the Indonesian air force. Singapore is using India's land and air base for their training.

Although Japan has not long supported armed force in Southeast Asia, it has supported many systems, including anti-piracy systems, tsunami warning systems, cyber-defence systems, building infrastructure such as air and sea ports, and so on. These systems are indirectly related to maritime security in the South China Sea. In addition, under the current Prime Minister Shinzō Abe, Japan has also started arms donation to these countries. For example, Japan will donate patrol ships to Vietnam and the Philippines.

Thus, if Japan and India collaborate with each other, we can support countries around the South China Sea more effectively. For example, if Japan built an airport in Vietnam and the Indian air force trained Vietnam's fighter pilots, Vietnam could get both an airport and fighter pilots. Hence, under the Japan–India–Vietnam cooperation, we can create a win-win-win situation.

To achieve this goal, what kind of systems would be most suitable? In January 2014, when Prime Minister Abe visited Delhi, the two prime ministers 'welcomed the launch of a bilateral dialogue on ASEAN [Association of Southeast Asian Nations] affairs'. It will be useful if such dialogue promotes a more practical trilateral strategic dialogue: for example, Japan–India–Vietnam, Japan–India–Philippines, Japan–India–Singapore, Japan–India–Indonesia, Japan–India–Malaysia and so on. Through such dialogue, both Japan and India can share information, better identify the needs of these Southeast Asian countries and decide how to cooperate with or support these countries.

Reasons why Japan believes that India is a responsible great power

If Japan–India cooperation can contribute to maintaining military balance, there is still one question that needs attention. How responsible is India's behaviour likely to remain? If India challenges the status quo and disturbs stability in the region like China, India will no longer be trustworthy for Japan. However, because of three factors, it can be inferred that India will remain trustworthy.

First, India is a democratic country, which Japan trusts. A holistic understanding and assessment of the military strategy of other countries is based not only on government assessment but also on exchanging opinions among experts both in and outside government. In some countries, researchers are not 'allowed' to have divergent views on such matters; in India, there is no such regulation. This factor helps to maintain the trustworthiness of information regarding India, because opinions are expressed in a free democratic environment.

Second, India is not likely to challenge the status quo in South Asia. To understand this, it is important to analyse why India's use of military force towards countries around India is relatively self-restraining. Table 4.1 shows the list of India's military operations since independence. This list proves that most of India's operations are *reactive*, and the Indian army has not crossed the borders since 1972 except for peacekeeping or peace building operations.[1] India's restraint in using force is a consistent strategy. In addition, India also accepted a UN tribunal ruling in favour of Bangladesh regarding the India–Bangladesh sea boundary dispute in 2014 (Table 4.1).

India's foreign policy has been regarded by other countries as relatively generous and one of 'strategic restraint'. If we focus on the power balance in South

Table 4.1 The list of India's military operations

	Active or reactive	Type of operation	Area of operation
Junagadh (1947)	Active	Limited war	Outside
India-Pakistan (1947–1948)	Reactive	Limited war	Outside
Hyderabad (1948)	Active	Limited war	Outside
Northeast (1956–now)	Reactive	Counterinsurgency	Inside
Goa (1961)	Active	Limited war	Outside
India-China (1962)	Reactive	Limited war	Inside
Kutch (1965)	Reactive	Limited war	Inside
India-Pakistan (1965)	Reactive	Limited war	Outside
Nathu La and Chola (1967)	Reactive	Limited war	Inside
Maoist (1967–now)	Reactive	Counterinsurgency	Inside
India-Pakistan (1971)	Active	Limited war	Outside
Siachen (1984)	Active	Limited war	Inside
Falcon and Checkerboard (1986–1987)	Reactive	Coercive diplomacy	Inside
Punjab (1984–1992)	Reactive	Counterinsurgency	Inside
Brasstack (1987)	Active	Coercive diplomacy	Inside
Sri Lanka (1987–1990)	Active	Peace building	Outside
Maldives (1988)	Reactive	Peace building	Outside
Kashmir (1989–)	Reactive	Counterinsurgency	Inside
1990 crisis (1990)	Reactive	Coercive diplomacy	Inside
Kargil (1999)	Reactive	Limited war	Inside
Parakram (2001–2002)	Reactive	Coercive diplomacy	Inside
UNPKO	Reactive	Peace keeping	Outside

See: Nagao, 2012. In this list, I have divided India's military operations into three categories. First is 'Active' or 'Reactive', referring to who sent combat troops first. Second, there are five types of operation: 'Limited war' (the probabilities of total wars may have reduced after World War II. Thus, most wars are limited wars); 'Coercive diplomacy' (Coercive diplomacy is not war or deterrence but a kind of diplomatic persuasion by using military intimidation). In a war, one country compels its opponent by using military operations. In coercive diplomacy, it attempts to persuade the opponent. 'Whereas deterrence represents an effort to dissuade an opponent from undertaking an action that has not yet been initiated, coercive diplomacy attempts to reverse actions which have already been undertaken by the adversary' (Craig and George, 1983: 196); 'Peace building' (forceful operations for peacekeeping); 'Peacekeeping' (a military operation based on the agreement of all warring parties); and 'Counterinsurgency' (a domestic operation to maintain law and order). Third is the 'area of operation', which refers to either 'Inside' or 'Outside' of India.

Asia, we can find one fitting explanation. Because India has already been the only great power in South Asia, it cannot garner more benefit from bullying smaller neighbours. India's gross domestic product (GDP) has been more than seven times bigger than Pakistan's since the 1971 Indo-Pakistan war.[2] Today, about 80 per cent of the total defence budget spent in South Asia is spent by India alone. If India tries to attack small neighbours, the size of the opponent being far smaller, India can get only marginal benefit at best. Instead of bullying its neighbours, India has shown a generous attitude to persuade them to cooperate. This policy reflects a much-expected maturity on the part of a leader in South Asia (Nagao, 2015). Thus, such generosity encourages Japan to trust India as a responsible country that will neither challenge the status quo nor disturb peace. To put it simply, India's attitude in South Asia is not China's attitude in the West Pacific.

Third, international cooperation inevitably leads to greater Indian influence, since the country has a long experience of joint international military operations. Why is international cooperation so important for an influential country? There are three reasons. First, an open society builds a secure feeling for other countries. Second, the experience gained through several multi-national operations, such as peacekeeping operations (PKO), joint exercises and military capacity-building activities, contributes to acquiring the know-how to manage the multilateral cooperation necessary for becoming a leading country in this region. Third, rich experience of international cooperation implies sufficient contribution towards global problems as a responsible great power.

The Indian army has been participating in UN PKO since the 1950s, with over 180,000 Indian soldiers in many parts of the world. Many of these were 'difficult operations', and over 156 Indian army officers sacrificed their lives while serving in UN PKO (Izuyama, 2013; Permanent Mission of India to the UN, 2017). Anti-piracy measures and joint exercises also indicate India's collaboration with other military organisations for achieving objectives. India organised the multilateral joint exercise Miran, and there are annual joint exercises or joint patrols with Singapore, Thailand and Indonesia. There have been more than 60 joint Indo-US exercises over the foregoing decade. Japan and India have also so far implemented six joint exercises.

Military capacity-building measures are another form of international cooperation. India's support for Southeast Asia has already been mentioned in the preceding sections. Besides, many foreign military personnel from Afghanistan, Bangladesh, Bhutan, Sri Lanka, the Maldives, Myanmar, Singapore, Vietnam, Oman and so on have been trained by Indian armed forces institutions such as the Counter-Insurgency and Jungle Warfare School and INS *Satavahana* for submariners (Chaudhury, 2014). India has given, and is planning to give, patrol vessels and planes to the Maldives, the Seychelles and Mauritius with relevant training courses. All the aforementioned factors fulfil India's credibility in having the rich experience of international cooperation necessary to be a responsible great power.

Conclusion

China's rise has had both a positive and a negative impact, but lately, the negative ramifications have gained leverage. The main reason lies in the changing US–China military balance. Countries around China, including Japan, want to deter China's assertiveness by maintaining a military balance and persuading China to show more responsible behaviour. In this joint security endeavour, cooperation between proactive Japan and rising India will be the decisive factor. To maintain military balance, Japan and India can cooperate by using the linkage of the East China Sea and the Indo-China border, share the burden in the Indian Ocean and collaborate to support countries around China in the South China Sea. India's behaviour is also likely to remain that of a responsible power, because India is a democratic country with a consistent history of restrained military action against its neighbours. Furthermore, India's experience of multilateral operations has aided both its reputation and its experience regarding responsible behaviour in international society. Collectively speaking, then, these are the reasons why Japan is seeking more cooperation with India. The time has come to proactively further this cooperation to ensure prosperous stability in the whole of the Indo-Pacific region.

Notes

1   Even if the intervention in Sri Lanka is a relatively large operation, the main purpose of this operation was peacekeeping.
2   World Bank database at: http://data.worldbank.org/indicator/NY.GDP.PCAP.CD (accessed 12 March 2017).

References

Abe, S., 2012. 'Asia's Democratic Security Diamond', *Project Syndicate*, 27 December, at: project-syndicate.org/commentary/a-strategic-alliance-for-japan-and-india-by-shinzo-abe#Vd6yytDokZJCiwtv.01 (accessed 12 March 2017).
Anon, 2014. 'Chinese N-Sub Prowled Indian Ocean: Two-Month Patrol Demonstrated Glitch-Free Deployment', *Indian Military Review*, 5(4): 8.
Chaudhury, D. R., 2014. 'Global Strategic Move: India Increases Defence Trainings in Asia, Africa and Latin America', *The Economic Times*, 5 September.
Craig, G. A. and George, A. L., 1983. *Force and Statecraft: Diplomatic Problems of our Times*, Third Edition (New York: Oxford University Press).
Izuyama, M., 2013. 'India's Foreign and Security Policy: Expanding Roles and Influence in the Region and Beyond', *East Asian Strategic Review 2013*, The National Institute for Defense Studies, at: www.nids.mod.go.jp/english/publication/east-asian/pdf/2013/east-asian_e2013_01.pdf (accessed 15 September 2017).
Jacob, J., 2016. 'Japan Willing to Fund Two More Road Projects in Northeast India', *Hindustan Times*, 24 May.
Khilnani, S., Kumar, R., Mehta, P. B., Menon, P., Nilekani, N., Raghavan, S., Saran, S. and Varadarajan, S., 2012. Nonalignment 2.0: A Foreign and Strategic Policy for India

in the Twenty-First Century, at: cprindia.org/sites/default/files/NonAlignment%20 2.0_1.pdf (accessed 12 March 2017).
Mahan, A. T., 1890. *The Influence of Sea Power upon History* (Boston: Little, Brown).
Matheswaran, M., 2015. 'China's Tibet Build Up', *Deccan Herald*, 5 May.
Ministry of Defence of India, 2016. *Annual Report 2015–2016*, at: https://mod.gov.in/sites/default/files/AnnualReport1617.pdf (accessed 12 March 2017).
Ministry of Defense of Japan, 2015. *China's Activities in the South China Sea* (Japanese), 22 December, at: mod.go.jp/j/approach/surround/pdf/ch_d-act_20151222.pdf (accessed 12 March 2017).
Ministry of Defense of Japan, 2016. Defense of Japan 2016 (Annual White Paper) (Tokyo: Government Printing Office).
Ministry of Foreign Affairs of Japan, 2016. *Annual Report of Statistics on Japanese Nationals Overseas 2017* (Japanese), at: www.mofa.go.jp/mofaj/files/000260884.pdf (accessed 15 September 2017).
Nagao, S., 2012. 'The Emerging India Is Not a Threat, Why? An Assessment from Japan', *Asia Pacific Journal of Social Science*, III(July–December): 99–109.
Nagao, S., 2015. *Indo no gunji senryaku: Kinchō suru shūhen-koku to no pawābaransu* [India's Military Strategy: Strained Relations and Power Balance with Neighbours] (Tokyo: Minerva).
Nagao, S., 2016. 'The Importance of a Japan-India Amphibious Aircraft Deal', *The Diplomat*, 12 December, at: thediplomat.com/2016/12/the-importance-of-a-japan-india-amphibious-aircraft-deal (accessed 12 March 2017).
Pandit, R., 2012. 'India Boring Border Tunnels to Take on China, Pakistan', *The Times of India*, 16 August, at: https://timesofindia.indiatimes.com/india/India-boring-border-tunnels-to-take-on-China-Pakistan/articleshow/15509722.cms (accessed 1 March 2018).
Permanent Mission of India to the UN, 2017. 'India and United Nations: Peacekeeping and Peacebuilding', New York, at: www.pminewyork.org/pages.php?id=1985 (accessed 15 September 2017).
Reuters, 2015. 'China Submarines Outnumber U.S. Fleet: U.S. Admiral', 25 February, at: www.reuters.com/article/2015/02/25/us-usa-china-submarines-idUSKBN-0LT2NE20150225 (accessed 12 March 2017).
Singh, R., 2013. 'India Far behind China's Combat Power', *Hindustan Times*, 12 December, at: www.hindustantimes.com/india/india-far-behind-china-s-combat-power/story-Y5Wbgfo59Wr7WFl6DBVeyI.html (accessed 12 February 2017).
Singh, R., 2014. 'Japan Gets Contract to Build Strategic Roads on Indo-China Border', *Daily News and Analysis*, 3 November, at: dnaindia.com/india/report-japan-gets-contract-to-build-strategeic-roads-on-indo-china-border-2031590 (accessed 12 March 2017).
Singh, S. and Yamamoto, L., 2015. 'Spectre of China's Artificial Islands', *Indian Defence Review*, July–September: 78–82.
Subramanian, K. S., 2016. 'Bridge the Gap between Plan and Execution: What Ails Warship Building in India', *Indian Military Review*, 7 (12): 10–12.
Times of India, 2013. 'Indian Navy to Have 200 Warships in Next 10 Years', 13 November, at: https://timesofindia.indiatimes.com/india/Indian-Navy-to-have-200-warships-in-next-10-years/articleshow/25708914.cms (accessed 12 March 2017).
Tiwary, D., 2013. 'Chinese Clearing Forest Cover to Grab Border Land', *The Times of India*, 26 August, at: https://timesofindia.indiatimes.com/india/Chinese-clearing-forest-cover-to-grab-border-land/articleshow/22057537.cms (accessed 13 February 2018).
Yoshida, R., 2012. 'Beijing's Senkaku Goal: Sub "Safe Haven" in South China Sea: Quest for Isles a Strategic Aim: Former MSDF Rear Admiral', *The Japan Times*, 7 November.

Part III

Japan–Southeast Asia security partnership

5

Japan's multilateral security cooperation with East Asia

Paul Midford

Introduction

THE SHARP CHANGE in Tokyo's strategy towards regional security multilateralism well illustrates Japan's decentring from the US after the Cold War, even while nonetheless serving, at least so far, to support, if not strengthen, the Japan–US alliance. This chapter examines how Japan has used regional multilateralism since 1991 for several purposes: to help keep the US engaged in the region; to reassure Japan's neighbours that Tokyo would not again threaten their security, even as it began playing a direct role in regional and international security and sent its military overseas for the first time since 1945; to ameliorate security threats, both traditional and non-traditional; to hedge against potential US abandonment; and to achieve a modicum of diplomatic independence (*Jishu Gaikō* in Japanese). It shows that Japan has even promoted multilateral security, and especially political, forums on several occasions that have excluded the US, as exemplified by the Hashimoto Doctrine, the ASEAN Plus Three (APT) Forum, and its promotion of Northeast Asian Cooperation (NEA 3). Japan has continued to promote regional security multilateralism even when faced with US anxiety that Tokyo's focus on multilateral cooperation would drain attention and resources away from the alliance and become a *de facto* hedging strategy.

The rest of this chapter consists of nine sections. The next section explains Japan's Cold War era strategy of regional security isolationism. The following section demonstrates that Japan started to abandon its regional security isolationist strategy and began decentring from the US as its exclusive security partner beginning with the 1991 Nakayama proposal. The section after that examines the Miyazawa initiatives, which were a follow-up to the Nakayama proposal, and which, together with the Nakayama proposal, significantly contributed to the creation of the ASEAN Regional Forum (ARF) in 1993. The next section considers rising US fears in the mid-1990s about Japan's decentring from the US and embrace of regional security multilateralism. The following section presents the Hashimoto Doctrine as another Japanese initiative for promoting regional political and even security multilateralism that did not include the US, and how this laid the groundwork for the establishment of the APT summit. The section after that looks at Japan's promotion of political multilateral cooperation in Northeast Asia, another venue that excludes the US. The next section examines Japan's role in the ARF since the turn of the century, and the following section examines Tokyo's initiative to establish a new specialized multilateral security institution to tackle the threat of piracy in Southeast Asia. The final section presents this chapter's conclusions.

Regional security isolationism during the Cold War

During the Cold War, Japan pursued a strategy of regional security isolationism. This isolationism rested on two pillars. First, Japan abstained from direct involvement in regional security. Tokyo refused even to discuss regional security with other East Asian countries. Second, Japan entrusted its stake in regional security to American hands. Tokyo's contribution to regional security was indirect and passive. Japan passively served as the major Asian platform for American military power.[1]

The 1977 Fukuda Doctrine (Sudo, 1992: 241–247) served to formalise Japan's strategy of regional security isolationism. At its core, the Fukuda Doctrine was a promise to Southeast Asian nations, and more broadly to East Asian nations, that Japan would not again become a military power capable of threatening its neighbours militarily, with the expectation that on this basis these nations would accept a Japanese regional political role. The Fukuda Doctrine promise meant that Japan would refrain from acquiring offensive military or power projection capabilities (Lam, 2012; Sudo, 1992). This also meant that Japan would avoid even discussing security issues with its neighbours. The Fukuda Doctrine was thus a formalisation of Japan's post-war strategy of regional security isolationism (Midford, 2000).

Given this strategy, it is not surprising that during the Cold War Tokyo followed the US lead in opposing proposals for establishing regional security multilateralism in East Asia. The East Asia of the 1980s stood in sharp contrast to Europe, where various like- and unlike-minded multilateral security institutions coexisted, including the Council on Security Cooperation in Europe (CSCE), NATO, the Warsaw Treaty Organization and so on. Although the US had promoted a NATO-style Pacific Pact in the 1950s, Washington subsequently decided that its system of bilateral alliances (spokes converging on a US hub) was more advantageous (Hemmer and Katzenstein, 2002; Press-Barnathan, 2000).

The US opposed an unlike-minded multilateral forum, an Asian equivalent of the CSCE (also known as CSCA), because of Soviet support for the idea (Youtz and Midford, 1992). The US sought to lock the Soviets out of the region, leaving them diplomatically isolated and depriving them of access to East

Asia's dynamic capitalist economies. The US also feared that Moscow would use security multilateralism as a means to drive a wedge between the US and its Asian allies. Above all, Washington feared that a multilateral security process would lead inevitably to naval arms control, reflecting the expectation that the US navy would be pressured to make large asymmetrical cuts.

Consequently, as the Cold War was winding down, the US even rejected multilateral security initiatives proposed by allies, including South Korea, Australia and Canada. As late as August 1991, the US unconditionally rejected security multilateralism for East Asia (Pacific Research, 1991a, b).

Given its dependent regional security posture, Japan followed Washington in opposing security multilateralism in East Asia. Tokyo, like Washington, feared that Soviet multilateral security initiatives, including several made by Mikhail Gorbachev in the late 1980s, were designed to drive a wedge between the US and its Asian allies and promote disadvantageous multilateral naval arms control. Moreover, because of the Fukuda Doctrine's *de facto* taboo against discussing regional security with its neighbours, Japan did not believe that it could meaningfully participate in a regional multilateral security forum. Japan could only discuss security with the US.

Thus, Tokyo closely followed Washington's line of opposing regional security multilateralism, even when the initiative came from US allies. In August 1990, shortly after Australia and Canada made high-profile proposals for establishing a regional security forum (Youtz and Midford, 1992: 11–12), Japan rejected both: 'Japan is negative toward a plan for an Asia-Pacific security grouping similar to the Conference on Security and Cooperation in Europe (CSCE) ... Japan doubts if such a grouping could produce fruitful results ... Conflicts in the Asia-Pacific region would be better settled through meetings of the concerned parties rather than at an international security forum' (Dewitt and Evans, 1992; Youtz and Midford, 1992: 20–21).

Japan begins decentring from the US on regional multilateralism

The Nakayama proposal

Despite following the US position of opposing a growing number of regional multilateral security proposals, including from US allies, Japan came to adopt a new and independent position by July 1991. In particular, Tokyo broke with Washington when Foreign Minister Tarō Nakayama proposed adding security to the agenda of the ASEAN Post Ministerial Conference (ASEAN PMC) of foreign ministers, and creating a senior officials meeting (SOM) to support this dialogue. In effect, the Nakayama proposal called for creating a like-minded multilateral security forum that only included US allies and US-friendly states, a forum that excluded the Soviet Union and other socialist nations.

As discussed elsewhere (Midford, 2000), the Nakayama proposal was a bold initiative, as it not only contradicted long-standing US policy on regional security multilateralism, but also came despite adamant US opposition to East Asian regional economic multilateralism in the form of Malaysia's call for creating an East Asian Economic Caucus (EAEC).[2] The US initially opposed the Nakayama proposal. Nonetheless, Japan persevered in the face of opposition from Washington and eventually convinced the US to change its position.[3]

Initial US opposition was ironic, given that Tokyo's two major motivations for making the Nakayama proposal served Washington's interests. First, Japan wanted to create a like-minded multilateral security forum of US-friendly states to help keep the US engaged in East Asian security, and perhaps even to coordinate and share the burden of hosting US military forces. Second, in response to US demands that Japan begin to shoulder military burdens commensurate with its status as the world's second largest economy, Tokyo sought a regional multilateral security forum where it could reassure neighbouring countries about Japan's decision to begin sending the Self-Defense Forces (SDF) overseas for non-combat operations, not only to the unstable Middle East, but notably, to participate in UN peacekeeping operations in Cambodia. Regional security multilateralism was thus a means to facilitate new and direct involvement by Japan in regional and global security, involvement that would largely support US interests.

The Nakayama proposal can be considered Japan's first post-war regional security initiative, one that represented a decisive break from its previous strategy of regional security isolationism and the *de facto* Fukuda Doctrine taboo against discussing security issues with its neighbours. The Nakayama proposal effectively inverted the logic of the Fukuda Doctrine: whereas the Fukuda Doctrine identified regional mistrust of Japan as a military power as a reason to avoid any regional security role, including involvement in security dialogue, the Nakayama proposal saw regional distrust of Japan itself as the very reason for establishing a regional multilateral security dialogue. As a consequence, Japan would now begin regular high-level security dialogue with countries other than the US for the first time in the post-war era.[4] Although the US and even ASEAN initially reacted negatively to the Nakayama proposal, the January 1992 ASEAN Summit Meeting in Singapore decided to add security to the agenda of the PMC, a position the US endorsed.

Furthering regional security multilateralism: The Miyazawa initiatives

Tokyo followed up on the Nakayama proposal of July 1991, and ASEAN's decision to initiate a security dialogue within the ASEAN PMC, with further initiatives for regional security cooperation. In particular, Prime Minister Kiichi Miyazawa gave several speeches and formed a study group. In a speech before the Foreign Press Club in Washington in July 1992, Miyazawa went well beyond the

Nakayama proposal by explicitly holding out the possibility of including China and Russia in the new dialogue at some point. He stated that it was important 'to build a region wide framework for political dialogue encompassing a broader spectrum of countries … The task remains for the future to involve China and Russia in such process of dialogue and cooperation as constructive participants' (Ministry of Foreign Affairs of Japan, 1992b: 430–431). Miyazawa argued that the ASEAN PMC, which did not include China or Russia at that time, 'may, for now, most usefully serve this purpose'. Nonetheless, Miyazawa's decision to mention the possibility of including China and Russia in a regional dialogue marked an important departure for Japanese diplomacy, and his wording suggested that the inclusion of China and Russia might not lie very far in the future.

Miyazawa's proposal for possibly including China and Russia created controversy within Japanese policy-making circles. A foreign ministry official subsequently denied that Miyazawa had proposed including China and Russia any time in the near future. Another 'government source' even claimed that Miyazawa had been labouring under a 'misunderstanding' by thinking that an Asian version of CSCE, a CSCA, was needed for Asia (Tomiyama, 1992: 78).

A broader concern about Miyazawa's call for possibly including China and Russia was that this would undercut one of the two major goals for promoting regional security multilateralism in the first place, namely, keeping the US militarily engaged in East Asia. Miyazawa himself emphasised the importance of this goal in his speech: 'It is earnestly desired that the United States will maintain its forward deployment in the region.' Reciting Japan's unparalleled host nation support of US forces, then projected to reach 70 per cent of non-salary costs by 1995, Miyazawa even pledged 'further improvement of its host nation support' (Ministry of Foreign Affairs of Japan, 1992a: 428). Nonetheless, domestic critics of Miyazawa were not convinced, with one suggesting that Miyazawa's proposal for an Asian security framework would be seen in Washington as a shift towards 'anti-Americanism'. This same critic suggested that if Japan doubted America's military commitment and wanted to study a multilateral alternative for the long run, this discussion should be conducted in private within the confines of the government or a think-tank.[5]

In view of the controversy that Miyazawa's July 1992 Washington initiative generated within Japan, it is not surprising that his next speech on security multilateralism avoided explicitly mentioning China and Russia. Addressing a Center for Strategic and International Studies (CSIS) Councillors meeting in Tokyo in October 1992, he emphasised the importance of making a high-profile commitment to building an Asia-Pacific region-wide cooperative security framework. Referring back to his July speech, Miyazawa asserted: 'I believe that it is about time for Japan, the United States and other Asia-Pacific countries to further contemplate a framework of such Asia-Pacific regional cooperation.' Again, the primary purpose of this framework would be to promote 'a region-wide political dialogue promoting mutual reassurance'. And again, Miyazawa coupled this initiative with a reaffirmation of the centrality of Japan's security arrangement with the US (*Japan Times*, 1992a; Ministry of Foreign Affairs of Japan, 1992a). Although not openly broaching the issue of including China and Russia in a regional security dialogue, Miyazawa's emphasis on contemplating a regional framework for such a dialogue clearly signalled dissatisfaction with the ASEAN PMC as the vehicle for this dialogue.

Miyazawa's commitment to promoting regional security multilateralism was manifested in an informal advisory panel he assembled, entitled 'Japan and the Asia-Pacific Region for the 21st Century', organised in May 1992 and led by the president of Keio University. This group's final report suggested that region-wide dialogue would be useful for promoting transparency and reassurance, and building confidence. Going beyond even Miyazawa's Washington speech, the panel advised that it was 'important to actively consider how to ensure the participation of China and Russia in this dialogue' (21 *Seiki no Ajia-Taiheyō to Nihon wo Kangaeru Kondankai*, 1992a: 15).[6]

Beyond the need for a regional dialogue for the sake of reassurance, the report also reaffirmed the need to keep the US militarily engaged in the Asia-Pacific region. Strikingly, the report linked these two objectives by noting that American military engagement in East Asia strengthens 'confidence in Japan's fundamental position': that, paraphrasing the Fukuda Doctrine, Japan 'will not become a military great power capable of threatening other nations'. More generally, the report claimed that the US military presence helps to 'stabilise' relations between Japan and the nations of the Asia-Pacific (21 *Seiki no Ajia-Taiheyō to Nihon wo Kangaeru Kondankai*, 1992: 7).

Despite the advice of his advisory panel, Miyazawa backed away from explicitly promoting the inclusion of China and Russia in his third and final speech on regional security cooperation in Bangkok in January 1993. Although Miyazawa's address to the CSIS Councillors meeting in October 1992 was relatively low key, his third speech was built up as a major diplomatic initiative. Touted by some as 'the Miyazawa Doctrine' (see Morley, 1993), Miyazawa's speech in Bangkok was in fact not as bold as his Washington Press Club speech of the previous July had been.

Miyazawa's initiatives on expanding regional security multilateralism helped pave the way for the creation of a regional consensus to create a new unlike-minded security forum that would include China, Russia and Vietnam. This consensus was reached at the first security-focused SOM held under the PMC in May 1993. By this time, the US, under the new Clinton administration, also supported including China and Russia in a regional security dialogue. Thus, the decision to create the ARF, reached informally by this SOM meeting in May, and formally by the PMC in July 1993,[7] did not cause Tokyo to again challenge US regional security policy. Nonetheless, the creation of the ARF would soon produce tension between the two, as Washington began to suspect that Tokyo was prioritising the ARF over alliance relations.

US fears about Japan's promotion of security multilateralism

Responding to the end of the Cold War, Japan began preparing to issue a new National Defense Program Outline (NDPO) to replace the first one ever issued in 1976. In preparation for this, Prime Minister Morihiro Hosokawa organised a study group to debate the contents of the new NDPO. This study group came to be known as the Higuchi report, named after its chairman Hirotarō Higuchi, president of Asahi Beer. The Higuchi report emphasised the importance of regional multilateral security cooperation for Japan's security. Notably, it discussed this before discussing the US–Japan alliance, and seemed to some observers to give too much emphasis to regional and even global multilateralism. This created alarm among some Japan hands in Washington, most notably Patrick M. Cronin and Michael J. Green, who wrote an influential paper warning about the dangers of Japan's engagement with multilateralism for the alliance.[8]

According to Cronin and Green, the Higuchi report signalled that 'momentum and energy in Japanese policy planning are flowing away from the alliance' (Cronin and Green, 1994: 2). The two set up a zero-sum trade-off between the alliance and multilateralism, claiming that 'bureaucrats in the Japan Defence Agency (JDA) and Ministry of Foreign Affairs are increasingly distracted from alliance concerns by other matters. In the 1980s, the best and the brightest worked on the alliance; now they work on peacekeeping, Asian relations' (Cronin and Green, 1994: 2). Later in the report, they characterise multilateralism as 'a distraction (in terms of political and financial resources) from bilateral defence cooperation' (Cronin and Green, 1994: 9). They identify UN peacekeeping, the ARF, and even the Track Two (non-state centric) Council for Security Cooperation in the Asia-Pacific (CSCAP) as the sources of this distraction. Here we see, in perhaps in its most direct and articulate form, American fear that Japan's decentring from the US, in this case by engaging with new multilateral security partners, could lead to fewer resources and less attention being devoted to the Japan–US alliance.

Cronin and Green argue that Japan's new focus on multilateralism is a possible 'hedge' against 'possible U.S. withdrawal or fatigue' or 'waning U.S. commitments to the alliance' (Cronin and Green, 1994: 22). Their report also warned that the Higuchi report was advocating the development of greater autonomous capabilities, capabilities that might prove 'redundant' with US capabilities. Again, they identified greater engagement in multilateralism as a major justification, if not a driver, of this trend, such as the report's call for Japan to develop greater autonomous airlift capabilities to support participation in UN peacekeeping operations.[9]

Ultimately, Cronin and Green suggest that Japan's pursuit of multilateral security partners can be made acceptable if it takes place through the US: 'We want Japan to play a more active role *in partnership with the United States*', including 'increased bilateral coordination' on UN peacekeeping (Cronin and Green, 1994: 14, emphasis in the original). More strikingly, they called for Japan's activism within the ARF to take place only through bilateral coordination with the US: 'Coordinating regional multilateral security initiatives (at the ASEAN Regional Forum (ARF), etc.) *before* presenting them to the rest of the region' (emphasis in original).[10] One can see the Cronin and Green paper as an attempt to adjust to Japan's decentring from the US by ensuring that Japan's new security partnerships only operated through bilateral coordination with the US, or at least that the US had some say in how they developed.

This reaction[11] to the Higuchi report illustrates a previously latent US sensitivity to Japan's decentring from the US in its regional security strategy and moving towards greater security engagement with its East Asian neighbours. Takao Sebata claims that the Cronin and Green paper indicated 'the real objective of the Security Treaty from the United States viewpoint [is] ... to prevent the growth of Japan's power projection capabilities known as the "Cork in the Bottle" argument' and the fear 'that Japan might become a country which is beyond the control of the United States' (Johnson, 1996; Sebata, 2010: 263). At the same time, the Cronin and Green paper proved to be very influential, and their message of alarm was arguably a major factor behind the 1995 Nye report. Joseph S. Nye himself shared many of the concerns of Cronin and Green, arguing that without a new institutional framework, Japan might rearm, achieve a '"normal" great power status' and 'act unilaterally in ways contrary to American interests' (Nye, 1992/93: 32–33, 37; Sebata, 2010: 263). The Nye report called for strengthening and redirecting the US–Japan alliance to deal with new post-Cold War regional contingencies in East Asia. This in turn led to the April 1996 Clinton–Hashimoto joint declaration reaffirming the importance of the bilateral alliance, and to the revised US–Japan Defense Guidelines of 1997.

The US reaction also illustrates the pressure that Washington could exert over Japanese policy, as one of the most notable differences between the Higuchi report and the 1996 NDPO was that the US alliance was mentioned before the ARF and regional multilateral security cooperation, and was given far greater emphasis. Indeed, the US–Japan Security Treaty was mentioned 13 times in the 1995 NDPO, versus only three times in the 1976 NDPO that it replaced (Sebata, 2010: 280).

Nonetheless, this incident occurred at a time when Japan was less concerned about US abandonment and more concerned about US entrapment. For example, Akio Watanabe, an academic and member of the Higuchi panel, 'argues the 1995 NDPO was formulated as a brake so that Japan would not be drawn into United States Strategy'. Watanabe also claims that the Higuchi report forced the US to abandon its focus on trade frictions and refocus on the security treaty (Sebata, 2010: 270). This was also a period when prominent members of the Liberal Democratic Party (LDP) were calling for the gradual withdrawal of US forces and bases from Japan.[12] During the May–June 1994 crisis over North Korea's development of nuclear weapons, Japan was reluctant to strongly support the US and potentially get pulled into a military conflict. Japan was also interested in pursuing new avenues for diplomatic independence, as became clear two years later with the Hashimoto Doctrine.

The Hashimoto Doctrine

From its inaugural meeting in 1994, Japan actively participated in the ARF, often cooperating with the US, especially in pushing China for greater transparency and to discuss disputes in the South China Sea. Nonetheless, Japan also enthusiastically continued to participate and promote the PMC as a like-minded multilateral security forum of US-friendly countries. Japan, despite its best efforts, could not stop the PMC being broadened into an unlike-minded forum by 1996 at ASEAN's behest.

Japan often acted far more independently of US regional policy than it had during the Cold War. Tokyo promoted regional political and security multilateralism that was often independent of the US. Perhaps the leading example of this was the Hashimoto Doctrine, named for then Prime Minister Ryūtarō Hashimoto, and whose ultimate outcome was the formation of a new East Asian political multilateral forum that excluded the US. In making the Hashimoto proposal, Japan was addressing two challenges it confronted. First, following China's admission to the PMC, how could Tokyo recreate a special relationship between ASEAN and Japan that would privilege Japan–ASEAN relations above China–ASEAN relations? Second, could Japan simultaneously reassert an independent diplomacy and identity in Southeast Asia vis-à-vis the US?

Like Prime Minister Miyazawa's visit of four years earlier, Hashimoto used the occasion of his visit to make a high-level diplomatic initiative, which, like Miyazawa's, was dubbed a 'doctrine'. However, the Hashimoto Doctrine proved to be more controversial than the Miyazawa Doctrine. The Hashimoto Doctrine essentially consisted of a proposal to institutionalise an annual Japan–ASEAN summit.[13] In an initiative reminiscent of the Nakayama proposal of more than five years earlier, the Japanese Ministry of Foreign Affairs, in a subsequent elaboration, even suggested creating an annual SOM to prepare for these summits.[14] Hashimoto also proposed discussing Asia-Pacific security with ASEAN nations on a bilateral basis, apparently avoiding the open suggestion of Japan–ASEAN talks on security (Ministry of Foreign Affairs of Japan, 1998: 189). Later, however, the Japanese Ministry of Foreign Affairs, in a low-key way, elaborated on the Hashimoto Doctrine by suggesting that Japan–ASEAN talks on 'regional security' as well as responding to the Asian financial crisis were a priority.[15]

As Green argues, this was a clear attempt 'to build a more explicit strategic relationship with ASEAN' (Green, 2003: 171). Similarly, Takeshi Yuzawa claims that the Hashimoto Doctrine 'envisaged a broader and more profound political and security relationship between Japan and ASEAN beyond mere economic cooperation. The main motivation behind the Hashimoto proposal was the desire to counterbalance growing Chinese power in East Asia with ASEAN support' (*Financial Times*, 1997; Yuzawa, 2007: 113). At the same time, the Hashimoto Doctrine also revealed reduced concern about US abandonment, in sharp contrast to the Nakayama proposal of five years earlier. It was an independent initiative that contained no role for the US, would create a political forum excluding the US, and came on the heels of the creation of the Asia–Europe Meeting (ASEM), which also excluded the US, and anticipated the APT, another forum excluding the US. If anything, the Hashimoto Doctrine suggested a desire to avoid being entrapped by American policy in Southeast Asia. As Green notes, 'When Prime Minister Hashimoto travelled throughout ASEAN in January 1997 to propose broader strategic relations with the region ... The key for Hashimoto was to maintain a balance between Japan's alliance with the United States and sympathy for ASEAN's position' (Green, 2003: 181). With this doctrine and these new forums, but also through policies that differed from Washington's on Cambodia and Burma, among others, Japan demonstrated a continued and, indeed, a growing appetite for an independent diplomacy in Southeast Asia. Sueo Sudo argues that the Hashimoto Doctrine effectively broke a 'deadlock' in Japan's ASEAN policy that had resulted from 'the lingering after-effects of the East Asian Economic Caucus Debate' (Sudo, 2002: ch. 3, 2009b: 139).

Nonetheless, the Hashimoto Doctrine reaffirmed Japan's position that the US forward military presence and the US–Japan alliance were crucial for regional security. Overall, the Hashimoto Doctrine represented an attempt to re-establish a special relationship with ASEAN, a relationship that had become attenuated over the previous 18 months after ASEAN decided to expand the membership of the PMC to include China, India and Russia. The Hashimoto Doctrine implicitly asserted a special role for Japan as ASEAN's closest economic and even political partner. At the same time, it also carved out a special role for the US as the regional provider of military security, even while attempting to deepen a security dialogue between Japan and ASEAN that did not include the US. The implicit hierarchy in this vision of regional order was made clear by the definition of China as a semi-outsider just emerging into international society, one that needed tutoring to ensure that this emerging engagement would be constructive (Ministry of Foreign Affairs of Japan, 1998: 192).

The Japanese Ministry of Foreign Affairs proclaimed the Hashimoto Doctrine a success, based on the ASEAN decision to hold an informal summit meeting with Japan in December of the same year during the celebrations for the 30th anniversary of the association's founding.[16] The reality, however, was different, as ASEAN effectively brushed aside Hashimoto's attempt to re-establish a special Japan–ASEAN relationship, reflecting its desire to maintain equidistant relations with all the great powers. According to Teo Poh Keng, 'Japan is not the only big power operating in Southeast Asia. The other powers like China and the US may wonder why Japan should be the only country to have the regular summit with ASEAN and not China or the US' (Keng, 1997).

Instead, ASEAN moved to broaden Hashimoto's initiative for an annual ASEAN–Japan summit into one that would include China and South Korea as well, nonetheless revealing in the process that excluding the US was not a concern. Jeannie Henderson rightly refers to this as a 'reinterpretation' of Hashimoto's proposal (Henderson, 1999: 64). In mid-May 1997, Malaysian Foreign Minister Abdullah visited Japan and, during a meeting with Japanese Foreign Minister Ikeda, reported that ASEAN members had by consensus agreed to Hashimoto's proposal for having regular summits with Japan, but added that this consensus extended beyond Japan to include a desire for summit dialogue that also included China and South Korea. At the end of May, a special ASEAN foreign ministers' meeting was convened, followed by a meeting that included the foreign ministers of Japan, China and South Korea, where the final decision was reached to establish the APT summit.[17]

Although the APT, with a regular Japan–ASEAN summit as one part, undoubtedly served Japan's national interest,[18] it is also clear that this represented a polite and creative ASEAN rejection of Japan's bid to re-establish a special ASEAN–Japan relationship. As Michael Green notes, 'Though not exactly what Tokyo had in mind, Japan nevertheless joined the first official ASEAN Plus Three meeting in late 1997' (Green, 2003: 171). While many observers argued that ASEAN was primarily concerned about China's reaction (Green, 2003: 171; Tanaka, 2000: 282–284), a more accurate characterisation would be that ASEAN was no longer interested in having a special relationship with Japan that was closer than its relationship with China. Indeed, ASEAN members have always been leery about having anything other than an equidistant relationship with the great powers. According to a senior Philippine foreign policy intellectual, ASEAN wants 'an equidistant relationship with all the big powers'.[19]

Thus, ASEAN reshaped Hashimoto's initiative by inviting China and South Korea to join an annual summit with ASEAN and Japanese leaders, giving birth to the annual APT summit. The membership of this forum was especially significant, since it exactly matched the proposed membership of the EAEC. This made the exclusion of the US, the only major Asia-Pacific power (unless one counts Russia) not to be included in ASEAN+3, all the more obvious (Smith, 2006: 191). Japan's willingness to quickly embrace a multilateral forum with this membership stands in clear contrast to its opposition to EAEC in the early 1990s, and with its more general concern about promoting any multilateral forum that might potentially alienate the US. This suggests that Japan's fear of abandonment, and its desire to use multilateralism as a means for keeping the US militarily engaged in East Asia, had clearly declined. It also indicates that other concerns, such as competing with China for influence in ASEAN, had become more important priorities. On the other hand, Japan's acceptance of the ASEAN+3 summit framework might also suggest a continued desire to create a multilateral diplomatic channel for political dialogue, if not security dialogue, with its principal East Asian partners absent the US. The trilateral summit involving China and South Korea that more recently precedes the ASEAN+3 suggests a similar desire as concerns Northeast Asia (see later in this chapter).

Even before the launch of ASEAN+3, another multilateral diplomatic initiative suggested Japan's growing interest in pursuing multilateral political, if not security, venues that do not include the US. Responding to European overtures, Singaporean Prime Minister Goh Chok Tong called for 'Europe and East Asia to engage in a dialogue at the highest level to forge the third link in the tripolar world' (Henson, 1994: 1). After some additional lobbying by Goh, the ASEAN SOM meeting, held on 18 March 1995, endorsed the ASEM proposal and decided to hold the first summit during the first half of 1996 in Bangkok (Hua, 1995: 10; Tanaka, 2007: 57). Although Japan pushed to include Australia and New Zealand, it did not try to include the US. Moreover, Japan bowed to opposition from Malaysia, which argued that Australia and New Zealand 'do not share our Asian values' (Ngoo and Song, 1995: 3). At the end of February 1996, heads of government from Asian members of ASEM held a pre-ASEM meeting, marking, according to Akihiko Tanaka, 'the first meeting of the heads of government in East Asia', at least since the wartime Greater East Asian Co-prosperity Sphere (Tanaka, 2007: 57).

With Japan's support, ASEM thus brought together Asian and European countries in a diplomatic forum that excluded the US. Strikingly, the Asian membership again exactly reproduced the membership of Mahathir's proposed EAEC, with the Asian and European sides meeting in two separate groups before the 26 Asian and European countries met together as a group. As a result of the ASEM process, the leaders that Malaysia had tried to get together for the EAEC met for the first time in history, although the term EAEC was not used and ASEM had a far broader agenda than economics, including cultural, social and political issues (Tanaka, 2007: 58). Although Japan did not take the initiative in this case, its willingness to accept this formula suggests at the very least that Tokyo no longer feared that political multilateralism excluding the US could encourage an American military withdrawal from Asia.[20] At maximum, Japan's enthusiastic support for ASEM suggests a willingness to explore multilateral diplomatic channels excluding the US.

Japan's promotion in 1997 of an Asian Monetary Fund, or AMF, which would serve many of the functions of the US-dominated International Monetary Fund (IMF) but without the same harsh conditionality, is another indicator of Japan's reduced concern about abandonment by the US at this time (Miyashita, 2001: 158). Japan pushed this proposal despite strong US opposition (Dwyer, 2000: 87; Wessel and Davis, 1998). Even after the US succeeded in defeating Tokyo's AMF proposal, Japan remained surprisingly undeterred. Tokyo quietly reconstructed some of the elements of the AMF, most notably through the New Miyazawa Initiative (named after former prime minister and then Finance Minister Miyazawa Kiichi), through which Japan provided funds to East Asian nations stricken by the Asian financial crisis, ignoring IMF conditionality and US opposition (Dwyer, 2000: 98, 120, note 31; Hughes, 2000: 222, 245–248; *Nihon Keizai Shimbun*, 1999: 3).

Although it was not a result of the Asian financial crisis per se, the crisis accelerated the development of the APT, especially in terms of financial and monetary cooperation. Political issues were on the agenda from day one, although economic cooperation dominated in the beginning. As the Asian financial crisis gradually abated, political issues became more prominent. At the Fourth APT in 2000, Prime Minister Yoshirō Mori proposed beginning a 'comprehensive' dialogue and cooperation regarding political and security issues (Tanaka, 2007: 66; Togo, 2008: 173). Although security was thus formally added to the APT agenda, not much happened in the subsequent years regarding security.

Northeast Asian political multilateralism

Since the ARF and other ASEAN-centric security forums are ostensibly Southeast Asian centric, Northeast Asian nations, especially Korea and Japan, have at times seen the ARF as being too Southeast Asia focused, and have striven to create a Northeast Asian multilateral forum. The Institute on Global Conflict and Cooperation (IGCC) at the University of California San Diego sponsored a planning meeting in July 1993 to establish a Track Two Northeast Asia Cooperation Dialogue (NEACD). The first NEACD meeting was held in October 1993. North Korea participated in the planning meeting and the first dialogue meeting, but did not attend subsequent sessions (Fukushima, 1999: 155–156; Togo, 2005: 213).

The second NEACD dialogue was held in May 1994 in Tokyo. Subsequent NEACD meetings were held in Moscow in April 1995, Beijing in January 1996 and New York in April 1997, with a return to Tokyo in December 1997 (Fukushima, 1999: 156). Paralleling developments at the ARF the following year, in May 1994, the NEACD in Tokyo agreed to establish a standing group on mutual reassurance measures (Fukushima, 1999: 156), a development that paralleled the ARF's establishment of the Inter-Sessional Group on Confidence Building Measures.

At the fourth ARF meeting in 1997, Japanese Foreign Minister Ikeda proposed transforming the NEACD into a Track One forum. It was envisaged that this forum would supplement the work of the ARF in Northeast Asia. Ikeda's proposal received little attention from other ARF participants, with the partial exception of South Korea, which floated its own proposal. China did not support the proposal because of North Korea's refusal to participate in NEACD (Matsuda, 1997: 37–38; Yuzawa, 2007: 115).

A Northeast Asian multilateral forum, after several failed starts, finally gained traction as a result of the APT, which linked ASEAN with the three Northeast Asian states. Then Prime Minister Keizō Obuchi 'surprised everybody' by proposing a breakfast meeting of the three Northeast Asian leaders at the third APT summit in 1999 in Manila.[21] Summit meetings among the Northeast Asian Three thereafter became a regular feature on the sidelines of the APT meetings. Tripartite governmental cooperation began in 2002, and on the sidelines of the Bali APT meeting in 2003, the three issued a 'Joint Declaration on the Promotion of Tripartite Cooperation', which was 'the first agreement among just those three countries' (Togo, 2008: 174).

From this point multilateral cooperation among what has been called the Northeast Asian 3 (NEA 3) developed rapidly. In 2008, the first Northeast Asian Summit not connected to the APT was held in Dazaifu, Japan. This marked what was supposed to become an annual Northeast Asian Summit. Nonetheless, due to political conflicts, mostly between China and South Korea, on the one hand, and Japan, on the other, over historical memory issues, summits to date have been less than regular. As yet, NEA 3 Summits still have limited connection with security multilateralism, but they do feature political dialogue. Moreover, like the APT, NEA multilateralism is a regional multilateralism that Japan played a leadership role in establishing, and one that excludes the US.

Japan and the ARF in the 21st century

By the end of the 1990s, Japan's enthusiasm for the ARF had waned according to some (Yuzawa, 2007: 150–157). Nonetheless, this waning revealed not an underlying lack of interest, but a quiet, patient and long-term interest in the ARF as a valuable means to reduce the chance of accidental conflict through misperception, the essence of common security.[22] As Togo observes, 'Japan has not taken a notable leadership role, but continued to be a stable supporter' of multilateralism in the ARF and Northeast Asia (Togo, 2005: 212). Although Japan was not as active at taking the initiative within the ARF itself, it continued to take multilateral security initiatives in Southeast Asia, especially as regards counter-piracy (see later in the chapter) and creating a defence ministers' dialogue. In June 2002, Japanese Defence Minister Gen Nakatani proposed establishing an annual inter-governmental-level Asia-Pacific defence ministers' forum. A new framework was needed, Nakatani asserted, because the participation of defence officials in the ARF was 'limited'. Starting with dialogue and an exchange of information, Nakatani saw this forum going further to include 'concrete cooperation' on peacekeeping, maritime safety, large-scale disaster relief, and policies for countering terrorism, piracy and drug trafficking (*Asahi Shimbun*, 2002; *Japan Times*, 2002; Togo, 2005: 212). This was, according to Togo, 'a proposal from Japan that had not been heard since Nakayama's ill-fated initiative in 1991' (Togo, 2005: 212). Unlike the Nakayama proposal, however, the Nakatani proposal did not suggest an ASEAN venue for this dialogue. This difference reflects ASEAN's by then well-known reluctance to have a non-ASEAN country propose an entirely new ASEAN-sponsored body, and perhaps a desire to create a non-ASEAN-centric forum that would be less focused on Southeast Asia. Nakatani's proposal did not produce any tangible results, however.

Nakatani made his proposal at the first meeting of the so-called 'Shangri-La Dialogue', an unofficial defence officials' dialogue sponsored by the International Institute for Strategic Studies (IISS). Nakatani was thus implicitly arguing that this dialogue, because it was unofficial and hence unable to conclude binding agreements or even non-binding joint policy positions of participants, was insufficient. When the Shangri-La Dialogue was started, it was 'touted as the "the real" regional forum' (Chongkittavorn, 2004: 10A) that could replace the ARF. However, sponsored as it was by the London-based IISS, and due therefore to 'a preponderance of Western-led security think-tanks' and their hostility towards 'China's strategic outlook', China was not alone in expressing its dissatisfaction with the Shangri-La Dialogue. Yukio Satō, the brains behind the Nakayama and Miyazawa proposals, argued in February 2004 that although the ARF had already established the foundations of mutual trust among members, it had a significant weakness because it lacked a defence ministers' dialogue. Like Nakatani, he further argued that the Shangri-La Dialogue, because it was not at the inter-governmental level, could not be as effective. Consequently, Satō proposed that Japan again take the initiative, ten years after the establishment of the ARF, by proposing the establishment of a forum for defence ministers' dialogue (Satō, 2004: 3).

Others shared the concern that the ARF was too focused on national foreign ministries and diplomats, and that defence ministry and uniformed officers, although increasingly involved after 1995, continued to have a relatively marginal role in the ARF.[23] Over the course of the first decade of the 21st century, ASEAN moved to develop an ASEAN Defense Ministers' Meeting, or ADMM. The design of the ADMM was finalised in 2009 (ASEAN Secretariat, 2006). By 2010, a consensus was reached to supplement the ADMM with an

ADMM Plus consisting of the ASEAN 10 plus eight partners, thus coinciding with the membership of the EAS (but significantly smaller than the ARF membership). The first ADMM Plus was held in Vietnam in October 2010. ADMM Plus represented the culmination of efforts by Satō, Nakatani and others to fully establish a defence ministers' dialogue, thereby deepening the regional security dialogue. Consistent with Satō's proposal, but unlike Nakatani's, what emerged was another ASEAN-centric cooperative security institution, once again reinforcing ASEAN's centrality.

In the meantime, over the course of the first decade of the 21st century, the ARF itself moved its focus away to some extent from hard security issues and towards non-traditional security issues, especially maritime security, anti-terrorism (especially after 9/11) and migration issues.[24] A major new focus after 2004 was military-to-military cooperation in humanitarian assistance/disaster relief (HA/DR) operations. This even resulted in ARF-sponsored small-scale military exercises that highlighted the capacities of member states' militaries to engage in and cooperate in disaster relief operations. According to a Singaporean-based analyst, with HA/DR the ARF 'can go beyond CBMs' (confidence-building measures) and into concrete military cooperation. This analyst also noted that China had taken a leadership role in promoting HA/DR cooperation, and had proposed that the ARF countries come up with an inventory of member nations' military equipment available for disaster relief.[25]

This shift in the ARF's focus towards HA/DR also illustrates that China's and Japan's interests in regional security multilateralism are by no means always a zero-sum game, as this shift has also well suited Japan's interests and abilities, enabling Tokyo to expand its role and activism in the ARF. As a leading Filipino defence intellectual noted, what Japan was trying to do was to work in areas where the SDF can help, and not in military areas.[26]

Japan's promotion of East Asian multilateral counter-piracy cooperation

Counter-piracy is a 'non-traditional' security area where Japan has again taken the initiative in promoting regional security multilateralism. As early as 1999, Japan proposed joint multilateral 'anti-piracy patrols' with ASEAN members. ASEAN disagreed and suggested establishing a multilateral mechanism for sharing data and 'coordinating' national patrols (Green, 2003: 189; Kin, 2000).

Two years later, in November 2001, following up on ASEAN's counter-proposal, then Prime Minister Junichirō Koizumi proposed the establishment of an information sharing centre in Southeast Asia to better coordinate anti-pirate patrols in Asian waters. Negotiations began 'under Japan's leadership', and included a two-day conference of Asian Coast Guard heads in Tokyo in June 2003 (Ministry of Foreign Affairs of Japan, 2010; Samuels, 2007/2008: 104).

Sixteen Asian nations participated in negotiating the agreement, which came to be known as the Regional Cooperation Agreement on Combating Piracy and Armed Robbery against Ships in Asia (ReCAAP). This agreement was concluded in November 2004 (Ministry of Foreign Affairs of Japan, 2010).[27]

With the agreement coming into force in September 2006, the ReCAAP Information Sharing Centre (ISC) was established in Singapore in November 2006 (Ministry of Foreign Affairs of Japan, 2010). A Singapore-based security expert described Japan as 'the driving force' behind ReCAAP.[28] During its first decade of operation, all ISC heads have been Japanese.[29] Another Southeast Asian security expert also saw ReCAAP as 'very Japanese driven' as well as funded, and noted that the ReCAAP ISC works very closely with the Singaporean Navy's 'naval fusion centre' at Changi, which monitors regional maritime traffic. Not surprisingly, the ISC's main role is reportage to member countries.[30]

ReCAAP illustrates how Japan has promoted its security interests through narrow functional regional security multilateralism, and has thereby avoided playing a direct military role in Southeast Asia and reassured regional states about Japan's intentions and behaviour. This is especially important given that Japan has been a leading foreign user of Singapore's Changi naval base. Nonetheless, the Japanese Coast Guard presence in the region has been more prominent,[31] with many of the Maritime Self-Defense Force (MSDF) ships simply passing through on their way to or from the Indian Ocean. ReCAAP has in turn supported the multilateral counter-piracy mission off Somalia, in which Japan is a major participant, both as a model and by providing capacity-building support to regional nations (see Vosse's chapter in this volume and Midford, 2015). ReCAAP is another example of Japan promoting regional security multilateralism, albeit in an area of non-traditional security, without including the US.

Conclusions

Since July 1991, Japan has been pursuing a policy on regional security multilateralism that has involved discussing security issues with its neighbours and even more concrete forms of security cooperation, thereby ending Japan's regional security isolationism and involving Tokyo in security dialogues and cooperation with countries other than its ally, the US. In the process, Japan has often acted independently of the US and has even promoted the creation of political and security venues that exclude the US, most notably the Hashimoto proposal, the APT, the NEA 3, and ReCAAP. In other cases, Japan's promotion of regional security multilateralism has often been coordinated with the US, and has rarely been explicitly at odds with US policy. Moreover, a major goal of Japan's independent security multilateralism from the beginning has been to keep the US forward deployed and engaged in East Asia. Multilateralism has thus generally been used as a supplement to, or support for, the Japan–US alliance.

However, the fact that Japan has been willing from time to time to promote forms of political and security multilateralism that exclude the US reflects the waxing and waning of the priority Tokyo has placed on using security multilateralism as a tool for keeping the US engaged in East Asia. Behind this has been variation over time in Japan's fears of abandonment versus entrapment by its powerful ally. Fear of abandonment tended to predominate during 1990–1993, 2006–2009 and 2011–2017, with fear of entrapment tending to be stronger during 1994–2005 and 2009–2010.

Japan has come a long way since it abandoned regional security isolationism, beginning with the Nakayama proposal in 1991. This abandonment was the result of having outgrown security isolationism; Japan had become the world's second largest economy and a global powerhouse that its US ally could no longer afford to see sitting on the sidelines of global and regional security. At the same time, Japan's growing economic weight and US pressure on Japan to play a larger security role alarmed East Asian nations with memories of Japan's invasion and occupation of its neighbours up to 1945. Tokyo was also motivated to shed its previously reactive stance and demonstrate that it could play a leadership role.

Overall, this chapter demonstrates that Japan has decentred from the US since the Cold War, when the US was Japan's sole security partner. Japan has built security cooperation with non-US partners through regional multilateralism in order to achieve several goals: to keep the US engaged in East Asian security, to hedge against US abandonment and entrapment, to promote regional transparency and reduce the risk of war, to promote regional collective goods, such as sea lanes free from the scourge of piracy, and to reassure neighbouring countries about Japan's own disposition as a military power, lest it provoke counter-balancing by its neighbours.

Notes

1. For classic studies of Japan's Cold War defense posture, see Weinstein (1971) and Welfield (1988).
2. Regarding this opposition, see Baker (1995: 610–611). Yukio Satō, the intellectual driving force behind the Nakayama proposal, emphasized in a classified internal Ministry of Foreign Affairs document the importance of distinguishing this proposal from the EAEC, fearing that linking them would provoke implacable US opposition. See Jōhō chōsa kyokuchyō, 'Ajia taiheiyō chiiki no antei kakuho to anzenhoshō ni tsuite— fukugōteki (marutipurekkusu) mekanizumu no unyō,' 25 June 1991, document found by the author at the Diplomatic Archives of the Ministry of Foreign Affairs of Japan, pp. 1–2. Sudo argues that Japan's ASEAN diplomacy was effectively in 'deadlock' from 1990 until the Hashimoto Doctrine of 1996, a result of 'the lingering after-effects of the East Asian Economic Caucus Debate' (Sudo 2002: ch. 3, 2015: 139). The Nakayama proposal and subsequent multilateral security proposals were the exception to this deadlock.

3 See Midford (2000: 384, 387). This new position was enshrined in the January 1992 Tokyo Declaration on the US–Japan Joint Global Partnership, in which the US and Japan endorsed a regional multilateral dialogue through existing forums such as the ASEAN-PMC or APEC. See 'The Tokyo Declaration on the US–Japan Joint Global Partnership,' 9 January 1992. In one paragraph, the Declaration identifies APEC as 'the forum for enhanced regional efforts to ... build political cooperation,' whereas a few paragraphs later it recommends promoting 'political dialogue among Asia-Pacific countries through the ASEAN Post Ministerial Conference'. The latter reference is an endorsement of the Nakayama proposal.
4 The beginning of regular bilateral security talks with the Soviet Union/Russia is a partial exception, as it predates the Nakayama proposal by about eight months. See Midford (2000: 377).
5 Tomiyama (1992: 79). This observer's warning proved prescient two years later, when Japan was debating the contents of its new National Defense Program Outline in 1994–1995; see later in the chapter.
6 Also see *Japan Times* (221992b).
7 Interview with a Singaporean diplomat who attended this meeting, 30 November 2011.
8 Cronin and Green (1994: 21–60). The full report appears on pp. 21–60 of this publication. Also see Sebata (2010: 261–266).
9 See Advisory Group on Defense Issues, 'The Modality of the Security and Defense Capability of Japan: The Outlook for the 21st Century' (report submitted to the Prime Minister of Japan, 12 August 1994), as reproduced in Cronin and Green (1994: 52); Green (1995: 148).
10 Cronin and Green (1994: 16). Emphasis in the original.
11 The Cronin and Green report was also criticized as the overreaction of inexperienced dilettantes, and the State Department pushed back against their conclusions. See Johnson (1996).
12 MITI Minister and later Prime Minister Ryūtarō Hashimoto, and LDP Diet member Shintarō Ishihara, later governor of Tokyo, submitted a paper to the LDP leadership calling for the eventual removal of US bases from Japan. Similarly, the deputy chairman of the LDP's Foreign Affairs Research Council, stated: 'The time has come for us to review the existence of all these [US] bases.' See Cronin and Green (1994: 11, 19) and Sterngold (1994: 16).
13 Ministry of Foreign Affairs of Japan (1998: 186–193) at p. 189. Sudo places this proposal in the context of Hashimoto's visit to several countries rather than his Singapore speech per se. See Sudo (2009b: 139).
14 This suggestion was made in an anonymous side-bar article published in *Gaikō Forum*, the Ministry's unofficial mouthpiece, in November. See *Gaikō Forum* (1997: 15).
15 *Gaikō Forum* (1997: 15). In addition to his Singapore speech, during each of his stops in ASEAN capitals, Hashimoto reiterated his proposal for a regular summit and wider dialogue between Japan and ASEAN. See Tanaka (2007): 59.
16 *Gaikō Forum* (1997). ASEAN informed Japan of this decision in early May 1997. See *Asahi Shimbun* (1997).
17 *Nihon Keizai Shimbun* (1997, morning edition: 2) and Sudo (Sudo (2009a: 165), who notes that the APT had already effectively become a reality through the creation of ASEM.
18 Additionally, as Akihiko Tanaka argues, from the perspective of Malaysia's campaign to realize the EAEC, the APT undermined Japan's negative position towards the EAEC (Tanaka 2000, 2007: 60). Referring to the formation of the APT, Malaysian Prime Minister Dr Mahathir claimed: 'This is EAEC though we do not call it as such', as quoted by Sudo (2009b: 104).

19 Interview of 24 September 2010. Also making a similar point is Smith (2006: 191): 'The Hashimoto administration also promoted a separate ASEAN–Japan summit, but had to be content with ASEAN's desire not to afford Japan special treatment at the time.'
20 Similarly, Tanaka notes that after the ASEM membership was decided, 'Japan became less reluctant to the grouping of ASEAN, China, Japan, and South Korea' (Tanaka 2007: 58).
21 Togo (2005: 212), who also notes that President Kim Young-Sam attempted to hold a summit meeting among the Northeast Asian three during his tenure as president, 1992–1997, but this did not materialize. Also see Tanaka (2007: 64).
22 The claim that Japan's enthusiasm for the ARF had ebbed is largely based upon a passage from an internal Ministry of Foreign Affairs of Japan document of 20–21 May 1999 evaluating the ARF SOM. According to this document, it was difficult to think that there was much hope for significant progress in institutionalizing and building an ARF organization, because China had a cautious, go slow approach (Anzenhoshō seisaku-ka (Security Policy Division) 1999: 2). Yet this was an evaluation of a single meeting, and this assessment was soon mooted by China's own activism in promoting the institutionalization of the ARF, including the development of a secretariat (see later).
23 The so-called ASEAN Special Senior Officials' Meeting (ASEAN Special SOM), starting in 1996, brought together ASEAN diplomats and defense officials, especially in a Working Group on Security Cooperation (ASEAN Secretariat 2006). Another milestone in ASEAN defense cooperation was the holding of a 'golf day' for ASEAN defense ministers in 1997. On the latter, see Henderson (1999: 82, note 28).
24 Interview of 24 September 2010. A Philippines-based analyst further observed that 'It is not very good for analysts, especially ASEAN analysts to continue talking about the ARF as a talk shop. Because it suggests that they have not been watching the movements from talk-shop to action.'
25 Interview of 28 September 2010.
26 Ibid.
27 Although Norway did not participate in negotiations, it became the first non-Asian nation to sign the agreement in August 2009, thereby making ReCAAP a 15-nation agreement. The Netherlands subsequently joined in July 2010, Denmark shortly thereafter, and the UK in 2012.
28 Interview of 27 September 2010.
29 www.recaap.org, and interview with ReCAAP ISC officials, Singapore, 30 November 2011. Also see Midford (2015).
30 Interview of 28 September 2010. This expert noted that naval officers from several ARF countries, including the US, are posted at Singapore's naval fusion centre.
31 Interview of 27 September 2010.

REFERENCES

Anzenhoshō seisaku-ka [Security Policy Division], 1999. 'ARF-SOM (Gaiyō to hyōka)', 24 May.
Asahi Shimbun, 1997. 'Nihon to ASEAN, 12 gatsu ni mo shunou kaigi', Asahi Shimbun, 8 May, morning edition, p. 2.
Asahi Shimbun, 2002. 'Ajia taiheiyō shokoku no kokubōsho kaigi wo teshō-anpō kaigi de Nakatani chōkan', 3 June, morning edition, p. 1.
Association of Southeast Asian Nations (ASEAN) Secretariat, 2006. 'Concept Paper for the Establishment of an ASEAN Defence Ministers' Meeting', May, at:

https://admm.asean.org/dmdocuments/1.%20Concept%20Paper%20for%20 the%20Establishment%20of%20an%20ASEAN%20Defence%20Ministers.pdf (accessed 7 February 2017).

Baker, J. A. III, 1995. *The Politics of Diplomacy: Revolution, War and Peace 1989–1992* (New York: G.P. Putnam's Sons).

Chongkittavorn, K., 2004. 'China Takes the Lead in Pushing Asian Security Dialogue', *The Nation*, 19 July, p. 10A.

Cronin, P. and Green, M. J., 1994. *Redefining the Alliance: Tokyo's National Defense Program* (Washington, DC: National Defense University).

Dewitt, D. B. and Evans, P. M., 1992. 'The Changing Dynamics of Asia Pacific Security: A Canadian Perspective', *NPCSD Working Paper* Number 3, pp. 8–9.

Dwyer, J. H., 2000. 'US-Japan Financial-Market Relations in an Era of Global Finance', in Curtis, G. (ed.), *New Perspectives on US-Japan Relations* (Tokyo: Japan Center for International Exchange), p. 87.

Financial Times, 1997. 'Hashimoto Designs a Grander Foreign Policy: Changing Balance of Power in Asia Has Led to a More Active Development of Regional Links', *Financial Times*, 14 January, p. 6.

Fukushima, A., 1999. *Japanese Foreign Policy: The Emerging Logic of Multilateralism* (London: Macmillan).

Gaikō Forum, 1997. "Fukuda "dokutorin" kara "Hashimoto dokutorin" made', November, p. 15.

Green, M., 1995. *Arming Japan: Defense Production, Alliance Politics, and the Postwar Search for Autonomy* (New York: Columbia University Press).

Green, M., 2003. *Japan's Reluctant Realism: Foreign Policy Challenges in an Era of Uncertain Power* (New York: Palgrave Macmillan).

Hemmer, C. and Katzenstein, P. J., 2002. 'Why Is There No NATO in Asia? Collective Identity, Regionalism, and the Origins of Multilateralism', *International Organization*, 56(3): 575–607.

Henderson, J., 1999. *Reassessing ASEAN*, Adelphi Paper 328 (London: International Institute for Strategic Studies).

Henson, B., 1994. 'PM: Time to Forge Europe-E.Asia Link', *The Straits Times*, 20 October, p. 1.

Hua, L. S., 1995. 'Thailand Agrees to Hold First Europe-Asia Summit', *The Straits Times*, 10 March, p. 10.

Hughes, C. W., 2000. 'Japanese Policy and the East Asian Currency Crisis: Abject Defeat or Quiet Victory?', *Review of International Political Economy*, 7(2): 219–253.

Japan Times, 1992a. 'Miyazawa Bids Asia-Pacific Weigh Security "Framework"', *Japan Times*, 23 October, p. 2.

Japan Times, 1992b. 'Prime Minister's Council Calls for Active Asian Role', *Japan Times*, 26 December, p. 1.

Japan Times, 2002. 'Japan Proposes Asia-Pacific Defense Chief Forum', *Japan Times*, 3 June.

Johnson, C., 1996. 'The Okinawan Rape Incident and the End of the Cold War in East Asia', *JPRI Working Paper*, 16 February.

Jōhō chōsa kyokuchyō, 1991. 'Ajia taiheiyō chiiki no antei kakuho to anzenhoshō ni tsuite— fukugōteki (marutipurekkusu) mekanizumu no unyō.' 25 (June). Document found by the author at the Diplomatic Archives of the Ministry of Foreign Affairs of Japan.

Keng, T. P., 1997. '"Hashimoto Doctrine" Takes Japan Step Closer to ASEAN', *The Nikkei Weekly*, 20 January, p. 19.

Kin, K. W., 2000. 'Asian Governments Not Keen on Joint Piracy Patrols', *The Straits Times*, 4 May.
Lam, P. E., 2012. *Japan's Relations with Southeast Asia: the Fukuda Doctrine and beyond* (New York: Routledge).
Matsuda, M., 1997. 'ARF no chūchōkiteki arikata', in Kokusai Mondai Kenkyujo, *Aijiataiheiyō no Anzenhoshō Heisei 8 nendo jishu kenkyu hōkokusho* (Tokyo: Nihon), pp. 37–38.
Midford, P., 2000. 'Japan's Leadership Role in East Asian Security Multilateralism: The Nakayama Proposal and the Logic of Reassurance', *The Pacific Review*, 13(3): 370–372.
Midford, P., 2015. 'Japan's Approach to Maritime Security in the South China Sea', *Asian Survey*, 55(3): 525–547.
Ministry of Foreign Affairs of Japan, 1992a. 'Senryaku kokusai mondai kenkyūjyo (CSIS) Kokusai hyōgiin kaigō (10/22) ni okeru Miyazawa sori kōen Nihon no kokusaiteki yakuwari-—Atarashii kyōryoku kankei no wakugumi wo motomete' [Speech of Prime Minister Miyazawa before a Counselors Meeting of the Center for Strategic and International Studies (CSIS) (10/22) on Japan's International Role—Seeking a New Framework for Cooperative Relations]. Text compliments of the Japanese Ministry of Foreign Affairs.
Ministry of Foreign Affairs of Japan, 1992b. *Diplomatic Bluebook 1992: Japan's Diplomatic Activities* (Tokyo: Ministry of Foreign Affairs).
Ministry of Foreign Affairs of Japan, 1998. 'Shingapo-ru rekuchya ni okeru Hashimoto sōri enzetsu "Nichi-ASEAN shinjidai he no kaikaku-yori hirogaku yori fukai pa-tona-shippu"', *Gaikō Seisho 1998*, Dai 1 bu (Tokyo: Gaimushō). pp. 186–193.
Ministry of Foreign Affairs of Japan, 2010. 'Ajia kaizoku taisaku chiiki kyōryoku kyōtei', May, at: www.mofa.go.jp/mofaj/gaiko/kaiyo/kaizoku_gai.html (accessed 27 May 2017).
Miyashita, A., 2001. 'Japanese Foreign Policy: The International-Domestic Nexus', in Beasley, R., Kaarbo, J., Lantis, J. S. and Smarr, M. T. (eds), *Foreign Policy in Comparative Perspective: Domestic and International Influences on State Behavior*, First Edition (Washington, DC: CQ Press), pp. 144–169.
Morley, J. W., 1993. *Japan and the Asia-Pacific: Defining a New Role*, Asian Updates (New York: The Asia Society).
Ngoo, I. and Song, T. K., 1995. 'Japan Wants NZ, Aussies in Asia-EU Summit', *The Straits Times*, 25 July, p. 3.
Nihon Keizai Shimbun, 1997. 'ASEAN to teiki shunō kyōgi', *Nihon Keizai Shimbun*, 22 May, morning edition, p. 2.
Nihon Keizai Shimbun, 1999. 'Shin Miyazawa kousou wo kakudai, Okurasho, Vietonamu ni tekiyō-IMF nado ni senkōshi shien mo', *Nihon Keizai Shimbun*, 3 May, morning edition, p. 3.
Nye, J. S. Jr., 1992/93. 'Coping with Japan', *Foreign Policy*, 89(Winter): 32–37.
Pacific Research, 1991a. 'Summary of Regional News', February, p. 20.
Pacific Research, 1991b. 'Summary of Regional News', November, p. 26.
Press-Barnathan, G., 2000. 'The United States and Regional Security Cooperation in Asia and Europe', *Security Studies*, 10(2): 49–97.
Samuels, R. J., 2007/2008. 'New Fighting Power! Japan's Growing Maritime Capabilities and East Asian Security', *International Security*, 32(3) (Winter): 84–112.
Satō, Y. 'ARF ni Kokubō daijin no sanka wo', *Seikai Shuhō*, 10 February, p. 3.
Sebata, T., 2010. *Japan's Defense Policy and Bureaucratic Politics, 1976–2007* (Lanham, Maryland: University Press of America).

Seiki no Ajia-Taiheyō to Nihon wo Kangaeru Kondankai [Japan and the Asia-Pacific in the 21st Century Roundtable], 1992. 21 Seiki no Ajia-Taiheyō to Nihon-—Kaihōsei no Suishin to Tayōsei no Sonchyō [Japan and the Asia-Pacific in the 21st Century: Promoting Openness and Respecting Diversity], 25 December, Tokyo.

Smith, A. L., 2006. 'Japan's Relations with Southeast Asia: The Strong Silent Type', in Sato, Y. and Limaye, S. (eds), *Japan in A Dynamic Asia: Coping with the New Security Challenges* (Lanham, MD: Lexington Books), pp. 179–198.

Sterngold, J., 1994. 'Some Leaders in Japan Begin to Question U.S. Bases', *The New York Times*, 28 August, p. 16.

Sudo, S., 1992. *The Fukuda Doctrine and ASEAN: New Dimensions in Japanese Foreign Policy* (Singapore: Institute of Southeast Asian Studies).

Sudo, S., 2002. *International Relations of Japan and South East Asia* (London: Routledge).

Sudo, S., 2009a. 'ASEAN ni yoru higashi ajia chiikishugi seisaku: Shin chikishugi keisei ni itaru taigai kōdō no setsumei'. *Akademia*, 88(January): 143–174.

Sudo, S., 2009b. 'Japan's ASEAN Policy: Reactive or Proactive in the Face of a Rising China in East Asia?', *Asian Perspective*, 33(1): 137–158.

Sudo, S., 2015. 'Japan's ASEAN Policy: In Search of Proactive Multilateralism' (Singapore: Institute of Southeast Asian Studies).

Tanaka, A., 2000. 'The International Context of U.S.-Japan Relations in the 1990s', in Curtis, G. L. (ed.), *New Perspectives on U.S.-Japan Relations* (Tokyo: Japan Center for International Exchange), pp. 265–294.

Tanaka, A., 2007. 'The Development of the ASEAN+3 Framework', in Curley, M. G. and Thomas, N. (eds), *Advancing East Asian Regionalism* (Oxon, UK: Routledge), pp. 52–73.

Togo, K., 2005. *Japan's Foreign Policy, 1945–2003: The Quest for a Proactive Policy* (Third Extended Edition) (Leiden: Brill).

Togo, K., 2008. 'Japan and the New Security Structures of Asian Multilateralism', in Calder, K. E. and Fukuyama, F. (eds), *East Asian Multilateralism: Prospects for Regional Stability* (Baltimore: Johns Hopkins University Press), pp. 168–197.

Tomiyama, Y., 1992. 'Miyazawa Shushō no Teishō Ajia Anpo Kōsō ni Gimon ari', *Chūō Kōron*, 107(1288) (November): 78–79.

Weinstein, M. E., 1971. *Japan's Postwar Defense Policy, 1947–1968* (New York: Columbia University Press).

Welfield, J., 1988. *An Empire in Eclipse: Japan in the Postwar American Alliance System* (London and Atlantic Highlands, NJ: The Athlone Press).

Wessel, D. and Davis, B., 1998. 'Global Crisis Is a Match for Crack US Economists', *Wall Street Journal*, 25–26 September, p. 8.

Youtz, D. and Midford, P., 1992. *A Northeast Asian Security Regime: Prospects after the Cold War* (New York-Prague: Institute for East West Studies).

Yuzawa, T., 2007. *Japan's Security Policy and the ASEAN Regional Forum: The Search for Multilateral Security in the Asia-Pacific* (Abingdon: Routledge).

6

The East Asia perspective on the security partnership with Japan

Stephen R. Nagy

Introduction

JAPAN'S APPROACH TO international relations has been highly influenced by the evolution of the global world order from a bipolar to a unipolar to a multipolar system, an acknowledgement of limited ability of traditional power projection (in particular in Japan's case) and the realisation of the importance of 'complex interdependence' between nation states via the implementation of institutions and an increased number of trading agreements (Keohane and Nye, 1998). In this context, since the end of World War II, Article 9 of the Japanese Constitution has limited Japan's military capabilities and compelled it to develop other strategies to achieve its foreign policy objectives (Katzenstein and Okawara, 1993). These have included the signing of the 'Treaty for Mutual Cooperation and Security', a treaty that provides for the execution of joint military training exercises as well as the promise of mutual security (Manyin, 2012). Complementing that approach has been a foreign policy approach that stressed economic engagement as a means to achieve Japanese foreign policy objectives (Hughes, 2000).

Notwithstanding its alliance with the US, Japan has demonstrated realist tendencies in the post-World War II period and since the return of Prime Minister Abe in 2012 (Auslin, 2016). Emerging threats such as North Korea's missile and nuclear tests and a growingly assertive China in the East and South China Seas (Valencia, 2007) have brought to light structural and normative factors that limit Japan's capability to effectively manage and respond to these increasingly contentious relationships, namely Article 9 and a largely pacifist citizenry that is deeply against the use of the military and revision of the so-called pacifist constitution (Miyashita, 2007). As a consequence of the decreasing efficacy of traditional tools of Japanese foreign policy such as economic incentives, regional challenges have deepened Tokyo's view not only of the salience of the US–Japan security partnership, but also of the importance of deepening its partnerships in Southeast Asia through economic, political and security linkages (Nagy, 2017). In line with this view, Japan has been actively courting Southeast Asian countries through official development assistance (ODA) and economic partnerships (Asplund, 2015). This engagement has accelerated in intensity and scope, beginning in December 2012 with the return of the Abe administration (Shiraishi, 2014).

Historically, Japan's relations with Association of Southeast Asian Nations (ASEAN) countries have been based on mutual benefit and, until recently, could be understood in terms of three categories: 1) developmental economics; 2) product hubs; and 3) shared values. Myanmar, Cambodia, Laos and to a certain degree Thailand represent the first category, where large amounts of ODA were injected into these three countries as part of Japan's commitment to contributing to its Southeast Asian neighbours' economic development (Stubbs, 1999). They are also resource-rich countries that Japan strives to develop relationships with to secure access to resources for its industries at home and abroad (Jomo, 2006).

Vietnam, the Philippines, Indonesia, Malaysia and Thailand represent the second category. These countries have become large manufacturing centres for Japanese businesses. From here, Japanese products are produced for global export (Felker, 2003). Singapore, Indonesia, Malaysia and the Philippines represent the third category of relationship between Japan and ASEAN countries, one that is rooted in democracy, the rule of law and a commitment to international norms and laws. Brunei is the outlier among the ASEAN member states, as its oil resources, monarchy and level of wealth mean that Japan has forged a relationship to secure access to oil resources while not having to engage in developmental economic policies (Islam and Odano, 2010).

With the bitter experience of Japan's imperial past reconciled, forgotten or deprioritised (Takeda, 1992), up until the early 2000s, Japan's relationship with ASEAN countries could be considered non-securitised (Yang, 2003). This long-standing economic-focused relationship has shifted with two related changes in the region: China's growing economic hegemony in the region and China's military modernisation and expansion (Reilly, 2016). Hand-in-hand with these endogenous regional drivers has been the exogenous factor of the US's declining ability to singly maintain the burden of the East Asia security framework (Goh, 2011). Endogenous and exogenous factors have led to what some scholars call bipolarisation of the South China Sea (Burgess, 2016). Lastly, political stability under the Abe administration has enabled a more sustained, engaged and proactive foreign policy, making Japan a more reliable partner in the areas of economic, political and security cooperation (Mark, 2016).

The objective of this chapter will be to examine Japanese–Southeast Asian security partnerships from a 'Southeast Asian perspective'. In this process, the author will divide Southeast Asian countries into two categories: peripheral-core countries and core-peripheral countries. The author will argue that Japanese–Southeast Asian security partnerships cannot be understood with a blanket formula; rather, we must divide ASEAN countries into 'peripheral-core' and 'core-peripheral' countries, which have different security challenges and political-economic relationships vis-à-vis China. This bifurcation into two categories also encompasses the different competitive advantages each grouping has in terms of its position in the regional and global economic chain, its economic relationship with China, and its threat perception of China as the latter continues to extend its economic, political and military influence in the region. It is the combination of these factors that drives and shapes Southeast perspectives of Japanese Southeast Asian security partnerships.

Defined as ASEAN core countries in terms of their geographic location but peripheral in terms of their economic largesse and influence, core-peripheral countries, which include Cambodia and Laos, will remain client states to China and see growing security partnerships with Japan by ASEAN countries as a difficult tightrope to walk.

In contrast, geographically at the periphery of ASEAN yet at the core of ASEAN's economic growing strength, peripheral-core states such as the Philippines, Indonesia, Vietnam, Malaysia and Brunei, and to a lesser extent Singapore and Thailand, will continue to welcome all forms of engagement from Japan, including security and economic partnerships to attenuate Chinese regional hegemony and/or prevent it from taking root.

This chapter poses several questions related to Southeast Asian countries' views on Japanese security partnerships within the region. For instance, how does the Japan–China security rivalry positively or negatively affect the evaluation of Japanese security partnerships in the region? What is the relationship between Japanese security partnerships, trade, and the advocacy of protecting freedom of thought, expression and speech in Southeast Asia, and the protection and promotion of the so-called universal values of freedom, democracy and human rights? What differences and similarities do ASEAN nations have in their perspectives on Japanese security cooperation in the region?

To analyse the perspectives of Southeast Asian countries on Japanese–Southeast Asian security partnerships, this chapter will examine strategic choices of Southeast Asian countries by investigating the link between the economic relations Southeast Asian countries have with China and their relative threat perception of China. Based on the relationship of these two variables, this chapter argues that Southeast Asian states will engage in bandwagoning, soft and hard hedging, engagement and other balance of power arrangements or fall prey to the pressure of client state relations, depending on the interaction of these two variables. These approaches have been selected because they explain security choices and growing security ties with Japan. Collectively, these theories will enable us to distinguish various factors that drive and shape Southeast perspectives of Japan–Southeast Asia security partnerships.

This chapter is divided into five sections. The preceding first section briefly introduces Japan–Southeast Asian relations and how they have evolved from a non-securitised framework to one that is in the process of securitising. The second section introduces the theoretical framework that will be used to evaluate Southeast Asian countries' views on Japanese–Southeast Asian security partnerships. Specifically, economic dependency versus threat perception concepts such as bandwagoning, client state relations and balance of power politics will be used to better clarify Southeast Asian countries' perspectives on Japan's changing role in the region. The third section examines the perspectives of the core-peripheral countries of Cambodia and Laos, whereas the fourth section then examines the peripheral-core countries of the Philippines, Indonesia, Malaysia and Vietnam. Brunei is excluded from the discussion, as there is no security cooperation between Japan and Brunei beyond a commitment to watch the situation in the South China Sea. Singapore, Thailand and Myanmar are not included in this section, as they do not face immediate security issues in the South China Sea, despite Singapore's concerns about territorial friction in the South China Sea. The last section will then contextualise Japanese security partnerships in Southeast Asia and their relationship with the Trans-Pacific Partnership (TPP) or new regional trade agreements and norm-diplomacy.

Theoretical framework

States respond to changes in the balance of power by making strategic choices about how they can benefit from the change, counter the change or maintain their status quo. They do this through the strategies of bandwagoning, soft and hard hedging, engagement and balance of power arrangements or fall prey to the pressure of client state relations.

According to Johnston and Evans (2006), we define engagement as 'influencing the target's behaviour through promise of boon rather than threat to punish'. The tools of engagement depend on a state's capacity and include enhanced cooperation, military exchanges, security cooperation and bolstering economic ties. Economic and security cooperation through engagement aims to provide reassurances as to each state's intentions.

Whereas the engagement approach is centred on reassurances, according to Hurrell (2006), balancing consists of external and internal components. Internal balancing may consist of self-strengthening of the economy and/or the military in order to attenuate or restrain a potential threat. In contrast, external balancing generally is understood as an attempt to restrain a potential threat from becoming a regional (or global) hegemon through a process of alliance formation and the development of 'special relationships' that bolster security, economic and political capabilities.

Another strategy often employed as statecraft to manage changing power dynamics is hedging. Goh (2005, 2011) discusses hedging in terms of a strategic middle-of-the-road approach that strives to create a relationship in which the state in question does not have to choose between engagement and balancing. Koga (2011) further bifurcates hedging into soft and hard components, with the former stressing continued engagement with a state that is seen as a potential security threat while maintaining ties with the current power centre (US) with the intention of socialising the potential threat nation into the US-led system. The latter, in contrast, still stresses engagement; however, the degree of commitment to the current security guarantor (the US) remains much more significant.

In the context of security relations in Southeast Asia, the security calculus and choice of the above strategies are closely tied to economic relations rather than tangential or non-tangential military concerns or threat perception (see Table 6.1). In this sense, we would expect states in the region with the closest economic relations with China (the country that is changing the balance of power in the region) to have limited choices concerning their security and thus to be subject to the pressures associated with client state relations. Countries with less economic dependency on China may either choose to bandwagon or form an economic, security and/or political alliance with neighbouring countries.

Using the matrix in Table 6.2, we could argue four different scenarios in terms of response choices vis-à-vis strengthening relations with Japan. The first category is the case of high economic dependency on China and high

Table 6.1 Balance of power strategy as an outcome of the interaction of economic dependency and threat perception

		Threat perception	
		High	Low
Economic dependency on China	High	Japan	Cambodia, Laos, Thailand, Malaysia
	Low	Philippines, Vietnam, Singapore	Indonesia, Brunei

Table 6.2 Country categorisation regarding economic dependency v. threat perception

		Threat perception	
		High	Low
Economic dependency on China	High	Engagement, soft and hard hedging, balancing	Engagement under client state relations
	Low	Soft and hard hedging	Engagement, soft hedging

threat perception. In this case, a country would engage in a hedging process of security alignments, in which a strategy of engagement and hedging occurs synergistically to maximise benefits while preventing conflict. This approach may simultaneously engage in soft and hard hedging strategies. The second case concerns those countries that have high economic dependency and low threat perception. Countries in this category, depending on geographic proximity, could be considered client states and as a result, their security choices would be highly influenced by Beijing. Here, security partnerships with Japan would be seen as a liability rather than a strategic advantage and consequently would be avoided. The third category comprises those countries with low economic dependency but high threat perception. Here, economic distance allows them to engage in a bandwagoning strategy to balance China or perhaps contain China. Security partnerships, whether they are formal alliances or strategic partnerships, would be seen as a strategic imperative to avoid being dominated. Lastly, the fourth category is the situation in which there is both low threat perception and a low level of economic engagement. Countries in this category, when considering security partnerships, would choose the path of engagement if the current trajectory was symbiotically beneficial or neutral.

It can be argued that based on the matrix in Table 6.2, Southeast Asian states, depending on their threat perception and economic relationship with China, will engage in security relationships with Japan using strategies that may include the various permutations of hedging (soft or hard hedging), balancing/bandwagoning, institutional engagement through enmeshment or other tactics.

ASEAN core-peripheral countries: Japan's security partnerships as a risk to political independence

Cambodia and landlocked Laos remain at the lowest end of socio-economic development in the region (Pink, 2016). Although they are beneficiaries of Japanese ODA, their largest trading partner is China, and as China's economy continues to grow in dominance in the region, so does their dependency on Chinese demand (Council for the Development of Cambodia, 2016). This economic dependency has created a client state relationship with China in which both states find it difficult to deviate from Beijing's influence (Ciorciari, 2013).

To illustrate, the 45th ASEAN Ministerial Meeting (AMM) on 9–13 July 2012 in Phnom Penh was concluded without issuing ASEAN's traditional Joint Communiqué (Ministry of Foreign Affairs & International Cooperation, Kingdom of Cambodia, 2014). At the meeting, ASEAN foreign ministers agreed on ASEAN's Six-Point Principles to deal with the South China Sea issue. ASEAN countries attempted to put forth the following proposal that they would agree to territorial disputes only in a multilateral forum.

Statement of ASEAN Foreign Ministers on ASEAN's Six-Point Principles on the South China Sea

ASEAN Foreign Ministers reiterate and reaffirm the commitment of ASEAN Member States to:

1. the full implementation of the Declaration on the Conduct of Parties in the South China Sea (2002);
2. the Guidelines for the Implementation of the Declaration on the Conduct of Parties in the South China Sea (2011);
3. the early conclusion of a Regional Code of Conduct in the South China Sea;
4. the full respect of the universally recognised principles of the International Law, including the 1982 United Nations Convention on the Law of the Sea (UNCLOS);
5. the continued exercise of the self-restraint and non-use of force by all parties; and
6. the peaceful resolution of disputes, in accordance with universally recognised principles of International Law, including the 1982 United Nations Convention on the Law of the Sea (UNCLOS).

The ASEAN Foreign Ministers resolve to intensify ASEAN consultations in the advancement of the above principles, consistent with the Treaty of Amity and Cooperation in Southeast Asia (1976) and the ASEAN Charter (2008).

(Ministry of Foreign Affairs and International Cooperation, Kingdom of Cambodia, 2012)

Under Chinese pressure, Cambodia refused the proposal, preventing it from coming into effect due to the so-called ASEAN way of consensus or nothing. The result was that Beijing's preference for bilateral negotiations over territorial disputes was maintained, allowing it to exert overwhelming pressure on its negotiating counterpart. With so many smaller countries engaged in disputes with China over territory, a multilateral approach would severely weaken Beijing's position.

This example is illustrative of two ASEAN core-peripheral countries' sensitivities to Beijing's security concerns and thus, their position on Japan's more sustained and qualitatively proactive security partnerships in the region. In this sense, Cambodia's approach towards security partnerships with Japan can be viewed as representative of an approach that is based on high economic dependency and a low threat perception emanating from its relationship with China in the security realm. As a consequence, it views a security partnership with Japan as a liability but other forms of engagement with China as a boon.

Japan's engagement includes ODA, commitments to shared norms, principles of engagement, peace, technological aid, economic incentives, and the provision of coast guard vessels and surveillance technologies (Pajon, 2013). This increasing number of commitments has real benefits for the beneficiaries but has the effect of increasing China's presence and pressure in the region. For Cambodia and Laos, this pushes the boundaries of client state relations to what may be unacceptable.

As a result of this conundrum, Cambodia and Laos, while potential beneficiaries of increased competition between Japan and China for their support, view Japanese security partnerships in Southeast Asia as having the potential to increase Chinese influence on their polities and thus decrease their political independence. This also decreases the effectiveness of ASEAN as a regional institution, as the ASEAN way of consensus decision making becomes vulnerable to the influence of non-ASEAN countries with strong and unbalanced economic relations with weaker members such as Laos and Cambodia.

ASEAN peripheral-core countries: Security through trade

Members of the ASEAN peripheral-core countries, with the exception of Malaysia, see Japanese–Southeast Asian security partnerships in a positive light. Malaysia has a more nuanced view due to the influence of Beijing on the large number of ethnic Chinese Malaysians with strong, trans-regional business ties to China (Smart and Hsu, 2004). Thus, Malaysia strives towards a relationship with China that is characterised as a 'productive relationship in both economic and diplomatic areas with China, but with whom she has unresolved territorial issues' (Izzuddin, 2016).

With low to moderate threat perceptions and deepening economic ties to China, Hughes (2015) and Nagao (2015) assert that Malaysia is actively engaging China while at the same time engaging in a soft hedging strategy by holding joint naval exercises with Japan and the US focusing on maritime cooperation. Moreover, Malaysia–Japan security cooperation includes the initiation of negotiations on the framework for cooperation on the transfer of defence equipment and technology, and both countries have elevated their relations to a strategic partnership (Ministry of Foreign Affairs of Japan, 2015a). Focusing on peacekeeping, humanitarian assistance and disaster relief, and maritime security, according to our model, this security partnership can be understood as soft hedging with Japan wedded to a commitment to continued engagement with China.

While not large scale, the symbolic nature of the cooperation can be interpreted at several levels. First, Malaysia recognises that multilateral cooperation is crucial to ensuring its maritime security and territorial integrity. Second, having Japan and the US as the major partners in these activities demonstrates not only that Malaysia sees these countries as being best able to contribute to its security needs but also that it views these partners in a constructive light as bringing stability, capability and experience to the region. Third, by remaining in a peripheral position within maritime security cooperation, Malaysia aims to allay concerns that it is proactively engaged in an encirclement of China.

The other driving factors behind other peripheral-core countries' support for Japanese security partnerships in the region are at least twofold. The first level relates to Beijing's practice of opening or closing its economic market with countries that engage in practices that deviate from Beijing's preferred approach (Reilly, 2012). To illustrate this in both Asian and non-Asian contexts, we can examine how France was temporary penalised by Beijing for meetings with the Dalai Lama, which caused bilateral trade to decrease by 8.1 per cent to 16.9 per cent (depending on the measuring tool) (Fuchs and Klann, 2010). Numerous other examples of applying damaging economic sanctions on states that have political disagreements with China include China stopping the import of the Philippines' bananas; disruption of travel by Chinese tourists to the Philippines (Brooks, 2012; Takungpao, 2012), France (Traynor, 2008) and Norway; and stopping the import of Norwegian salmon and removing Norway from the list of countries allowed visa-free visits to Beijing after the Nobel Peace Prize was awarded to Liu Xiaobo (Anderlini and MacCarthy, 2012; *Apple Daily*, 2011).

In 2010 and then in 2012, Japan was also punished for political differences with Beijing. The first case involved the imprisonment of a Chinese fishing boat captain after the ramming of a Japanese coast guard vessel. The imprisonment resulted in a rare earths embargo against Japan (Johnston, 2013). The second case of punitive economic measures followed the September 2012 nationalisation of the Senkaku/Daioyu Tai Islands and was characterised by vandalism and arson against Japanese businesses in some parts of China (Nagy, 2013, 2014).

A vulnerability to punitive economic measures applied by Beijing (directly or indirectly) has compelled Southeast Asian countries and Japan to strengthen economic ties (Garrison and Wall, 2016). At the business level, corporations see political risk as 'the plus alpha' that business contingency plans cannot inculcate well into their strategic vision.

> The anti-Japanese riots are another example of the risk of doing business in China. This risk has been known for some time and our company has made adjustments. There is definitely a rise in anti-Japanese sentiment but in addition to this, the increasing cost of labor and doing business has made ASEAN states such as the Philippines, Indonesia, Vietnam and Myanmar attractive business destinations and as a result we are building manufacturing centers there. (Manager, Sales and Marketing, Japanese Manufacturing Company, interview, May 2013)

With the acknowledged geopolitical risk associated with China, corporations are realigning their foreign direct investment (FDI) to maintain their current footprint in China but also build another footprint in Southeast Asia, where geopolitical risk is less of a concern.

At the second level, countries in Southeast Asia have growing concern over China's territorial claims in the South China Sea and activities associated with those claims. With territorial disputes with several countries in the South China Sea; island building and militarisation of those islands; the placement of oil platforms in claimants' territorial waters; and a growing number of Chinese fishing vessels conducting fishing activities in Indonesia's, the Philippines' and other countries' waters (Tanner and Wang, 2016), peripheral-core Southeast Asian countries welcome security and other forms of cooperation with Japan and other extra-regional powers such as the US (Oishi, 2016). That being said, as with the previous cases of Cambodia, Laos and Malaysia, security cooperation is being calibrated to take into consideration threat perceptions and levels of economic dependency on China.

The Vietnamese view on security cooperation with Japan is highly favourable and is based on a high threat perception and China being Vietnam's largest trading partner (*China Daily*, 2015). In terms of the high threat perception, this is based on a history of Vietnamese–Chinese conflict, including not only the most recent war between the two in 1979 but also the colonialisation of Vietnam by China in the distant past. This threat perception is further enhanced by territorial disputes between the two claimants, incursions into Vietnamese territory and other incidents. These tensions seem to be on the rise despite China being Vietnam's largest trading partner.

Whereas the role of China as the largest trading partner of Cambodia and Laos resulted in an aversion to security partnerships with Japan, in the case of Vietnam, with a rapidly diversifying and growing economy and large expected gains from its participation in the TPP or a similar agreement, Vietnam has economic space to prioritise its security issues and commit to security partnerships with Japan and other countries such as the US. Thus, in the case of Vietnam, the variables of high threat perception and moderate (but declining) economic dependency on China have resulted in a soft and hard hedging approach to security calculation and a positive approach to cooperation with Japan in the form of a strategic partnership, the provision of second-hand marine vessels to enhance surveillance, and visits by Japanese destroyers to Vietnam's Cam Ranh Bay, which faces the South China Sea, as well as a commitment to deepen cooperation on maritime security as China's militarisation of the South China Sea continues (*Japan Times*, 2016b). Other initiatives, such as the signing of a memorandum in September 2015 to bolster defence-related cooperation and the provision of new marine patrol vessels, are meant to buttress the strategic partnership, not only to strengthen their bilateral ties but also to meet their overlapping and national security interests in the South China Sea (Ministry of Foreign Affairs of Japan, 2016).

The Philippines has a similar threat perception when it comes to China, but its economic dependency is relatively low, with Japan and the US ranking first and third in terms of trade volume and China ranking second (Philippine Statistics Authority, 2015). The outcome has been a greater commitment to both soft and hard hedging strategies and a proactive outreach to Japan (and the US) to help with its security. The end result includes agreements 'in principle to negotiate the transfer of defence equipment and technology from the Japan

Self-Defence Forces to the Armed Forces of the Philippines (AFP)' (De Castro, 2016). This commitment has been further buttressed by joint naval exercises, transfer to the Philippine Navy three JMSDF Beechcraft TC-90 King Air patrol planes with basic surface and air surveillance radar, to be followed in the near future by P-3C Orions, allowing access of Japanese Marine Self-Defense Forces (JSDF) to military bases, the formulation of a Visiting Forces Agreement and other cooperation (De Castro, 2016).

While not declaring a formal alliance, the Philippines sees Japan as a useful partner to engage in its own soft and hard hedging strategies vis-à-vis China based on its threat perception and also an implicit understanding of its own limitations. This engagement is expected to increase as the South China Sea becomes more volatile. This is evidenced by President Rodrigo Duterte's visit to Tokyo in October 2016 (Nagy, 2016b), the reciprocal visit by Prime Minister Abe to the Philippines in January 2017 and the Japanese Imperial Family's visit to Manila on 27 January 2016 (Imperial Household Agency, 2016), all of which demonstrates the importance that both countries place on each other as regional partners.

Indonesia's views on Japanese security partnerships have been evolving. Until recently, Indonesia held a low to moderately low threat perception towards China and experienced positive economic relations prior to the slowdown in the Chinese economy and accompanying commodities bust (Global Business Guide Indonesia, 2015). Indonesia has managed and de-prioritised its territorial dispute with China through diplomacy, preferring to prioritise comprehensive relations with China. This approach has been fairly constant, but changing economic relations as a result of the commodities bust, a more assertive China, and the 19 March 2016 incident in which an Indonesian Maritime Affairs and Fisheries patrol ship intercepted a Chinese trawler lowering its nets in waters at coordinates that placed it within Indonesia's Exclusive Economic Zone (EEZ) north of the Natuna Islands have shifted the strategic calculus of the Indonesian security establishment (Weatherbee, 2016).

Whereas the Philippines and Vietnam have actively courted Japanese aid and expressed a desire to have more security dialogue, Indonesia has been caught unprepared as to how to maintain its economic ties with China in the face of China's track record in the South China Seas and now in its backyard of the Natuna Islands. Notwithstanding, on 17 December 2015 at the Japan–Indonesia Foreign and Defence Ministerial Meeting, Indonesia and Japan agreed to hold politico-military (PM) and military-military (MM) dialogues in 2016 and initiate negotiations on an agreement on the transfer of defence equipment and technology, and stated that going forward, Japan would strive to develop security and defence cooperation, including in the area of defence equipment, and further promote its effort to enhance Indonesia's capability to secure the safety of its oceans and skies and to respond to disasters through active participation in the multilateral joint exercise KOMODO 2016 (Ministry of Foreign Affairs of Japan, 2015b).

These Japanese-driven initiatives are less about direct security cooperation and more about creating the institutional linkages that can be utilised for further defence cooperation, not only in the Straits of Malacca but, importantly, in the South China Sea. Indonesia's 'March 19th Shock' and changing economic relationship have shifted what the model in this paper would have predicted in terms of Indonesia's security choices: that is, continued engagement with China and at best soft hedging because of its previous low threat perception and mutually beneficial economic relationship. Instead, we see the threat perception of China on the rise and the previously mutually beneficial economic relations deteriorate, shifting Indonesia's approach to security towards soft and hard hedging, as evidenced through expanding security ties with Japan, as explained earlier.

Linking security and trade: TPP or rebranded trade agreement

The then TPP was a trade pact linking participating countries in the Asia Pacific. It was formulated to also strengthen ASEAN's importance as a manufacturing export hub. The peripheral-core countries that form the central nexus in this trade framework almost exclusively export their products through the South China Sea. With additional members such as the Philippines and Thailand receiving support for their ascension to the TPP (*Japan Times*, 2016a), more and more peripheral-core countries will have not only territorial stakes within the region but economic stakes that will require a multilateralisation of security partnerships to ensure that the South China Sea export/import lanes are not disrupted by territorial disputes or unilateral claims of sovereignty (Nagy, 2016a).

From this point of view, peripheral-core countries see increased Japanese security partnerships in Southeast Asia as an extension of Japan's economic strategy based on the TPP or a revamped version of the agreement. Security partnerships that anchor Japan into the region consolidate smaller countries' positions on territories in dispute with China. In this sense, peripheral-core countries interpret Japanese security partnerships in the region as the embedding of a multitude of bilateral security partnerships based on the TPP or a similar agreement.

Peripheral-core countries view Japanese security partnerships as a pyramidal structure consisting of the promotion of international norms (human rights, freedom and human security), trade and security. They are interrelated and mutually self-reinforcing. The promotion of international norms in the region, especially since Prime Minister Abe's visit to Southeast Asia in 2013, in which he espoused the view that Japan will protect and promote human rights, freedom and democracy (Kantei (The Prime Minister of Japan and His Cabinet), 2013), creates the foundation for building stronger, deeper and broader economic relations between Japan and Southeast Asian countries based on shared norms and rules. The TPP or revamped trade agreement is the most illustrative aspect of this.

Whereas the promotion and the protection of international norms create the conditions to strengthen economic cooperation, intensified and deepened trade not only increases the number of stakeholders in the region but also increases and multilateralises those who stand to lose from conflict or destabilisation in the region of the South China Sea. The potential loss or disruption of trade flows in the region thus strengthens the incentives for Southeast Asian countries to form security partnerships not only among each other but also with Japan.

Conclusion

This chapter has shown that Southeast Asian perspectives on Japanese security policy in the region are not uniform. Indeed, they are divided into peripheral-core and core-peripheral countries, and their views on Japanese–Southeast Asian security cooperation are influenced by their threat perception associated with the rise of China and their economic relationship with China. The core-peripheral countries view Japanese security partnerships as a destabilising influence that could further deepen their client state relationship with China, leading to a further erosion of their sovereignty due to China's economic influence. Peripheral-core countries, on the other hand, view Japanese security partnerships favourably, as they inculcate more stakeholders into the South China Sea through increasing trade ties based on international norms, the protection of human rights, democracy and freedom. Norms form the basis for trade, and increased trade creates the incentive to invest in security relationships. A plethora of bilateral security partnerships thus strengthens smaller countries' security interests within the region, as does the adherence to international law in the forms of international conventions such as the United Nations Convention for the Law of the Seas (UNCLOS).

Returning to the questions posed at the beginning of this chapter, the Japan–China security rivalry both positively and negatively affects the evaluation of Japanese security partnerships in the region, as demonstrated by the peripheral-core and core-periphery division outlined earlier. The core-peripheral nations of Cambodia and Laos particularly are facing a difficult choice in how to balance their bilateral relations with an influential China and a generous Japan.

This tug-of-war, which China is winning, also has implications not only for the role of Cambodia and Laos in ASEAN but also for the future of ASEAN as a regional institution. If the ASEAN way of consensus-based decision making continues to be influenced by China through Cambodia and Laos, the institution itself may lose its raison d'être in the region.

The relationship between Japanese security partnerships, trade, and the advocacy of protecting freedom of thought, expression and speech in Southeast Asia and the protection and promotion of the so-called universal values of freedom, democracy and human rights is an intentional shift by the Japanese government, but one that has enabled some countries to come together and join the TPP or a similar agreement.

ASEAN nations have both shared and different perspectives on Japanese security cooperation in the region, as evidenced by the bifurcation of ASEAN into peripheral-core and core-periphery groupings. Among these groupings, there are further divisions depending on the influence of overseas Chinese communities in the local polities and also regional trade flows. Malaysia's influential overseas Chinese-Malaysian community with trans-regional business interests plays a moderating role in Malaysian responses to expanding Chinese economic and military power in the South China Sea.

Asian countries from the peripheral-core see Japanese security partnerships at the bilateral level in four ways. First, bilateral security partnerships help smaller Southeast Asian neighbours in their territorial disputes with China. Second, the now defunct TPP and other trade agreements between Japan and Southeast Asian countries in bilateral and now multilateral trade agreements mean that Japan has a much larger stake in what happens in the South China Sea. With a significant volume of Japanese trade and a large percentage of its energy resources flowing through the South China Sea, it would be a national security miscalculation not to have at least bilateral ties in the region. Third, peripheral-core countries understand that security partnerships with Japan are not necessarily exclusively focused on the security dimension of cooperation. The wedding of development aid, bolstering infrastructure, increasing FDA and promoting values diplomacy to security cooperation is seen as a comprehensive approach to achieving development strategies while also dealing with a growingly assertive China in the South China Sea. Fourth, by virtue of expanding security partnerships with Japan, Southeast Asian countries implicitly understand that they are also expanding their security and other ties with Japan's most important security partner, the US.

At the time of writing this chapter, the security situation in the South China Sea has been evolving. The outcome of proceedings against the People's Republic of China (PRC) under Annex VII to UNCLOS by the Philippines and China's reaction to that judgement have influenced the direction of Japanese–Southeast Asian security partnerships in the future. The outright rejection of the judgement has increased the threat perception vis-à-vis China. China is now seen as a regional power that aims to overturn the status quo power and as a country not willing to follow international law. This has resulted in Southeast Asian countries strengthening their engagement and a preference for soft hedging over hard hedging strategies. At the same time, the rejection of the judgement has heightened the threat perceptions of Southeast Asian countries, Japan and other countries within the region, leading to an increase in soft and hard hedging against China through the strengthening of security partnerships with Japan.

Further militarisation on the South China Sea by building military facilities, through incidents at sea like the 'March 19th Shock', or through the declaration of an Air Defence Identification Zone (ADIZ) will also erode confidence among Southeast Asian states that China's rise will not be at their expense, increasing the incentive to form security and other partnerships with Japan.

There is at least one other factor that may affect Southeast Asian countries' approaches to security cooperation with Japan, and that is the Chinese economy. As the Chinese economy continues to transform away from an export-led, manufacturing-based economy that requires commodities from the region (and the world) towards a service-based economy that does not require commodities, commodity exporters in the region (Indonesia, Thailand, Philippines, Myanmar and Vietnam) will have decreasing economic interests with China. This decline in economic dependency may result in more robust approaches to dealing with bilateral issues and increase their commitment to deeper security cooperation with Japan and extra-regional powers such as the US, Australia and India.

References

Anderlini, J. and MacCarthy, C., 2012. 'China Snubs Norway in Visa Reforms', *Financial Times*, 6 December, at: www.ft.com/content/7aa84f82-3f6a-11e2-b0ce-00144feabdc0 (accessed 17 June 2013).

Apple Daily, 2011. 'Nuojiang ban Liu Xiao Bo, Zhong jin Nuowei guiyu' [Nobel Prize Was Conferred to Liu Xiao Bo, China Prohibits Imports of Norwegian Salmon], 6 October, at: appledaily.com.tw/appledaily/article/international/20111006/33719120/ (accessed 18 June 2013).

Asplund, A., 2015. Values vs. Interest: Strategic Use of Japanese Foreign Aid in Southeast Asia. No. 241. The European Institute of Japanese Studies.

Auslin, M., 2016. 'Japan's New Realism', *Foreign Affairs*, 95(2): 125.

Brooks, B. R., 2012. 'Asia-Pacific Economic Update 2012', Vol. 3, Honolulu, US Pacific Command, at: pacom.mil/documents/pdf/2012-APEU-Vol_3_091612_.pdf (accessed 17 June 2013), p. 23.

Burgess, S. F., 2016. 'Rising Bipolarity in the South China Sea: The American Rebalance to Asia and China's Expansion', *Contemporary Security Policy*, 37(1): 111–143.

China Daily 2015. 'Vietnam, China Trade Ties Seeing New Momentum', 15 July, at: http://europe.chinadaily.com.cn/world/2015-07/15/content_21287091.htm (accessed 23 April 2016).

Ciorciari, J. D., 2013. 'China and Cambodia: Patron and Client?', *International Policy Center Working Paper* No. 121, at: ssrn.com/abstract=2280003 (accessed 23 February 2016).

Council for the Development of Cambodia, 2016. 'Investment Trends', at: www.cambodiainvestment.gov.kh/why-invest-in-cambodia/investment-enviroment/investment-trend.html (accessed 10 March 2016).

de Castro, R. C, 2016. 'Philippines and Japan Strengthen a Twenty First Century Security Partnership', The Asia Maritime Transparency Initiative and the Center for Strategic and International Studies, at: amti.csis.org/philippines-and-japan-strengthen-a-twenty-first-century-security-partnership (accessed 23 May 2016).

Felker, G. B., 2003. 'Southeast Asian Industrialisation and the Changing Global Production System', *Third World Quarterly*, 24(2): 255–282.

Fuchs, A. and Klann, N.-H., 2010. 'Paying a Visit: The "Dalai Lama Effect" on International Trade', *Center for European Governance and Economic Development Research Paper*, No. 113.

Garrison, J. and Wall, M., 2016. 'The Rise of Hedging and Regionalism: An Explanation and Evaluation of President Obama's China Policy', *Asian Affairs: An American Review*, 43(2): 47–63.

Global Business Guide Indonesia (GBGI), 2015. 'What China's Slowdown Means for Indonesia: A Trade Perspective', 15 September, at: gbgindonesia.com/en/main/business_updates/2015/what_china_s_slowdown_means_for_indonesia_a_trade_perspective_11313.php (accessed 6 May 2016).

Goh, E., 2005. 'Meeting the China challenge: The US in Southeast Asian Regional Security Strategies', East-West Center, Washington, DC, at: www.eastwestcenter.org/publications/meeting-china-challenge-us-southeast-asian-regional-security-strategies (accessed 11 January 2016).

Goh, E., 2011. 'How Japan Matters in the Evolving East Asian Security Order', *International Affairs*, 87(4): 887–902.

Hughes, C. W., 2000. 'Japanese Policy and the East Asian Currency Crisis: Abject Defeat or Quiet Victory?', *Review of International Political Economy*, 7(2): 219–253.

Hughes, C. W., 2015. 'Japan's Relations under Abe with China, the Korean Peninsula and ASEAN', in Hughes, C. W. (ed.), *Japan's Foreign and Security Policy under the 'Abe Doctrine': New Dynamism or New Dead End?* (Basingstoke and New York: Palgrave Macmillan), pp. 79–90.

Hurrell, A., 2006. 'Hegemony, Liberalism and Global Order: What Space for Would-Be Great Powers?', *International Affairs*, 82(1): 1–19.

Imperial Household Agency, 2016. 'Addresses by Their Majesties the Emperor and Empress on the Visit to Philippines', 27 January, at: www.kunaicho.go.jp/e-okotoba/01/address/speech-h28e.html (accessed 2 January 2017).

Islam, S. and Odano, S., 2010. 'LNG Exports from Brunei to Japan', *Center for Risk Research Faculty of Economics Working Paper*, A-20.

Izzuddin, M., 2016. 'China–Malaysia Relations and Foreign Policy by Abdul Razak Baginda (Review)', *Contemporary Southeast Asia: A Journal of International and Strategic Affairs*, 38(1): 167–170.

Japan Times, 2016a. 'Twelve Countries to Discuss Expanding TPP to More Nations', 23 January.

Japan Times, 2016b. 'Maritime Security Ties to Grow, Hanoi and Tokyo Say Twelve Countries to Discuss Expanding TPP to More Nations', 6 May.

Johnston, A. I., 2013. 'How New and Assertive Is China's New Assertiveness?', *International Security*, 37(4): 7–48.

Johnston, A. I. and Evans, P., 1999. 'China's Engagement in International Security Institutions', in Johnston, A. I., Ross, R. S. (ed.), *Engaging China: The Management of an Emerging Power* (London and New York: Routledge), pp. 241–278.

Jomo, K. S. (ed.), 2006. *Japan and Malaysian Economic Development: In the Shadow of the Rising Sun* (Abingdon: Routledge).

Kantei (The Prime Minister of Japan and his Cabinet), 2013. 'The Bounty of the Open Seas: Five New Principles for Japanese Diplomacy', at: japan.kantei.go.jp/96_abe/statement/201301/18speech_e.html (accessed 10 April 2016).

Katzenstein, P. J. and Okawara, N., 1993. 'Japan's National Security: Structures, Norms, and Policies', *International Security*, 17(4): 84–118.

Keohane, R. O. and Nye Jr, J. S., 1998. 'Power and Interdependence in the Information Age', *Foreign Affairs* 77: 81–94.

Koga, K., 2011. 'The US and East Asian Regional Security Architecture: Building a Regional Security Nexus on Hub-and-Spoke', *Asian Perspective*, 35(1): 1–36.

Manyin, M. E., 2012. 'Senkaku (Diaoyu/Diayutai) Islands Dispute: US Treaty Obligations', *Current Politics and Economics of South, Southeastern, and Central Asia*, 21(3/4): 231.

Mark, C., 2016. *The Abe Restoration: Contemporary Japanese Politics and Reformation* (Lanham: Rowman & Littlefield).

Ministry of Foreign Affairs & International Cooperation, Kingdom of Cambodia, 2014. 'Statement of ASEAN Foreign Ministers on ASEAN's Six-Point Principles on the South China Sea', at: www.cambodianembassy.jp/web2/?p=188&lang=en/ (accessed 21 March 2016).

Ministry of Foreign Affairs of Japan (MOFA), 2015a. 'Japan-Indonesia Foreign and Defense Ministerial Meeting', at www.mofa.go.jp/s_sa/sea2/id/page3e_000437.html (accessed 10 May 2016).

Ministry of Foreign Affairs of Japan (MOFA), 2015b. 'Japan-Malaysia Joint Statement on Strategic Partnership', at www.mofa.go.jp/s_sa/sea2/my/page3e_000342.html (accessed 10 May 2016).

Ministry of Foreign Affairs of Japan (MOFA), 2016. 'Japan-Viet Nam Foreign Ministers' Meeting', at: www.mofa.go.jp/s_sa/sea1/vn/page3e_000488.html (accessed 15 May 2016).

Miyashita, A., 2007. 'Where Do Norms Come From? Foundations of Japan's Postwar Pacifism', *International Relations of the Asia-Pacific*, 7(1): 99–120.

Nagao, S., 2015. 'Maritime Security and Multilateral Cooperation: A Japanese Perspective', *Maritime Affairs: Journal of the National Maritime Foundation of India*, 11(2): 16–24.

Nagy, S. R., 2013. 'Territorial Disputes, Trade and Diplomacy: Examining the Repercussions of the Sino-Japanese Territorial Dispute on Bilateral Trade', *China Perspectives*, 2013/14: 49–57.

Nagy, S. R., 2014. 'Japanese Business in China – Alive in the Bitter Sea', *China Economic Quarterly*, 18(1): 31–36.

Nagy, S. R., 2016a. 'The South China Sea in 2016. Towards Recognising the Global Public Good of the SCS', *World Commerce Review*, 10(1): 50–53.

Nagy, S. R., 2016b. 'Duterte in Tokyo: An Unraveling Security Strategy', *Policy Forum, Asia and the Pacific Policy Society*, 25 October, at: www.policyforum.net/duterte-tokyo-unraveling-security-strategy (accessed 21 January 2017).

Nagy, S. R., 2017. 'Proactive Pacifism: Investing in Multilateralization and Omnidirectional Hedging', *Strategic Analysis*, 41(3): 223–235, doi:10.1080/09700161.2017.1295607.

Oishi, M., 2016. 'The South China Sea Dispute: Formation of a Mediation Regime and Challenges for Management', in Oishi, M. (ed.), *Contemporary Conflicts in Southeast Asia* (Singapore: Springer Singapore), pp. 157–180.

Pajon, C., 2013. 'Japan and the South China Sea. Forging Strategic Partnerships in a Divided Region', *Asie.Visions Policy Papers*, Institut français des relations internationales, Center for Asian Studies, 60.

Philippine Statistics Authority, 2015. 'Foreign Trade Statistics of the Philippines', 15 July, at: https://psa.gov.ph/content/foreign-trade-statistics-philippines-2015 (accessed 12 December 2016).

Pink, R. M., 2016. 'Laos: The Poorest Country in Asia', in *Water Rights in Southeast Asia and India* (New York: Palgrave Macmillan US), pp. 119–138.

Reilly, J., 2012. 'China's Unilateral Sanctions', *The Washington Quarterly*, 35(4): 121–133.

Reilly, B., 2016. 'In the Shadow of China: Geography, History and Democracy in Southeast Asia', *Policy: A Journal of Public Policy and Ideas*, 32(1): 24.

Shiraishi, M., 2014. 'Nihon no "senryaku-teki pātonāshippu" gaikō – zentai-zō no fukan' [Japan's 'Strategic Partnership' Diplomacy: An Overview of the Overall Picture], Waseda daigaku: Ajia taiheiyō kenkyū sentā (ed.), *WIAPS Research Series*, 2(1): 585.

Smart, A. and Hsu, J. Y., 2004. 'The Chinese Diaspora, Foreign Investment and Economic Development in China', *The Review of International Affairs*, 3(4): 544–566.

Stubbs, R., 1999. 'War and Economic Development: Export-Oriented Industrialization in East and Southeast Asia', *Comparative Politics*, 31(3): 337–355.

Takeda, I., 1992. 'Anzenhosho Daiarogu no Teishyoh-Nihon ni totte ASEAN to Oseania' [Advocacy of Security Dialogue for Japan for ASEAN and Oceania], *Gaiko Forum*, 49(October): 16–26.

Takungpao, 2012. 'Chukou zoujiang, Feilubin xiangjiaoshang xiexin xiang Zhongguo qiuzhu' [Export Suddenly Decrease, Philippines Banana Dealers Write Letters to China to Seek Help], 26 October, at: takungpao.com.hk/finance/content/2012-10/26/content_1293478.htm (accessed 17 June 2013).

Tanner, T. and Wang, D. (eds), 2016. 'U.S.-China Relations in Strategic Domains', *The National Bureau of Asian Research*, NBR Special Report No. 57, Seattle.

Traynor, I., 2008. 'China Cancels EU Summit over Dalai Lama Visit', *The Guardian*, 27 November.

Valencia, M. J., 2007. 'The East China Sea Dispute: Context, Claims, Issues, and Possible Solutions', *Asian Perspective*, 31(1): 127–167.

Weatherbee, D. E., 2016. 'Re-Assessing Indonesia's Role in the South China Sea', *ISEAS-Yusof Ishak Institute Perspective*, 18: 1–13, at: iseas.edu.sg/images/pdf/ISEAS_Perspective_2016_18.pdf (accessed 25 January 2016).

Yang, J., 2003. 'Sino-Japanese Relations: Implications for Southeast Asia', *Contemporary Southeast Asia*, 25(2): 306–327.

7

The Philippine perspective on the security partnership with Japan

Renato Cruz De Castro

Introduction

IN EARLY JUNE 2015, President Benigno Aquino III made his first state visit to Japan. The event was doubly significant. First, it was a state visit. Second, it was indicative of the increasing tempo of security cooperation between these two US allies in Asia in confronting a common security threat – China's maritime expansion in the East China and South China Seas. President Aquino and Prime Minister Shinzō Abe discussed how they could strengthen their countries' strategic partnership in the face of China's aggressive behaviour in the aforesaid maritime area. They also signed 'A Joint Declaration on a Strengthened Strategic Partnership for Advancing the Shared Principles and Goals of Peace, Security, and Growth in the Region and beyond.' The five-page document provides a detailed action plan for bolstering the two countries' strategic partnership. Before he left for Manila, President Aquino announced that the two countries would soon start negotiations for a Status of Forces Agreement (SOFA) that would allow the Japan Self-Defense Forces (JSDF) access to Philippine military bases. Examining President Aquino's observation on his country's newfound security partnership with Japan, Professor Simon Sheldon notes: 'Of all Southeast Asian countries, Japan's security relations with the Philippines are the most advanced. Because it is a close ally of U.S., Japan is seen by Manila as an important security partner' (Sheldon, 2015: 5).

This chapter examines the external and domestic forces behind the increased security cooperation between the Philippines and Japan, and explores the status of this security partnership. It addresses these two corollary problems: What are the external and domestic factors that account for the increasing security cooperation between the Philippines and Japan? And what is the state of this security partnership? It also looks into these related issues: What is the origin of the Philippine–Japan security partnership? How has China's maritime expansion in East Asia affected the security policies of these two countries? What are the components of the Philippine–Japan security cooperation? And finally, how will this security partnership evolve over time?

An accidental strategic partnership?

The Philippines and Japan actively supported their common ally, the US, during the Cold War era. Both countries hosted several American military facilities during this period and relied on American military power to deter communist external aggression and prevent domestic disorder caused by internal insurgency (Buckley, 2002: 74). Both countries were also affected by China's emergence in East Asia in the early 21st century. In the face of China's growing economic and political clout, Japan found it necessary to strengthen its security relations with the US as a strategic hedge. The country developed the military capabilities to enable the JSDF to interface with the US armed forces in any major overseas operations away from the Japanese homeland. This signified that Japan was assuming the geo-strategic role of the 'new South Korea' – a leverage point of the US against China in first the decade of the 21st century (Auer and Lim, 2004: 282). The Philippines, meanwhile, was simultaneously renewing its alliance with the US through the latter's global anti-terror campaign and more significantly, developing an entente with China. From 2005 to 2009, security ties between Manila and Beijing thrived amidst their intensified economic and political relations. This created the perception that Manila was taking into account Beijing's political and strategic interests in making any major strategic decisions involving Washington. Consequently, these developments caused a cleavage between the Philippines and Japan, making them separate, exposed and vulnerable to China's diplomatic gambit in East Asia. Fortunately, China's emergence as an economic power and its maritime adventurism filled the gap between these two American allies. These realities augured well for a Philippines–Japan security partnership.

China's remarkable progress during the first decade of the 21st century made it into an engine of economic growth in East Asia and in the wider world. With its gross domestic product (GDP) surpassing Japan's in 2010, and its economy becoming the second largest next to that of the US, China's external behaviour has become more proactive and assertive, boosted by the confidence generated by its economic success (National Institute for Defense Studies, 2014: 2).

In the military area, China has had an annual double-digit increase in defence spending since 2006. Recently, the Chinese government increased its defence budget by 13 per cent to boost the People's Liberation Army Navy (PLAN)'s capability to accomplish a range of military functions, including 'winning local wars under information age conditions'. Consequently, in the past few years, the PLAN has acquired a growing fleet of Russian-made diesel-electric Kilo-class submarines and Sovremmeny-class destroyers, along with several types of indigenously built destroyers, frigates and nuclear-powered attack submarines. The PLAN has also upgraded its operational capabilities across the waters surrounding Taiwan and has deployed two new classes of ballistic and attack submarines.

With a booming economy and a formidable navy, China no longer focuses on pre-empting possible US intervention in a Taiwan Straits crisis but on denying the US Navy access to the East China Sea and South China Sea or inside the first island chain. China's naval forces can generate regional tension by challenging the claims of its small neighbouring states over parts of the South China Sea, and in the long run, by changing the strategic pattern of the maritime commons of East Asia and the western Pacific, from where the US Navy can be eased out. Interestingly, Chinese media commentators have repeatedly emphasised the significance of China's blue-water navy and the exigency of protecting its territorial claims in the South China Sea.

Judging from its recent behaviour, China's aggressive pursuit of its territorial claim over the South China Sea has increased in tandem with the expansion of its navy and maritime services (Dutton, 2011: 6). It conducts regular naval exercises that utilise modern surface combatants and even submarines.[1] These activities reflect China's intention to unilaterally and militarily resolve the maritime issue, flaunt its naval capabilities, and impress upon the other claimant states its *de facto* ownership of the disputed territories (The International Institute for Strategic Studies, 2011: 196). Over the long haul, China's naval capabilities will be directed not only to expand its maritime domain but also to deny foreign navies – especially that of the US – access to the East China and South China Seas. In time, it will be capable of depriving the US 7th Fleet of access to the western Pacific inside the so-called first island chain (Kato, 2010: 19). Eventually, China will be able to project its growing naval power not only in its near seas but to the far seas – the sea adjacent to the outer rim of the first island chain and those of the north Pacific (Sharman, 2015: 6).

This pattern of Chinese actions suggests that China has taken the top hierarchical position in the regional pecking order. It also fulfils all the requirements (economic and military might, diplomatic prowess, and carrying a lot of weight with the smaller powers) of a traditional great power determined to change the power game in East Asia. Strong economically and militarily, China has taken a series of maritime manoeuvres relative to the South China Sea dispute. These include the unilateral declaration of an East China Sea Air Defence Identification Zone (ADIZ), the active conduct of several live-fire naval exercises by the PLAN and People's Liberation Army's Air Force (PLAAF) in the western Pacific/South China Sea, and the hard-line responses by the PLAN in coordination with other Chinese maritime law-enforcement agencies on territorial rows with the Philippines and Vietnam in the South China Sea (National Institute for Defense Studies, 2015: 3).

These moves heightened the apprehension of the other littoral states about China's maritime design in the region (National Institute for Defense Studies, 2015: 3). From their viewpoint, these manoeuvres smacked of Chinese maritime expansionism/adventurism in the East China and South China Seas (Scott, 2007: 104). However, from China's perspective, it is a case of the country outgrowing its subordinate status in the past and feeling confident enough to press its case in the western Pacific and to stand resolute in managing its territorial and sovereignty issues in the disputed seas (Swaine, 2015: 146–147).

Bearing the brunt of China's maritime expansion

On 8 September 2010, the Japanese Coast Guard (JCG) arrested a Chinese fishing boat captain after his vessel collided with a JCG patrol boat that had ordered his trawler to stop in Japanese territorial waters near the Senkaku Islands in the East China Sea (Jiji Press English News Service, 2010). The following day, the Japanese public prosecutor sought a court approval for the detention of the Chinese boat captain for 10 days to investigate the incident and identify the waters in which the trawler was operating. The Chinese government demanded that Tokyo immediately release the Chinese captain. Seiji Maehara, then Japanese foreign minister, justified the handling of the case by a Japanese court on the grounds that the islands are an 'integral part of Japanese territory' (Johnson, 2010: 1). The Chinese Foreign Ministry then summoned the Japanese ambassador in Beijing and demanded the unconditional release of the Chinese fishing boat captain. In an official statement, the Chinese Foreign Ministry accused Japan of seriously damaging Sino-Japanese bilateral relations. China suspended top-level exchanges with Tokyo, all relations between provincial and central Chinese government units and their Japanese counterparts, and the bilateral negotiations on increasing the number of commercial flights between the two countries.

In time, Tokyo released the Chinese fishing boat captain. However, Beijing demanded an apology and compensation from Tokyo for the captain's detention, which Japanese Prime Minister Naoto Kan firmly rejected. The September 2010 incident happened amidst Tokyo's apprehension over China's increasing military spending and its unrelenting efforts to explore and secure new sources of energy in the East China Sea. As a result, the Japanese government decided to peg its 'host nation support' for the 'US bases at the 2010 level, amounting to US$ 3.3 billion.' (Heginbotham, Ratner and Samuels, 2011: 245). Furthermore, it relaxed its long-standing restrictions on arms exports, and cooperated with the US in developing high-technology weapon systems and in reviving the Japanese defence industry (Heginbotham, Ratner and Samuels, 2011: 146). More significantly, the Senkaku incident reignited Japanese anxiety over China's aggressive pursuit of its expansive claims in the South China Sea and its hostile encounters with several claimant Southeast Asian states (Feckler and Johnson, 2010: A–1).

China claims almost 80 per cent of the South China Sea, along with the Paracels and Spratly Islands, which are also claimed by the Philippines, Brunei, Malaysia and Vietnam. In March 2010, China declared the South China Sea as one of its 'core interests', which indicated its determination to assert its rights over the disputed areas. Meantime, the Chinese navy backs the official claim that the South China Sea is in Chinese territorial waters. Hence, Vietnamese and Philippine vessels are harassed, detained or even fired upon by Chinese patrol craft. These incidents are proof of China's aggressiveness and coercive diplomacy to pressure the two claimant states to steer clear of the contested area (Sutter and Huang, 2011: 1).

China became relentlessly assertive against the Philippines in early 2011. On 2 March 2011, two Chinese patrol boats confronted a survey ship commissioned by the Philippine Department of Energy (DOE) to conduct oil exploration in the Reed Bank (now called the Recto Bank), 150 km east of the Spratly Islands and 250 km west of the Philippine island of Palawan. Prior to this incident, the British-based Forum Energy – in a joint exploration venture with its Philippine partner Philex Mining Corporation – announced its completion of a geographic survey of a potential gas field near the Reed Bank off the western part of Palawan (McIndoe, 2011: 3). The survey ship was identifying sites for possible appraisal wells to be drilled in the next phase of the DOE–Forum Energy–Philex Mining Corporation contract when it was accosted by the two Chinese patrol boats.

The 2 March 2011 incident at the Reed Bank underscored the volatility of the South China Sea dispute and the tension generated between China and the Philippines despite their entente in the early 21st century. On 8 April 2012, the Philippine navy (PN)'s flagship, the *BRP Gregorio del Pilar*, tried to apprehend several Chinese fishing boats in the Scarborough Shoal. However, two Chinese maritime surveillance vessels arrived and blocked the arrest of the Chinese fishermen, who were hauling corals, clams and live sharks into their boats. To prevent the incident from escalating into an armed clash, the Philippines replaced its surface combatant with a smaller coast guard vessel. Instead of reciprocating, China deployed the *Yuzheng 310* – its most advanced and largest patrol ship, equipped with machine guns, light cannons and electronic sensors. The Scarborough Shoal stand-off lasted for two months. It was a tense situation in which four Chinese civilian vessels confronted a lone Philippine coast guard ship. During the stand-off, China did not show any desire to de-escalate or end the crisis (Yung and McNulty, 2015: 9). After a two-month stand-off, China and the Philippines eventually agreed to remove their civilian ships near the shoal after a deal brokered by the US. Subsequently, however, China redeployed its maritime surveillance ships to block Philippine access to the shoal, and has maintained a presence there ever since (Yung and McNulty, 2015: 9).

Although Japan is not a party in the South China Sea dispute, it has inevitably paid attention to China's actions in this territorial row. This stemmed from Japan's concern that if China achieves its expansionist goal in the South China Sea dispute, it will also adopt a similar objective and strategy in the East China Sea. Hence, Japan should monitor Chinese actions not only in the South China Sea but also in the waters surrounding the country, such as the East China Sea and the western Pacific (National Institute for Defense Studies, 2011: 26). On 11 July 2012, after the Japanese government decided to buy the Senkaku Islands from their private owner, three ships from the China Maritime Surveillance (CMS) and Fisheries Law Enforcement Command (FLEC) entered Japanese waters off the Senkakus (Przystup, 2012: 7). Immediately, Vice-Minister Sasae Kenichiro summoned the Chinese ambassador in Tokyo and denounced the incursion as 'extremely serious' and unacceptable. Instead of backing out of the confrontation, China deployed another ship into Japan's contiguous zone. Eventually, to assert its claims over the Senkakus, China regularised its maritime presence in the areas off the island. On 13 December 2012, the JCG reported 17 Chinese intrusions into Japanese territorial waters since 11 September 2012 (Przystup, 2013a: 6). Consequently, Japanese Foreign Ministry officials concluded that Chinese maritime intrusions were aimed at chipping away at Japan's effective administrative control over the islands and forcing it to recognise the existence of a dispute (Przystup, 2013a: 6).

Converging strategic priorities – constraining an assertive China

Upon assuming the presidency in June 2010, President Benigno Simon Aquino vowed to modernise the Armed Forces of the Philippines (AFP) in line with shifting its focus from internal security to maritime/territorial defence. The 2 March 2011 incident at the Reed Bank and China's dismissive response to the Philippines' diplomatic queries prompted the Aquino administration to hasten the AFP's modernisation. China has claimed a wide maritime territory. In fact, it badgered the Philippines and other claimant states to recognise Chinese sovereignty over the South China Sea. China's haughty and hostile attitude towards the Philippines and Vietnam in the first half of 2011 escalated the territorial dispute. By then, President Aquino unmistakably saw that the Philippines was potentially on a direct collision course with China regarding the South China Sea issue. Hence, the current modernisation of the Philippine military is externally influenced by a changing balance of power in East Asia, generated by a geo-strategic reconfiguration of national capabilities in the light of an emergent China (Salvador and Santiago, 2012: 13).

In building up the country's territorial defence capabilities, the Aquino administration is sinking its teeth into challenging China's expansive claims in the South China Sea, as the latter directly encroaches into the country's Exclusive Economic Zone. The Philippines' territorial defence goal is very modest – to develop a credible posture for territorial defence and maritime security by organising a competent force capable of safeguarding the country's interests and the land features it occupies in the South China Sea (Gazmin, 2015: 4). Despite this unpretentious objective, the Aquino administration is still immobilised by scant financial resources. Given its current pace and budget allocation, the AFP's territorial defence build-up would hardly deter the PLAN in the contested sea, because the latter has been procuring modern surface combatants and submarines since the start of the 21st century (Bitzinger, 2011: 24). The military imbalance between the Philippines and China will not be resolved in the foreseeable future even if the AFP develops a credible defence posture. Thus, the Philippines has no recourse but to seek a security guarantee from its only strategic ally, the US, and at the same time, to request military assistance and diplomatic support from other American allies that share a common interest with the country in maritime security.

Prime Minister Shinzō Abe came into power amidst an intense territorial row between Japan and China over the Senkaku Islands. After the 16 December parliamentary election, Prime Minister Abe declared 'that the islands are the inherent territory of Japan ... We own and effectively control them. There is no room for negotiations about them' (Przystup, 2013b: 9). In the first few months of his term, the Senkaku Islands dispute occupied the centre stage of the Japan–China relationship, which became extremely strained. Prime Minister Abe continued his predecessor's policy of not acknowledging the existence of a dispute over the islands. China responded by increasing the number and frequency of civilian ships deployed around the islands. In the face of heightened tension in the Senkakus, Prime Minister Abe took several significant steps to expand Japanese security policy. From his point of view, China's assertive behaviour in East Asia is a source of grave security concern for Japan (Singh, 2015: 57). On 28 February 2013, without mentioning China by name, he cautioned against the use of force to change the status quo on account of territorial issues (Przystup, 2013b: 9). He called on China to refrain from any dangerous acts with regard to the Senkakus, and underscored that Japan's interests are immutable forever, that aggression must be prevented at all costs, and that international law, the fundamental rule for the entire world, must prevail against the use of force (Przystup, 2013b: 2).

During his first few months in office, Prime Minister Abe announced an increase in the defence spending in the last 11 years and a review of the 2010 National Defense Program Guidelines (NDPG) (Przystup, 2013b: 9). In October 2013, Japan and the US convened a meeting of the Security Consultative Committee (SCC) or two-plus-two in Tokyo. Both sides issued a joint statement reaffirming the importance of the alliance and announcing a review of the US–Japan Defense Cooperation Guidelines, last updated in 1997, to reflect the changes in the regional and global security environment (Green and Szechenyi, 2014: 3). The communiqué mentioned several priorities for cooperation, which included ballistic missile defence, space and cyber-defence, joint intelligence surveillance and reconnaissance (ISR) activities, dialogue on extended deterrence, joint training and exercises, realignment of US forces in Okinawa, and convening trilateral and multilateral security cooperation among US allies in East Asia (Green and Szechenyi, 2014: 8). Finally, Japan launched the 'multi-layered security cooperation' on a regional and global scale with like-minded countries including US allies in the region, such as South Korea and Australia, as well as with US alliance/partner countries whose coastal territorials are critical to Japanese sea lanes of communications (SLOC) (Matsuda, 2012: 116). The *2013 National Security Strategy of Japan* specifically mentioned that Japan would strengthen diplomacy and security cooperation with ASEAN countries concerned to settle disputes in the South China Sea, not by force, but in accordance with the rule of law (Government of Japan, 2013: 60–61). Although the document did not name specific countries, two states are located along Japan's SLOC and have ongoing disputes with China in the South China Sea: Vietnam and the Philippines.

Exploring a strategic partnership

Historically, the Philippines and Japan have maintained vigorous economic and transnational relations. Both countries adhere to democratic governance, civil and political liberties, free trade, freedom of navigation and respect for human rights. Furthermore, they are US allies whose maritime domains are threatened by China's assertiveness (National Institute for Defense Studies, 2012: 25). In April 2012, at the start of the two-month Scarborough Shoal stand-off, then Japanese ambassador to the Philippines, Toshio Urabe, stressed the 'close-knit triangular relationship among Japan, the Philippines, and their closest (mutual) ally – the U.S.' (*Asia News Monitor*, 2012: 1). Then, in May 2012, three Japan Maritime Self-Defense Force (JMSDF) surface combatants arrived in Manila for a four-day port call (*BBC Monitoring Asia-Pacific*, 2012: 1). The visit came after Tokyo announced its plans to provide the Philippines with 10 new patrol vessels to boost the latter's maritime patrol capability. The newspaper *Yomiuri Shimbun* linked the ship visit to the ongoing Scarborough Shoal impasse and editorialised that Japan could not just stand idly by and wait for China and the Philippines to clash openly (*BBC Monitoring Asia-Pacific*, 2012: 1). It also underscored that it was in 'Japan's national interest to ensure that its sea-lanes remain safe' (*BBC Monitoring Asia-Pacific*, 2012: 1). Curiously, the JMSDF's ship visit to the Philippines happened just a few days after the US navy's Virginia-class attack submarine, the USS *North Carolina*, made a supposed port call at Subic Bay in

Luzon. Actually, these ship visits were routine port calls. However, they were made during the Scarborough stalemate and were extensively publicised. In a sense, Washington and Tokyo were insinuating that they would not hesitate to act jointly if the Philippines were threatened by any form of Chinese armed aggression (Almazan, 2012: 1).

Consequently, in the aftermath of the Scarborough Shoal stand-off, Tokyo became more forthright in extending security assistance to the Philippines. In July 2012, then Japanese Defence Minister Satoshi Morimoto and his Filipino counterpart, Defence Secretary Gazmin, inked a bilateral agreement on maritime security. The agreement called for high-level dialogues between defence officials and reciprocal visits by the MSDF chief of staff and the PN flag commander. It also featured various security-related activities such as the Multinational Cooperation Program in the Asia-Pacific (MCAP); multilateral logistic staff talks (MLST); training exchanges and subject matter exchanges on humanitarian assistance/disaster relief (HA/DR) and logistics; and exchange visits and student exchanges in the two countries' respective staff colleges. A few days later, Philippine Foreign Affairs Secretary Albert del Rosario announced that Tokyo was likely to provide the PCG with ten 40-metre boats as part of Japan's official development assistance (ODA) to the Philippines by the end of the year. Newspapers also reported that two additional bigger vessels were being considered for transfer to the Philippine government under a grant.

A few weeks after his return to power, Prime Minister Abe sent Foreign Minister Fumio Kishida on a four-country Asia/Pacific diplomatic tour to convey Japan's growing concern over Beijing's expansive territorial claims in the South China Sea. In Manila, Minister Kishida met with Philippine Foreign Secretary Del Rosario. They discussed the difficulties China's neighbours faced in defending their positions vis-à-vis the East China and South China Sea issues while managing their economic relations with China, which was now a major economic power (Larano and Cuneta, 2013). The two foreign ministers agreed to work closely together on enhancing cooperation in maritime security. Minister Kishida pledged 10 multi-role response vessels to the PSG to better patrol Philippine maritime territories. He also announced Japan's provision of essential communication system equipment to the PCG for maritime safety (*Asia News Monitor*, 2013a).

On 27 June 2013, Japanese Defence Minister Itsunori Onodera and Philippine Defence Secretary Gazmin confirmed the continuous 'exchanges of information aimed at strengthening Philippine–Japan defence relations and on working together to make U.S. strategic rebalancing a reality in Asia' (*BBC Monitoring Asia-Pacific*, 2013). To further defence cooperation, the two security partners undertook the following activities (Embassy of Japan in the Philippines, 2013): reciprocal visits between the chiefs of staff of the JMSDF and the flag officer of the PN; the holding of the Japan–Philippines Maritime Chief of Staff Meeting; port calls in the Philippines of JMSDF vessels; and active participation in the Pacific

Partnership 2012. The two defence ministers also extended the two countries' security cooperation to the field of aviation, which was highlighted by the visit to the Philippines by the chief of staff of the Japanese Air Self-Defense Force (JASDF). During the same meeting, Secretary Gazmin raised the possibility of allowing the Japanese SDF access to the former American military bases in the Philippines if Tokyo was interested in such an arrangement (Embassy of Japan in the Philippines, 2013).

Japan's willingness to extend security assistance to the Philippines became apparent during its participation in the multilateral HA/DR operations in Tacloban City, which was heavily devastated by a category five typhoon with the international name of Haiyan in mid-November 2013. Locally known as Yolanda, the super-typhoon killed more than 6,000 people and left more than three million Filipinos without homes in five major island-provinces – Leyte, Samar, Panay, Cebu and Palawan. It destroyed nearly 550,000 residential houses and damaged several farmlands and fishponds in these island-provinces, which account for about 12 per cent of the country's GDP (Cuneta, 2013).

Japan immediately joined a US-led international coalition that immediately provided humanitarian assistance to the victims of typhoon Yolanda. It sent three JMSDF destroyers carrying nearly 1,000 Japan Ground Self-Defense Force (JGSDF) personnel to deliver emergency supplies to the remote areas of Samar and Leyte (Obe, Hayashi and Martine, 2013). Japan also dispatched three CH-46 transport helicopters, three UH-1 utility helicopters, the transport vessel *Osumi*, two KC-767 air tankers, seven C-130 transport aircraft and U-4 utility support aircraft to assist multinational forces involved in the international HA/DR operations in the Central Philippines (*Asia News Monitor*, 2013b). The ASDF C-130s ferried typhoon victims, US Marines, aid agency officials and Philippine government officials between Manila and Tacloban. In addition to its military assistance, Tokyo also gave Manila more than US$50 million in direct aid and grants (Murtagh, 2013).

During his state visit to Japan in early June 2015, President Aquino continued his thorough consultation with Prime Minister Abe on peace and stability in the Asia-Pacific region (Philippines News Agency, 2015). The two leaders signed a joint declaration on 'A Strengthened Strategic Partnership for Advancing the Shared Principles and Partnership and Goals for Peace, Security, and Growth in the Region and beyond.' They also agreed to further enhance the strategic partnership between their countries on the basis of shared principles and goals (Philippines News Agency, 2015). The document also expressed the two countries' commitment to ensuring maritime safety and security in the South China Sea and their serious opposition to unilateral actions to change the status quo in the South China Sea, including large-scale reclamation and building of outposts. This was especially directed against China's construction of artificial islands in the contested sea. Specifically, the communiqué commits

Japan to the following: 1) enhancing the capacity of the PCG; 2) cooperating with the Philippines on maritime security and on maritime domain awareness; and c) exploring the prospects for the transfer of Japanese defence equipment and technology to the Philippines (Ministry of Foreign Affairs of Japan, 2015).

21st-century Philippine–Japan strategic partnership

With China bent on pursuing its goal of maritime expansion in East Asia, the Philippines and Japan have explored a strategic partnership to complement their respective bilateral alliances with the US. This strategic partnership is made operational by the following:

(a) *Political/security consultations* – As part of their security cooperation, the Philippines and Japan have conducted high-level meetings and consultations to solidify their security cooperation in the face of China's military assertiveness. These high-level consultations enable both countries to discuss common challenges that they face in terms of the apparent assertions of China as well as the possibility of sharing strategies in dealing with those issues (Larano and Cuneta, 2013). *The 2012 Statement of Intent on Defense Cooperation and Exchanges* between the Department of National Defense of the Philippines and the Japanese Ministry of Defense provides the institutional framework for defence exchanges and cooperation at the ministerial level, between senior officers of the AFP and the JSDF, at working level, at unit-to-unit level and so on. The two sides have discussed international armaments cooperation during United Nations peacekeeping operations (UNPKO), security assistance, humanitarian assistance, combined operations support, and international training and education (Hernandez, 2014: 73). As of 2014, the PN and JMSDF have conducted two staff-to-staff talks that had facilitated numerous ship visits, education, and training exchanges, and visits of high-level officials from both the PN and JMSDF (Hernandez, 2014: 75). As a result of these high-level talks, both sides have considered expanding the exchanges to include subject matter expert exchange (SMEE) on HA/DR and the conduct of UNPKO, and research collaboration between the JMSDF Fleet Research and Development Command and the PN Naval Research Development Centre (Hernandez, 2014: 75). At the level of unit-to-unit exchanges, both sides discussed possible 'training activities and exercises during the occasional and mutual ship visits between the PN and JMSDF on HA/DR operations and maritime security' (Hernandez, 2014: 75). Unfortunately, the conduct of joint exercises by both countries is constrained by the limitations imposed by the 1947 Constitution on the overseas deployment of the JSDF and the absence of a SOFA between the Philippines and Japan (Hernandez, 2014: 73).

(b) *Naval exercises and port visits* – Despite the constitutional limitations on the JSDF and the absence of a SOFA between the two countries, the Philippines and Japan held a joint naval exercise in the South China Sea on 12 May (Philippines News Agency, 2015). Japan sent two JMSDF destroyers – the JS *Harusame* and *Amigri* – which conducted a training exercise with the PN frigate BRP *Ramon Alcaraz* on communication strategies to respond to 'unplanned encounters at sea' (Hayasho, 2015: 1). Known as the Code for Unplanned Encounters at Sea (CUES), the joint JMSDF–PN 12 May naval exercise was an offshoot of a security agreement signed by Tokyo and Manila in January 2015 to tighten security cooperation between the two US allies (Kelly and Mogato, 2015: 1). Japan announced that it was sending surveillance planes and naval vessels to assist the US 7th Fleet in conducting maritime patrols in the South China Sea (Kelly and Mogato, 2015: 1). Security analysts noted the significance of this low-key naval exercise, which signalled Japan's growing interest in the Southeast Asian region.

A few weeks after President Aquino's June 2015 state visit to Japan, a JMSDF reconnaissance plane landed on the westernmost Philippine island of Palawan and took part in a training exercise with the PN from 22 June to 26 June 2015. On 21 June 2015, the JMDSF P3-C Orion with 20 crew members from Kanoya Air Base in Kagoshima Prefecture arrived in the Philippines to participate in yet another training exercise, proving the increasing tempo of Philippine–Japan maritime security cooperation. According to the PN press release, the training activity would focus on developing the fleet skills and the interoperability of the two countries' navies in HA/DR operations, particularly on the search-and-rescue of stricken vessels or downed aircraft in the high seas. It would involve one fixed wing maritime aircraft from the two navies and a PN patrol vessel. The activity would be conducted in the high seas about 140 km northwest of Palawan. Officials from both countries emphasised that the training activity was primarily a disaster relief and search-and-rescue exercise, not a reconnaissance operation. They also added that the activity aimed to foster camaraderie and strengthen the budding PN–JMSDF partnership in fostering maritime security. Aside from these joint naval activities, JMSDF ships have conducted port visits to the Philippines.[2] In 2012, four JMSDF ships visited the country. The following year, two JMSDF ships made a port call in Manila. In 2014, seven JMSDF ships visited the Philippines. As of October 2015, a total of seven JMSDF ships had made port calls in Manila and Subic Bay.

(c) *Arms transfer* – A crucial component of Japan's relations with the Philippines has been its provision of ODA and other grass-roots assistance to this country since 1956. The JSDF conducted its most massive overseas HA/DR operations in the Philippines in the aftermath of typhoon Haiyan. Japan has also pledged to provide the PCG with 10 patrol vessels. A new set of initiatives vis-à-vis the Philippines must be built on the existing relationship and must be widened to help the country develop its capacity for HA/DR and maritime security (Tatsumi, 2015). During a bilateral meeting at the end of the 2015 Asia Pacific Economic Cooperation (APEC) Leaders' Summit in Manila, Philippine President Benigno Aquino III and the Japanese prime minister agreed in principle that their two countries should negotiate an agreement for the transfer of SDF defence equipment and technology to the AFP. Both leaders agreed that such an agreement would commit both sides to discussing the type and scale of Japanese security assistance to the Philippines but would not include the specific type of security assistance.

Barely three months after President Benigno Aquino III's and Prime Minister Abe's meeting on the side of the Asia Pacific Economic Community Leaders' Meeting in mid-November 2015, Philippine Defence Secretary Gazmin and Japanese Ambassador to the Philippines Kazuhide Ishikawa inked 'The Agreement between the Government of Japan and the Government of the Republic of the Philippines concerning the Transfer of Defense Equipment and Technology' on 29 February 2016. The new defence agreement establishes the legal parameters for the transfer of defence equipment and technology from Japan to the Philippines. It also provides for the Philippines and Japan to conduct joint research and development, and even joint production of defence equipment and technology (Ministry of Foreign Affairs of Japan, 2016b: 1). The *Asahi Shimbun* revealed that Japan plans to supply the Philippines with five second-hand Beechcraft TC-90 King Air reconnaissance aircraft, currently used by JMSDF aviators, which can be equipped with basic surface and air-surveillance radar. These short-range reconnaissance aircraft will enable the PN to patrol the disputed waters of the South China Sea (*Asahi Shimbun*, 2016: 1). The Philippines also expressed interest in the purchase of Japanese-made defence equipment.

(d) *Tentative negotiations for a Philippine–Japan SOFA* – In a press briefing after his June 2015 state visit to Japan, President Aquino announced the forthcoming negotiation on a SOFA that would allow the JSDF access to Philippine military bases. He disclosed that a Philippine–Japan SOFA is possible, since the two countries have boosted their security relationship significantly over the past few years. President Aquino explained that only the US and Australia have a visiting forces agreement (VFA) with the Philippines. Adding Japan to the list would make sense, as it has been one of the Philippines' strategic partners since 2011. The SDF's use of Philippine bases, on a limited and rotational basis, will be useful as Japan actively pursues a policy of proactive contribution to peace in East Asia. With refuelling and basing facilities in the Philippines, units of the JASDF and JMSDF can conduct joint patrols with their American counterparts for a longer period of time and over a larger area of the South China Sea.

Philippine–Japan security partnership and the Duterte administration

Since becoming the 16th president of the Philippines on 30 June 2016, former Davao City Mayor Rodrigo Roa Duterte has steered his country's foreign policy away from its traditional close security alliance with the US and has sought closer diplomatic and economic relations with its foremost rival in the South China Sea dispute, China (*Asia News Monitor*, 2016: 1–2). He is pursuing a balanced and calibrated policy characterised by gravitating closer to China while crafting some diplomatic distance from the Philippines' only strategic security ally, the US (Baviera, 2016: 203). On the one hand, he declared that he is open to direct bilateral negotiations with China. President Duterte's then foreign secretary, Perfecto Yasay declared 'that the relationship between the two countries (China and the Philippines) was not limited to the maritime dispute' (Katigbak, 2016: 1). 'There were other areas of concern in such fields as investment, trade, and tourism, and discussing them could open the doors for talks on the maritime issues.' On the other hand, President Duterte called for the withdrawal of American Special Forces, who are operating in Mindanao to support the AFP's counter-terrorism operations. He also ordered the PN not to conduct joint patrols with the US navy in the South China Sea, since these activities could be seen by China as a provocative act (on the part of the Philippines), making it more difficult to peacefully resolve the territorial dispute.

President Duterte's foreign policy gambit of gravitating closer to Beijing while alienating Washington has unsettled both the US and Japan (Baviera, 2016: 204–205). Puzzled by the changes in Philippine foreign policy, the Japanese government decided to persevere with its nuanced or unique approach in dealing with the Philippines. A senior Japanese official admitted that while Tokyo and Washington share the same goal in the Philippines, Japan takes a different approach in its relations with the Philippines, as there are some things that Manila can only accept when Japan provides them (Wanklyn and Mie, 2016: 1). Unlike the US, which has been taken aback by President Duterte's anti-American pronouncements, Japan continued its comprehensive engagement with the Philippines (Wanklyn and Mie, 2016: 1). Japan is strengthening its relations with the Duterte administration by fostering periodic consultations between the two countries, and strengthening its navy's and coast guard's maritime domain awareness capabilities, as it is aware that strained Philippine–US relations benefit China.

During the ASEAN summit in Laos, Prime Minister Abe held his first meeting with President Duterte, during which he unveiled Japan's plan to provide two 90-metre patrol vessels in addition to the 10 multi-role vessels (MRRV) that were delivered to the PCG to boost its search-and-rescue and fisheries protection capabilities (Ministry of Foreign Affairs of Japan, 2016a: 2). These two large patrol vessels have thick armour to protect the crews from shells, and therefore they are likely to be treated as warships. This will be the first time Japan has provided this type of large patrol vessels to a country. He also informed his Filipino counterpart about Japan's decision to lend the Philippines five JMDSF TC-90 training aircraft, which will useful for reconnaissance missions, disaster relief operations and transporting supplies (Ministry of Foreign Affairs of Japan, 2016a: 2). Japan's goal is to assist the Philippines in improving its maritime surveillance capabilities in the light of increasing Chinese maritime activities in the South China Sea.

During his three-day official visit to Japan, President Duterte engaged Prime Minister Abe in a discussion of greater politico-social and defence cooperation, particularly in maritime domain awareness and maritime security (Cabacungan, 2016: 1–2). During his visit, he signed the Exchange of Notes on Japanese Official Development Assistance for the provision of two large-scale patrol vessels, which were given in addition to the 10 patrol vessels that Tokyo is in the process of delivering to the PCG. Japan's provision of the two 90-metre patrol vessels will boost the capabilities of the PCG, since white ships are often used on the front line of the various territorial disputes in maritime East Asia, given that the deployment of grey ships in disputed waters is seen as too provocative.

Significantly, Japan has also started to provide the Philippines with military equipment and training. President Duterte witnessed the signing of the Memorandum of Implement and Letter of Arrangement for the transfer of JMSDF training aircraft TC-90 maritime reconnaissance planes for the PN. Japan will also provide the training for PN aviators and will develop the infrastructure for these reconnaissance aircraft, which will be patrolling the South China Sea. Interestingly, President Duterte also hinted that the Philippines could conduct naval exercises with Japan, but he repeated that there would be no more joint exercises with the US (Funakoshi, 2016: 1). The most significant accomplishment of Duterte's working visit to Japan was the two security partners' signing of the 26 October 2016 Japan–Philippine Joint Statement. The statement commits both countries to the maintenance of the freedom of navigation and overflight in the South China Sea, which contains the sea lanes that are vital for global economic activity and viability (Embassy of Japan in the Philippines, 2016). The two leaders also reaffirmed that stronger (security) ties between Japan and the Philippines would promote the peace, stability and maritime security of the region.

For the Philippines, keeping its security partnership with Japan intact is necessary because Japan remains the nation's most important trading partner, its largest investor, and the home of several thousand overseas Filipino workers (OFWs), who are sending their remittances to their home country to boost the local economy. Currently, Japan is the only Western country with a healthy and cordial relationship with the Philippines, making it an important countervailing force to an expected increase in Chinese influence in the light of President Duterte's efforts to forge a new economic partnership with China. A functioning security partnership with Japan also enables the Philippines to effectively play its classic diplomatic gambit of equi-balancing, or the art of pitting one great power against another.

Conclusion

Confronted by an expansionist China in their maritime domains, the Philippines and Japan have explored a security partnership as a result of their experience in dealing with Chinese aggression in the East China and South China Seas. The Philippines was involved in a stand-off with Chinese civilian vessels at the Reed Bank in 2011 and again at the Scarborough Shoal. Japan experienced the same rough treatment from China over the Senkaku Islands, first in the latter part of 2010 and second, during a longer impasse between Chinese and Japanese coast guard vessels from the latter part of 2012 to mid-2013. This strategic alignment, however, is still at a tentative and evolving stage. It consists primarily of political and security consultations between Filipino and Japanese political leaders, ranking defence officials and high-level military officers. Japan's constitutional limitations on the sale of military materiel to other countries and the overseas deployment of JSDF personnel, along with the absence of a SOFA, have hampered both countries' efforts to expand their partnership, especially in the transfer of military materiel and the conduct of joint military exercises and HA/DR training activities.

President Duterte's efforts to gravitate closer to China at a time when Philippine–US security relations are at rock bottom create a popular misconception that the Philippines is about to embark on a major pivot towards China. However, while President Duterte is seeking a fresh relationship with Beijing, he is also fostering a security partnership with China's foremost rival in East Asia, Japan. President Duterte has been very critical about the Philippine–US alliance, but he has never criticised or even mentioned the Philippine–Japan security partnership. Japan is the only Western country with a healthy and cordial relationship with the Philippines, making it an important countervailing force to an expected increase in Chinese influence in the light of President Duterte's efforts to forge a new economic partnership with China.

NOTES

1. For details on China's training exercises in its surrounding waters, see National Institute for Defense Studies (2011: 14–21).
2. Data on the JMSDF ship visits were provided by the Political Section of the Japanese Embassy in Manila, 5 October 2015.

REFERENCES

Almazan, A., 2012. 'U.S. N-Sub in Subic a Strong Signal to China: Routine Visit Comes amid Reports China is Mobilizing Fleet for Philippines Ops', *The Business Times*, 18 May, p. 1.

Asahi Shimbun, 2016. 'MSDF Convoy to Make Friendly Call at Subic Bay with Real Attention Focused on China', *Asahi Shimbun*, 3 March.

Asia News Monitor, 2012. 'Japan/Philippines/United States: Japan Envoy Notes Close-Knit Relations among Philippines, Japan, and U.S.', *Asia News Monitor*, 11 April.

Asia News Monitor, 2013a. 'Philippine/Japan: Philippines, Japan Agree to Enhance Cooperation in Maritime Security', *Asia News Monitor*, 14 January.

Asia News Monitor, 2013b. 'Philippines: Fumigation Starts in Evacuation Centers in Tacloban', *Asia News Monitor*, 27 November.

Asia News Monitor, 2016. 'Philippines President Steers New Foreign Policy Path', *Asia News Monitor*, 15 September.

Auer, J. E. and Lim, R., 2004. 'Japan: America's New South Korea?', *Current History*, 103: 674.

Baviera, A., 2016. 'President Duterte's Foreign Policy Challenges', *Contemporary Southeast Asia*, 38(2): 202–207.

BBC Monitoring Asia-Pacific, 2012. 'Philippine Navy Says Japan Sending Three Warships for Port Call to Manila', *BBC Monitoring Asia-Pacific*, 26 May.

BBC Monitoring Asia-Pacific, 2013. 'Philippines, Japan Agree to Strengthen Defense Ties', *BBC Monitoring Asia-Pacific*, 27 June.

Bitzinger, R. A., 2011. 'Recent Developments in Naval and Maritime Modernization in the Asia-Pacific: Implication for Regional Security', in Saunders, P., Yung, C., Swaine, M. and Yang, A. N.-D. (eds), *The Chinese Navy: Expanding Capabilities, Evolving Roles* (Washington DC: National Defense University).

Buckley, R., 2002. *The United States in the Asia-Pacific since 1945* (Cambridge, UK: Cambridge University Press).

Cabacungan, G., 2016. 'Duterte, PM Abe to Discuss Maritime Defense Cooperation', *Philippine Daily Inquirer*, 26 October.

Cuneta, J., 2013. 'Typhoon Left Nearly $13 Billion in Damage: Government Report Details Losses along with a Rebuilding Plan', *Wall Street Journal*, 18 December.

Dutton, P., 2011. 'Three Disputes and Three Objectives: China and the South China Sea', *Naval War College Review*, 54(4): 42–67.

Embassy of Japan in the Philippines, 2013. 'Press Release on the Visit of His Excellency Mr. Itsunori Onodera, Minister of Defense of Japan to the Philippines', 27 June.

Embassy of Japan in the Philippines, 2016. 'Japan–Philippines Joint Statement', 26 October, at: www.ph.emb-japan.go.jp/itpr_en/00_000168.html (accessed 2 February 2018).

Feckler M. and Johnson, I., 2010. 'Arrest in Disputed Sea Riles China and Japan', *The New York Times*, 20 September, pp. A–1.

Funakoshi, M., 2016. 'Duterte Says Philippines Could Join Sea Exercise with Japan, again Vents Anger at U.S', *Reuters*, 27 October.

Gazmin, V. T., 2015. *Defense Planning Guidance 2016–2021* (Quezon City: Department of National Defense).

Government of Japan, 2013. *The National Security Strategy of Japan* (Tokyo: Office of the Prime Minister).

Green, M. J. and Szechenyi, N., 2014. 'U.S.–Japan Relations: Big Steps, Big Surprises', *Comparative Connections*, 15(3): 1–8.

Hayasho, Y., 2015. 'Japan, Philippines Hold Naval Drills in the South China Sea', *The Wall Street Journal*, 13 May.
Heginbotham, E., Ratner, E. and Samuels, R., 2011. 'Tokyo's Transformation: How Japan Is Changing – and What It Means for the United States', *Foreign Affairs*, 90(5): 138–148.
Hernandez, E. V., 2014. 'Philippines–Japan Defense Cooperation: Implications to National Maritime Security', Master's Thesis submitted to the National Defense College of the Philippines, Camp Aguinaldo (unpublished work).
The International Institute for Strategic Studies, 2011. *The Military Balance 2011: The Annual Assessment of Global Military Capabilities and Defence Economics* (London: The International Institute for Strategic Studies).
Jiji Press English News Service, 2010. 'Japan Prosecutors to Seek Extension of China Skippers' Detention', 16 September.
Johnson, I., 2010. 'Japan–China Rift Grows as Captain Kept in Detention: In Conflict over Islands, Beijing Threatens to Take Strong Counter-Measures', *International Herald Tribune*, 20 September.
Katigbak, J., 2016. 'Philippines Eyes Talks with China sans Condition', *The Philippine Star*, 28 September.
Kato, Y., 2010. 'China's Naval Expansion in the Western Pacific', *Global Asia*, 5(4) (Winter 2010): 18–21.
Kelly, T. and Mogato, M., 2015. 'Japan and the Philippines Are about to Upset China in the South China Sea', Reuters, 8 May.
Larano, C. and Cuneta, J., 2013. 'Japan, Philippines Pledge Greater Cooperation', *Wall Street Journal*, 10 January.
Matsuda, Y., 2012. 'Engagement and Hedging: Japan's Strategy toward China', *SAIS Review*, 32(2): 109–119.
McIndoe, A., 2011. 'Philippines Stirs Waters off Spratlys', *McClatchy-Tribune Business News*, 31 March.
Ministry of Foreign Affairs of Japan, 2015. 'Japan–Philippines Joint Declaration: A Strengthened Partnership for Advancing the Shared Principles and Goals of Peace, Security, and Growth in the Region and Beyond', 4 June.
Ministry of Foreign Affairs of Japan, 2016a. 'Japan–Philippines Summit Meeting', 26 October, at: www.mofa.go.jp/s_sa/sea2/ph/page3e_000608.html (accessed 1 February 2018).
Ministry of Foreign Affairs of Japan, 2016b. 'Signing of the Agreement between the Government of Japan and the Government of the Philippines concerning the Transfer of Defense Equipment and Technology', 29 February, at: www.mofa.go.jp/mofaj/files/000152490.pdf (accessed 2 February 2018).
Murtagh, P., 2013. 'Typhoon Opens New Chapter in Relations between Philippines and Japan: A New Welcome for the Japanese Military Was Unthinkable', *Irish Times*, 25 November.
National Institute for Defense Studies, 2011. *China Security Report 2010* (Tokyo: National Institute for Defense Studies).
National Institute for Defense Studies, 2012. *NIDS China Security 2011* (Tokyo, Japan: National Institute for Defense Studies).
National Institute for Defense Studies, 2014. *NIDS China Security Report 2014* (Tokyo: National Institute for Defense Studies).
National Institute for Defense Studies, 2015. *China Security 2014: Diversification of Roles of the People's Liberation Army and the People's Armed Police* (Tokyo: National Institute for Defense Studies).

Obe, M., Hayashi, Y. and Martine, A., 2013. 'Japan Deploys Self-Defense Forces to Aid Philippines', *Wall Street Journal*, 21 November.

Philippines News Agency, 2015. 'Japan Shares Philippines Serious Concern over China's Reclamation Activities in West Philippines Sea', *The Philippines News Agency*, 5 June.

Przystup, J. J., 2012. 'Japan–China Relations: Happy 40th Anniversary..? Part 2', *Comparative Connections*, 14(2): 105.

Przystup, J. J., 2013a. 'Japan–China Relations: 40th Anniversary 'Fuggetaboutit!', *Comparative Connections*, 14(3): 109.

Przystup, J. J., 2013b. 'Japan–China Relations: Treading Troubled Waters', *Comparative Connections*, 15(1): 111.

Salvador A. M. O. and Santiago, J., 2012. 'Defense Budget and Spending: Alignment and Priorities', in Oreta, J. S. (ed.), *Philippine Defense Spending* (Quezon City: Ateneo De Manila University Press).

Scott, D., 2007. *China Stands Up: The PRC and the International System* (Oxon; New York: Routledge).

Sharman, C. H., 2015. *China Moves Out: Stepping Stones toward a New Maritime Strategy* (Washington DC: National Defense University Press).

Sheldon, S., 2015. 'U.S.–Southeast Asia Relations: Courting Partners', *Comparative Connections*, 17(2): 53–64.

Singh, B., 2015. 'The Development of Japanese Security Policy: A Long-Term Defensive Strategy', *Asian Policy*, 19(1): 49–64.

Sutter, R. and Huang, C.-H., 2011. 'Managing Rising Tension in the South China Sea', *Comparative Connections*, 13(2): 67.

Swaine, M. D., 2015. 'The Real Challenge in the Pacific: A Response to "How to Deter China" ', *Foreign Affairs*, 94(3): 145.

Tatsumi, Y., 2015. 'The Emerging Japan–Philippines Security Partnership', *The Diplomat*, 6 June.

Wanklyn, A. and Mie, A., 2016. 'Japan Tries to Decode Duterte after Joint U.S. Patrol Halted', *TCA Regional News*, 15 September.

Yung, C. D. and McNulty, P., 2015. 'An Empirical Analysis of Claimant Tactics in the South China Sea', *Strategic Forum*, 289: 1.

8

The Vietnamese perspective on the security partnership with Japan

Swee Lean Collin Koh

Introduction

Tensions in the South China Sea (SCS) have taken a turn for the worse, with China's push to consolidate its position in the disputed waters – especially the ambitious island and infrastructure construction programme – and corresponding moves undertaken by Washington to challenge such expansive claims, notably through freedom of navigation operations. Indeed, the headlines of media reports on arguably the Indo-Pacific region's most volatile geopolitical flashpoint have been mainly preoccupied with actions undertaken by the major players to date – first and foremost, China and the US. But less emphasis has been given to what other, 'lesser' extra-regional powers have been doing in the grander scheme of things in the SCS thus far.

But to call these 'lesser' players second fiddle to the Great Powers may miss the point. While carrying out their roles in the latter's shadow, these players are no less significant. One of them is Japan. Though geographically distant from the SCS, Japan is a major player. One just needs to recall the keen strategic interest Tokyo had in Southeast Asia to sustain its expansionist policy prior to 1945. After all, imperial Japanese forces conducted a wildly successful military campaign in this region in 1941, colonising it, including the SCS, from where it staged its operations across wider Asia – including into the Indian Ocean. Fast forward to today; Tokyo continues to have a keen, though benign, strategic and economic interest in this region, including the SCS, through which its energy imports from the Middle East pass.

Since 1945, Japan's security role in Southeast Asia has largely been relegated to the shadows, to assisting the newly sovereign countries in the region to build their economies, primarily through the official development assistance (ODA) programme. In no small part, this could be attributed to Tokyo's post-war pacifist constitution. However, this has changed under recent administrations, notably the one led by Prime Minister Shinzō Abe, who possesses the conviction to put into effect what can be deemed Japan's version of 'pivot' to Southeast Asia, and a maritime-flavoured one at that. In order to implement this 'maritime pivot' effectively, Japan needs partners in Southeast Asia. Besides the Philippines, Vietnam fits the role nicely.

Yet this Southeast Asian country also stands out prominently when one considers at first glance the obvious strategic convergences it shares with Japan, foremost the fact that both countries have their fair share of maritime rivalries with China. Is this factor decisive in charting the path ahead for Vietnam's defence and security relationship with Japan, in the maritime realm especially? Few studies have been conducted on Vietnam–Japan maritime security engagement. In part, that is because this engagement has only recently begun to see significant activity. Nevertheless, this chapter seeks to examine these recent developments and to derive observations on the future trajectory of the Vietnam–Japan maritime security partnership.

This chapter first examines Vietnam's approach to dealing with post-Cold War and contemporary maritime security challenges, which revolve primarily around the SCS disputes. Besides threat perception, another aspect of this challenge has been the capacity shortfalls Hanoi has long faced. This leads to the discussion about Japan's role, examining the enablers and constraints on this burgeoning bilateral maritime security partnership. The chapter then concludes with some policy recommendations for the future of this relationship.

Setting the stage: Vietnam's maritime security conundrum

One cannot escape from mentioning the SCS when discussing the maritime security challenges Vietnam faces, even though in recent years, new threats have emerged. These included the ship hijacking incidents in the SCS, notably when the tanker MT *Orkim Harmony* was boarded by Indonesian pirates in June 2015 and Vietnamese maritime authorities were mobilised to respond. Also, Vietnam was prompted to respond in March 2014 when Malaysia Airline passenger jet MH370 was first reported missing over the SCS.

Notwithstanding these new emergent challenges, it is clear that Vietnam remains preoccupied with the SCS disputes, and this shapes its long-term defence planning. Since May 2009, when Vietnam submitted new maritime baseline claims to the Commission on the Limits of the Continental Shelf (CLCS), tensions have worsened in the SCS (Commission on the Limits of the Continental Shelf, 2009). Chinese maritime forces have repeatedly seized Vietnamese fishing boats and their crews in disputed waters close to the Chinese-occupied Paracel Islands, which are claimed by Hanoi. On 26 May 2011, the Vietnam National Oil and Gas Group seismic survey ship *Binh Minh-02* reportedly had its 7 km-long towed cable severed by Chinese patrol boats in overlapping Exclusive Economic Zone waters near the Paracels (BBC Monitoring Asia Pacific, 2011; Reuters News, 2011). Less than a week later, the French-owned seismic survey ship *Viking-2*, contracted by Hanoi, was allegedly harassed by a pair of Chinese vessels (Dow Jones International News, 2011; Platts Commodity News, 2011).[1]

Amid the Chinese coastguard and military build-up in the SCS, Hanoi's wariness towards Beijing was inevitably heightened when the latter seized control of Scarborough Shoal following a stand-off with the Philippine Coast Guard in April 2012. When the deep-sea oil rig HYSY981, owned by the China National Offshore Oil Corporation (CNOOC), was installed unilaterally in disputed waters some 120 nm off the Vietnamese coast in May 2014, Vietnam engaged in a stand-off with China for almost two months. The ordeal involved ramming and water-cannoning one another's fishing and government vessels. Fortuitously, this did not lead to a repeat of the bloody Sino-Vietnamese naval clashes that took place in 1974 and 1988. Nonetheless, this particular stand-off was an excruciating one for both disputants.

Against up to 122 Chinese government vessels of various types from multiple agencies, including the People's Liberation Army (PLA) navy, about 63 Vietnamese government vessels were deployed.[2] Both sides, exhausted by the sustained, gruelling face-off, gradually de-escalated tensions, culminating with the eventual withdrawal of the incriminating oil rig from the scene. The experience showed that both countries' maritime forces can be severely over-stretched by a prolonged stand-off. However, the material and manpower preponderance clearly favours China, given its vast size and resources. As such, the stand-off is a harbinger of what the future might hold for Hanoi. Nonetheless, when the same oil rig reappeared in June 2015 to carry out, in Beijing's words, 'ocean drilling operations' some 75 nm south of Sanya on Hainan Island,[3] thankfully there was no repeat of the May 2014 stand-off, even though Vietnamese civilian maritime law enforcement (CMLE) forces maintained a watchful eye on Chinese activities.

The May 2014 stand-off, which was arguably the worst Sino-Vietnamese maritime incident in the SCS since the end of the Cold War, amplified the persistent challenge posed by Beijing's growing assertiveness in waters so close to the Vietnamese coast. But the disputed waters surrounding the Paracels are not the only area of concern, for in recent years fresh, unsettling events have emerged in the Spratly Islands further out in the SCS, where Beijing has carried out a massive and rapid spate of island-building and fortification activities. In all, Vietnam finds itself in a maritime security conundrum, simply because its existing forces – the Vietnam People's Navy (VPN), Vietnam Coast Guard (VCG) and Vietnam Fisheries Resources Surveillance Force (VFRSF) – will be stretched to their limits. It is conceivable that the VPN, which owns more offshore-capable assets, is primarily tasked with operations in the more distant Spratlys waters, whereas the 'shorter legged' CMLE forces are preoccupied with waters closer to Vietnamese coast and the Paracels.

Despite this conceivable geographical division of labour, which arises mainly out of pragmatic considerations over the composition of Vietnam's maritime forces, capacity shortfalls look set to persist, for a number of reasons. The first is that Vietnam's maritime forces have endured a sustained period of Cold War neglect. The VPN did not receive as much attention as its sister services, especially the dominant ground forces. This land-centric defence strategy centred on the 'people's war' notion, which was particularly relevant back then given the conflicts Vietnam had fought, including the border war with China in 1979. The VPN played a minor supporting role, as its North Vietnamese predecessor had done for most of the Vietnam War, when it facilitated the seaborne version of the 'Ho Chi Minh Route' Viet Cong infiltration into American-backed South Vietnam.

Following the 1988 SCS clash with Chinese forces, there was an attempt to reinvigorate the maritime forces. But the post-Cold War priority has been socio-economic development, centred on the *Doi Moi* (Renovation) philosophy. Funds were limited, especially when the defence budget pie had to be shared between the various armed services. It also does not help that the entire Vietnamese armed forces, not just the navy, are in need of refurbishment. For the VPN in particular, post-1991 modernisation has been 'resource challenged' because of widespread obsolescence and the need for replacement (and in appreciable quantities) in various force categories.

Therefore, the VPN's complete overhaul will take time. It also does not help that VCG and later VFRSF have had to fight for the same limited resources with the VPN since the former were established. However, the creation of these 'white hull' agencies is politically expedient, for such forces convey a far less militaristic image compared with their 'grey hull' navy counterpart in the context of maritime disputes (Kearsley, 1992: 46). As far as possible, Hanoi would avoid using 'grey hulls' in order to maintain the 'moral high ground' in future SCS tussles with Beijing. As such, Vietnam's CMLE forces have received no less attention, even as Hanoi persists in boosting the VPN's war-fighting capabilities. Unlike the 'big ticket' submarine and frigate purchases for the VPN, the equivalent for these CMLE forces has been offshore patrol vessels (OPVs) and smaller coastal craft. Dutch shipbuilder Damen has been at the forefront of Vietnam's CMLE force build-up efforts, aiding the Vietnamese shipbuilding industry in churning out new-build OPVs.

However, even here, operationally and technically, Vietnam finds itself unable to match the speed at which the China Coast Guard (CCG) is expanding its capacity. While the CCG is still inducting converted, hand-me-down vessels from the PLA navy, it is also increasingly populating its stable with new-builds, aided by its colossal and vastly more developed shipbuilding industry, which has long been producing a diverse range of military and CMLE vessels. Using modern shipbuilding concepts such as modularity, China has been able to produce increasingly capable OPVs at a rapid rate, for instance a modified Type-056 *Jiangdao*-class corvette design using basically the same hull and some superstructure similarities, but painted in CCG colours and equipped 'light' for maritime law enforcement duties (just water- and auto-cannons and no heavy offensive armaments). The recent introduction of a 12,000-ton CCG patrol vessel – built to military standards and ostensibly designed to supersede the 6,000-ton Japanese *Shikishima* class – is another testament to how far CCG capacity-building efforts have come.

By contrast, Vietnam has been relying largely on foreign sources for its CMLE agencies, while simultaneously building up its domestic shipbuilding capacity. A robust relationship has been established with Damen, for example, with local shipyards such as Song Thu building Dutch-designed vessels under licence. However, the pace is much slower than that of China. Moreover, cost is not on Vietnam's side. The Chinese can tap cheaper domestic sources of labour and raw materials, while Hanoi has to rely more heavily on foreign components. One may argue that Vietnamese new-builds ought to be of superior quality, given that they benefit from Western technology. But this comes at a huge premium – one that Vietnam cannot possibly sustain if it hopes to build more to match, if not exceed, the CCG.

All in all, the asymmetry between China and Vietnam is just too insurmountable, especially when the former already enjoys a comfortable lead in CMLE capacity, not to mention the navies. Vietnam's CMLE forces muster only about 22 offshore-capable assets out of slightly over 100 vessels in service, compared with at least 118 offshore-capable assets out of the CCG's 448-plus vessels (International Institute of Strategic Studies, 2018: 258, 311). Under such circumstances, the extent to which Hanoi can rely on self-help is severely limited. It needs external assistance, and Japan features within this strategic equation.

Vietnam–Japan security cooperation acquires a maritime flavour

A major part of external assistance comes in the form of financial, technical and training aid provided by the foreign donor governments. In recent years, Vietnam has received a range of these assistances from a number of countries, including the US, with which Hanoi has cultivated increasingly warmer relations. Nonetheless, American assistance to Vietnam has been limited for various reasons, not least the existing arms embargo imposed by Washington – a relic of the Cold War – and only partially lifted in 2015.[4] What Washington has offered so far may fall short of Vietnam's maritime security capacity-building requirements. The Defiant 75-type patrol craft, to be built under an $18 million grant inked in June 2015, is optimised for coastal patrol but not for operations in distant SCS waters. Washington's Southeast Asia Maritime Security Initiative (MSI) may promise better assets for Vietnam.[5] However, there is also scepticism as to whether this new initiative can make a real difference in bolstering Vietnam's physical capacity to exercise sovereign control in the SCS.[6]

Therefore, it becomes imperative for Vietnam not to rely on a single source of external support, but to diversify. Moreover, diversification fits well with the long-avowed post-Cold War Vietnamese foreign policy principles of independence and non-alignment, which emphasise both collaboration and struggle against domination and exclusion politics (*vua hop tac, vua dau tranh*). Japan's role in this context is therefore critical. However, suffice it to say that Japan is by no means the only extra-regional power Vietnam relies on. There are a number of enabling factors behind the growing Vietnam–Japan security cooperation, especially in the maritime sphere – a step up from previous cooperation, which had been largely diplomatic and economic in nature.

There is, first of all, a fading of residual World War II memories, especially among older Vietnamese, who resented the Japanese for deeds such as starving some two million Vietnamese by taking food to support the Japanese Imperial Army. Vietnam had also harboured suspicions towards Japan, in particular after the Japanese National Diet tried to pass a bill in October 1990 that proposed deploying troops overseas to assist in international peacekeeping operations following the Persian Gulf crisis.[7] However, a turning point came in August 1994, when Japanese Prime Minister Tomiichi Murayama visited Hanoi and expressed his personal remorse for Japan's World War II atrocities in the region. Top officials, including Prime Minister Vo Van Kiet, responded that they were willing to close the chapter on the past and have appealed for greater investment and cooperation with Japan.

The second enabling factor is the post-Cold War foreign policy principle mentioned earlier, which calls for Vietnam to wean itself off reliance on any one extra-regional power – as was the case with the Soviet Union during the Cold War. Nonetheless, as will be discussed later, this foreign policy principle in a way also constrains the scope of the defence and security partnership Vietnam can pursue with Japan. Third, strategic engagement in defence and security issues constitutes a natural progression from long-standing diplomatic and economic engagement, including the generous aid Japan has been providing to Vietnam. This also fits generally within Hanoi's broader aims towards enhancing defence diplomacy with foreign partners. In June 2013, for example, Vietnam's then Deputy Defence Minister Senior Lieutenant General Nguyen Chi Vinh affirmed that Hanoi wished to further strengthen friendship and cooperation with countries, including defence ties (*Vietnam News Summary*, 2013). Perhaps the most crucial of all is the fourth factor, which is nothing other than common maritime security concerns, especially over China's growing assertiveness. This factor facilitates a common world view, including the desire to play a proactive role for peace, safety and prosperity in Asia and the international community; to uphold the freedom and safety of navigation and overflight; to enhance the rule of law at sea; and for the peaceful maintenance of the status quo.

Nonetheless, Vietnam's maritime security partnership with Japan is far from being a recent development; bilateral relations in this field date back to the 1990s, starting with low-level defence exchanges. Events that took place in the SCS and the East China Sea (ECS) contributed in no small way to propelling the further development of these ties.

For example, in January 1997, Japanese Prime Minister Ryutaro Hashimoto and his Vietnamese counterpart Vo Van Kiet agreed to strengthen security dialogue, including vice defence ministerial-level exchange visits. In March of the same year, during his visit to Tokyo, Vietnamese Vice Defence Minister Lieutenant General Tran Hanh called for acceptance of Vietnamese students at Japan's National Defense Academy, and reiterated support for Japan's security arrangements with Washington, viewing those as contributing to regional stability. In fact, these exchanges began around the time of growing tensions in the SCS, following China's seizure of Mischief Reef in 1995. In January 1998, Fumio Kyuma became the first Japanese defence chief ever to visit Vietnam, and he expressed interest in Japanese naval ships conducting port calls to Vietnam, with which his Vietnamese counterpart Pham Van Tra expressed 'basic agreement'. In December of the same year, when Tra visited Tokyo, an agreement was reached for Japanese warships to make a port call in Vietnam, whereas Japan's National Defense Academy would accept three Vietnamese students annually from April 1999 onwards. Besides the fact that Tra's visit to Japan was also the first ever by a Vietnamese defence chief, this meeting was interesting because it took place not long after tensions escalated once more in the SCS following the discovery of new Chinese structures being built at Mischief Reef the same year.

After Japanese warships conducted their first ever port call to Vietnam in May 1999, the following year, Hanoi proposed bilateral maritime search-and-rescue (SAR) cooperation and joint operations in the SCS, on the grounds that many Japanese vessels ply SCS waters and Vietnam could not deal with marine accidents alone (Japan Economic Newswire, 2000). Even though Tokyo agreed to consider this proposal, there was little traction thereafter, except for the joint search-and-rescue exercise (SAREX) conducted when a Japanese coastguard vessel visited Vietnam in January 2007.[8] Nonetheless, in the interim, general defence exchanges were enhanced. Most notably, Vietnam and Japan have held expert-level meetings to exchange views on defence and foreign affairs since 2002, under an agreement between the Defence and Foreign Affairs Ministries of the two countries. However, Vietnam has expressed keen interest in stepping up defence and security cooperation with Japan. Enhanced cooperation between the two militaries, according to Vietnamese Prime Minister Phan Van Khai in July 2003, would help in stabilising peace and development in the region and the world (Vietnam News Brief Service, 2003).

Following the Sino-Japanese diplomatic fallout over the September 2010 trawler incident off the Senkaku/Diaoyu Islands, Vietnam and Japan elevated their ties to a strategic partnership, and in the same year they conducted their first Strategic Partnership Dialogue (Ministry of Foreign Affairs of Japan, 2010). Part of this agreement was a long-term partnership to jointly survey, explore and exploit Vietnam's rare-earth minerals.[9] Exactly a year later, the Japan–Vietnam Joint Statement on the Actions Taken under Strategic Partnership for Peace and Prosperity in Asia was issued (Ministry of Foreign Affairs of Japan, 2011). Japan by then ranked among the biggest investors in Vietnam and also as the country's largest ODA provider, including such crucial projects as Hanoi's plan to build a second nuclear power plant in Ninh Thuan. Coinciding with the issuance of the joint statement in October 2011 was the signing of a 'Memorandum between the Ministry of Defense of Vietnam and the Ministry of Defense of Japan on Bilateral Defense Cooperation and Exchanges', which calls for regular dialogue at the deputy defence ministerial level, joint training, and cooperation in the areas of the defence industry, humanitarian assistance/disaster relief (HA/DR) and maritime security (Jiji Press English News Service, 2011).

Based on the memorandum, bilateral defence and security ties accelerated. In January 2012, the two militaries held their first general-level dialogue. When Japanese Vice Defence Minister Shimojo Mitsu visited Hanoi around the same time, both governments agreed to foster military exchanges, training cooperation and marine SAR (Vietnam News Agency Bulletin, 2012). July the same year saw signs of qualitative enhancement to the bilateral maritime security partnership when, during his visit to Hanoi, Japanese Foreign Minister Koichiro Gemba pledged support for Vietnam's maritime security capacity-building effort, in response to Vietnam's request for Tokyo's assistance in training coast guard personnel and bolstering physical capabilities. Barely two months after Sino-Japanese tensions flared up again in 2012, the first deputy ministerial-level defence strategic dialogue was held in November, during which both countries agreed to draft a roadmap to implement initiatives spelt out in the 2011 memorandum (Ministry of Foreign Affairs of Japan, 2011).

The most significant and substantial bilateral maritime security engagement has been taking place under Prime Minister Shinzō Abe, who seeks to reinvigorate Japan's influence in Southeast Asia in an apparent countervailing move against China's growing assertiveness in the ECS. In fact, after Shinzō Abe retook the post of prime minister in December 2012, the first stop of his three-nation Southeast Asia tour the following month was Vietnam. During that visit, Abe and his counterpart Nguyen Tan Dung agreed to promote dialogue and cooperation in the political and security fields, while stressing the importance of rule of law and opposing changing the status quo by force (Ministry of Foreign Affairs of Japan, 2013), in apparent reference to China's actions in the ECS and

SCS. A month after Chinese ships allegedly opened fire on a Vietnamese fishing boat in the SCS in March 2013, a high-powered Vietnamese military delegation visited Japan, and both countries' military chiefs agreed to bolster defence ties to cope with rising regional challenges, again in oblique reference to China. Vietnam suggested close coordination with Japan in regional and international forums, such as the Association of Southeast Asian Nations (ASEAN) Regional Forum and ASEAN Defense Ministers Meeting-Plus, whereas Japan called for boosting defence ties for their mutual benefit in view of their many common interests. In May, both navies agreed to enhance bilateral ties. During that same month, the first bilateral maritime security dialogue was held in Hanoi, focusing on China's growing expansionism in the western Pacific, especially its naval presence in the ECS and SCS. Vietnam's purchase of patrol ships from Japan was also discussed.

When the second Vietnam–Japan Defence Policy Dialogue was held in Tokyo in August 2013, both countries agreed to focus on maritime security cooperation, which includes supporting each other in research capacity-building and management of maritime areas, developing defence industrial linkages, and counter-piracy capacity-building (Vietnam News Agency Bulletin, 2013c; Vietnam News Brief Service, 2013a). The following month, during his visit to Tokyo, Vietnamese Foreign Minister Pham Binh Minh affirmed that Hanoi has long considered Japan as one of its leading strategic partners.[10] The same month, Japanese Defence Minister Itsunori Onodera called on his Vietnamese counterpart Phung Quang Thanh, and both agreed to boost maritime security cooperation amid concern over China's growing naval activities, according to Japanese officials (Kyodo News, 2013b). That was when Onodera also pledged Tokyo's commitment to support Vietnam's coast guard capacity-building, which did not appear to have gained much traction following Gemba's visit to Hanoi in 2012. Onodera also became the first Japanese defence minister to visit Cam Ranh Bay.[11] This pledge to strengthen the maritime security partnership was further reinforced in October, on the sidelines of the 21st APEC Summit held in Bali, by Vietnamese President Truong Tan Sang and Abe.

The subsequent years from 2014 onward saw intensified maritime security engagement between Japan and Vietnam, coinciding with the latter's increasing concerns about China's SCS moves, especially following the May 2014 oil rig stand-off and the spate of Chinese island-building and fortification activities. These developments impressed upon Hanoi the need to bolster its own maritime security capacity in two ways. The first is to build national capacity through foreign assistance. The second is to attract extra-regional involvement in facilitating regional peace and stability. India, Japan and the US especially have been involved in these two aspects, albeit to varying degrees. With Japan, there are evident limitations, notwithstanding the rapid pace of developing bilateral defence and security exchanges in recent years.

Naval diplomacy: Just one-way?

The most basic form of maritime security engagement between Vietnam and Japan is port visits by maritime forces – a traditional type of naval diplomacy that governments have long conducted as part of foreign policy. The idea here is to 'show the flag' in support of the other party, in much the same way as the Soviet navy sent one of its aircraft carriers to Cam Ranh in 1979 after the Sino-Vietnamese border conflict erupted. In the context of the simmering SCS disputes with China, having vessels from the Japan Maritime Self-Defense Force (JMSDF) and the Japanese Coast Guard (JCG) visit Vietnamese ports acquires politically symbolic importance. It signals a common Japan–Vietnam stance towards SCS issues, especially towards China's activities. Also, in a way, facilitating port calls by JMSDF and JCG enables Japan to play a more active security role in Southeast Asia – a move supported by Hanoi.[12] Table 8.1 highlights the visits to Vietnam by JMSDF and JCG based on the 1998 agreement.

The frequency of Japanese visits after the inaugural port call in May 1999 was low, with considerable intervals of a few years. However, port calls to Vietnam picked up in frequency from 2011 onwards, coinciding with the flaring up of ECS and SCS tensions. To be sure, this increased frequency of port calls to Vietnam is also enabled by Tokyo's participation in multinational counter-piracy operations in the Gulf of Aden; JMSDF escort flotillas have ample opportunity to stop over at Vietnamese ports while en route to the Indian Ocean and back to Japan after completing their missions. This opportunity thus spawned yet another qualitative upgrade of Vietnam–Japan maritime security partnership, when in March 2014 the JMSDF's aviation arm made its first ever stopover in Vietnam. The JMSDF's P-3C Orion long-range maritime patrol aircraft (LRMPA) has since become a frequent visitor. Somewhat coincidentally, this took place barely a year after Hanoi first evinced interest in acquiring this very same type of aircraft to bolster aerial maritime surveillance over the SCS.[13] During their stopover in Vietnam in February 2016, the P-3C aircrews also held a table-top SAREX with their Vietnamese hosts, who were also given a tour on board the aircraft.

Japan's port calls to Vietnam were given another qualitative upgrade in June 2014, when JS *Kunisaki*, one of its landing platform ships – one of the largest warships in JMSDF service – visited in another step forward beyond sending destroyer-sized ships. This visit was part of the US-led Pacific Partnership Program, which seeks to help build regional HA/DR capacities following the December 2004 Indian Ocean earthquake and tsunami, embarking also Australian and American personnel. In November 2015, Vietnam agreed to allow Japanese warships to dock in Cam Ranh and to hold joint naval exercises in the SCS, though details are lacking (Kyodo News, 2015a). With this agreement, JMSDF and JCG can make use of more Vietnamese facilities. Especially following

Table 8.1 Visits to Vietnam by JMSDF and JCG

Date	Visiting Assets	Port of Call
7 May 1999	JS *Kashima*; JS *Hamagiri*	Ho Chi Minh City
14 April 2003	JS *Asayuki*; JS *Shirayuki*	Ho Chi Minh City
January 2007	JCGS *Yashima*	Danang
March 2008	JS *Yamayuki*; JS *Matsuyuki*	Ho Chi Minh City
17 September 2011	JS *Uraga*; JS *Tsushima*	Danang
12 March 2012	JS *Hamagiri*; JS *Sawayuki*; JS *Asayuki*	Haiphong
7 September 2012	JCGS *Shikishima*	Haiphong
30 July 2013	JCGS *Kojima*	Danang
19 October 2013	JS *Kashima*; JS *Shirayuki*; JS *Isoyuki*	Danang
March 2014	P-3C Orion	Ho Chi Minh City
7 June 2014	JS *Kunisaki*	Danang
15 April 2015	JS *Asayuki*; JS *Kirisame*	Danang
May 2015	P-3C Orion	Danang
10 May 2015	JCGS *Yashima*	Danang
18 February 2016	P-3C Orion	Danang
12 April 2016	JS *Ariake*; JS *Setogiri*	Cam Ranh Bay
29 May 2016	JS *Uraga*, JS *Takashima*	Cam Ranh Bay
16 July 2016	JS *Shimokita*	Danang
25 July 2016	JCGS *Kojima*	Danang

Source: Author's database compiled from various sources, including news reports.[1]

[1] See, for example, Vietnam News Brief Service (1999); Kinh Luan (2003); Vietnam News Brief Service (2007); Vietnam News Brief Service (2012b); Vietnam News Brief Service (2011); Vietnam News Brief Service (2012a); Vietnam News Agency Bulletin (2013a); Vietnam News Agency Bulletin (2013b); Vietnam News Brief Service (2014d); Vietnam News Brief Service (2015); Vietnam News Agency Bulletin (2015a); Jiji Press English News Service (2016); Manabu Sasaki (2016); *Tuoi Tre Newspaper* (2016).

China's moves to militarize the SCS, including deployment of missiles in the Paracels soon after the US Navy conducted freedom of navigation operations, Japan's ship visits to such a strategic port as Cam Ranh take on a highly visible, politically symbolic importance. April 2016 saw JMSDF warships calling on the Cam Ranh International Port, which had been inaugurated by Hanoi a month earlier, for the first time – the second foreign naval visitor following Singapore's visit.

Notwithstanding Hanoi's support, greater JMSDF and JCG presence in Southeast Asian waters, especially the SCS, remains to be seen following passage of the new security legislation in mid-September 2015. Japanese defence authorities have professed a lack of capacity to maintain regular military aerial presence over the SCS. 'It may be possible for our airplanes to just shuttle between Naha and the SCS, but it would be difficult for them to stay in the area long enough to conduct surveillance activities', a senior Japanese military official remarked in July 2015 (Akita, 2015). It is more feasible, from the operational and technical point of view, for JMSDF and JCG to exert presence in the region only when Tokyo sustains its involvement in its Indian Ocean counter-piracy activities,[14] on top of the JMSDF overseas training cruises undertaken from time to time. Vietnam can therefore serve as a convenient stopover for replenishment, rest and recreation, and maritime security engagements.

For now, this engagement will be one-way, since neither VPN nor Vietnamese CMLE forces possess the requisite capabilities for undertaking 'out-of-area' operations in distant waters, given the primary operational focus on immediate waters since the Cold War. This may change in the foreseeable future, especially as Hanoi acquires more long-range force projection assets. Moreover, in February 2016, a VPN frigate participated in the India-hosted International Fleet Review in Visakhapatnam (Vietnam News Agency Bulletin, 2016). It is therefore not inconceivable that Vietnamese maritime forces may undertake similar cruises to Japan to effect a 'two-way' engagement, thereby creating more chances for both countries to bolster joint naval exchanges and training to build interoperability. Until then, such engagements will have to be confined to whenever JMSDF and JCG assets call on Vietnam, thereby limiting 'face time' between both countries' maritime forces. This is also contingent on Japan's political will and resource capacity.

Technical assistance: Slow and steady?

Given the operational constraints on exchanges and training engagement through routine deployment of JMSDF and JCG, Tokyo's primary approach may be limited to mainly technical and financial assistance towards Vietnam's maritime security capacity-building efforts. Japan's ODA policy in February 2015 prescribes such aid as one of its priorities, namely, the 'sharing of universal values and realising a peaceful, stable and secure society', which, among various aspects, includes an explicit maritime security dimension:

> In view of the fact that threats to stability and security can hamper socio-economic development, Japan will also provide assistance to enhance capacities in developing countries such as: the capacity of law enforcement authorities including capabilities to ensure maritime safety; the capacity of security authorities including capabilities to combat terrorism and transnational organised crime including drug trafficking and trafficking in persons; and the capacity of developing countries in relation to global commons such as seas, outer space, and cyberspace. (Ministry of Foreign Affairs of Japan, 2015a: 6)

Following the Gemba visit to Hanoi in 2012, when the supply of patrol vessels to Vietnam was first mulled, there had been little progress throughout 2013. There was, however, modest progress in the related area of maritime domain awareness, such as Hanoi's launch of the PicoDragon microsatellite, designed with Japanese technical assistance, for remote-sensing purposes in August 2013.[15] There was evidently a strong push by Hanoi for capacity-building in the area of providing patrol assets, which would prove so pivotal for Vietnam to enforce its sovereignty claims in the SCS. During a joint press conference with then visiting Vietnamese Prime Minister Nguyen Tan Dung in Tokyo in December 2013, Abe said that talks would begin soon on providing patrol vessels to VCG (Kyodo News, 2013a). This pledge was made barely a month after Beijing promulgated an Air Defence Identification Zone (ADIZ) over the ECS, sparking concerns that a similar zone could be declared over the SCS. Indeed, given the building up of SCS tensions, obtaining timely Japanese assistance had acquired a new sense of urgency. In March 2014, two months before the Sino-Vietnamese stand-off flared up, Hanoi and Tokyo further elevated their bilateral relations to 'Extensive Strategic Partnership for Peace and Prosperity in Asia' (Ministry of Foreign Affairs of Japan, 2014), on which occasion a bilateral pact was reached for the latter to dispatch a fact-finding team to Vietnam to assess plans to provide VCG with patrol vessels (Yoshida, 2014). Nonetheless, progress was not as quick as Hanoi expected. It was not until late May, while Chinese and Vietnamese maritime forces faced off over the oil rig, that this assistance acquired a newfound sense of urgency. During the 20th Nikkei International Conference on the Future of Asia held in Tokyo, plans were mooted for Foreign Minister Fumio Kishida to visit Hanoi the following month to discuss ways to hasten the transfer of the patrol vessels.[16]

Nonetheless, Hanoi seems to have had a grasp of the reality – that Japanese assistance might not come in the amount and at the time expected, thus making it imperative not to put all its eggs into the Japanese basket. Vietnamese Deputy Prime Minister Vu Duc Dam said during that 20th Nikkei event that 'Vietnam has a long coastal line. So we are in the great need for equipment, facilities, so that we can better manage our coastlines. Therefore, we'd like to seek assistance, not only from Japan, but also from other countries' (Sieg and Takenaka, 2014). Vietnam's prudence was proven warranted about a week later; when asked during a National Diet session about the possibility of providing decommissioned patrol ships to Vietnam to expedite the process of helping the latter build its coastguard capacity, Abe admitted that Tokyo was unable to immediately supply used patrol vessels to Vietnam, because of the increasing surveillance burden on the JCG. He remarked that 'regrettably, our country is not in a situation where we can retire all vessels that have reached such age' (Reuters News, 2014).

Soon afterwards, on the sidelines of the 13th Shangri-La Dialogue held in Singapore, during which Abe pledged assistance to Southeast Asian countries' maritime security capacity-building efforts, Vietnamese Vice Defence Minister Nguyen Chi Vinh sounded an upbeat note about Japan's aid to Vietnam in this respect. Vinh remarked that 'the process is developing very well and we are planning to receive the ships by early next year' (Armstrong, 2014). But Hanoi was evidently not too pleased with the lethargic progress of technical cooperation. During the visit to Ho Chi Minh City by Major General Naohisa Fukase, vice president of the National Institute for Defense Studies, a think-tank of the Japanese Ministry of Defense, in late June 2014, Deputy Chief of the General Staff, Lieutenant General Vo Van Tuan, called for stronger defence links with Japan, opining that bilateral defence cooperation, especially in the defence industry and science and technology, remained modest (Vietnam News Agency Bulletin, 2014). A consensus was reached at the meeting to beef up bilateral cooperation in defence-related research and training (Vietnam News Brief Service, 2014j). The planned visit to Hanoi by Kishida in June to discuss the patrol vessel transfer was also delayed until July, when he co-chaired the 6th Meeting of the Vietnam–Japan Cooperation Committee, during which he assured his Vietnamese hosts of Tokyo's commitment to bolstering maritime security cooperation (Kyodo News, 2014b; Vietnam News Brief Service, 2014c).

Most importantly, Kishida agreed on the specifics of the patrol vessels. In all, Japan would furnish Vietnam with six second-hand vessels (all displacing 600–800 tons; two from the Fisheries Agency and four commercial fishing vessels) modified for patrol duties, along with associated equipment such as lifeboats – altogether totalling a value of 500 million yen (US$4.9 million), and originally slated for delivery by the end of 2014 (Kyodo News, 2014a). Nonetheless, the delivery lapsed, so much so that high-ranking Vietnamese government officials repeatedly impressed upon their Japanese counterparts during 2015 the need to expedite or even enhance assistance. Tokyo had to assure Hanoi of its commitment towards such endeavours. In January 2015, Katayama Satsuki, chairwoman of the Japanese Diet Committee for Foreign Affairs and Defense, assured her Vietnamese hosts during her visit to Hanoi that Tokyo was willing to enhance military cooperation with Vietnam, especially in the defence industry (Kyodo News, 2015c). Two months later, on the sidelines of the UN World Conference on Disaster Risk Reduction, Vietnamese Vice President Nguyen Thi Doan and Kishida agreed to bolster maritime security cooperation (*Japan Times*, 2015b).

Nonetheless, developments unfolding along the way appeared to point to a pessimistic outlook regarding the prospects for Japan supplying more assets to Vietnam. In July 2015, Tokyo announced plans to bolster JCG capacity in order to cope with not just the regular CCG forays into territorial waters surrounding the disputed Senkaku/Diaoyu islands, but also scores of intruding Chinese fishing vessels (*Japan Times*, 2015a). Naturally, Japan's own maritime interests within its immediate waters would have to take precedence. So, it was laudable that Tokyo still followed through on its commitment regarding the six second-hand vessels; the first was delivered in August.[17] By the following month, Japan completed delivery of the first pair. These are not new-builds, but the time taken for their transfer and modification exceeded the envisaged timeline. This aid can be seen as a stop-gap measure, which also showed how stretched the Japanese are in providing assets to foreign countries while themselves being in need of capacity to deal with their own ECS conundrum. Nevertheless, by November, Japan delivered the second pair of patrol vessels to Vietnam (Kyodo News, 2015b).

Despite its own difficulties, Japan continued to pledge assistance to Vietnam's maritime security capacity-building efforts. Notably, when Nguyen Phu Trong, general secretary of the ruling Communist Party of Vietnam (CPV), visited Japan in September 2015, a Joint Vision Statement on Japan–Vietnam Relations (Ministry of Foreign Affairs of Japan, 2015b) and a Memorandum on Cooperation between Coast Guard Agencies were signed. While sharing 'serious concerns' with Vietnam over China's activities in the SCS, Japan promised to provide additional used patrol vessels (Jiji Press English News Service, 2015a). Interestingly, this visit came less than three months after Dung met Abe in Tokyo, where he reiterated Hanoi's desire to ramp up the maritime security relationship, including the prospect of acquiring new patrol vessels from Japan. Beyond the six second-hand vessels, it seemed that the prospects for Japan to supply new and more capable ones to Vietnam would have to wait at least until the JCG satisfied its own operational requirements, especially when Beijing started to deploy armed patrol vessels, backed by such PLA navy assets as intelligence-collection ships, into waters surrounding those ECS isles. The situation appeared gloomy, as Tokyo warned in January 2016 that JMSDF ships would be deployed to back up the JCG, which might not be able to handle the situation alone (*Japan News*, 2016; *Mainichi Shimbun*, 2016).

In May 2016, during talks between Kishida and his counterpart Minh and newly appointed Prime Minister Nguyen Xuan Phuc, Hanoi sought new patrol vessels from Japan. This was urgent given the perceived persistence of Chinese aggression in the SCS, in particular the alleged ramming and sinking of a Vietnamese fishing boat by a Chinese vessel in waters off Danang, which occurred at the same time as the talks. 'Vietnam wants new vessels', Japanese government spokesman Masato Otaka told reporters, adding that the timing, methods of delivery, costs and quantity of vessels had not yet been decided, and that 'Vietnam feels it needs to strengthen its coastguard generally, and that's why we've responded' (Reuters News, 2016). But it became clear that new vessels would take time, such that Kishida gave assurances that Tokyo would swiftly provide more second-hand vessels – most plausibly as a stop-gap measure – to boost Vietnam's sea patrol capabilities, in addition to the six already handed over (Kyodo News, 2016b).

Indeed, the JCG evidently could not yet sufficiently fill the shortfalls with new-builds, such that existing assets from other JCG regional commands had to be reassigned to duties around the ECS isles.[18] As such, the supply of second-hand vessels to Vietnam looked set to be the way to go, at least until JCG acquired enough new assets for itself. Therefore, it became prudent on Vietnam's part to stick to this current policy of diversifying sources as best it could, aided in no small part by its existing foreign policy principles.

Conclusions: A balance of interests

There are certainly a host of enabling factors that bring about the strategic convergences between Vietnam and Japan, foremost being their common concerns towards China in the ECS and SCS. Under the energetic Abe administration, Japan has exerted tremendous efforts in cultivating more holistic defence and security relations with Vietnam, with a predominant focus on the maritime arena. Vietnam is naturally one of the crucial partners, like the Philippines, of Tokyo's 'maritime pivot' to Southeast Asia. Indeed, from the post-Cold War foreign policy standpoint of Hanoi, having Japan close by its side proves to be beneficial insofar as maritime security capacity-building efforts are concerned.

However, there are evident limitations to the extent of this maritime security partnership between Vietnam and Japan. Naval diplomacy remains one-way, mainly because of Vietnam's own inherent limitations when it comes to force projection capabilities. This could change over time as it accumulates the requisite means to make this interaction with Japan 'two-way' in the future. Japan's technical assistance to Vietnam's maritime security capacity-building, while realising some noteworthy progress, nonetheless falls short of Hanoi's expectations. Japan has its own set of challenges in the ECS that limit the extent to which it can furnish newer and more capable physical assets, the foremost priority being patrol vessels, to Vietnam's CMLE forces. Given the persistent Chinese military and coastguard challenge in the ECS, it is safe to assume that Tokyo will continue to prioritise satisfying its own operational requirements. As such, Vietnam will need to continue to diversify its sources beyond Japan.

Perhaps the most interesting factor determining the future trajectory of the Vietnam–Japan maritime security partnership is Hanoi's post-Cold War foreign policy, which is premised on independence and non-alignment. This forms an enabling basis for the burgeoning bilateral maritime security partnership. Yet it also imposes a limitation on how far Vietnam can afford to bring this relationship further afield. In fact, this limitation is observed in the calibrated and cautious approach Vietnam undertakes in cultivating defence and security relations not only with Japan, but also with India and the US. At the end of the day, geography, history and economics determine the pivotal status of China within Hanoi's strategic calculus.

China, being a proximate neighbour with shared land and sea boundaries, constitutes an immutable geographical fact that Vietnam has to live with.

Notwithstanding the misgivings Vietnam has had towards China over the centuries – dating to the era of imperial Chinese expansionism – it makes sense to maintain cordial relations with Beijing. Historically, also, the two ruling communist parties continue to enjoy warm fraternal ties, dating back to the Cold War, when Beijing supported the North Vietnamese government in its struggle against the French and the Americans. CPV leaders still continue to talk fondly about, and express gratitude for, CPC material and personnel assistance during those conflicts. The depth and entrenchment of this inter-party relationship is well demonstrated in the aftermath of the May 2014 stand-off.[19]

Finally, it needs to be pointed out that China remains Vietnam's biggest trading partner, so much so that Hanoi took urgent steps in the aftermath of anti-China protests over the SCS to maintain buoyant trade links with Beijing.[20] It also does not help that while bilateral trade has been expanding, Vietnam's trade deficit with China has also been widening (General Statistics Office of Vietnam, 2016).[21] And Beijing has obviously used this as leverage on Vietnam. For example, in the midst of the May 2014 stand-off, a Chinese Commerce Ministry official, Zhang Ji, warned that the anti-China protests in Vietnam would 'definitely damage the healthy development of Sino-Vietnam trade, which China does not want to see, and will also be detrimental to the Vietnamese economy' (ANN Asia News Network, 2014). Within the Vietnamese bureaucracy, there has been strong concern about the country's heavy economic dependence on China.[22]

Taking all these factors together, Vietnam faces an interesting situation in which it has to balance its national interests – possessing the ability to stand up to Chinese aggression, while at the same time not pushing the envelope so far as to provoke Beijing and completely sour relations. Speaking with Deputy Chief of General Staff of the Chinese PLA, Lieutenant General Wang Guanzhong, on the sidelines of the 13th Shangri-La Dialogue in June 2014, as the Sino-Vietnamese stand-off over the oil rig continued, Vietnamese Vice Minister of Defence Nguyen Chi Vinh said: 'Vietnam doesn't want to hold tensions with China. We dare not to be winner or loser, but all we want is peace and integrity of the country's sovereignty' (Vietnam News Brief Service, 2014f). Even since the stand-off, as Vietnam sought closer security links with other extra-regional powers, it has also been cautious. In August 2014, Nguyen Xuan Thang, a member of the CPV central committee, called for strategic balance in the region through better trilateral cooperation with India and Japan with respect to China. 'There is a need for better cooperation between the three countries by sharing their experiences on how they deal with China on border issues as the three countries face similar kind of problems', he said. However, when asked whether they should form a bloc against China, he clarified: 'no I don't think it would be good to form a bloc against any country as that might lead to a conflict situation' (Press Trust of India, 2014).

The foreign policy statements made by the new Vietnamese leadership reflect this quest for balance. Nguyen Phu Trong pledged to continue prioritising the comprehensive strategic partnership with China after being re-elected as CPV general secretary (Vietnam News Brief Service, 2016c). New Vietnamese President Tran Dai Quang identified the development of friendly cooperation with China as a priority in Vietnam's foreign policy during a meeting with Chinese ambassador Hong Xiaoyong in Hanoi on 5 May 2016 (Zhang Jianhua, 2016). Earlier, Quang had said that Vietnam treasures its relations with Japan and considers the country a high-priority partner in its foreign policy (Vietnam News Brief Service, 2016b). Meanwhile, on the very same day as Quang met Hong, Prime Minister Nguyen Xuan Phuc emphasised Japan as Vietnam's close long-term strategic partner (Vietnam News Brief Service, 2016a).

Therefore, by establishing inclusive ties with multiple extra-regional partners, not just Japan, and sustaining 'traditional friendship' with China, Vietnam maintains some 'geopolitical buoyancy' for itself, exploiting the unprecedented flexibility it derives from the post-Cold War foreign policy principles that enable Hanoi to court whichever extra-regional power it deems fit to suit its national interests, while not necessarily being beholden to any of them. Naval diplomacy, technical assistance and capacity-building look set to be the 'safest' way forward for this burgeoning maritime security partnership between Vietnam and Japan. However, further enhancements will foreseeably be hampered by Hanoi's continued cautious gaze towards its northern neighbour. As long as it preserves and stays consistent with its avowed post-Cold War foreign policy, Vietnam will continue to seek incremental, but not overly bold, enhancements to this partnership. Hanoi will avoid anything that denotes a formal military alliance – with Japan.

NOTES

1. The same ship was later rammed by a Chinese vessel the following month, in what Hanoi called a 'premeditated and calculated attack' by Beijing (Agence France Press, 2011; Timberlake, 2011).
2. The author derived this estimate by tracking the progress of the incident through Chinese and Vietnamese state-controlled media reporting.
3. This activity came after a Chinese seismic survey vessel Number 517 reportedly came within 20 nm of Phy Quy Island off the central Vietnamese province of Binh Thuan and 40 nm off the mainland Vietnamese coast – a move Hanoi deemed a violation of its sovereignty (Reuters News, 2015).
4. At the time of writing, there are already reports of a possible complete lifting of the arms embargo, a move that had been lobbied for by influential American politicians, many of whom felt that a complete abolishment of this policy would strengthen Washington's rebalancing efforts in Asia by facilitating a more robust defence and security relationship with Vietnam in order to counter China.

5 According to open-source reports and author's discussion with those with insider knowledge of the policy thinking behind this initiative, MSI is primarily designed to bolster maritime domain awareness, which essentially means bolstering surveillance capabilities, with the aim of promoting information-sharing among Southeast Asian countries and thereby attaining a common maritime awareness picture. Of course, many such capabilities can be mobile instead of static, such as radars. However, MSI may limit the scope of capabilities that can be supplied to the recipient Southeast Asian countries in cases where exact specific needs may not be matched.

6 The question revolves around whether MSI can facilitate Vietnam's acquisition of such physical assets as patrol vessels, which matter when it comes to exerting presence, which is so central to the idea of exercising sovereign control in disputed waters. If all MSI does is to merely furnish surveillance systems, it will be of no use if better maritime domain awareness does not translate into real, practical action of enforcing sovereignty, which requires physical mobile assets such as patrol vessels. Discussion with Vietnamese defence analyst, Jakarta, 29 March 2016.

7 Then Vietnamese Foreign Minister Nguyen Co Thach said Vietnam was deeply concerned: 'the existence of Japanese troops in areas outside Japan will revive the memory of the Japanese army during World War II' (Japan Economic Newswire, 1990).

8 This SAR training carried on as a regular feature whenever JCG vessels visited Vietnam.

9 According to Japan Foreign Affairs Ministry spokesman Satoru Sato, Japan is keen to tap rare earth minerals in Vietnam to diversify its sources of supply after Beijing announced a slashing of exports by 40 per cent (Vietnam News Brief Service, 2010).

10 During that visit, Tokyo pledged an additional US$500 million in ODA for Vietnam in FY2013, on top of the same amount Abe pledged during his January visit to Hanoi (Kyodo News, 2013d; Vietnam News Agency Bulletin, 2013d).

11 On that occasion, Onodera appeared to refer to China being the common problem both countries face when he remarked that 'Japan's situation in the East China Sea is similar to Vietnam's in the South China Sea', adding that 'there are many things that Japan should learn from Vietnam' (Kyodo News, 2013c).

12 This includes Vietnam's support for the security legislation proposed by Abe's cabinet, and which was later passed by the National Diet in September 2015. This legislation paves the way for Japan to deploy its troops overseas to exercise the right of collective self-defence – a prospect much abhorred by Beijing, which views this as Japan's attempt at remilitarization. 'Politics: Vietnam Expects Bigger Role of Japan in East Asia: Spokesman' (Vietnam News Brief Service, 2014e; Jiji Press English News Service, 2015b).

13 According to Clay Fearnow, Lockheed Martin's director of maritime patrol programmes, Hanoi has 'expressed a lot of interest' in acquiring up to six surplus P-3s from US Navy stocks (Jennings, 2013).

14 When asked whether the JMSDF could possibly expand its involvement in the SCS, such as by conducting freedom of navigation operations (FONOPS) with the US Navy, a Japanese defense analyst who has insider knowledge of policy remarked that this prospect is feasible whenever JMSDF counter-piracy task forces – including warships and LRMPAs – transit through Southeast Asia to and from the Gulf of Aden. Q&A session during an academic conference on promoting maritime domain awareness and maritime security capacity-building in Southeast Asia, held in Jakarta, 29 March 2016.

15 Vietnam's plan to launch a series of remote-sensing microsatellites, as part of the broader space programme till 2020, has the explicit intent of bolstering its intelligence, surveillance and reconnaissance (ISR) suite to improve maritime domain awareness over the SCS (*Japan News*, 2013; Koh, 2016).

16 This agreement came about during the 20th Nikkei International Conference on the Future of Asia, when Deputy Prime Minister Vu Duc Dam reached a consensus with Abe on enhancing maritime security cooperation (Vietnam News Brief Service, 2014i).
17 The 56-m-long former tuna fishing vessel *Hayato* is to be equipped for fishery surveillance and assigned to VFRSF. When commissioned, it will be one of the service's most modern vessels, being capable of offshore fishery patrol over a sustained period without the need for refueling (Vietnam News Agency Bulletin, 2015b, c).
18 Notably, of the special unit of 12 patrol vessels established in April 2016 to be exclusively deployed for patrolling the waters of the Senkaku/Diaoyu Islands, 10 are newly built, 1,500-ton patrol vessels, but there is also a pair of helicopter-equipped patrol vessels transferred from other JCG regional commands and refurbished (Kyodo News, 2016a).
19 For example, during the stand-off, a high-ranking CPV delegation visited China. And not long after the oil rig stand-off died down, the CPV dispatched a special envoy, Le Hong Anh, a member of the party's Politburo, to Beijing (Vietnam News Brief Service, 2014k, l).
20 For example, not only did the Vietnamese government forcibly disperse the anti-China protests, but Vietnam's northern province of Ha Giang and China's Yunnan province inked a pact to boost cross-border economic cooperation. Hanoi also urged the northernmost province of Quang Ninh to preserve economic ties and trade with China. 'Politics: Vietnam Northern Province to Boost Economic Ties with China's Yunnan' (Vietnam News Brief Service, 2014g); and 'Politics: Vietnam PM Asks Northernmost Province to Maintain Economic Ties with China' (Vietnam News Brief Service, 2014h).
21 In 2014, Vietnam's exports to China amounted to US$14.9 billion, while imports from China stood at US$43.9 billion. These figures increased in 2015 to US$16.9 billion and US$50.3 billion, respectively. At the same time, Vietnam's trade deficit with China rose from almost US$29 billion in 2014 to US$33.5 billion in 2015. Data extracted and compiled from the General Statistics Office of Vietnam. Available at: https://www.gso.gov.vn/default_en.aspx?tabid=626.
22 Even though China ranked ninth among foreign investors in Vietnam in 2014, the greatest concern stemmed from the fact that Chinese contractors held up to 90 per cent of Vietnam's engineering, procurement and infrastructure construction projects. Vietnamese lawmakers reportedly blamed Chinese contractors for stymying the implementation of 30 national power and transport infrastructure projects (Vietnam News Brief Service, 2014b). Vietnam's apparel industry is another example, having found it difficult to wean itself off reliance upon China in the garment and textile sector (Vietnam News Brief Service, 2014a).

REFERENCES

Agence France Press, 2011. 'Vietnam Says China Fishing Boat Rams Research Ship', 9 June.
Akita, H., 2015. 'Japan's "Submarine Killer" Tantalizes West', *Nikkei Asian Review*, 23 July.
ANN Asia News Network, 2014. 'Vietnam Riots: China Warns Vietnam Trade Will Suffer', 21 May.
Armstrong, R., 2014. 'Interview: Vietnam Expects Japan Coastguard Ships Next Year – Vice Defence Minister', Reuters News, 1 June.
BBC Monitoring Asia Pacific, 2011. 'Vietnam Issues Statement on 26 May South China Sea Incident', 31 May.

Commission on the Limits of the Continental Shelf (CLCS), 2009. 'Outer Limits of the Continental Shelf beyond 200 Nautical Miles from the Baselines: Submissions to the Commission: Submission by the Socialist Republic of Viet Nam, Division for Ocean Affairs and the Law of the Sea, United Nations', at: www.un.org/Depts/los/clcs_new/submissions_files/submission_vnm_37_2009.htm.

Dow Jones International News, 2011. 'Foreign Ships Harassed Norwegian Ship near Vietnam Oil Field – Report', 1 June.

General Statistics Office of Vietnam, 2016. Import-Export Turnover, at: www.gso.gov.vn/default_en.aspx?tabid=626 (accessed 1 February 2016).

International Institute of Strategic Studies, 2018. *Military Balance 2018* (Oxford, UK: Oxford University Press).

Japan Economic Newswire, 1990. 'Vietnam Concerned about Japan Sending Troops Abroad', 27 October.

Japan Economic Newswire, 2000. 'Japan, Vietnam Agree to Study Joint Rescue of Civilian Ships', 4 May.

The Japan News, 2013. 'Kounotori Carries Vietnam's Mini-Satellite', 7 August.

The Japan News, 2016. 'MSDF Seaborne Patrolling Action Planned to Guard Senkakus', 13 January.

The Japan Times, 2015a. 'Japan to Bolster Ship Patrols near Senkakus', 1 January.

The Japan Times, 2015b. 'Japan, Vietnam Affirm Partnership on Maritime Security', 16 March.

Jennings, G., 2013. 'LAAD Defence and Security 2013: US Mulls P-3 MPA Sale to Vietnam', *Jane's Navy International*, 11 April.

Jiji Press English News Service, 2011. '(Update) Japan, Vietnam to Beef Up Defense Cooperation', 24 October.

Jiji Press English News Service, 2015a. 'Japan to Provide Vietnam with More Ships for Maritime Security', 15 September.

Jiji Press English News Service, 2015b. 'Japan, Vietnam Foreign Ministers Share Concerns over China', 31 July.

Jiji Press English News Service, 2016. '2 Japanese MSDF Patrol Planes Visit Vietnam', 17 February.

Kearsley, H. J., 1992. *Maritime Power and the Twenty-First Century* (Aldershot, UK: Dartmouth).

Koh, S. L. C., 2016. 'Vietnam's Master Plan for the South China Sea', *The Diplomat*, 4 February.

Kyodo News, 2013a. 'Japan Eyes Providing Patrol Ships to Vietnam amid S. China Sea Row', 15 December.

Kyodo News, 2013b. 'Japan, Vietnam Agree to Beef Up Maritime Security Cooperation', 16 September.

Kyodo News, 2013c. 'Japanese Defense Chief Visits Cam Ranh Bay Naval Base in Vietnam', 17 September.

Kyodo News, 2013d. 'Vietnam, Japan Consolidate bilateral Ties', 13 September.

Kyodo News, 2014a. 'Japan to Give 6 Ships to Vietnam to Help Boost Security Capability', 1 August.

Kyodo News, 2014b. 'Japan Foreign Minister Eyes Vietnam Trip Later This Month: Sources', 10 July.

Kyodo News, 2015a. 'Japan Defense Vessel to Stop at Vietnam Naval Base in S. China Sea', 6 November.

Kyodo News, 2015b. 'Japan Delivers 2 Boats to Vietnam to Help Boost Security Capability', 3 November.

Kyodo News, 2015c. 'Politics: Japan Ready to Boost Defense Ties with Vietnam: Senior Legislator', Vietnam News Brief Service, 21 January.
Kyodo News, 2016a. 'Japan Deploys 12 Coast Guard Ships to Patrol Senkakus', 4 April.
Kyodo News, 2016b. 'Update 1: Japan, Vietnam to Step Up Maritime Security Cooperation', 5 May.
Luan, K., 2003. 'Japanese Escort Ships Visit City', *The Saigon Times Daily*, 14 April.
The Mainichi Shimbun, 2016. 'Japan Signals Readiness to Deploy SDF Vessels to Senkakus to Counter Chinese Incursions', 12 January.
Ministry of Foreign Affairs of Japan, 2010. 'Japan-Viet Nam Joint Statement on the Strategic Partnership for Peace and Prosperity in Asia', 31 October, at: www.mofa.go.jp/region/asia-paci/vietnam/joint1010.html (accessed 1 February 2018).
Ministry of Foreign Affairs of Japan, 2011. 'Japan-Viet Nam Joint Statement on the Actions Taken under Strategic Partnership for Peace and Prosperity in Asia', 31 October, at: www.mofa.go.jp/mofaj/kaidan/s_noda/vietnam1110/pdfs/1.pdf (accessed 1 February 2018).
Ministry of Foreign Affairs of Japan, 2013, 'Prime Minister Shinzo Abe's Visit to Viet Nam (Overview)', 17 January, at: www.mofa.go.jp/region/asia-paci/pmv_1301/vietnam.html (accessed 1 February 2018).
Ministry of Foreign Affairs of Japan, 2014. 'Japan-Viet Nam Joint Statement on the Establishment of the Extensive Strategic Partnership for Peace and Prosperity in Asia', 18 March, at: www.mofa.go.jp/files/000031617.pdf (accessed 1 February 2018).
Ministry of Foreign Affairs of Japan, 2015a. 'Cabinet Decision on the Development Cooperation Charter', at: www.mofa.go.jp/policy/oda/page_000138.html (accessed 1 February 2018).
Ministry of Foreign Affairs of Japan. 2015b. 'Joint Vision Statement on Japan-Viet Nam Relations', 15 September, at: www.mofa.go.jp/files/000099707.pdf (accessed 1 February 2018).
Platts Commodity News, 2011. 'Second Vietnamese Seismic Ship Harassed in South China Sea: Report', 1 June.
Press Trust of India, 2014. 'India, Vietnam and Japan Should Have Better Cooperation on Issues with China', 13 August.
Reuters News, 2011. 'Update 1 – Vietnam Says Chinese boats Harassed Oil Exploration Ship', 27 May.
Reuters News, 2014. 'Japan PM Says Will Take Time to Provide Patrol Ships to Vietnam', 28 May.
Reuters News, 2015. 'China Moves Controversial Oil Rig back towards Vietnam Coast', 26 June.
Reuters News, 2016. 'Vietnam Asks Japan for Vessels to Strengthen Coastguard', 5 May.
Sasaki, M., 2016. 'Maritime SDF Destroyers Visit Port in Vietnam for 1st Time', Asia & Japan Watch, 12 April.
Sieg, L. and Takenaka, K., 2014. 'Vietnam Eyes Philippine Court Case while Weighing Options on China Row', Reuters News, 22 May.
Timberlake, I., 2011. 'Vietnam Complains to China as Sea Tensions Rise', Agence France Presse, 9 June.
Tuoi Tre Newspaper, 2016. 'Japanese Naval Ships Visit Cam Ranh Port in Vietnam', 13 April.
Vietnam News Agency Bulletin, 2012. 'Minister Lauds Growing Military Cooperation with Japan', 18 January.

Vietnam News Agency Bulletin, 2013a. 'Japan Coast Guard Vessel Visits Da Nang', 30 July.
Vietnam News Agency Bulletin, 2013b. 'Japan's Naval Defence Ships Visit Da Nang', 19 October.
Vietnam News Agency Bulletin, 2013c. 'Vietnam, Japan Hold Second Defence Policy Dialogue', 9 August.
Vietnam News Agency Bulletin, 2013d. 'UPDATE1: Japan Pledges 54 Bil. Yen in Loans to Vietnam for Infrastructure-Building', 12 September.
Vietnam News Agency Bulletin, 2014. 'Vietnam Proposes Stronger Defence Ties with Japan', 23 June.
Vietnam News Agency Bulletin, 2015a. 'Japanese Patrol Ship Anchors in Da Nang', 10 May.
Vietnam News Agency Bulletin, 2015b. 'Politics: Vietnam Fisheries Surveillance Receives First Patrol Ship Donated by Japan', 5 August.
Vietnam News Agency Bulletin, 2015c. 'Japanese-Funded Ship Handed Over to Vietnam', 5 August.
Vietnam News Agency Bulletin, 2016. 'Vietnam Attends Int'l Fleet Review in India', 6 February.
Vietnam News Brief Service, 1999. 'Two Japanese Ships Arrive in Vietnam', 7 May.
Vietnam News Brief Service, 2003. 'Politics & Law – Vietnam, Japan Bolster Military Cooperation', 11 July.
Vietnam News Brief Service, 2007. 'Politics: Vietnam, Japan Tightening Military Ties', 24 January.
Vietnam News Brief Service, 2010. 'Politics: Vietnam Partners with Japan to Tap Rare Earth', 1 November.
Vietnam News Brief Service, 2011. 'Politics: Two Japan Naval Ships to Visit Vietnam Port on Sept 17–19', 16 September.
Vietnam News Brief Service, 2012a. 'Politics: Japanese Shikishima Ship Visiting Vietnam Northern Port', 7 September.
Vietnam News Brief Service, 2012b. 'Politics: Three Japanese Warships Dock at Vietnam Northern Port', 12 March.
Vietnam News Brief Service, 2013a. 'Politics: Vietnam, Japan Affirm Maritime Cooperation at 2nd Defense Dialogue', 12 August.
Vietnam News Brief Service, 2013b. 'Politics: Vietnam, Japan Enhance Defense Ties amid Escalating Tensions in West Pacific', 16 April.
Vietnam News Brief Service, 2014a. 'Business: Vietnam Apparel Sector Finds Hard to Reduce Reliance on China: Economist', 12 June.
Vietnam News Brief Service, 2014b. 'Business: Vietnam Borrows Little from China for Development Projects: Minister', 11 June.
Vietnam News Brief Service, 2014c. 'Politics: Defense Cooperation to be Focus of Japan FM's Trip to Vietnam', 31 July.
Vietnam News Brief Service, 2014d. 'Politics: Japanese Landing Ship with Marines of Allies Arrives in Vietnam Central City', 7 June.
Vietnam News Brief Service, 2014e. 'Politics: Vietnam Expects Bigger Role of Japan in East Asia: Spokesman', 4 July.
Vietnam News Brief Service, 2014f. 'Politics: Vietnam Expects to Receive Patrol Ships from Japan Next Year', 2 June.
Vietnam News Brief Service, 2014g. 'Politics: Vietnam Northern Province to Boost Economic Ties with China's Yunnan', 22 May.

Vietnam News Brief Service, 2014h. 'Politics: Vietnam PM Asks Northernmost Province to Maintain Economic Ties with China', 5 June.

Vietnam News Brief Service, 2014i. 'Politics: Vietnam, Japan Enhance Maritime Security amid East Sea Escalating Tension', 23 May.

Vietnam News Brief Service, 2014j. 'Politics: Vietnam, Japan to Enhance Defense Research, Training amid Sea Tensions', 24 June.

Vietnam News Brief Service, 2014k. 'Politics: Vietnam Politburo Member to Visit China', 25 August.

Vietnam News Brief Service, 2014l. 'Vietnam Sends More Cadres to China to Learn Party Building amid Sea Tensions', 30 June.

Vietnam News Brief Service, 2015. 'Politics: Two Japanese Warships Dock at Vietnam Danang Port for Five-day Visit', 16 April.

Vietnam News Brief Service, 2016a. 'Politics: Japan Remains Close Long-term Strategic Partner of Vietnam: Newly-elected PM', 6 May.

Vietnam News Brief Service, 2016b. 'Politics: Vietnam Newly-Elected President Reaffirms to Strengthen Bilateral Ties with Japan', 22 April.

Vietnam News Brief Service, 2016c. 'Politics: Vietnam Re-Elected Communist Leader Reaffirms Special Ties with China', 1 February.

Vietnam News Summary, 2013. 'Vietnam Reinforces Defence Ties with Countries', 3 June.

Yoshida, R., 2014. 'Vietnamese Leader Welcomes Fresh Aid from Japan', *Japan Times*, 19 March.

Zhang Jianhua, 2016. 'Developing Bilateral Ties with China Priority in Vietnam's Foreign Policy: President', Xinhua News Agency, 5 May.

9

The Japanese perspective on the security partnership with Vietnam

Bjørn Elias Mikalsen Grønning

Introduction

IN A MARCH 2000 meeting between the foreign ministers of Japan and Vietnam, the Japanese side proposed the establishment of bilateral politico-military consultations (Ministry of Foreign Affairs of Japan, 2000). The proposal marked the entry of security cooperation with Vietnam on Japan's public and official security agenda. While irregular bilateral working-level security consultations ensued in the decade to come, 2011 marks a turning point, as Japan–Vietnam security relations refocused markedly towards substantial cooperation with an explicit maritime orientation. As of 2017, the security partnership stands on the verge of military significance.

This development marks one of the emerging security partnerships in a Japanese unidirectional turned multidirectional security diplomacy, as scrutinised in this volume. Putting this particular case front and centre, this chapter examines the nature and objectives of Japan's emerging security partnership with Vietnam and the incentives and constraints operating on Tokyo.

The chapter argues that Japan's emerging security partnership with Vietnam primarily reflects an aspiration to assist and induce Vietnam's continued resistance against Chinese maritime coercion. China's maritime rise and erosion of the maritime order represents its fundamental driver, but it has been further provoked, invited and facilitated by Japan–US alliance dynamics and domestic nationalism. Recent changes in Japan's domestic context vastly expand its potential for developing the security partnership, but this potential is severely negated by considerable constraints operating on Tokyo. Consistently with its limited objectives, Japan is likely to seek to broaden bilateral maritime security cooperation on the verge of military significance.

China's maritime rise and the erosion of the regional order

With the exception of the Taiwan Straits, China has traditionally asserted its national interests primarily inward on the Asian continent. In the last decade, this has changed, as China's two most recent presidents have publicly declared (China Internet Information Center, 2012; Yoon, 2015), and increasingly projected emerging maritime ambitions. China has turned towards the Asian seas as a domain in which to assert its national interest.

China's vast investment in naval warfare capabilities is the single most telling indicator of Beijing's forceful turn to the Asian seas as a new domain in which to pursue its national interests. As naval specialist O'Rourke (2016) reported to the US Congress, China is 'building a modern and regionally powerful navy' through a 'naval modernization effort [that] encompasses a broad array of platform and weapon acquisition programs'. Another indication is the growing presence of Chinese military and paramilitary assets in the seas and maritime airspace of East Asia and the mounting number of reports of Chinese vessels engaged in manoeuvres that are harassing or dangerous towards their foreign counterparts (Dickie and Hille, 2011; Fackler, 2013, 2014; *New York Times*, 2009). Yet another is China's increasingly forceful pursuit of maritime territorial claims that conflict with its neighbours, promoting its claim using military assets (Dominguez and Tsuneoka, 2016), paramilitary assets (Kyodo, 2016a; Takenaka, 2012), land reclamation on disputed maritime features and fitting military-grade infrastructure and assets atop them (*Guardian*, 2016). Finally, China in 2013 established a maritime East China Sea Air Defence Identification Zone (ADIZ) (BBC News, 2013), interpreted by many as a move to support its sovereignty claims in these seas. As Dutton (2014) reports, China's establishment of an East China Sea ADIZ 'was entirely consistent with this strategy to use legal language to increase Chinese jurisdictional control incrementally over the near seas' (p. 13). The same would ostensibly apply to the much-anticipated Chinese ADIZ in the South China Sea (Chan, 2016).

In this context, the immediate concern for Japan is China's assertion of its claims of sovereignty to East Asian maritime territory. China has mounted an increasingly staunch challenge against Japan's administrative control over maritime territory over which both parties claim inherent sovereignty. Specifically, this applies to the East China Sea islands that go by the name of Senkaku in Japan (Ministry of Foreign Affairs of Japan, 2016b) and Diaoyu in China (State Council Information Office, 2012).

However, the broader long-term implications of China's maritime rise are more worrisome for Japan. The collapse of the Soviet Union and the end of the Cold War left Japan in the relatively comfortable position of being the protectee of the sole global superpower. Since then, China's vast accumulation of wealth and its translation of this into military capabilities have shifted the power balance dramatically in China's favour (Grønning, 2014). Recognising this development,

Japan's National Security Strategy (NSS) notes that 'Since the beginning of the twenty first century, the balance of power in the international community has been changing on an unprecedented scale' (National Security Council of Japan, 2013: 6). In its most recent annual White Paper, the Ministry of Defense (MOD) observes that 'a shift in the global balance of power beginning with the military rise of China' is significantly changing the patterns of US global involvement (Ministry of Defense of Japan, 2016b: 9).

China's maritime ambitions and vast investment in sea power reveal that the rising power is positioning itself and rapidly developing the capabilities to contest US naval predominance in maritime East Asia. This represents a major strategic challenge for Japan, as it threatens to undo the very fundament of Japan's national security structure. Supported by its own considerable naval and paranaval forces, Tokyo relies on US regional naval dominance as the bulwark of a regional maritime order that protects its top-ranked national interests. This entails the security of Japan's territory and its nationals (National Security Council of Japan, 2013: 20, 4) but also, as a nation 'surrounded by the sea on all sides', the security of its maritime trade routes, its sea lanes of communication (SLOCs) (National Security Council of Japan, 2013: 2). 'Sea lanes of communication', the NSS notes, 'are critical to Japan due to its dependence on the maritime transport of natural and energy resources from the Middle East' (National Security Council of Japan, 2013: 17). As 'the basis of peace and prosperity', the MOD presents maintenance and strengthening of the 'Open and Stable Seas order' as an integral part of Japan's defence policy (Ministry of Defense of Japan, 2013b: 4).

This explains why Japan is strategically mindful not only of events in the East China Sea, where territorial integrity is at stake, but also of events in the adjacent South China Sea, which is not only subject to the same maritime regional order but also represents the jugular connecting Japan to its vital overseas resource supplies (National Security Council of Japan, 2013: 17). Indicative of this sensitivity, in 2015 the MOD began publishing and updating a report dedicated to China's activities in the South China Sea and the implications thereof for Japan's security (Ministry of Defense of Japan, 2016a). Japan witnesses that the regional order is under Chinese siege in both of its near seas. As the NSS notes, 'China has taken actions that can be regarded as attempts to change the status quo by coercion based on their own assertions, which are incompatible with the existing order of international law, in the maritime and aerial domains, including the East China Sea and the South China Sea' (National Security Council of Japan, 2013: 12).

Defending the maritime order against Chinese coercion

Recognising that China's maritime emergence erodes the regional maritime order and its material anchor, Japan has ventured onto a diplomatic campaign to defend, support and strengthen its normative standing. Japan sees Vietnam as a valuable partner in this venture, as their interests align in resisting Chinese maritime coercion in the seas of East Asia. This is the nature of Japan's emerging security partnership with Vietnam.

Essentially, Japan's defence of the regional maritime order entails the promotion of the rule of law as the governing principle of the maritime domain. Japan, the NSS declares, 'will promote regional efforts and play a leading role in creating a shared recognition that reinforcement of the maritime order governed by law and rules and not by coercion is indispensable for peace and prosperity of the international community as a whole' (National Security Council of Japan, 2013: 29). Prime Minister Abe's three principles of the rule of law at sea render meaning to Japan's conception of the law based maritime order: 'The first principle is that states shall make and clarify their claims based on international law. The second is that states shall not use force or coercion in trying to drive their claims. The third principle is that states shall seek to settle disputes by peaceful means' (Abe, 2014).

The NSS clarifies that Japan will pursue leadership in promoting this maritime rule of law 'through close cooperation with other countries' (National Security Council of Japan, 2013: 16). While this, traditionally, has meant cooperation with the US, long its exclusive security partner, Japan has expanded its security cooperative ambitions to a broader set of partner states, testament to which is the present volume. Indeed, the NSS and the National Defense Program Guidelines (NDPG), respectively, declare that in order to manage security challenges and accomplish the objectives of its security policy, Japan *needs to* (National Security Council of Japan, 2013: 14) and *will* (Ministry of Defense of Japan, 2013b: 5) 'expand and deepen cooperative relationships with other countries' than the US. The NSS focuses this ambition on the maritime domain, stating that Japan will 'promote maritime security cooperation with other countries', placing particular emphasis on those 'partners on the sea lanes who share strategic interest with Japan' (National Security Council of Japan, 2013: 16, 17).

Vietnam sits along Japan's SLOC in the South China Sea. It moreover, as noted in Collin Lean's chapter in this volume, has overlapping territorial claims with China. Like Japan in the East China Sea, Tokyo observes Vietnam to be at the receiving end of China's coercive diplomacy over these overlapping claims. The MOD calls attention to how 'China's unilateral, large-scale, and rapid land reclamation and building of facilities have heightened tension' in the South China Sea (Ministry of Defense of Japan, 2016b: 98). In its report on Chinese activities in the South China Sea, the MOD highlights specific examples of Chinese maritime coercion targeting Vietnam, including the obstruction and sabotage of resource exploration activities, the ramming and sinking of fishing vessels, and the dispatch of an oil rig with naval and paranaval escort (Ministry of Defense of Japan, 2016a: 3).

Japan also observes that Vietnam shares its position that maritime disputes are to be settled not by force and coercion but by peaceful and legal means (Ministry of Foreign Affairs of Japan, 2014a, 2016a; National Security Council of Japan, 2013: 24). This, in Tokyo's view, aligns Japan's and Vietnam's strategic interests in resisting Chinese maritime coercion and defending the regional maritime order. However, considering Hanoi's geo-strategic vulnerabilities vis-à-vis Beijing, Tokyo does not take its alignment in this matter for granted. Coinciding with its own rising threat perceptions since 2010 (Grønning, 2014), Japan has accordingly developed the bilateral security partnership, aspiring to assist and induce by security and defence diplomatic means Vietnam's continued resistance against China's coercion and cement its alignment as a co-defender of the regional maritime order.

One element in this venture is Japan's public declarations, as displayed in successive joint statements since 2011, of its alignment with Vietnam's position on the maritime rule of law as the governing principle in the South China Sea and the peaceful settlement of its territorial disputes. In the most recent joint statement, Prime Minister Abe 'highly praised Viet Nam's efforts toward the settlement of issues including those in the area of maritime security based on the principle of the rule of law' and 'stressed that any unilateral and coercive action to challenge peace and stability should not be overlooked' (Ministry of Foreign Affairs of Japan, 2011, 2014a).

Tokyo's aspiration has also taken the form of maritime capacity-building. Commencing in 2012, this initially consisted of technical assistance in the form of seminars and training to enhance Vietnam's capacity in maritime security and safety, underwater medicine, peacekeeping operations, flight safety, and humanitarian assistance/disaster relief (Japan Coast Guard Academy, no date; Ministry of Defense of Japan, 2014). In 2014, however, Japan ventured into material capacity-building in agreeing to transfer six decommissioned patrol vessels to the Vietnam Coast Guard (VCG) in the form of grant aid at a value of 500 million yen for the enhancement of Vietnam's maritime law enforcement capabilities (Ministry of Foreign Affairs of Japan, 2014b, c). While this initial material capacity-building effort was rather modest (Thayer, 2014), Prime Minister Abe revealed following a Japan–Vietnam summit meeting in January 2017 that Japan, upon Vietnam's request, had decided to further equip the VCG with six newly built patrol vessels (Kantei (The Prime Minister of Japan and His Cabinet), 2017).

A third element has been increasing and increasingly substantive bilateral defence interaction. The 2011 joint statement introduced ambitions of engaging in high-level military visits and mutual naval port calls as new elements of bilateral military interaction, which had thus far been largely limited to irregular subcabinet and working-level dialogues. Reflecting their ambitions of jointly deflecting Chinese coercive advances in the seas of East

Asia, Prime Minister Noda and Prime Minister Dung, the joint statement noted, had agreed that such efforts would contribute 'to the peace and stability of the region' (Ministry of Foreign Affairs of Japan, 2011). During a September 2013 visit to Cam Ranh Bay, Vietnam's naval stronghold, Defence Minister Onodera stated his expectation that military interactions were set to expand (Ministry of Defense of Japan, 2013a). Indeed, two Japan Maritime Self-Defense Force (JMSDF) destroyers called port at Cam Ranh Bay for the first time amidst a South China Sea tour in April 2016 (Kyodo, 2016b), succeeded by a second port call by two JMSDF ships in May (Kajiwara, 2017). Reflecting the nature of these events, a government official noted in advance that Japan's naval presence at Cam Ranh Bay would 'help deter Chinese military activity in the South China Sea' (Nikkei Asian Review, 2015).

Japan's ambition of vitalising its defence interaction with Vietnam is also reflected in its dispatch of additional defence attachés to its diplomatic mission in Hanoi (Jiji, 2016). More importantly, Japan reached a bilateral agreement to refuel JMSDF P-3C Orion maritime patrol aircraft at air bases in Vietnam as they return to Japan from anti-piracy missions in the Gulf of Aden, seeing Japanese P-3Cs touching down at Da Nang in February 2016 (Nikkei Asian Review, 2016a). While these interactions are of limited military significance, they may serve as a stepping-stone to future interaction of greater military significance. One such possibility is a bilateral military intelligence-sharing agreement Japan is reportedly pursuing, which, depending on its configuration, would potentially add elements of military significance to the Japan–Vietnam security partnership by enabling exchange of classified information on defence equipment and, notably, Chinese military movements and activities in the South China Sea (Nikkei Asian Review, 2016b).

Alliance politics by new means

US alliance dynamics further incentivise and facilitate Japan's development and substantiation of the Vietnam security partnership. In response to China's emerging challenge to US regional dominance, Japan has sought to augment the aggregate power output of the Japan–US alignment by strengthening its own defence capabilities, promoting and facilitating the expansion of US defence capabilities in the region, and enhancing defence cooperation between them (Grønning, 2014). US interests overlap with those of Japan on this point, as the Obama administration had pursued its 'rebalancing' to Asia while expecting from regional allies, not least Japan, greater engagement in and contributions to their own and regional security (Bowers and Grønning, 2017: 160).

Japan's embrace and substantiation of security partnerships beyond the US thus appear to answer Washington's expectations of Tokyo's more active role in regional security (Ministry of Defense of Japan, 2016a: 25). The

Guidelines for Japan–US Defense Cooperation, released in 2016, advocates this linkage, declaring that '[p]roactive cooperation with partners will contribute to maintaining and enhancing regional and international peace and security' (Ministry of Defense of Japan, 2015). Moreover, Japan's material capacity-building of the VCG, the most substantial feature of their security partnership to date, implements policies initially outlined within the parameters of the Japan–US alliance. Specifically, the bilateral Security Consultative Committee issued a joint statement in April 2012 declaring that 'the Government of Japan [...] plans to take various measures to promote safety in the region, including strategic use of official development assistance, for example through providing coastal states with patrol boats' (Security Consultative Committee, 2012).

Moreover, US alliance dynamics appear to invite the specific directionality of Japan's new security proactivity towards Vietnam. Japan observes a steady forging of stronger US–Vietnam defence ties and cooperation since 2005 (Ministry of Defense of Japan, 2010: 85). Japan highlights US capacity-building of Vietnamese maritime forces, joint naval exercises with and port calls by the US navy, the partial and, in the end, full lifting of the US-imposed arms embargo, and joint declarations to proceed with bilateral trade in defence equipment and technologies as particularly notable developments (Ministry of Defense of Japan, 2016b: 96). These developments in US–Vietnam security relations legitimise Hanoi as a recipient of the Japanese regional security partnership outreach stipulated within the parameters of the Japan–US alliance. Moreover, they underscore that Japan's security partnership policies towards Vietnam represent new features of the Japan–US alliance itself. As Japan itself consistently stresses, its new security partnerships are being developed with the Japan–US alliance as the cornerstone (Ministry of Defense of Japan, 2013b: 5; National Security Council of Japan, 2013: 14). The US factor accordingly serves as an international facilitator of Japan's new international security partnership approach in general and partly explains the selection of Vietnam as a recipient.

Domestic nationalism

Domestic processes in Japan have invited the recent progression in its security partnership with Vietnam. For one, partaking in and shaping the international security environment in pursuit of national interests is consistent with core ideas in the nationalism associated with much of the Japanese political elite: Japan as a tier one nation in terms of means and extent of influence in international politics. As Prime Minister Abe himself proclaimed shortly after the election that brought him back to power, 'Japan is not, and will never be, a Tier-two country. [...] I am back, and so shall Japan be' (Abe, 2013). These elite nationalist currents have energised Japan's security partnership outreach to Vietnam.

Moreover, Japanese nationalism has further stoked Chinese maritime coercion against Japan in the East China Sea, thus helping to explain Tokyo's consolidation of Vietnam security ties. In 2012, the Government of Japan was forced, it claims (Ministry of Foreign Affairs of Japan, 2012), to intervene in the planned purchase of the East China Sea islands by Tokyo's outspoken Governor Shintaro Ishihara, whose motives they believed to be of nationalist nature and severely damaging to Sino-Japanese relations, by themselves appropriating the islands. The intervention failed to achieve its declared objective, as the number of Chinese vessels identified as operating within the territorial sea (12 nautical miles) and contiguous zone (24 nautical miles) of the islands in an apparent challenge to Japan's administrative control increased markedly (Ministry of Foreign Affairs of Japan, 2017).

Great opportunities, greater constraints

Developments in the domestic context present Japan with the opportunity to vastly expand its security partnership with Vietnam. Implementing intentions outlined in the NSS (National Security Council of Japan, 2013: 30), Japan in 2015 broadened the scope of its strategic use of official development assistance (ODA) by allowing the provision of aid to foreign militaries for non-military purposes (Cabinet of Japan, 2015: 10–11). Moreover, Japan in 2014 established a new arms exports regime conditionally permitting Japan's foreign exports of arms, defence equipment and military technology (Ministry of Foreign Affairs of Japan, 2014d). These new domestic paralegal arrangements significantly broaden the potential of Japan's security partnership with Vietnam within arms trade and capacity-building.

Another major domestic development broadening the scope of the bilateral security partnership is the loosening of Japan's constitutional constraints upon the application of military power. A 2014 Cabinet decision formally and officially reinterpreted Japan's Constitution to conditionally permit its exercise of the right of collective self-defence (Cabinet of Japan, 2014). In 2015, the Japanese Diet passed a package of bills aligning Japan's security legislation with the new constitutional provisions (Ministry of Defense of Japan, 2016b: 213–227). This new legal framework, legalizing the use of armed force on behalf of a 'foreign country that is in a close relationship with Japan', permits, at Japanese decision makers' discretion, a vast expansion of Japan's bilateral security cooperation by operating the Japan Self-Defense Forces (JSDF) in defence of Vietnam.

However, powerful constraints and disincentives largely counter these new opportunities to expand the bilateral security partnership into uncharted military terrain. A mandatory Diet approval clause was inserted into the new legal provisions on the exercise of the right to collective self-defence to secure the support of the junior government party Komeito (Komeito, 2015). This, coupled with a Japanese public still deeply sceptical about military escapades, as reflected in the persistent disapproval of the new legislation (Kyodo, 2015), implies a high threshold for engaging the JSDF in collective self-defence in general and, in particular, beyond operations in defence of its US ally. A more plausible scenario involving a much more modest application of Japanese military power is the contemplated dispatch of naval assets to conduct declared freedom of navigation operations (FONOPs) in the South China Sea (Hayashi and Tsuneoka, 2015; Kelly and Kubo, 2015; Lubold and Page, 2015).

Furthermore, Japan's own limited capacity constrains its ability to expand significantly its ODA-based maritime capacity-building efforts. China's staunch challenge to Japan's administrative control over the East China Sea islands puts unprecedented pressure on the Japan Coast Guard (JCG), forcing it to extend the service life of assets to meet the Chinese challenge. This dynamic has already interfered with Japan's capacity-building efforts towards Vietnam, as the increasingly demanding surveillance duties of the JCG in the East China Sea forced Japan to postpone its planned decommissioning and transfer of JCG patrol ships to the VCG (Reuters News, 2014). Further substantiating and strengthening the bilateral security partnership via trade in arms is likely the preferable option for Japan, as this could not only strengthen the capacity of Vietnam to resist Chinese coercion but also stimulate Japan's struggling defence industry and economy.

Conclusion

This chapter has depicted the Japan–Vietnam security partnership as one developing from a security talk shop in its early days to the verge of military significance after 2011. It interprets Japan's development of this security partnership as a response to the Chinese challenge to US naval hegemony and the maritime order in East Asia. It has also, however, been further catalysed by US alliance dynamics and Japanese nationalism. Japan's primary motive in developing this particular security partnership is to defend the regional maritime order from Chinese maritime coercion by assisting and inciting Vietnam's continued alignment in this matter. Domestic security reform has opened up new avenues by which Japan can legally assist Vietnam militarily, but as material realities and political constraints linger, the Japan–Vietnam security partnership continues to remain on the verge of military significance.

References

Abe, S., 2013. 'Japan Is Back', Ministry of Foreign Affairs of Japan, 22 February, at: www.mofa.go.jp/announce/pm/abe/us_20130222en.html (accessed 11 April 2016).

Abe, S., 2014. 'The 13th IISS Asian Security Summit -The Shangri-La Dialogue-Keynote Address by Shinzō Abe, Prime Minister, Japan', 30 May, at: www.mofa.go.jp/fp/nsp/page4e_000086.html (accessed 1 March 2018).

BBC News. 2013. 'China Establishes "Air-Defence Zone" over East China Sea', 23 November, at: bbc.com/news/world-asia-25062525 (accessed 10 March 2017).

Bowers, I. and Grønning, B. E. M., 2017. 'Protecting the Status Quo: Japan's Response to the Rise of China. Strategic Adjustment and the Rise of China', in Ross, R. S. and Tunsjø, Ø. (eds), *Strategic Adjustment and the Rise of China: Power and Politics in East Asia* (Ithaca: Cornell University Press).

Cabinet of Japan, 2014. 'Cabinet Decision on Development of Seamless Security Legislation to Ensure Japan's Survival and Protect Its People', at: www.mofa.go.jp/fp/nsp/page23e_000273.html (accessed 25 May 2015).

Cabinet of Japan, 2015. 'Cabinet Decision on the Development Cooperation Charter', 10 February, at: www. mofa.go.jp/files/000067701.pdf (accessed 24 October 2016).

Chan, M., 2016. 'Beijing Ready to Impose Air Defence Identification Zone in South China Sea Pending US Moves', 1 June, at: www.scmp.com/news/china/article/1960954/beijing-ready-impose-air-defence-identification-zone-south-china-sea (accessed 22 October 2017).

China Internet Information Center, 2012. 'Report of Hu Jintao to the 18th CPC national Congress', 16 November, at: www.china.org.cn/china/18th_cpc_congress/2012-11/16/content_27137540.htm (accessed 8 September, 2016).

Dickie, M. and Hille, K., 2011. 'Japan Protests over China Military Incident', *Financial Times*, 8 March.

Dutton, P. A., 2014. 'China's Maritime Disputes in the East and South China Seas', *Naval War College Review*, 67(3): 7–18.

Fackler, M., 2013. 'Japan Says China Aimed Military Radar at Ship', *New York Times*, 5 February, at: www.nytimes.com/2013/02/06/world/asia/japan-china-islands-dispute.html.

Fackler, M., 2014. 'Japan Protests Chinese Flybys over East China Sea', *New York Times*, 11 June, at: nytimes.com/2014/06/12/world/asia/japan-protests-chinese-flybys-over-east-china-sea.html (accessed 10 March 2017)

Grønning, B. E. M., 2014. 'Japan's Shifting Military Priorities: Counterbalancing China's Rise', *Asian Security*, 10(1): 1–21.

The Guardian, 2016. 'China Has Reclaimed 3,200 Acres in the South China Sea, says Pentagon', 13 May, at: theguardian.com/world/2016/may/13/pentagon-report-china-reclaimed-3200-acres-south-china-sea (accessed 10 March 2017).

Hayashi, Y. and Tsuneoka, C., 2015. 'Japan Open to Joining U.S. in South China Sea Patrols', *The Wall Street Journal*, at: wsj.com/articles/japan-may-join-u-s-in-south-china-sea-patrols-1435149493 (accessed 1 March 2018).

Japan Coast Guard Academy, no date. 'The Coast Guard Capacity Improvement Program to Secure Safety and Environmental Conservation in Asian Oceans', at: ajoc.jcga.or.jp/programs_en.html (accessed 17 January 2016).

Jiji, 2016. 'Japan to Increase Defense Attaches in Philippines, Vietnam', *The Japan Times*, 11 August.

Kajiwara, M., 2017. 'MSDF Helicopter Carrier Arrives for Major Pacific Naval Exercise', *Asahi Shinbun*, 21 May, at: www.asahi.com/ajw/articles/AJ201705210030.html (accessed 23 February 2018).

Kantei (The Prime Minister of Japan and His Cabinet), 2017. 'Press Conference by Prime Minister Shinzo Abe Following His Visit to the Philippines, Australia, Indonesia and Viet Nam', 16 January, at: japan.kantei.go.jp/97_abe/statement/201701/1221207_11567.html (accessed 29 March 2017).

Kelly, T. and Kubo. N., 2015. 'INTERVIEW – U.S. Would Welcome Japan Air Patrols in South China Sea', Reuters UK, at: uk.reuters.com/article/japan-southchinasea-idUKL4N0V63HM20150129 (accessed 31 January 2016).
Komeito, 2015. 'Security bills and Komeito', at: www.komei.or.jp/en/policy/stands/20150516.html (accessed 27 January 2016).
Kyodo, 2015. 'Cabinet's approval rating sinks to 38.9% over unpopular security laws', 21 September, at: www.japantimes.co.jp/news/2015/09/21/national/politics-diplomacy/cabinets-approval-rating-sinks-38-9-unpopular-security-laws/#. WofrooPOWUk (accessed 17 February 2018).
Kyodo, 2016a. 'Japan Protests after Swarm of 230 Chinese Vessels Enters Waters near Senkakus', *Japan Times*, 6 August.
Kyodo, 2016b. 'Japanese Destroyers Visit Vietnam's Cam Ranh Bay', *The Japan Times*, 12 April.
Lubold, G. and Page, J., 2015. 'U.S. Navy Ship Sails Near Islands Claimed by China', *The Wall Street Journal* (26 October), at: wsj.com/articles/u-s-navy-ship-sails-near-islands-claimed-by-china-1445908192 (accessed 31 January 2016).
Mie, A., 2016. 'First Chinese Warship to Skirt Senkaku Triggers Protest from Tokyo', *Japan Times*, 9 June, at: www.japantimes.co.jp/news/2016/06/09/national/chinese-frigate-sails-near-senkakus-russian-military-vessels?utm_content=buffer8e657&utm_medium=social&utm_source=twitter.com&utm_campaign=buffer#.Wofu8o-POW02 (accessed 17 February 2018).
Ministry of Defense of Japan, 2010. *Defense of Japan* (Tokyo: Urban Connections).
Ministry of Defense of Japan, 2013a. 'Extra Press Conference by the Defense Minister (04:00–04:09 P.M. September 17, 2013 (Japan time))', at: www.mod.go.jp/e/press/conference/2013/09/17.html (accessed 16 January 2016).
Ministry of Defense of Japan, 2013b. 'National Defense Program Guidelines for FY 2014 and beyond', 17 December, at: www.mod.go.jp/j/approach/agenda/guideline/2014/pdf/20131217_e2.pdf.
Ministry of Defense of Japan, 2014. 'Special Feature: Capacity Building Assistance', at: www.mod.go.jp/e/jdf/no55/specialfeature.html (accessed 17 January 2016).
Ministry of Defense of Japan, 2015. 'The Guidelines for Japan-U.S. Defense Cooperation', at: www.mod.go.jp/e/d_act/anpo/shishin_20150427e.html (accessed 30 January 2016).
Ministry of Defense of Japan, 2016a. 'China's Activities in the South China Sea', at: www.mod.go.jp/j/approach/surround/pdf/ch_d-act_20161222e.pdf (accessed 15 March 2017).
Ministry of Defense of Japan, 2016b. *Defense of Japan* (Tokyo: Urban Connections).
Ministry of Foreign Affairs of Japan, 2000. 'Press Conference by the Press Secretary 14 March 2000', at: www.mofa.go.jp/announce/press/2000/3/314.html (accessed 14 January 2016).
Ministry of Foreign Affairs of Japan, 2011. 'Japan-Viet Nam Joint Statement on the Actions Taken under Strategic Partnership for Peace and Prosperity in Asia', at: www.mofa.go.jp/mofaj/kaidan/s_noda/vietnam1110/pdfs/1.pdf (accessed 15 January 2016).
Ministry of Foreign Affairs of Japan, 2012. 'Position Paper: Japan-China Relations Surrounding the Situation of the Senkaku Islands', 9 November, at: www.mofa.go.jp/region/asia-paci/senkaku/position_paper_en.html (accessed 11 April 2016).
Ministry of Foreign Affairs of Japan, 2014a. 'Japan–Viet Nam Joint Statement on the Establishment of the Extensive Strategic Partnership for Peace and Prosperity in Asia', at: www.mofa.go.jp/files/000034408.pdf (accessed 16 January 2016).

Ministry of Foreign Affairs of Japan, 2014b. 'Minister for Foreign Affairs Fumio Kishida's Visit to Viet Nam', at: www.mofa.go.jp/s_sa/sea1/vn/page3e_000215.html (accessed 29 March 2017).

Ministry of Foreign Affairs of Japan, 2014c. 'Signing on Exchange of Notes concerning Japan's Non-Project Grant Aid to Viet Nam', at: www.mofa.go.jp/press/release/press4e_000386.html (accessed 29 March 2017).

Ministry of Foreign Affairs of Japan, 2014d. 'Three Principles on Transfer of Defense Equipment and Technology', at: www.mofa.go.jp/press/release/press22e_000010.html.

Ministry of Foreign Affairs of Japan, 2016a. 'Japan-Viet Nam Summit Meeting', 20 November, at: www.mofa.go.jp/mofaj/s_sa/sea1/vn/page3e_000624.html.

Ministry of Foreign Affairs of Japan, 2016b. 'Japanese Territory', 13 April, at: www.mofa.go.jp/region/asia-paci/senkaku/ (accessed 10 March 2017).

Ministry of Foreign Affairs of Japan, 2017. 'The Numbers of Chinese Government and Other Vessels That Entered Japan's Contiguous Zone or Intruded into Territorial Sea Surrounding the Senkaku Islands (PDF)', 6 March, at: www.mofa.go.jp/files/000170838.pdf (accessed 21 March 2017).

National Security Council of Japan, 2013. 'National Security Strategy', 17 December, at: japan.kantei.go.jp/96_abe/documents/2013/__icsFiles/afieldfile/2013/12/18/NSS.pdf (accessed 19 April 2016).

New York Times, 2009. 'U.S. Accuses the Chinese of Harassing Naval Vessel', 9 March.

Nikkei Asian Review, 2015. 'Japan Plans Vietnam Port Call to Check Chinese Expansion', 30 October, at: asia.nikkei.com/Politics-Economy/International-Relations/Japan-plans-Vietnam-port-call-to-check-Chinese-expansion (accessed 28 March 2017).

Nikkei Asian Review, 2016a. 'Japan Calls for More US Surveillance', 19 February, at: asia.nikkei.com/print/article/153881 (accessed 31 October 2017).

Nikkei Asian Review, 2016b. 'Japan Eager for Security Agreements with Philippines, Vietnam', 15 January, at: asia.nikkei.com/Politics-Economy/International-Relations/Japan-eager-for-security-agreements-with-Philippines-Vietnam (accessed 16 January 2016).

O'Rourke, R., 2016. 'China Naval Modernization: Implications for U.S. Navy Capabilities – Background and Issues for Congress', 31 March, CRS Report for Congress, at: www.fas.org/sgp/crs/row/RL33153.pdf (accessed 1 October 2017).

Reuters News, 2014. 'Japan PM Says Will Take Time to Provide Patrol Ships to Vietnam', 28 May.

Security Consultative Committee, 2012. 'Joint Statement of the Security Consultative Committee', at: www.mofa.go.jp/region/n-america/us/security/scc/pdfs/joint_120427_en.pdf (accessed 29 January 2016).

State Council Information Office, 2012. 'Diaoyu Dao, an Inherent Territory of China', at: english.gov.cn/archive/white_paper/2014/08/23/content_281474983043212.htm (accessed 10 March 2017).

Takenaka, K., 2012. 'Japan Scrambles Jets as Chinese Plane Flies over Disputed Isles', Reuters, 13 December, at: reuters.com/article/us-china-japan-scramble-idUSBRE8BC07920121213 (accessed 10 March 2017).

Thayer, C., 2014. 'Vietnam's Extensive Partnership with Japan', *The Diplomat*, at: thediplomat.com/2014/10/vietnams-extensive-strategic-partnership-with-japan/ (accessed 18 January 2016).

Yoon, S., 2015. 'Implications of Xi Jinping's "True Maritime Power": Its Context, Significance, and Impact on the Region', *Naval War College Review*, 68(3): 40.

Part IV

Japan–Europe security partnership

10

The Japanese perspective on the security partnership with the EU

Akiko Fukushima

Introduction

Japan–Europe relations were centred initially on cultural exchanges after World War II and then on the economy, in particular trade. Security ties, on the other hand, have emerged more recently as an area for cooperation. Symbolically, this emerged as an area for cooperation in 1991, when the European Community (EC) and Japan announced the Hague Declaration. Both sides agreed to 'strengthen their cooperation' in broader areas beyond trade. Included in the areas of cooperation were peace and security (Ministry of Foreign Affairs of Japan, 1991). One should note that the Hague Declaration alluded to 'common values and shared interests' as the reasons for Japan and the EC to promote overarching cooperation ranging from the economy and security to education.

Since the Declaration, Japan and the EC, and European countries and other regional institutions more widely, have consistently sung this tune of common values and shared interests up to now in promoting security cooperation. In the 2013 National Security Strategy (NSS), Japan acknowledged: 'Japan and European countries ... share universal values of freedom, democracy, respect for fundamental human rights and the rule of law, and principles.' The Strategy stated that Japan will further strengthen 'its relations with Europe including cooperation with the European Union (EU), the North Atlantic Treaty Organization (NATO), and the Organisation for Security and Co-operation in Europe (OSCE) in order to ensure a peaceful and prosperous international community.' (Government of Japan, 2013: 62). Thus, Japan has maintained and enhanced its political will to promote security cooperation with Europe.

The security partnership, however, did not develop substantially in the eyes of some observers. A decade after the Hague Declaration, in December 2001, the EU and Japan released a Joint Action Plan for EU–Japan Cooperation entitled 'Shaping our Common Future.' The Action Plan aimed to further the cooperation between the EU and Japan that had been announced in the Hague Declaration.

In facing criticism on the lack of progress in pledged cooperation after the enunciation of the Declaration, the Plan enumerated issues to be addressed and noted that they should further 'tap the unrealized potential for cooperation to achieve our common objectives' (Ministry of Foreign Affairs of Japan, 2001: 1). The Action Plan included a chapter on promoting peace and security with a list of concrete issues to be covered. In the chapter, the Plan included UN reform with a focus on UN peace operations as well as UN finances. It also included arms control, disarmament and non-proliferation to eliminate weapons of mass destruction as well as the spread and accumulation of small arms and light weapons. It also listed conflict prevention and peace building as an area for cooperation, with a specific mention of dialogue among civilisations. As for regional issues, the Action Plan mentioned the Korean Peninsula and expressed concerns on nuclear development of the Democratic People's Republic of Korea (DPRK) and, therefore, support for closer engagement with the Republic of Korea (South Korea).

The Action Plan with a list of concrete issues to be addressed generated higher hopes, in both Europe and Japan, that actual concrete cooperation would take place. Nevertheless, after a few years, it was perceived, particularly from the EU side, that 'the momentum behind this shopping list of grand ambitions soon dissipated in benign neglect, [although] persistent prompts regarding the logic of such efforts at partnership continued' (Raine and Small, 2015: 4).

Thus, when the Japanese side proposed to draft a new Action Plan in 2010, a decade after the first Action Plan, the EU side were not forthcoming on another round of an action plan, but instead insisted on a legally binding agreement so as to produce tangible results of cooperation rather than what they termed 'rhetorical cooperation'. The Japanese side formed a wise men's group to draft a recommendation for a new plan, but the EU side did not echo this.[1]

This stalemate eventually settled into parallel negotiations for an Economic Partnership Agreement (EPA) and a Strategic Partnership Agreement (SPA) in 2012. At the May 2016 Ise-Shima G7 Summit, the heads of state of the UK, Germany, France, Italy and the EU met with Prime Minister Shinzō Abe and agreed to accelerate the EPA negotiations so that the parties could agree on an outline of the agreement, preferably by the end of that year. In July 2017, Japan and the EU finalized negotiations on the EPA, which is scheduled to be ratified in 2018. The Strategic Partnership Agreement (SPA) is scheduled to be signed in 2018.

This chapter asks whether Japan–Europe cooperative relations can develop into substantive security partnership. It first takes stock of Japan–Europe security relations in the past three decades since the seminal 1991 Hague Declaration and gives observations on drivers, twists and inhibitors of cooperation. It then examines the impact of changes taking place in security undertakings, both in Europe and in Japan, as the background for future Japan–Europe security ties. Finally, the chapter concludes with some observations on potential security ties that can be forged between Japan and Europe, bearing in mind the geopolitical changes.

Trajectory of Japan–Europe security cooperation

Pushing Japan–Europe relations beyond trade

While Japan–Europe relations immediately after World War II were limited to cultural exchanges, they were gradually extended, most notably to the economy, as Japan recovered from war damage and developed its trade-led economy. By the end of the 1960s, Japan had achieved its post-war economic recovery and increased its exports to Europe, particularly in the car, electronics, ball bearings, steel and shipbuilding sectors. In the 1970s, Japanese exports to Europe soared by 330 per cent. In 1981, the EC had a record high trade deficit of $10.3 billion with Japan. This sudden surge of Japanese exports irritated European countries, which was illustrated by the leaked internal EC document that portrayed Japan as a nation of 'workaholics' living in 'rabbit hutches' (Watanabe, 2013).

The mounting trade deficit led France to take action to delay the customs clearance of Japanese home-use videocassette recorders (VCRs) in 1982. France announced that it was moving its customs clearance point for Japanese VCRs from the coastal port of Le Havre to the inland city of Poitiers, and demanded that the Japanese prepare all customs documents in French. This decision brought Japanese export of VCRs to a *de facto* halt. The media dubbed this case 'the Second Battle of Poitiers'. Both Japanese and French governments made efforts to solve the dispute, and Japan decided to voluntarily control the volume of VCR exports for three years. With the solution of this trade dispute, the dust over Japan–Europe relations gradually settled. This incident led the Japanese government to review how it should shape its relations with Europe, and to transform its relationship from confrontational to cooperative, and from one exclusively focused on trade to one including broader issues.

Driving the Japan–Europe security cooperation

Several events were behind the expansion of the sphere of cooperation beyond trade, most notably to peace and security. One major driving force was the perceived ramifications of European security decisions for Japan. This was first triggered by the negotiations over the deployment of American Pershing II intermediate-range nuclear missiles to Western Europe in response to the Soviet deployment of SS 20 in Eastern Europe, and the subsequent negotiations between the US and the Soviet Union over the reduction of these missiles. Although the negotiation was in the European theatre, Japan was concerned about the possible impact of the decision on Japan's security interests. Such a decision might lead countries to deploy these missiles to Asia instead, at the expense of Japanese security interests. Thus, at the G7 Summit held in May 1983 in Williamsburg in the US, then Prime Minister Yasuhiro Nakasone explained his concern and managed to include the phrase that security is 'indivisible' among the G7 members. This event strongly motivated Japan to explore substantive security relations with Europe to prevent similar events from recurring. Subsequently, the indivisibility of security has been another tune used to enhance Japan–Europe security ties.

This indivisibility was also behind Japan's initiative on the 'Arc of Freedom and Prosperity', which was enunciated by then Japanese Foreign Minister Taro Aso in 2008. Aimed at promoting cooperation with NATO and the EU as partners to enhance peace and prosperity from Europe to Asia, this also sang the tune of indivisibility and common universal values (Aso, 2008). Although this particular label of the Arc of Freedom and Prosperity had been dropped, the awareness that the security of Japan is linked to that of Europe remained.

Another event that motivated Japan to strengthen security ties with Europe took place between 2004 and 2005. Europe attempted to lift the arms embargo it had imposed on China at the time of the Tiananmen Square incident. This move startled the US and Japan, who aired strong opposition to lifting the embargo on the grounds that such an action by Europe might have an impact on the arms race and subsequently security in the Asia-Pacific. It sent a strong message to the Japanese security community that Europe did not appreciate the intricate nature of the Asian security environment and was simply attracted to the sheer size of the Chinese market. Japan perceived the move as a way to improve the relations between China and European countries by expanding trade with China.

This concern led to rounds of strategic dialogues between Japan and Europe, particularly with the EU, as well as on a bilateral basis with EU member states.[2] Japan tried to give Europe a better understanding of the strategic situations in its neighbourhood and in Asia more widely. The decision on lifting the ban was subsequently postponed, but the concern still lingers that there may be a new move to lift it.

Although the Japan-Europe relations in earlier decades were the history of trade disputes, events from the 1980s, as described above, encouraged Japan to expand the horizon of its relations with Europe to include political and security issues. After the settlement of the trade friction and the end of the Cold War, the EC and Japan agreed to expand the horizon of their sphere of cooperation from economic issues to much broader areas, including security.

In July 1991, Prime Minister Toshiki Kaifu and European Commission President Jacques Delors declared in The Hague that 'we have common attachment to freedom, democracy, the rule of law and human rights' and agreed to expand their relations beyond trade. The areas of cooperation included a whole spectrum of ties, including security, education and culture (Ministry of Foreign Affairs of Japan, 1991). This Hague Declaration of 1991 was a milestone in their relations and was the origin of Japan–Europe security cooperation. The Declaration noted their growing interdependence and their common interest in the security, peace and stability of the world as the reasons why Japan and Europe would cooperate to 'set up a just and stable international order'. These shared values and interests have been the driver of Japan–Europe security cooperation ever since, and remain as a shared premise of cooperation. The Declaration also created a consultative follow-up mechanism, including the annual Japan–EC Summit – now the Japan–EU Summit. Thus, Japan and Europe have harnessed cooperation with institutional linkages. In order to improve cooperation, Japan has enhanced its institutional frameworks with the EU and NATO.

A decade after the Hague Declaration in 2001, in order to further implement the Hague Declaration, Japan and the EU adopted the Japan–EU Joint Action Plan, entitled 'Shaping Our Common Future'. The Plan included the four major objectives of 'promoting peace and security, strengthening the economic and trade partnership, utilizing the dynamism of globalisation for the benefit of all, coping with global and social challenges and bringing together people and cultures'. On peace and security, under the heading of 'promoting peace and stability', the Action Plan stated that we should 'tap the unrealized potential for cooperation in security' and enumerated agendas such as 'the promotion of regional dialogue and political stability, the enhancement of international and regional organizations for conflict prevention, and the engagement of specific regional issues such as Korean Peninsula' (Ministry of Foreign Affairs of Japan, 2001).

After the adoption of the Action Plan, further cooperation was sought, and annual follow-up conferences on the Plan were held. However, the EU side observed that the cooperation promised in the Plan stayed in the comfort zone of rhetoric and did not bring tangible results. When Japan sought to draft a new action plan a decade later in 2011 on the recommendation of the wise men's group described in the Introduction, the EU insisted that such a plan must be based on binding resolutions to produce concrete results.[3] In the end, the Japanese failed to launch another action plan.

Instead, in 2012, Japan and the EU agreed to launch a negotiation on legally binding agreements, including an EPA to further liberalise trade and investment. EPA negotiations took time due to differing positions. For example, Japan aims to expand the export of cars and consumer electronics to Europe, while the EU calls for total liberalisation of agricultural trade. Also at issue are food safety standards and tariff measures for chemical products and pharmaceutical products. All of these differing positions have made the EPA negotiation a protracted process.

In 2011, Japan and the EU also agreed to start negotiations on a SPA in parallel with the EPA in order to promote politico-security cooperation. Although EPA negotiations take time, by the time of the G7 Summit in Ise-Shima, Japan, leaders from Japan and Europe had agreed to accelerate the negotiations.

When these two agreements are concluded, the overall Japan–Europe cooperation will be harnessed, including security cooperation with institutional frameworks of legally binding agreements.

The narrative of 'common values' and 'shared values' has also been employed with another institution in Europe, namely, NATO. With NATO, institutional relations are a more recent incarnation than those with the EU. The relations were initially developed during mutual visits of heads of governments. It was Prime Minister Shinzō Abe, in his first administration, who started the ball of cooperation between Japan and NATO rolling when he spoke at the North Atlantic Council in January 2007. In a speech entitled 'Japan and NATO: Toward Further Collaboration', Prime Minister Abe stated that shared values are the premise of Japan–NATO cooperation. He invited the attention and support of NATO for regional issues in Asia, particularly DPRK issues, including nuclear development and abduction; arms build-up by China; and other Asian regional security issues. He further suggested: 'There is room to combine knowledge and experience to help in areas such as peace building, reconstruction and disaster relief.' Prime Minister Abe concluded his speech by saying that 'Japan and NATO should move on to a new phase of cooperation' (Ministry of Foreign Affairs of Japan, 2007).

In return, NATO Secretary General Jaap de Hoop Scheffer visited Japan in December 2007. During his visit, Prime Minister Yasuo Fukuda and Secretary General de Hoop Scheffer issued a joint press statement and affirmed a shared sense of responsibility towards global security challenges and a determination to continue cooperating to meet those challenges. They agreed that Japan and NATO would 'seek utmost synergy in utilizing their respective resources and capabilities' in the fight against terrorism as well as the stabilisation and reconstruction of Afghanistan.

These mutual visits were followed by the conclusion of the Agreement between Japan and NATO on Security of Information and Material in June 2010 to strengthen the basic rules and mechanisms for protecting classified information and materials that Japan and NATO share with one another. This was a major milestone in promoting security cooperation. Even during the Democratic Party of Japan (DPJ) government, foreign ministers visited NATO headquarters. Foreign Minister Matsumoto met Secretary General Rasmussen in May 2011 at the NATO headquarters, followed by Japanese participation in the NATO Chicago Summit in May 2012. Japan designated its ambassador to the kingdom of Belgium as a permanent representative of the government of Japan to NATO. Also, Japan and NATO together designated cyber-defence and maritime security as possible areas for further cooperation at the Chicago Summit.

In the second Abe government, when he spoke to the North Atlantic Council on 6 May 2014, Prime Minister Abe further stressed cooperation with NATO as a 'natural partner', quoting the remarks by Secretary General

Rasmussen. In his speech, Prime Minister Abe emphasised his policy of making 'proactive contribution to peace based on international cooperation', which was clearly mentioned in the NSS of 2013. During this visit, Prime Minister Abe and Secretary General Rasmussen signed the Individual Partnership and Cooperation Programme (ICPC) as a guiding principle of the cooperation between Japan and NATO. ICPC lists medium- and long-term priority objectives for bilateral cooperation. They also agreed to collaborate on global commons such as maritime security, cyber-security and disaster relief. In the speech, Abe also committed to cooperate with NATO in the areas of women, peace and security. Since women in many instances suffer wounds of the mind and body resulting from conflicts, Japan emphasises assisting women with maternal and child health as part of the protection and promotion of women's rights in the frame of Japan's efforts to enhance overall human security. In his speech, Prime Minister Abe committed to dispatching female government personnel with experience in international peace cooperation to the NATO headquarters. He kept his word, sending the first Japan Self-Defense Force (JSDF) officer, Lt Colonel Chizu Kurita, on secondment to NATO headquarters to work on gender issues in December 2014 (Ministry of Foreign Affairs of Japan, 2013).

Prime Minister Abe further proposed to set up a Joint Study Group on Humanitarian Assistance and Disaster Relief. The Joint Declaration stated: 'Japan and NATO are dedicated to the shared values and shared interest through pursuing a rules-based international order' (NATO, 2013). The two noted that they attached importance to deterring conflict and preventing crises through twinned cooperation and dialogue. Prime Minister Abe asserts that Japan and NATO are now reliable partners beyond their natural partnership. Thus, the institutionalization of Japan–NATO cooperation is on its way.

Security cooperation on the ground

The institutionalization of Japan–Europe cooperation is thus underway. The SPA is to provide an institutional framework for cooperation in the politico-security field in parallel with EPA. Meanwhile, security cooperation on the ground, particularly non-combat security cooperation on the ground between Europe and Japan, has been promoted in a wide spectrum of areas, including disarmament, demobilisation and reintegration (DDR), security sector reform (SSR) such as police training and border control in conflict-affected countries, disaster prevention and relief, and piracy control, to name a few.

As an illustration of such cooperation on the ground, in Afghanistan, NATO designated Japan as a contact country and subsequently 'a partner across the globe', a term applied to a smaller subset of external partners. Japan has assisted peace building in Afghanistan by leading DDR as a non-NATO partner. Also, Japan has contributed to job creation projects for former soldiers, such as water, road construction and irrigation, by providing vocational training. More than 10,000 former combatants have joined the project for reintegration. Japan also assisted the Provincial Reconstruction Teams (PRTs) by implementing 144 projects in 16 of Afghanistan's provinces, such as by sending liaison officers to the Lithuanian PRT in Chaghcharan and the Swedish PRT in Mazar-e-Sharif, to support these programmes on medical care and education. Japan's financial assistance to Afghanistan has totalled US$6 million since 2001.

In Afghanistan, even 15 years after the collapse of the Taliban government in 2001, internal safety has been the priority agenda. In order to support peace building in Afghanistan, Japan has committed to provide $3 billion in assistance for the development and security sector from 2012 for five years. In promoting SSR, Japan has shouldered 30 per cent of the salaries of Afghanistan's national police personnel, together with NATO and others. Moreover, Japan has thus supported the capacity-building of Afghan police officers and drug control. For example, Japan has assisted in the literacy training of the national army and the Afghanistan national police, along with NATO. Although literacy education is not a core part of the capacity-building of the national army and police, it has improved their efficiency and productivity.

Domestic violence is rampant in Afghanistan, and it was reported that female victims found it difficult to report to male police officers. In October 2015, the Japanese Policy Agency dispatched two Japanese female police officers to lecture on the role of female police in Japan as part of the empowerment training of the Afghan police. Also on SSR, Japan and the EU cooperated to enhance the border control of the Tajikistan–Afghanistan border in 2009, 2010 and 2012. Japan and the EU jointly hosted capacity-building seminars to train the border management capacity. Border control is important to halt illegal trafficking of drugs and arms. Enhancement of border control improves the peace and security prospects of the country as well as the region (Ministry of Foreign Affairs of Japan, 2009, 2010, 2012).

Another illustration of security cooperation on the ground is piracy control. Japan, NATO and EU are collaborating in countering piracy in the Gulf of Aden off the coast of Somalia (see Chapter 12 in this volume for a detailed analysis). The JSDF escorts not only Japanese commercial vessels but also other countries' vessels. In 2016, about 600 members of the JSDF were serving in the Gulf of Aden. In addition, Japan's P-3C maritime patrol aircraft cover 60 per cent of all warning and surveillance flights over the Gulf of Aden and have provided information to countries participating in NATO's Operation Ocean Shield. In January 2014, the JSDF and the EU worked in collaboration to seize five pirates, which was a tangible result of cooperation. Since October 2014, Japan has also conducted joint exercises with countries participating in piracy control, namely, with the Italian, German, Dutch and Spanish navies. In 2015, the JSDF also served as a commander of the Combined Maritime Forces (CTF) 151.

Japanese perspective on EU partnership

Japan also contributes to EU Common Security and Defence Policy (CSDP) missions using its official development assistance. In Niger, the EU CSDP civilian mission has engaged in capacity-building for security by providing advice and training. In December 2014, Japan provided provincial governments with radio communication equipment and radio-equipped vehicles for patrol in remote areas to the amount of 202 million yen through the United Nations Development Programme (UNDP). In Mali, an EU CSDP mission has been providing capacity-building for safety since July 2014. Mindful of such dispatch, in March 2015, Japan provided funding of 4.6 million US dollars through UNDP to repair the National Police Academy, provide IT equipment and support human resources development in Mali. These are not direct contributions to CSDP missions, but have produced synergy in assisting missions. The Joint Press Statement of the 23rd Japan–EU Summit meeting in May 2015 noted that these collaborations would potentially lead to 'a future participation of Japan in CSDP missions'.

Japan has also provided a total of $3.4 million to the OSCE Border Management Staff College in Dushanbe, Tajikistan since 2013. This college has provided member countries and partner countries of OSCE with training in the latest border control approaches and measures against illegal trafficking since 2009. In total, as of June 2016, 1,899 students from Central Asian countries and Afghanistan have attended the college. The Japanese contribution was $400,000 (7 per cent of the total project budget of the college) in FY 2013, $1 million (53 per cent) in FY 2014, $1 million (47 per cent) in FY 2015 and $1 million (59 per cent) in FY 2016.[4]

Thus, Japan and Europe are cooperating on security on the ground. In the past three decades, repeated dialogues, from summits to the working level, have been held to explore further cooperation. Yet it is still perceived as remaining in the rhetorical domain or consisting solely of funding. Some observers portray Japan–Europe security cooperation as limited to peripheral areas of security but not including core security issues. Or, Japan–Europe security cooperation is criticised as 'worthy-but-dull' or 'lacking reality' (Raine and Small, 2015: 1).

Inhibitors of substantive security cooperation

What are the inhibitors of substantive security cooperation between Japan and Europe? First and foremost, it is pointed out that Japan–Europe relations have not been 'at the centre of foreign and security policies' for either, despite shared values and shared interest narratives. Japanese experts on Japanese relations with Europe point out that the relations have been dismissed as marginal, overlooked and undervalued so much that substantive energy has not been devoted to enhancing the relations beyond the rhetorical level. Michito Tsuruoka (2012: 73) observes: 'The EU and Japan are not likely to be each other's partner of first choice.' It is more the US that remains the primary partner for both. Hirotaka Watanabe (2013) also observes that 'for Europe as well as for Japan, their mutual partnership was secondary to their respective strategic partnerships with the United States which were based on alliances in the Atlantic and the Pacific respectively'.

Second, lack of tangible results and only sporadic fruits of security cooperation generated this perception. Criticism from Europe was particularly strong on the 2001 Action Plan, that it did not achieve any substantive results. This even led the EU to refuse the drafting of a new action plan in 2011 when the Japanese government proposed it. This perception is well demonstrated by the description of the relationship by then European Commission President Jose Manuel Barroso (2006) as a 'mature relationship' but one with 'untapped potential'.

Third, on the Japanese side, there is a feeling that Europe, despite repeated security dialogues, does not understand the sensitivities of security matters in Asia. As Kent Calder observes, there is a perception that Europe does not appreciate the impact of Europe's strong rapprochement to China, in search of its market, on the balance of power in East Asia (Kent Calder, 2016).

Enhancing the third leg through trilateral cooperation

In spite of criticisms of the lack of substantive progress in Japan–Europe security cooperation, there has been a certain amount of progress, as described in the preceding section, in the form of cooperation on the ground. How will the relations further unfold to security ties in the future?

There emerge several factors that could move the Japan–Europe security partnership further, surmounting the inhibitors raised in the preceding section. On the European side, the EU, which was traditionally focused on the economic sector, has enlarged its activities in politico-security fields more notably since the Balkan wars. The EU developed the European Security and Defence Policy (ESDP), subsequently called the CSDP under the Lisbon Treaty.

On the other hand, NATO, which was created as a military alliance of collective self-defence, has enlarged the scope of its activities to the political realm, which entices Japan to enhance its relations with NATO. Michito Tsuruoka (2011) recommends that Japan should look at NATO as a 'political partner' – more than a military alliance – with which Japan should have cooperative relations. He brings it to Japanese attention that NATO members encompass all major powers from North America to Europe, and that NATO carries weight not only as a military alliance but also as a political institution. It is worth noting that the preamble and Article 2 of the North Atlantic Treaty refer to the promotion of well-being and economic collaboration among the member states, which coincides with Japanese interests. The economy was also included in its founding treaty. Moreover, in recent decades, NATO has come to engage in situations beyond the geographic area of the membership, in non-member conflict-affected areas such as the Balkans, Afghanistan and Africa. NATO operations are widening to cover peacekeeping and peace building operations. These changes within NATO enlarge the potential for Japan–NATO cooperation.

Japan has also begun to be more proactive rather than passive in making its contribution to international peace and security, most recently under the banner of 'the proactive contribution to peace based on international cooperation'. Thus, it now contributes not only in traditional economic areas but also in security. Japan's scope of engagement has enlarged both in terms of its content, ranging from logistical support to coalition forces to UN peacekeeping operations, as well as in terms of geography beyond the traditional area of Asia. For example, it was engaged in the Gulf of Aden and South Sudan, the former for piracy control, as described in the preceding section, and the latter for peace building, as part of a UN mission. Behind these moves is the awareness of the indivisibility of security internationally.

In March 2016, the Legislation for Peace and Security took effect. With this new set of laws, Japan no longer needs to introduce temporary-measures laws every time it needs to dispatch its SDF, for example to provide logistical support for piracy missions or other overseas missions. It also enables Japanese peacekeepers to operate under the same rules of engagement. Moreover, Japan can now participate not only in UN peacekeeping operations but also in peace operations organised by regional organisations such as the EU. The law opens a new avenue for cooperation with Europe. This law may also allow Japan and Europe to include new joint activities and areas of cooperation in the Framework Partnership Agreement for participation in CSDP missions.

Third, both Japan and Europe face difficult problems in their immediate neighbourhoods; for example, Ukraine and China and the DPRK, respectively. Europe has undergone the Russian annexation of Crimea and an intrusion into the eastern part of Ukraine. Japan acted in sync with Europe as a member of G7 by imposing sanctions against Russia and providing economic assistance of $1.5 billion to improve the Ukrainian economy. Japan has also provided assistance to improve humanitarian situations, including medical equipment, shelter and water for internally displaced persons in Crimea and the eastern part of Ukraine.

In Asia, Japan has recently witnessed heightened tensions in the East and South China Seas due to assertive actions by China. Moreover, it is concerned with aggressive military actions by the DPRK after its testing of nuclear weapons and ballistic missiles.

However, as Tom Wright (2016) observes, Japan and Europe have long preferred to deal with their own revisionist powers in their respective regions and avoid saying or doing much about each other. While Japan is on guard against China, Wright argues that European countries are eager to develop commercial ties with China. Similarly, Europe is on guard against Russia, while Japan is looking for ways to engage Russia and is keen to negotiate on the northern territories, a problem that has not been solved even 70 years after the end of World War II.

It is a solemn fact that the respective strategic landscapes differ. Although Japan and Europe face and wish to address their respective revisionist powers separately, they can no longer manage these powers within their geographical footprint. Threats to their security travel beyond their geographic zones. Terrorism affects citizens of countries as far away as Japan, as has been shown when Japanese nationals have been killed or injured in Europe, the Middle East and Africa. As an illustration, in January 2013, Japanese nationals of JGC Corporation, who had worked for the gas plant, were killed by Islamic militants in In Amenas in Algeria. The attack was reportedly by al-Qaeda-affiliated groups. This case sent a strong message that Japanese nationals can be victims of terrorism far from home. The advent of globalisation transcends traditional geographical regions. Even an aggression by a regional power against another country impacts other regions both directly and indirectly. For example, Japan and Europe share a common concern, though to a varying degree, with maritime security. As Joshua W. Walker (2016: 1) noted, 'Europe is inextricably linked to Asian geopolitics not just by Eurasia and Russia but also by strategic sea-lanes through which over 98 percent of all global trade traverse'.

Furthermore, there emerges a harbinger of change in their respective perceptions of peace and security in their neighbourhoods. This can be seen in the media report of the Ise-Shima G7 Summit in May 2016. It was reported that in conversations over dinner on 18 June 2016, heads of state had a meeting of minds or concerns on Chinese actions in the South China Sea. Meanwhile, at the 2015 G7 Summit, it was reported that there were gaps in perception between European countries and Japan, but in 2016 all agreed that international rule on maritime security should be respected, and a strong message should be expressed to those who do not obey the rules. European countries, which were more anxious to develop economic relations with China, have seemingly shifted their perception (*Nihon Keizai Shimbun*, 2016). This tone was reflected in the G7 Leaders Declaration 2016, which mentioned under the heading of maritime security that 'we reiterate our commitment to maintaining a rules-based maritime order in accordance with the principles of international law …. We reaffirm the importance of states' making and clarifying their claims based on international law, refraining from unilateral actions which could increase tensions and not using force or coercion in trying to drive their claims.' The declaration specifically mentioned G7 countries' concern about the East and South China Seas (Ministry of Foreign Affairs of Japan, 2016: 25).

Similar changes could be observed in speeches given by European defence ministers at the 2016 Shangri-La Dialogue. Jean-Yves Le Drian, French minister of defence, stated in his speech that 'if the Law of the Sea is not observed in the China seas today, it will be in jeopardy in the Arctic, the Mediterranean and elsewhere tomorrow. In order to keep the risk of conflict contained, we must defend the Law and defend ourselves with the Law' (Le Drian, 2016). He emphasised the impacts of incidents in Asia on Europe. Furthermore, he mentioned that 'we must stand firm against actions that undermine the foundations of the international order, stand firm against the rejection of the law and of dialogue'. Since the conversation at the Shangri-La Dialogue focused on the South China Sea, his message was received as referring to China, though he did not mention it by name.

At the Shangri-La Dialogue, Michael Fallon (2016), the defence secretary of the UK, stressed in his speech that 'our commitment is to the rules-based international system, international law and the maintenance of freedom of navigation and over flight – both of which we consider non-negotiable'. Referring to the South China Sea, he mentioned: 'we expect all parties to avoid actions which could further raise tensions, and to implement the UNCLOS [*United Nations Convention on the Law of the Sea*] tribunal's ruling'.

In addition, they share the broader challenge of whether or not a liberal international order should be left to decay (Fukushima, 2016; Twining, 2016; Wright, 2016). If they believe that their interests are in maintaining such an order, there remains room for an even closer partnership based on common values so as to collaborate beyond differences to protect their people's common interests. The alternative would be a more contested world.

In maintaining international peace and security, Japan truly needs global partners, and Europe is an important partner, as noted in the NSS. The Strategy specifically mentions that 'Japan will strengthen cooperative relations with countries outside the Asia-Pacific region that play an important role in ensuring the peace and stability of the international community.' It names Europe as the top partner in the section, and states that 'Europe has the influence to formulate international public opinions, the capacity to develop the norms in major international frameworks'. The Japanese NSS also notes universal values that Japan and Europe share and further mentions that Europe and Japan are

> partners which together take a leading role in ensuring peace, stability and prosperity of the international community. At a time when the power balance of the international community is changing, in order to establish an international order based on universal values and rules, to effectively address global challenges, and to accomplish Japan's initiative for peaceful and prosperous international community, Japan will further strengthen its relations with Europe. (Government of Japan, 2013: 62)

Judging from this politico-security outlook in the two regions, security cooperation seems to be in order rather than allowing security to pale into a simple rhetorical domain.

In designing future security ties between Japan and Europe, it is essential to surmount the inhibitors described. The perceived emerging changes may change the scene for both. Another way is to form a more robust trilateral cooperation of Japan, Europe and the US. Daniel Twining (2016) wrote that the trilateral should work to 'defend liberal democratic order which is now fraying'. He suggests closer cooperation to maintain liberal international order, which is in crisis in the wake of emerging countries eroding such an order. He suggests the three to cooperate systematically to protect global order.

By promoting such trilateral cooperation, both Japan and Europe can place their security cooperation at the centre of their foreign policy, rather than in the marginal position that has been an inhibitor of security cooperation. While the non-US aspects of Japan–Europe cooperation have been emphasised, it is time to switch our minds and to consider effective trilateral cooperation, mindful of the indivisibility of global security. As has been mentioned before, the weak third leg of Japan–Europe relations would make the three-legged chair unstable. In the days when global security is indivisible, it is incumbent upon Japan and Europe to strengthen their ties.

Conclusion

For Japan and Europe to make their security ties more realistic and to secure themselves from global threats, there is no other option but to enhance their partnership along with their respective ties with the United States. In addressing fragility in conflict-affected countries, when international actors impose their democracy and their governance methods, host countries often suffer from contradiction, if not friction, with their traditional way of life. This resulted in the argument of a hybrid peace that allows both liberalism and non-liberalism to coexist in building peace in fragile states, so-called 'hybrid peace'. If we are to pursue a hybrid peace, which involves a more flexible and dynamic process that fits each local case for preventing conflicts and building peace, Japan and Europe may find more room for their enhanced cooperation in missions. Although Japan–Europe security cooperation has not been substantive in terms of hard security, changing situations and a narrowing gap between perceptions should allow deeper cooperation in new areas. After their successful cooperation in fighting maritime piracy, peace building, and humanitarian assistance and disaster relief, Japan and the EU can now upgrade their cooperation to other fields, such as peace support operations.

Being aware of globally connected security concerns, Japan would benefit from the European experience of forging consensus in making rules and norms for peace and security. If Japan, Europe and the US can coordinate their strategies, they should be able to build an international order, which does not leave a vacuum in international society. Should there be a vacuum, it might further increase insecurity. Trilateral coordination would make all partners a more robust force against threats and pave the way to stabilising international security.

NOTES

1 Based on the author's experience of being a member of a wise men's group.
2 Based on personal interview by the author with French and British government representatives.
3 Based on the author's experience as a member of the wise men's group.
4 Based on the author's interview with Japanese government officials on 6 June 2016.

REFERENCES

Aso, T., 2008. 'Arc of Freedom and Prosperity: Japan's Expanding Diplomatic Horizons', Speech at the Japan Institute of International Affairs, Tokyo, 30 November 2008.
Barroso, J. M., 2006. 'EU-Japan: A Mature Relationship with Untapped Potential', Speech at the Tokyo Chamber of Commerce, 21 April.
Fallon, M., 2016. 'Speech at the Shangri-La Dialogue', 4 June, at: www.mofa.go.jp/files/000160266.pdf (accessed 3 March 2017).
Fukushima, A., 2016. 'Multilateralism Recalibrated: Japan's Engagement in Institution Building', CogitASIA, CSIS, 6 April, at: cogitasia.com/multilateralism-recalibrated-japans-engagement-in-institution-building/ (accessed 3 March 2017).
Government of Japan, 2013. *National Security Strategy* (print version). Tokyo.
Kent Calder, E., 2016. 'Minshushugi no kyoyu, Saikkunin wo' [Reconfirming the sharing of democracy], *Nihon Keizai Shinbun*, 20 May.
Le Drian, J. Y., 2016. Speech at the 15th Asia Security Summit, The IISS Shangri-La Dialogue, 5 June, at: www.iiss.org/-/media/documents/events/shangri-la%20dialogue/sld16/speeches%202016/20_sld16%204th%20plenary%20-%20jean%20yves%20le%20drian%20as%20delivered.pdf (accessed 3 March 2017).
Ministry of Foreign Affairs of Japan, 1991. 'Joint Declaration on Relations between the European Community and its Member States and Japan', The Hague, 18 July.
Ministry of Foreign Affairs of Japan, 2001. 'Shaping Our Common Future: An Action Plan for EU-Japan Cooperation', European Union-Japan Summit, Brussels, December.
Ministry of Foreign Affairs of Japan, 2007. 'Japan and NATO: Toward Further Collaboration', Prime Minister Shinzo Abe's Speech at the North Atlantic Council on 12 January, at: www.mofa.go.jp/region/europe/pmv0701/nato.html (accessed 3 March 2017).
Ministry of Foreign Affairs of Japan, 2009. 'Joint Press Statement', 18th EU-Japan Summit, Prague, 4 May, para. 23.
Ministry of Foreign Affairs of Japan, 2010. 'Joint Press Statement', 19th EU-Japan Summit, Tokyo, 28 April, para. 8.
Ministry of Foreign Affairs of Japan, 2012. 'Recommendation from the Japan-EU Conference on Tajikistan-Afghanistan Border Management and Cross-border Cooperation', Dushanbe, 28–29 February, at: www.mofa.go.jp/region/europe/eu/conference1202/pdfs/rec1202.pdf (accessed 3 March 2017).
Ministry of Foreign Affairs of Japan, 2013. 'Speech by Prime Minister Shinzo Abe, at the North Atlantic Council on May 6 2013', at: www.mofa.go.jp/mofaj/files/000037774.pdf (accessed 3 March 2017).

Ministry of Foreign Affairs of Japan, 2016. 'Ise-Shima G7 Summit Leaders Declaration', 26–27 May, at www.mofa.go.jp/files/000160266.pdf (accessed 3 March 2017).

NATO, 2013. 'Joint Political Declaration between Japan and the North Atlantic Treaty Organization', 13 April, at: nato.int/cps/en/natohq/official_texts_99562.htm (accessed 3 March 2017).

Nihon Keizai Shinbun, 2016. 'Sono Yoru Kawasareta Honne' [Frank Opinions Exchanged That Night], 19 June, p. 2.

Raine, S. and Small, A., 2015. *Waking Up to Geopolitics: A New Trajectory to Japan-Europe Relations*. Washington: The German Marshall Fund of the United States.

Tsuruoka, M., 2011. 'Japan-Europe Security Cooperation: How to "Use" NATO and the EU', *NIDS Journal of Defense and Security*, 12 (December): 27–43.

Tsuruoka, M., 2012. 'The Potential for EU-Japan Political and Security Cooperation: A Japanese Perspective', in *Japan and the European Union: Challenges and Cooperation in Times of Crisis* (Warsaw, Poland: Polish Institute of International Affairs (PISM)), pp. 71–82.

Twining, D., 2016. 'Trilateral Bloc Could Defend a Fraying Liberal Order', *Nikkei Asian Review*, 29 April.

Walker, J. W., Wright, T., Leonard, M., Takahara, A., Watanabe, Y. and Riecke, H., 2016. 'Cooperation in the Midst of Crisis', The German Marshall Fund of the United States, *Asia Policy Paper*, No. 22.

Watanabe, H., 2013. 'Takoku-kan wakugumi no naka no nichiō kankei' [Japan-European Relations at the Multilateral Level], in Kokubun, R. (ed.), *Nihon no Gaiko*, Vol. 4 (Tokyo: Iwanami Shoten), pp. 201–218.

Wright, T., 2016. 'The Problem of Revisionism and the European Japanese Relationship', in Walker, J. W., Wright, T., Leonard, M., Takahara, A., Watanabe, Y. and Riecke, H. (eds), 'Cooperation in the Midst of Crisis', The German Marshall Fund of the United States', *Asia Policy Paper*, No. 22.

11

The European perspective on the security partnership with Japan

Axel Berkofsky

Introduction

THE EU AND JAPAN have – at least on paper – big plans as regards cooperation in international politics and security. The instrument and agreement through which such increased and institutionalised cooperation is envisioned to take place is the so-called Strategic Partnership Agreement (SPA). The SPA will cover EU–Japan cooperation in regional and global politics and security and is envisioned to give the current EU–Japan ad hoc cooperation in the realms of politics and security an institutional framework. This chapter is confronted with the difficulty of having to analyse an agreement that has yet to be adopted, and hence it remains difficult to assess whether the SPA will turn out to be the 'Big Bang' of regional and global EU–Japan political and security cooperation.

As will be shown below, the adoption of the SPA is not necessarily the precondition for Brussels and Tokyo to get engaged in on-the-ground cooperation in regional and global security. However, the SPA – together with an EU–Japan free trade agreement (FTA) – will not be adopted separately but together as a 'package'. Throughout 2016, EU sources told this author that both agreements could be adopted by the end of 2016, but, like several other earlier self-imposed deadlines, the 2016 deadline, too, was missed.

During the 20th EU–Japan Summit in 2010, Brussels and Tokyo agreed to adopt two legally binding agreements: one to institutionalise and expand bilateral cooperation in international political and security and another to increase bilateral trade and investment ties through an FTA (Tyszkiewicz, 2013). In 2010, the so-called Framework Agreement (FA) (which was later renamed the SPA) and the EU–Japan Economic Partnership Agreement (EPA)/FTA were initially launched. The so-called 'scoping exercises' were launched after the EU–Japan 2011 Summit for both agreements as part of a parallel negotiation process: 'parallel' in the sense that it was agreed at the time that the two agreements would be adopted together and simultaneously. At the time, the European Commission sought the necessary authorisation from the

Union's member states for the negotiations of these agreements on the basis of a successful outcome of the 'scoping exercise'. The 'scoping exercise' was meant as a preparatory phase, during which the EU and Japanese sides both committed themselves to demonstrate their preparedness to agree on a common platform from which to negotiate both agreements. The scoping exercises for the SPA and the FTA were successfully concluded in April and May 2012, respectively.

The adoption of the SPA will be accompanied by the establishment of an inner-EU EU–Japan joint committee, that is, a committee through which the EU Commission informs the European External Action Service (EEAS) on the state and progress of the more than 40 EU–Japan sectoral dialogues.[1] So far, there are no regular exchanges between the EU Commission and the EEAS on EU–Japan sectoral dialogues, which is without much doubt a result of rivalry and struggle over competencies between the Commission and the EEAS. Either way, a joint EU–Japan committee – if used efficiently and effectively – is undoubtedly a relevant instrument and a way to allow the EU Commission and the EEAS to inform each other on their respective policies towards Japan. Indeed, the fact that such a committee has yet to be established, and that to date there is no regular forum for the EU Commission and the EEAS to exchange information and data on their respective exchanges with Japan, clearly hampers the EU's ability to formulate and adopt coherent and coordinated policies towards Japan.

The Strategic Partnership Agreement

The negotiations of the EU–Japan SPA were launched in 2013, and after the 11th round of negotiations in March 2016, the EU and Japan were able to agree on 31 out of the 54 articles of the agreement. The outstanding articles – referred to by the EU as 'politically sensitive'[2] – had to be adopted at the time. By July 2017, Brussels and Tokyo had agreed on all 54 articles. During the 24th EU–Japan Summit in July 2017, the EU and Japan announced that they had reached an agreement on all main elements of the SPA. However, negotiations on the SPA – together with the negotiations on the EU–Japan EPA/FTA – have yet to be finalised.[3] At the time of this writing (August 2017), this author has learned from Japanese sources that Brussels has requested additional time for what is referred to as 'final legal tuning'. Furthermore, the same Japanese sources explain, Brussels and the EU member states have yet to agree on and announce whether the SPA will be an EU-only or a mixed agreement. If it were an EU-only agreement, only the EU Commission would be competent. In the case of a mixed agreement, both the EU Commission and the EU member states would be competent. With that in mind, Japanese sources tell this author that Brussels and Tokyo aim at finalising negotiations by the end of 2017 in order to be able to sign the agreement over the course of 2018. The SPA is envisioned to be 'binding' in the sense that there will be – at least according to EU sources – a well-defined list of issues and areas the EU and Japan will be dealing with in the years ahead.

The SPA's 54 articles cover cooperation in over 30 areas, and the agreement will result in an upgrade of EU–Japan political and security cooperation, moving from sectoral agreements to a comprehensive, binding and forward-looking framework. The SPA will include political dialogue, regional dialogues, promotion of human rights and fundamental freedoms, and economic, scientific and cultural cooperation.

Unlike the previous EU–Japan Action Plan (adopted in 2011 and expired in 2011), the SPA will not be limited by a specific timeframe. The SPA will be a legally binding framework covering bilateral cooperation in politics and security. It will set out arrangements for regular meetings between respective political leaders and ministry officials.

What kind of agreement?

It has yet to be decided whether the SPA will be an EU-only agreement or a mixed agreement.[4] Obviously, the EU Commission is aiming for an EU-only agreement (with the Commission having exclusive competence), while a number of EU member states want a mixed agreement. A mixed agreement would have to be ratified by all EU member states, which would most probably further slow down the eventual adoption of the SPA.

Furthermore, and more importantly, Tokyo is opposed to the introduction into the agreement of the so-called 'Essential Elements Clause', a clause through which the EU reserves for itself the right to link issues such as human rights and non-proliferation to FTAs it adopts with other countries.[5] Through this clause, Brussels reserves for itself the right to interrupt an FTA with a partner country in the case of human rights violations in that particular country. EU sources tell this author that the EEAS is not 'happy' about having to insert that clause into an agreement with a democratic country either. That clause, the EU source emphasises, has been 'imposed' on Brussels by EU member states, and had it not been for EU member states' insistence on inserting that clause, it would not have been in the agreement with democratic Japan. EU sources furthermore stress that while individual EU member states do not have 'essential elements' clauses in their bilateral agreements with other countries, they expect the EU have such clauses in agreements. The treaty-based requirement for the EU to conduct a principled foreign policy is formulated in Article 21 of the Treaty of the Functioning of the European Union (TFEU). This requires the EU to stipulate in all agreements a respect for human rights and the non-proliferation of weapons of mass destruction, as well as to find a mechanism to link these political principles to the EU's trading concessions. This inclusion poses a special problem, not only with Japan but also with other like-minded and strategic partners such as South Korea, Singapore, Canada, Australia, New Zealand and other Southeast Asian countries with which negotiations have been concluded or are ongoing. While this approach may be a legal requirement of the EU, it has been contested by some of the EU's partners, including Japan.

The legal link Brussels wants between the FTA and the SPA was approved by the Union's Committee of Permanent Representatives (COREPER) in 2009. Through this link, the EU authorises itself to suspend an FTA in the case of, for example, human rights violations committed by the other party. To be sure, the possibility of Japan violating human rights, in turn leading to the interruption of negotiations with Brussels, was always very unlikely, but from a Japanese perspective such a clause is unambiguous and also understandably unwelcome, as it conveys a patronising message of Brussels 'supervising' the quality of Japanese foreign policies (Reiterer, 2013, 2015).

Hard security

In September 2005, Brussels and Tokyo began discussing Asian security issues on a regular basis by launching the 'EU–Japan Strategic Dialogue on East Asian Security' (Mykal, 2011). The establishment of that dialogue was preceded by the establishment of the 'EU–US Dialogue on East Asian Security' in 2004. Given that the EU weapons embargo imposed on China in 1989 was always the most central issue on the dialogue's agenda, it is accurate to conclude that the motivation for Tokyo to initiate regular exchanges on East Asian security in the framework of its dialogue with the EU on East Asian security was identical to Washington's motivations in 2004: institutionalising political pressure on Brussels not to lift the weapons embargo imposed on China after the Tiananmen Square massacre in 1989 (Berkofsky, 2012). Today, that dialogue continues, and its main objective is for the parties to informally consult with and inform each other on their respective security policies in East Asia. It has arguably not become – and was never intended to, as EU policymakers stress – a dialogue aimed at adopting EU–Japanese joint Asian security policies. In other words, those who expect the dialogue to be one leading to concrete joint EU–Japan policies will continue to be disappointed.

Today, Japan is governed by the Liberal Democratic Party (LDP), led by Prime Minister Shinzō Abe, who certainly has his doubts about the EU as a security actor able to help defend Japanese security interests in East Asia.[6] While bilateral defence relations with countries such as the UK and France have been expanded over the last two years (for details see following sections), it is accurate to conclude that the EU as a hard security policy actor with a role and influence in Asian hard security issues continues to have secondary importance in Tokyo's security policymaking circles (Pejsova, 2015); that is, unless Brussels – against the background of Chinese territorial expansionism in the South China Sea – decides to follow up on its verbal and written opposition against Beijing building civilian and military facilities on islands also claimed by other countries with concrete action (such as patrol missions in the South China Sea), as suggested by French Defence Minister Le Drian in 2016 (Panda, 2016).

Chinese unilateral territorial expansionism in disputed Asian territorial waters over the last three to four years has led Tokyo and Brussels to express joint concerns about China reclaiming and occupying disputed territories in the South China Sea. In April 2016, during the G7 Foreign Ministers' Statement on Maritime Security in Hiroshima, Brussels and Tokyo announced:

> We are concerned about the situation in the East and South China Seas and emphasise the fundamental importance of peaceful management and settlement of disputes. We express our strong opposition to any intimidating, coercive or provocative unilateral actions that could alter the status quo and increase tensions, and urge all states to refrain from such actions as land reclamations including large scale ones, building of outposts, as well as their use for military purposes and to act in accordance with international law including the principles of freedoms of navigation and overflight. (European External Action Service, 2016)

Even if China was not explicitly mentioned in this statement, it is very clear that it is China's unilateral territorial expansionism that was meant when the statement spoke of 'provocative unilateral actions'. However, this statement has not been followed up by joint EU–Japan policies aimed at deterring China. If the EU and Japan really maintain the 'natural alliance' mentioned below, then China's military rise and its very assertive and, indeed, aggressive policies related to territorial claims in the East and South China Seas could, or indeed should, lead to increased EU–Japan hard security cooperation. This, however, has not happened, even if some EU members recently (e.g. France during the International Institute for Security Studies Shangri-La Dialogue 2016 in Singapore.) called on fellow European countries to consider coordinated EU patrolling activities in the South China Sea (Roman, 2016). However, suggesting such joint patrol activities is one thing; doing the actual patrolling in the South China Sea is quite another, and it remains, indeed, very unlikely that there will be coordinated European patrolling activities in the South China Sea any time soon. Then again, should China continue to unilaterally reclaim disputed territories and render the passage of vessels through international waters in the South China Sea difficult in the months and years ahead, it is feasible that Europe – together with the US and/or Japan – might coordinate patrol activities in the South China Sea.

2016 was not the first time that Brussels and Tokyo expressed joint opposition to Chinese territorial expansionism. Already in 2015, in the joint press release of the EU–Japan Summit in May of that year, the EU and Japan stated:

> We continue to observe the situation in the East and South China Sea and are concerned by any unilateral actions that change the status quo and increase tensions. We support the full and effective implementation of the 2002 Declaration

on the Conduct of Parties in the South China Sea and the rapid conclusion of the negotiations to establish an effective Code of Conduct in the South China Sea. We highlight the constructive role of practical confidence-building measures, such as the establishment of direct links of communication in cases of crisis and crisis management mechanisms in this regard. (European Commission, 2015)

While such a joint statement is positive per se and to be understood as jointly expressing opposition against Chinese unilateral territorial expansionism, it certainly should have gone beyond 'highlighting the constructive role of confidence-building measures' if the purpose was to send a clear message that Brussels and Tokyo are prepared to be more than just 'concerned' about Chinese aggressive policies related to territorial claims in the South China Sea. Instead, the declaration should have called on China directly and unambiguously to stick to what it has promised to do in the past: talk and negotiate on territorial disputes it has with Southeast Asian nations. Instead, Beijing is, through the construction of civilian and also military facilities on disputed islands, rapidly and continuously creating facts on the ground, and a timid and very diplomatic EU–Japan joint statement is obviously not changing anything. To be sure, a stronger EU–Japan statement in 2016 and a statement that had directly called on China not to unilaterally change the territorial status quo in the region would not have changed anything about Beijing's territorial expansionism, but at least Beijing would have received a clearer message, to which it could have reacted (as opposed to ignoring the above-mentioned statement). The statement is indeed toothless, and it looks like a statement for the sake of making a statement as opposed to one that is expected to have an impact on Chinese regional policy behaviour.[7]

However, some EU–Japan hard/military security cooperation has already taken place in the recent past. Tokyo and Brussels have been working together to fight maritime piracy off the Coast of Somalia and in the Gulf of Aden since 2009. Japanese Maritime Self-Defense Force (MSDF) destroyers began their participation in March 2009, along with two P-3C maritime patrol aircraft added in June 2009. The MSDF unit has been providing data to and sharing information with other countries, and has been conducting operations in the field, including EU Naval Force (NAVFOR) Somalia Operation Atalanta, a Common Security and Defence Policy (CSDP) military mission operational since the end of 2008.[8] In January 2014, for example, cooperation between European and Japanese navies resulted in the arrest of pirates, and European and Japanese naval forces have been conducting joint exercises since October 2014. In October and November 2014, the Japanese navy participated in naval military exercises with Italian, German and Dutch naval vessels. Those exercises included activities such as tactical manoeuvring, helicopter take-off and landing, and boarding (Fukushima, 2015) (see also Chapter 12 in this volume).

Finally, both the EU and Tokyo are providing development assistance to Somalia and some neighbouring countries, and are also jointly helping to train

Somali maritime security officials. Akiko Fukushima (2015) argues that there is further potential for collaboration on capacity-building in Somalia.

Japanese contributions to CSDP missions

In August 2012, the EU deployed a civilian CSDP mission to Niger to provide training in the country's security sector. In December 2014, Tokyo decided to provide grant aid through the UN Development Programme to the EU's CSDP mission in Niger. At the time of writing, Tokyo has spent 202 million yen on wireless communication devices to connect regional government offices with bureaus under their jurisdiction, as well as wireless-equipped vehicles for patrolling in various locations in Niger's seven administrative regions (Berkofsky, 2017). In April 2014, Brussels deployed a civilian CSDP mission to Mali, assisting the country in the security sector. A year later, in March 2015, Japan started contributing to the same mission, providing grant aid amounting to 492 million yen for the rehabilitation of Mali's national police school. Japan's cooperation with CSDP missions, Akiko Fukushima (2015) argues, was facilitated by Tokyo's expertise in the rebuilding of infrastructure in Iraq since the early 2000s (for which Japan used part of the country's Official Development Assistance (ODA) budget at the time).

During the 22nd Japan–EU Summit in Brussels in May 2014, Japanese Prime Minister Shinzō Abe, then European Council President Herman Van Rompuy and President of the European Commission Jose Manuel Barroso announced the promotion of closer collaboration between the EU's CSDP missions and Japan's assistance and security cooperation initiatives in direct support of ongoing CSDP missions.

> At the 2014 EU–Japan Summit, Brussels and Tokyo furthermore announced that they would:
> 1. Promote the Anti-Personnel Mine Ban Convention
> 2. Counter the illicit trade in small arms and light weapons, especially in Libya and the Sahel region
> 3. Press for the early entry into force and effective implementation of the Arms Trade Treaty

Brussels and Tokyo also expressed their commitment to ensuring strict export controls of arms and dual-use items and technologies, particularly in conflict areas. Finally, Brussels and Tokyo also announced further intensification of collaboration between Tokyo's humanitarian and technical assistance operations and the EU's CSDP mission in Mali and the Democratic Republic of Congo. It was agreed to strengthen joint capacity-building measures for the national military forces of Mali, to jointly support the peacekeeping school of Bamako, and to jointly assist the improvement of security and anti-terrorism laws and the enhancement of judicial cooperation in Mali. It was also agreed to jointly assist capacity-building measures for police officers and judicial administrators in the Democratic Republic of Congo. Finally, it was agreed to jointly assist the improvement of security and anti-terrorism laws and the enhancement of judicial cooperation in Niger (European Commission, 2014).

Bilateral defence ties (France and the UK)

In January 2014, France and Japan held their first ministerial-level foreign affairs/defence ministers' (two-plus-two) meeting (Berkofsky, 2017). During the second French–Japanese two-plus-two meeting in 2015, the respective foreign and defence ministers discussed the so-called 'Plan of Action for Africa', which included the possibility of joint French–Japanese border security actions in Niger, Mali and Burkina Faso and joint peacekeeping policies and missions in Africa (*Japan Times*, 2015). In July 2014, Paris and Tokyo signed a memorandum of understanding (MOU) to increase cooperation in the area of defence, including the joint development of military equipment. This is envisioned to include, among other things, the joint development of unmanned underwater vehicles.

In April 2012, Tokyo and London had already signed a first joint weapons development agreement, which in July 2013 was followed by two additional British–Japanese agreements – the so-called 'Defence Equipment Cooperation Framework' to facilitate joint development of military equipment and the 'Information Security Agreement' facilitating increased cooperation in the area of intelligence (Government of the United Kingdom, 2013). This resulted in, among other things, British–Japanese joint developments of chemical and biological warfare suits and cooperation in the area of missile technology. In May 2014, London and Tokyo initiated negotiations on a bilateral Acquisition and Cross-Servicing Agreement (ACSA), which foresees the provision of logistical, material and technical support for each other's armed forces. Finally, in January 2015, London and Tokyo held their first two-plus-two meeting.

Given Prime Minister Abe's strong interest in upgrading Japan's military capabilities, competencies and partnerships (facilitated by the adoption of new national security laws in September 2015, which constitute the legal framework for the Japanese military to be able to execute the right to collective self-defence, as formulated in Chapter VII of the Charter of the United Nations[9] authorising Japanese armed forces to execute the right to collective self-defence), there is obviously a risk that Tokyo under Abe will focus on the development of bilateral hard security partnerships with European countries such as France and the UK. While this does not necessarily mean that Japan under the (very) pro-defence Prime Minister Abe will neglect the SPA with the whole of the EU, the expansion of bilateral defence ties with Paris and London is arguably an indication of Tokyo's security policy priorities. Indeed, Abe is very likely to continue focusing on pursuing the adoption of guidelines and the legal framework to facilitate ties between Japanese and European defence contractors, something Japanese defence lobbies have been urging the government to do for years.

Framework Partnership Agreement

Currently, Brussels and Tokyo are also negotiating the FPA, an agreement aimed at facilitating the deployment of Japanese armed forces troops within the framework of CSDP missions. Once adopted, the FPA will institutionalise Japanese contributions to European CSDP missions, such as the above-mentioned Japanese contributions to EU CSDP missions in Niger and Mali. However, at the time of writing (August 2017), there is no information publicly available on the current state of negotiations other than that negotiations are 'ongoing'. Without the FPA, the EU and Japan are, strictly and legally speaking, not conducting a joint mission but are engaged in what Brussels refers to as 'parallel coordinated action'. It is hoped in Brussels that the FPA will create stronger links between the development-security nexus and, as Andrea Fontini (2016) argues, synergies between the EU's 'comprehensive approach' to regional and global security and Japan's 'human security' concept in the Middle East and Asia. Fontini must have referred to the 2014 European Council[10] Conclusions (Council of the European Union, 2014), which declare that the EU and its member states can '[b]ring to the international stage the unique ability to combine, in a coherent and consistent manner, policies and tools ranging from diplomacy, security and defence to finance, trade, development and human rights, as well as justice and migration'. To be sure, the devil lies in the details, and time will tell whether or not the EU's 'comprehensive approach' and Tokyo's concept of 'human security' are compatible and can result in joint policies in the Middle East, Asia and elsewhere. Fontini also speaks of 'post-industrial security dossiers' such as counter-terrorism, maritime security, resource management (among other things, water, food and energy), natural disaster prevention and management, cyber-defence, arms control, and non-proliferation of weapons of mass destruction. Many of these areas and issues most probably will – one way or another – be part of EU–Japan security cooperation as formulated in the SPA.[11]

The China factor

If the EU is serious about increasing its involvement in Asian security, and if Japan is really the EU's 'natural ally' in Asia, then China's military rise and its increasingly assertive regional security policies in general, and policies related to territorial claims in the East and Southeast Asian territorial waters in particular, should be part of EU–Japan security cooperation. However, China's territorial expansion in the South China Sea over the last two to three years has not led to any concrete EU–Japanese policies directed at countering Beijing's unilateral territorial expansionism. Brussels will most probably continue to remain (very) reluctant to get involved in Asian territorial disputes beyond issuing statements urging all involved parties to solve disputes peacefully. Furthermore, it must not go unmentioned that the EU's EEAS is not an organisation operating independently of EU member states (some of which have strong reservations about getting involved in disputes with China due to business and economic ties with and in China). Furthermore, the EU continues to insist that it does not take sides in territorial disputes and arguably does not have – unlike the US – the resources and capabilities in the region (i.e. military troops and navy vessels) to deter China from building facilities and military bases on disputed islands in the South China Sea.

The more Beijing seeks to unilaterally change the territorial status quo in Asia in its favour, the more the EU and Japan should arguably realise that consulting with, let alone cooperating, with China on regional security is an illusion and is not something in which Beijing is in any way seriously interested. Indeed, Chinese assertive, and increasingly often aggressive, regional policies and policies related to territorial claims in Asia should, from Tokyo's perspective, inject a 'sense of urgency' into European interests in Asian regional security and encourage European policymakers to side with Japan in its efforts to keep China's regional territorial expansionism in the East and South China Seas in check.[12]

Doubts about the potential impact of European concerns and advice on Chinese regional and global security policy notwithstanding, in 2010 the EU and China set up an annual dialogue, which also covers Asian security. The last annual 'EU–China High-Level Strategic Dialogue' was held in June 2016,[13] and for years Brussels policymakers have hoped, among other things, that the dialogue would encourage Beijing to become more transparent about its defence expenditures and military equipment procurement and sales policies.[14] However, that clearly turned out to be a case of European wishful thinking, as China will not make any more information on its arms procurement policies available simply because the EU is requesting just that in a bilateral dialogue. When analysts[15] argue that the EU–China strategic dialogue on Asian security is nothing more than an annual window-dressing event as opposed to a dialogue that produces real results, let alone joint policies related to Asian security, EU policymakers typically explain that the dialogue's objective is not the adoption of joint policies but, rather, a platform to informally consult with each other on Asian security issues. While dialogue and consultations are positive as such, the raison d'être of such a dialogue must, however, be put in doubt if European advice and input on Chinese regional security policy conduct, such as Beijing's (very) assertive policies related to territorial claims in the East and South China Seas, are mostly ignored in Beijing. Indeed, the reality of Chinese regional security policy conduct and policies has shown that Beijing's preparedness to consult with the EU on security issues that fall under what Beijing refers to as its 'core interests' – the Taiwan and Tibet 'questions' and what Beijing refers to as 'territorial integrity' in Asia's disputed territorial waters – is *de facto* non-existent. If that is accurate, and if European views and advice on Chinese security policies in Asia are only endorsed during official encounters as opposed to in the 'real' world, then it is fair to question whether the dialogue on Asian security with China is an efficient use of EU resources and political capital (Berkofsky, 2015). Against this background, it is accurate to point out that security issues have become a passing mention on the agendas of the 'High-Level Dialogues' in April 2015 and the most recent in June 2016.

Even if, as indicated in the preceding paragraphs, the bilateral EU–Chinese dialogue on Asian security does not produce any real results, that is, does not lead to Beijing changing its regional security policy behaviour, Japanese policymakers (and scholars likewise[16]) have at times wondered how much substance there is to Brussels announcing that Japan is the EU's 'natural ally' in Asian politics and security[17] (Berkofsky, 2014). Indeed, even if Brussels (like Washington, at least for now) is officially not taking sides in the Sino-Japanese territorial dispute in the East China Sea, Tokyo's policymakers have not always had the impression that Brussels' support for Japan defending islands that since 1895 have been *de facto* part of Japanese territory is sufficient. To be sure, Tokyo is obviously aware of the EU's difficulties in formulating and implementing one 'set' of European policies towards China[18] and is equally aware of Chinese tactics of economic retaliation in the case of perceived 'interference' in Chinese domestic and foreign policies. Therefore, the 2016 joint EU–Japan statement on Chinese territorial policies and claims in the East and South China Seas (very outspoken by EU standards) must have been appreciated in Tokyo after previous EU statements on Chinese aggressive territorial policies in the East and South China Seas that had been far less outspoken and, in essence, limited themselves to urging all involved parties to solve outstanding territorial disputes peacefully.[19] Both Brussels and Tokyo are fully aware that such European 'interference' will be all but completely ignored by Beijing, and Japanese policymakers obviously know that Brussels has few illusions about influencing Chinese security policy behaviour in general, and Chinese aggressive policies related to territorial claims in the East and South China Seas in particular. Against the background of the described Chinese regional security policy behaviour and the lack of anything resembling tangible results coming out of the Union's security dialogue with Beijing, further institutionalised EU–Japan security cooperation as envisioned in the SPA is – at least in theory – an opportunity for Brussels and Tokyo to demonstrate that their own dialogue on Asian security is able to produce results and joint policies reflecting similar approaches of two like-minded democratic countries towards regional and global security. Whether Brussels and Tokyo will take advantage of such an opportunity remains to be seen, and mostly depends on whether policymakers in both the EU and Japan will be prepared to assign sufficient resources and political capital to producing not only joint statements but also, importantly, joint (security) policies.

Conclusion

Andrew Small and Sarah Raine (2015) argued in a paper for the German Marshall Fund that 'Japan's National Security Strategy of 2013 highlighted the convergence of interests and ideals that underlies these policies, namely that "Europe has the influence to formulate international public opinions, the capacity to develop norms in major international frameworks"' (Government of Japan, 2013, p. 26). While this sounds good on paper and can indeed be interpreted as Japanese (on paper) preparedness to work with the EU and Europe in promoting and enforcing shared norms, it remains to be seen where and to what extent such a declaration will translate into actual joint policies beyond the ones already taking place.

Michito Tsuruoka (2013) argued that intensifying cooperation requires both Japan and the EU to overcome what he calls an 'expectation deficit' in EU–Japan relations. Today, it is probably fair to conclude that such an 'expectation deficit' (if it ever existed) has been overcome after years of joint experience in non-military security cooperation. Both Brussels and Tokyo are undoubtedly aware that the SPA – if and when finally adopted – will not necessarily be the 'Big Bang' of EU–Japan cooperation in regional and global politics and security, but will, rather, give the existing cooperation and that envisioned in the future an institutional framework.

As elaborated earlier, it will be interesting to observe whether Chinese territorial expansionism will in the months and years ahead facilitate or, indeed, necessitate further EU involvement in Asian hard security through maritime patrolling. To be sure, whether such further involvement on Asian 'ground' could jointly take place with Japan remains to be seen (and is, indeed, rather unlikely any time soon), but if the EU and Japan really want to follow up on joint political rhetoric to increase their joint impact and role in global security, then it might become – depending on the level of Chinese preparedness to unilaterally claim and occupy disputed territories in the South China Sea – inevitable to jointly patrol international waters in the South China Sea. For Japan, hard EU–Japan security cooperation in Asia will continue to be complementary to security and defence cooperation with the US, at least for the foreseeable future.

Japan's solidarity with the US and the EU in 2014 in imposing economic sanctions in reaction to Russia's annexation of Crimea was an important indication of Tokyo's preparedness to support Western policies aimed at safeguarding international legal norms and standards. By doing so, Japan has taken a clear position and is – without doubt – counting on European countries' support for its efforts to deter and, indeed, contain Chinese territorial ambitions in the East and South China Seas.[20] Indeed, Japan is expecting more tangible European support as regards Tokyo's defence of its territorial integrity in the East China Sea in the case of Chinese intrusions into Japanese-controlled territorial waters, but is aware that Brussels is not prepared and, indeed, not able – due above all to strong opposition from (some) EU member states[21] – to get involved in a dispute that touches upon the (territorial) interests of a country that is able (and, indeed, willing) to retaliate against 'interference in its internal affairs'.[22]

In the meantime, the EU and Japan are advised to make a clear choice that is necessary to safeguard their respective individual and joint credibility: the choice of whether or not to limit bilateral cooperation strictly to cooperation of non-military nature (which would most probably exclude joint patrolling activities in the South China Sea) or to jointly respond to a more unstable security environment and also get involved in military security cooperation in East and Southeast Asia (which would be, as mentioned earlier, perceived by China as interference in its internal affairs). If EU–Japan military cooperation responding to increased Japanese concerns about aggressive and expansionist Chinese regional policies does not, in terms of resources and energy, come at the expense of the above-mentioned EU–Japanese non-military security cooperation, then there is arguably nothing against expanding bilateral EU–Japan security cooperation to include military cooperation also. To be sure, for Europe there would be a price to be paid for EU–Japan military security cooperation such as joint patrolling in the East or South China Sea, as Beijing is clearly acting in zero-sum terms in this context, and hence EU–Japan military security cooperation would almost inevitably lead to the interruption of EU–Chinese bilateral consultation on Asian security in the framework of the EU–China High-Level Strategic Dialogue.

In practical terms, however, that should not be a major problem. As mentioned earlier, the EU–China High-Level Strategic Dialogue has not led to any increased Chinese interest in letting the EU 'interfere' in Chinese regional and global security policies. In other words, the part of the bilateral dialogue that deals with security issues is, as mentioned earlier, nothing more than 'window-dressing' as opposed to a dialogue that produces actual results, even if Brussels (in official declarations) argues that China is prepared to take European advice and input on Chinese security policies into account. Consequently, Beijing's interrupting bilateral consultation on Asian security with Brussels is – speaking in realpolitik terms – not a loss, as Beijing never intended to include the EU in its security policy thinking and action in the first place.

As regards joint capacity-building assistance, the EU, NATO and Japan, it is sometimes suggested by scholars and policymakers likewise, could pool resources and consider a trilateral security cooperation.[23] Although such resource pooling has been suggested several times in the past, the idea of expanding bilateral to trilateral cooperation probably would not contribute to making EU–Japan cooperation less complicated and more efficient. 'Pooling resources' is easily said in international relations lingo, but much harder and complicated to do in real life. In fact, it is time for EU and Japanese policymakers to move beyond nice and high-sounding political rhetoric and announcements, and adopting the SPA sooner rather than (much) later could be a step in that (right) direction.

Notes

1. As told to the author by EU sources in conversations in 2016.
2. Conversation with an EEAS official in May 2016.
3. EU and Japanese official sources told this author that both Brussels and Tokyo hope to have concluded by the end of 2017.
4. As an EU official told this author in August 2017.
5. At the time of writing (August 2017), publicly accessible information on the wording of the 'Essential Elements Clause' is not available. When asked on the clause within the agreement, Japanese sources limited themselves to telling this author that Tokyo has sought to adopt an agreement that reflects 'mutual trust between Japan and the EU'.
6. For a prime minister who over recent years has invested and keeps on investing enormous resources and political capital into expanding Japan's hard security ties and cooperation with countries both inside and outside East Asia (such as the US, Australia and India), closer and more intense hard security and military ties (above all, obviously, those with Washington) remain the fundamental basis and instrument to protect and defend Japanese security and security interests.
7. When reaching such and similar conclusions regarding Chinese policy behaviour, analysts like this author are often confronted with the counter-argument and criticism that Beijing reacts very strongly to strong statements on its domestic and foreign policies, which in turn is counterproductive and does not achieve the desired results. While that might be true, it must be pointed out that attempts to influence Chinese foreign policy behaviour in general, and that related to territorial claims in the East and South China Sea in particular, diplomatically and attempts to take all Chinese sensitivities into account have not produced any results either.
8. EU NAVFOR's main tasks are to escort merchant vessels carrying humanitarian aid for the World Food Program, to protect ships in the Gulf of Aden and the Indian Ocean, and to deter and disrupt piracy. EU NAVFOR also monitors fishing activity off the coast of Somalia.
9. Until the Japanese government led by Prime Minister Shinzō Abe initiated the reinterpretation of the war-renouncing Article 9 of the Japanese constitution in 2014, Japan denied itself the right to execute the right to collective self-defence, that is, the right to militarily defend soldiers from other countries in the case of military conflict.
10. The EU institution representing the EU member states.
11. How many and to what extent remains to be seen (as the SPA has yet to be adopted).
12. Several interviews the author conducted with Japanese officials from the Ministry of Foreign Affairs of Japan and the Ministry of Defense of Japan in 2014, 2015 and 2016 confirm this.
13. For some (not many) details on the dialogue, see European External Actions Service (EEAS), China and the EU at: https://eeas.europa.eu/headquarters/headquarters-homepage/15394/china-and-eu_en#Political+relations.
14. Interviews and conversations with officials from the EEAS in 2015 and 2016. The argument that this dialogue with China grants the EU – at least within limits – more access to information on Chinese defence procurement policies, however, arguably does not correspond with reality. In reality, Chinese defence procurement policies and strategies are and remain a closed book to outsiders, and an annual informal security dialogue with the EU does not change this at all.
15. As this author has done many times in the context of roundtables, conferences and workshops dealing with EU–China relations. EU officials present at those events typically disagreed, but were at the same time not able to cite any significant results of the EU–China security dialogue that could qualify as going beyond the informal exchange of

16 Japanese policymakers, officials and scholars this author has spoken with in 2015 and 2016.
17 'Natural ally' is a term the EEAS uses when pointing to the (great) potential of EU–Japan cooperation in Asian politics and security.
18 Due to competing interests and China policy priorities among EU member states.
19 Indeed, an official from the EEAS told this author that the 2016 Hiroshima statement was the most outspoken and unambiguous EU statement on China's very assertive and, indeed, aggressive territorial policies in the East and South China Seas that Brussels has ever adopted. Chinese officials and scholars, on the other hand, were (far) less appreciative of that EU–Japan joint statement, and at the time, unsurprisingly, accused the EU of taking sides in the territorial dispute, in violation of what Beijing in such cases typically refers to as 'China's territorial integrity'.
20 As numerous conversations with Japanese policymakers and officials in 2015 and 2016 have confirmed.
21 EU policymakers confirmed in several interviews with this author that the economic and trade interests of the EU's bigger member states are at times an obstacle to Brussels voicing more outspoken protests against China not respecting international law and practice in Asian disputed territorial waters.
22 China is – at least in Japan's view – clearly such a country, as this author's interviews with officials from the Japanese Ministry of Defense in 2015 and 2016 confirm.
23 This author has heard this suggestion numerous times during conferences and roundtables on EU–Japan relations. However, such and similar suggestions have typically remained on the surface, and those who made such suggestions did not add any details of what exactly such a 'pooling of resources' would actually look like.

REFERENCES

Berkofsky, A., 2012. 'EU-Japan Relations from 2001 to Today: Achievements, Failures and Prospects', *Japan Forum*, 24(3): 265–288.
Berkofsky, A., 2014. 'The European Union (EU) in Asian Security: Actor with a Punch or Distant Bystander?', *Asia-Pacific Review*, 21(2): 61–85.
Berkofsky, A., 2015. 'EU-China Security Dialogue: Rhetoric versus a Very Different Reality', cogitAsia, Center for Security and International Studies (CSIS), Washington DC, at: www.cogitasia.com/eu-china-security-dialogue-rhetoric-versus-a-very-different-reality (accessed 1 March 2018).
Berkofsky, A., 2017. 'The EU for Japan – Primary or Secondary Partner in International Politics and Security?', Commentary Istituto per gli Studi di Politica Internazionale (ISPI), at: www.ispionline.it/en/pubblicazione/eu-japan-primary-or-secondary-partner-international-politics-and-security-16186 (accessed 1 March 2018).
Council of the European Union, 2014. 'Council Conclusions of the Union's Comprehensive Approach, Foreign Affairs Council Meeting Brussels', 12 May, at: www.consilium.europa.eu/uedocs/cms_Data/docs/pressdata/EN/foraff/142552.pdf (accessed 1 March 2018).
European Commission, 2014. 'The EU and Japan Acting Together for Global Peace and Prosperity', 22nd EU-Japan Summit Joint Press Statement Brussels, 7 May, at: europa.eu/rapid/press-release_STATEMENT-14–151_en.htm (accessed 1 March 2018).

European Commission, 2015. Fact Sheet: 23rd Japan-EU Summit, Tokyo, 29 May, Joint Press Statement, at: europa.eu/rapid/press-release_MEMO-15-5075_en.htm (accessed 1 March 2018).

European External Action Service (EEAS), 2016. G7 Foreign Ministers' Statement on Maritime Security, 11 April 2016, Hiroshima, at: http://eeas.europa.eu/statements-eeas/2016/160411_05_en.htm (accessed 1 March 2018).

Fontini, A., 2016. 'Advancing the EU-Japan Strategic Partnership in a Transforming Global Environment: Challenges, Opportunities and Prospects', European Policy Centre (EPC) Policy Brief, 3 March, at: epc.eu/documents/uploads/pub_6363_eu-japan_strategic_partnership.pdf (accessed 1 March 2018).

Fukushima, A., 2015. 'Japan-Europe Cooperation for Peace and Stability: Pursuing Synergies on a Comprehensive Approach', Policy Brief Asia Program, April, The German Marshall Fund of the United States.

Government of Japan, 2013. *National Security Strategy (NSS) (December 17, 2013)* (Tokyo: Government of Japan).

Government of the United Kingdom, 2013. 'Foreign Secretary Signs Groundbreaking Defence and Security Agreements with Japan', Press Release, 4 July 2013, at: gov.uk/government/news/foreign-secretary-signs-groundbreaking-defence-and-security-agreements-with-japan (accessed 1 March 2018).

Japan Times, 2015. 'France, Japan to Discuss Joint Counterterrorism Operations in Africa', 11 March.

Mykal, O., 2011. *The EU-Japan Security Dialogue: Invisible but Comprehensive* (Amsterdam: Amsterdam University Press).

Panda, A., 2016. 'French Defense Minister to Urge EU South China Patrols', *The Diplomat*, 6 June, at: http://thediplomat.com/2016/06/french-defense-minister-to-urge-eu-south-china-sea-patrols (accessed 1 March 2018).

Pejsova, E., 2015. 'The EU and Japan: Stepping up the Game', Brief Issue 15/2015, European Union Institute for Security Studies (EUISS), Paris, May, at: www.iss.europa.eu/sites/default/files/EUISSFiles/Brief_15_EU-Japan.pdf (accessed 1 March 2018).

Reiterer, M., 2013. 'The EU-Japan Relationship in Dynamic Asia', in Keck, J., Vanoverbeke, D. and Waldenberger, F. (eds), *From Confrontation to Global Partnership: EU-Japan Relations from 1970 to the Treaty of Lisbon and Beyond* (Abingdon and New York: Routledge), pp. 293–328.

Reiterer, M., 2015. 'EU Security Interests in East Asia: Prospects for Comprehensive EU – Japan Cooperation beyond Trade and Economics', NFG Policy Paper No. 6, June.

Roman, D., 2016. 'France to Push for Coordinated EU Patrols in South China Sea', *Bloomberg News*, 5 June, at: www.bloomberg.com/news/articles/2016-06-05/france-to-push-for-coordinated-eu-patrols-in-south-china-sea (accessed 1 March 2018).

Small, A. and Raine, S., 2015. *Waking Up to Geopolitics: A New Trajectory to Japan-Europe Relations*. Washington: The German Marshall Fund of the United States.

Tsuruoka, M., 2013. 'The EU and Japan: Making the Most of Each Other', European Union Institute for Security Studies (EUISS), Paris Alert, 36.

Tyszkiewicz, R., 2013. 'Towards New Political and Economic Agreements with Japan: Bringing New Dynamism into the Strategic Partnership between the EU and Japan', Policy Paper No. 9 (57), The Polish Institute of International Affairs (PISM), Warsaw, April, at: pism.pl/files/?id_plik=13357 (accessed 1 March 2018).

12

EU–Japan security partnership in practice: The counter-piracy mission off the coast of Somalia

Wilhelm Vosse

Introduction

AFTER THE PRECEDING two chapters provided an overview of EU–Japan security relations from the European and a Japanese perspective, this chapter will introduce the first example of an operational security cooperation, which was not confined to government-to-government cooperation but involved military-to-military cooperation in the field, namely, in the counter-piracy mission off the coast of Somalia. While neither the Japanese government nor the European Union considered the counter-piracy mission as a military mission, regarding it instead as a constabulary or law-enforcing measure,[1] the mission required both Japan and the EU to deploy their maritime forces and enabled them to cooperate in ways not unlike a limited military operation.

Maritime piracy has been an issue of concern for seafarers, shipping companies and governments for a long time. In East Asia, maritime piracy had already been a problem in the 1990s, but in East Africa and the Gulf of Aden, the problem became more serious between 2007 and 2009, when the number of incidences of maritime piracy increased from 44 to 218 (International Chamber of Commerce Commercial Crime Services (ICC-CSS) data). Most of these attacks occurred off the coast of Somalia, a country that had long suffered from civil wars and had no functioning government, and in the Gulf of Aden between Somalia and Yemen.

This chapter will introduce the main reasons and different stages of involvement of the Japanese government and the Maritime Self-Defense Force (MSDF) and Japan Coast Guard (JCG) in the counter-piracy mission off the coast of Somalia, before focusing on the question of the extent to which this mission provided opportunities for closer EU–Japan security cooperation, and what significance this case already has had and might have for the future EU–Japan security cooperation more broadly, at a time when their Strategic Partnership Agreement (SPA) is still being negotiated.

Japan's counter-piracy operations off the coast of Somalia

In October 2007, the *Golden Nori*, a Japanese-owned ship under Panamanian flag, was approached by pirates and hijacked off the Somali coast. After negotiations, there were unconfirmed reports and claims by the pirates that a US$1 million ransom had been paid.[2] In 2008, five Japanese-owned vessels were approached; in four cases they were hijacked, and in most of these cases the Japanese owner paid a ransom. Between June and December 2008, the United Nations Security Council began reacting to the growing crisis by passing a series of resolutions on maritime piracy off the coast of Somalia, authorising naval forces to enter Somali waters (UNSC 1816), to suppress piracy and reconfirm UNCLOS[3] (UNSC 1838), to criminalise piracy (UNSC 1846) and to set up the Contact Group on Piracy off the Coast of Somalia (CGPCS) (UNSC 1851).

These resolutions formed the legal justification for the international community to use military force against piracy. Until 2008, Japan had employed the Self-Defense Forces (SDF) only for United Nations Peacekeeping Operations (UNPKO), mine sweeping, and humanitarian and reconstruction missions (e.g. the Iraq mission), and was traditionally very hesitant to deploy the SDF. However, this case was different in two respects. First, the Japanese government joined the counter-piracy mission almost from the very beginning, and second, it was the first Japanese deployment to a mission that was not a UNPKO, humanitarian and reconstruction, or rear-area support mission, but one in which the potential use of force was integral to the mission rather than merely a risk of undertaking the mission. Japan joined the multilateral counter-piracy mission off the coast of Somalia and the CGPCS in 2009, and gradually became even more deeply involved in the political and military governing of the anti-piracy missions. Second, this was the first time the SDF had joined a non-PKO multilateral military operation with more than 40 other countries, which provided a major opportunity to engage and interact with militaries other than that of the US.[4]

Japan's active participation in the counter-piracy mission off the coast of Somalia began on 28 January 2009, when the Japanese minister of defence issued an order to the commander in chief of the MSDF Fleet and the director general of the Defense Intelligence Headquarters to begin preparations for a mission against piracy off the coast of Somalia and in the Gulf of Aden. The outline of the instructions asked the MSDF to prepare for (1) the formation of the unit; (2) information gathering; (3) training for the mission; (4) the procurement, replenishment, storage and maintenance of necessary means; and (5) coordination with relevant organisations.

Shortly thereafter, in February 2009, a Ministry of Defense (MOD) and SDF personnel field investigation team was sent to visit Yemen, Djibouti, Oman and Bahrain. In March 2009, the MOD and SDF were similarly commissioned to review possible bases for Japanese troops, aircraft and vessels (Japanese Ministry of Defense, 2009c), and only three weeks later, on 14 March 2009, the first two MSDF destroyers, the DD *Sazanami* and the DD *Samidare*, left their base in Kure with about 400 MSDF personnel and eight JCG officers for the Gulf of Aden (Japanese Ministry of Defense, 2009a, b). The destroyers also carried two helicopters. The legal framework of this first dispatch was Article 82 of the SDF Law, which allowed the deployment of MSDF personnel without Diet approval when 'special measures are deemed necessary to protect lives and property or maintain order at sea' (SDF Law, 1954, Article 82).

The Law on Punishment of and Measures against Acts of Piracy or Anti-Piracy Law came into force on 24 June 2009 after a fierce debate in the Japanese Diet (Black, 2012). It finally allowed the MSDF to protect ships owned by countries other than Japan, which made Japan a fully functioning independent deployer. The law provides a clear definition of acts of piracy, or attempted piracy, and the penalties that these incur (Government of Japan, 2009: Articles 1 to 4). Japan considers piracy a criminal offence and, therefore, regards the anti-piracy mission as a matter of policing and law enforcement, which is why the JCG plays a central role in enforcing the law. However, since the JCG does not have ships that would allow passage from Japan to Somalia, the MSDF is in charge of providing the necessary support activities, such as observation and transportation of JCG officers, while the JCG takes 'necessary measures pursuant to the provisions of this law', in line with the Japan Coast Guard Law (Law No. 28 of 1953) (Government of Japan, 2009: Article 5). Only JCG officials, and not the MSDF, may use weapons, provided the 'perpetrator or the ship disobeys other measures to deter and continues the acts of piracy and that there is probable cause to believe in the lack of any other appropriate measures to stop the navigation of that ship' (Government of Japan, 2009: Article 6) regulated by existing policing laws.[5] This law is different from special measures laws such as the Anti-Terrorism Law (October 2011) or the refuelling mission in the Indian Ocean (2001–2010), in that it gives the minister of defence, with the approval of the prime minister, the right to order units of the SDF to take 'actions against acts of piracy at sea in the case where there is extraordinary necessity to take measures against acts of piracy' and to 'draw up and submit to the Prime Minister the guidelines for response operations' (Government of Japan, 2009: Article 7).[6]

The EU and counter-piracy off the coast of Somalia

The European Union and its European naval forces (EU NAVFOR) as well as individual EU member states have a longer history of multilateral cooperation through EU NAVFOR, as well as through NATO missions and exercises, before the beginning of the EU mission Atalanta. Simultaneously, they also gained experience through other missions, such as Mission Sophia in the Mediterranean Ocean, which has tackled the refugee crisis since 2015 (Tardy, 2015).

The EU NAVFOR mission Atalanta was launched in December 2008. As in the case of Japan, it was a reaction to the UNSC Resolutions mentioned earlier and was considered part of the European Common Security and Defence Policy (CSDP). Initially, its main purpose was the protection of the World Food Programme (WFP) vessels delivering food aid to Somalia, and to protect the African Union Mission in Somalia. While the EU had conducted 22 European Security and Defence Policy (ESDP) missions since 2003, the majority were in policing, border monitoring and military peacekeeping. However, the EU NAVFOR mission Atalanta was a military operation against a defined culprit, which made it an 'important departure from the typical pattern of ESDP missions established since 2003', because it 'involved a direct threat to the interests of EU member states' (Germond and Smith, 2009: 575–576). Others found at this early stage that 'the EU used the increase in piracy outside Somalia as an opportunity to prove its self-sufficiency as a foreign policy actor' and as an important opportunity to work with the other participating nations, including China and Japan, in the designated coordinating bodies (particularly Shared Awareness and Deconfliction (SHADE) and CGPCS (Riddervold, 2011: 393).

EU and Japanese commitment in counter-piracy

After this short general introduction to the specific reasons, and the specific political and military context, for joining the maritime counter-piracy missions off the coast of Somalia in 2009, this chapter will return to the central question; namely, in what ways these missions provided opportunities for closer political and military cooperation between Japan and the EU and some of its member states. It will first focus on the operational cooperation before assessing its significance for closer political and security cooperation between Japan and the EU.

Comparison of military commitment

For an independent deployer, and one that was geographically located at a great distance from the theatre of operation, and for a country with traditionally strong anti-militarist values, even considering Japan's strong dependence on oil supplies from the Gulf States and its strong support for the *United Nations Convention on the Law of the Sea* (UNCLOS) and the rule of law, its military engagement in this case is still quite surprising. From the beginning, Japan had two surface vessels[7] deployed, while the multi-national EU NAVFOR mission Atalanta usually had around five vessels in service. In addition, the MSDF had two planes deployed to assist in searching for pirates, the same number as in the Atalanta mission. In 2015, the MSDF had about 390 personnel stationed in Djibouti and on surface vessels, while EU NAVFOR had around 1,200 personnel deployed. However, while the much larger EU NAVFOR contingency flew about 17,000 hours between 2009 and 2015, the MSDF flew 11,000 hours. This shows the strong Japanese commitment, even when compared with a mission that is supported by 28 EU member states. While the EU NAVFOR mission cost about US$ 37 million in 2015, Japan spent about US$ 37 million,[8] another indicator of Japan's strong commitment to counter-piracy operations.

MSDF and EU NAVFOR military-military contacts

Since Japan joined the counter-piracy mission off the coast of Somalia, there have been few encounters, and even fewer exercise or joint training opportunities between MSDF and EU navy forces. Between 2009 and 2013, there were only one or two such occasions every year. However, the number of such encounters increased to six in 2014, seven in 2015 and nine in 2016. A significant number of these encounters were visits of senior military EU NAVFOR and MSDF officers, who met their counterparts to demonstrate specific technology and to exchange thoughts. In 2015, there were six and in 2016, four such visits. While joint military exercises are mentioned in EU, Japanese Ministry of Defense (JMOD) and Japanese Ministry of Foreign Affairs (MOFA) documents as one of the achievements of EU–Japan cooperation, the actual number of these training exercises at sea has remained relatively limited. In 2014 and 2015, there was only one joint training exercise a year. The only time EU NAVFOR and MSDF units cooperated in an actual counter-piracy mission was in January 2014, when an MSDF helicopter assisted in freeing a crew member of an Indian Dhow.

The declining number of maritime piracy incidences opened opportunities to conduct more joint military exercises and navigation manoeuvres at sea (see Tables 12.1 and 12.2). However, in 2015, while there were six official ship visits, which gave some opportunities for ship captains and EU NAVFOR commanders to visit MSDF vessels and their base in Djibouti, these led to only one communications exercise at sea, involving a EU NAVFOR warship and the MSDF destroyer *Harusame* in the Gulf of Aden in March 2015. This number increased somewhat in 2016, with four training exercises conducted in January and July 2016, and a navigation manoeuvre in November 2016. In December 2016, a Spanish maritime patrol aircraft and the warship ESPS *Relampago* cooperated with an MSDF aircrew to rescue two men from a capsized skiff in the Gulf of Aden.

Table 12.1 EU NAVFOR–MSDF encounters in 2015 and 2016

	Activity	Type
2015		
January	EU NAVFOR force commander meets MSDF Escort Division 2 commander on board EU Naval Force Flagship ITS *Andrea Doria*	Visit
February	MSDF commander of Escort Division visits EU NAVFOR commander on board the EU NAVFOR flagship	Visit
March	EU NAVFOR visits MSDF base in Djibouti	Visit
	EU NAVFOR warship FGS *Bayern* conducts communications exercise with MSDF destroyer JDS *Harusame* in Gulf of Aden	Exercise
June	Operation ATLANTA force commander visits Japanese warship JDS *Ikazuchi* at sea	Visit
July	Operation ATLANTA Force headquarters staff visit Japanese detachment in Djibouti	Visit
December	Operation ATLANTA flagship hosts Japanese Navy	Visit
2016		
January	Japanese Escort Division 3 hosts Operation ATLANTA force commander	Visit
	Operation ATLANTA Flagship conducts training with JDS *Suzunami*	Training
	ATLANTA ESPS *Victoria* trains with MSDF Escort Division in the Gulf of Aden	Training
July	EU NAVFOR Italian sailors exercise with CMF Japanese counterparts	Training
August	MSDF sailors visit Operation ATALANTA Flagship	Visit
September	Operation ATALANTA Counter-Piracy force commander visits MSDF warship JDS *Suzutsuki*	Visit
November	Operation ATALANTA warships HNLMS *Tromp* and ESPS *Relampago* rendezvous at sea with JMSDF JS *Suzutsuki*	Navigation manoeuvres
	Operation ATALANTA force commander welcomes Japanese commander of the MSDF Escort Task Group on board Dutch flagship HNLMS *Tromp*	Visit
December	Operation ATALANTA Spanish maritime patrol aircraft and warship ESPS *Relampago* work with MSDF aircrew to rescue two men from upturned skiffs in Gulf of Aden	Rescue

European view on EU–Japan piracy cooperation

In her analysis of the EU–Japan SPA (see the two EU–Japan chapters in this volume for details), Julie Gilson (2016) argues that 'cooperation within international forums was always regarded as a core point of engagement for Japan and the EU and in these arenas there has been closer dialogue on, for example, piracy and the environment' (Gilson, 2016: 796). This is, in fact, something that resonates well

Table 12.2 EU NAVFOR–MSDF exercises and training between 2014 and 2016

Date	Joint Military Training Exercises
January 2014	EU NAVFOR Atalanta flagship FS *Siroco*, MSDF helicopter from the MSDF vessel JS *Samidare* freed crew of the Indian Dhow *Shane Hind*
October 2014	EU NAVFOR flagship ITS *Andrea Doria* and MSDF JS *Takanami* conduct counter-piracy exercise at sea in the Gulf of Aden. 1. Bridge-to-bridge communications exercise 2. 'Cross-deck' exercise
March 2015	EU NAVFOR warship FGS *Bayern* conducts communications exercise with MSDF destroyer JS *Harusame* in Gulf of Aden: joint tactical communications exercise
January 2016	Operation ATLANTA flagship conducts training with JDS *Suzunami* ATLANTA ESPS *Victoria* trains with MSDF Escort Division in the Gulf of Aden • Helicopters conducting landings on both ships to train flight crews and flight deck personnel • 'Light-weight' replenishment at sea • Ship handling and manoeuvring exercise • Small arms firing exercise
July 2016	EU NAVFOR sailors exercise with CMF Japanese counterparts • Practice boarding procedures • Sharing methods for stopping and searching vessels • Sailing together in close formation • Italian helicopter took the opportunity to practice cross-deck landings
November 2016	Operation ATALANTA warships HNLMS *Tromp* and ESPS *Relampago* rendezvous at sea with JMSDF JS *Suzutsuki* • Navigation manoeuvres to strengthen skills of navigation teams

with the EU's East Asian partners. In particular, the EU-led Atalanta mission to fight piracy off the coast of Somalia has provided a useful framework to promote cooperation between the EU, Japan, South Korea and China (Reiterer, 2014).

Some European countries, in particular the UK and France, have developed an even closer relationship with the Asia-Pacific region, including Japan. Since 2012, the UK and Japan discuss security issues at least once a year through so-called two-plus-two, or security consultative meetings of their respective foreign and defence ministers. Both countries have developed particularly close security ties (Simón and Klose, 2015). In 2012, the UK joined Regional Cooperation Agreement on Combating Piracy and Armed Robbery against Ships in Asia (ReCAAP) to combat piracy and armed robbery in Southeast Asia, and in October 2016 the British Royal Air Force (RAF) conducted the first joint drill with the Japanese Air Self-Defense Force (ASDF) in Tohoku (*Japan Times*, 2016). Other European member states with closer security ties with Japan are Denmark, the Netherlands and Norway.

Counter-piracy in EU–Japan Summit meetings

As the analysis of EU–Japan security cooperation (Chapters 9 and 10 in this volume) has demonstrated, security cooperation, although mostly non-traditional security, has been a major element in the two framework agreements of 1991 and 2001. Nonetheless, both entered into force before the EU and Japan began to cooperate in post-conflict areas, such as Afghanistan, and before the beginning of the counter-piracy mission in 2009. Since 2009, the counter-piracy mission off the coast of Somalia has not only led to closer military-to-military cooperation, but at the same time it has become a prime example of successful military and political cooperation between the EU and Japan.

The two most important diplomatic forums where EU and Japanese leaders and Foreign and Defence Ministry officials discuss security cooperation in the counter-piracy missions are (1) the EU–Japan annual summit meetings (bilateral summits) and (2) the meetings of Foreign and Defence Ministry officials in multilateral regimes, in this case in the CGPCS.

From the early days of the counter-piracy mission off the coast of Somalia, the EU and Japan considered it to be central as a test field for operational cooperation on the ground, and an ideal next step almost a decade after the 2001 Action Plan had failed to meet expectations for security cooperation.[9] Only a few months after the start of the counter-piracy mission, in May 2009, then Prime Minister Taro Aso met EU High Representative Javier Solana and the president of the European Commission, José Manuel Barroso, at the 18th EU–Japan summit in Prague. Both sides stressed that they wanted to assume greater global responsibility in a broad range of non-traditional security and policy fields and to cooperate more closely to promote peace and security, from Afghanistan and Pakistan, Central Asia and Africa to the Middle East peace process. One of the areas emphasised was the need to 'tackle the root causes of piracy and underlining their support for development activity in Somalia', which is why both sides promised to 'take appropriate steps to contribute to ensuring the safe passage of vessels in need through the Gulf of Aden, the EU through its deployment of NAVFOR Atalanta and Japan through the dispatch of escort ships of Maritime Self-Defence Forces' (Commission of the European Union, Government of Japan, 2009).

One year into the counter-piracy mission, in April 2010, after the change to a Democratic Party of Japan (DPJ)-centred government in Japan, then Prime Minister Yukio Hatoyama 'reiterated the importance of continuing their efforts to address the increasing threat posed by pirates to the safety of maritime navigation off the coast of Somalia and the Gulf of Aden and to stability in the region' and praised the 'fruitful interaction' of the MSDF and EU NAVFOR Operation Atalanta. In order to demonstrate its strong commitment to the counter-piracy mission, Japan also decided in April 2010 to jointly plan the Djibouti Regional Training Centre (DRTC) and the information sharing

The counter-piracy mission off the coast of Somalia

centres in Yemen, Kenya and Tanzania (Council of the European Union, 2010). EU–Japan counter-piracy cooperation continued under Prime Minister Naoto Kan. Both reiterated their intention to cooperate at the EU–Japan summit in May 2011 (Council of the European Union, 2011). This clearly demonstrated that intensifying security cooperation with Europe and the cooperation in the counter-piracy mission were supported by both major parties in Japan, and not just the conservative LDP.

EU–Japan cooperation in the counter-piracy mission off the coast of Somalia continued to be mentioned in the years of the Abe administration from December 2012, usually as a prime example of ongoing and future security cooperation. For example, at the 2013 EU–Japan summit meeting, both sides stressed that EU NAVFOR–SDF cooperation was 'strengthening counter piracy capabilities in Somalia and its neighboring countries' and the significance of EU–Japan cooperation in setting up the DRTC (Commission of the European Union, Government of Japan, 2013: 10). In 2014, the EU leadership praised Japan's newly expanded security role and its so-called 'proactive contribution to peace' because it enabled the two sides to develop even closer 'cooperation in counter piracy activity off the coast of Somalia and in the Gulf of Aden' and to conduct more joint counter-piracy exercises (Commission of the European Union, Government of Japan, 2014: 5). In 2015, the EU side stressed that it welcomed 'continuing concrete cooperation in anti-piracy activities off the coast of Somalia and in the Gulf of Aden within the relevant International Contact Group and through operational activities between the deployed units of Japan Self Defense Forces and the EU's Naval Force Somalia (EUNAVFOR)-Operation ATALANTA' (Commission of the European Union, Government of Japan, 2015).

The SPA is expected to include provisions about future security cooperation between the EU and Japan. The counter-piracy mission off the coast of Somalia has frequently been mentioned as an example of successful EU–Japan security cooperation. In the draft report containing the European Parliament's recommendations to the Council, the Commission and the European External Action Service on the negotiations for the SPA, counter-piracy was mentioned as one of the areas where the EU should deepen and enhance its cooperation with Japan (Commission of the European Union, 2016; European Parliament, 2014).

Counter-piracy as a catalyst for bilateral cooperation

The many years of operational military-military, civilian and political cooperation on the ground and in the waters around Somalia and the Gulf of Aden have been the first opportunity for regular encounters of Japanese and European diplomats together with military personnel managing a ground and sea operation for an extended period of time. While this was a multilateral as well as multi-stakeholder operation that also involved a large number of other countries and actors, the European as well as the Japanese government and many commentators frequently mentioned the significance and symbolic value of the counter-piracy mission off the coast of Somalia for bilateral cooperation. While the military-to-military encounters were certainly limited in number and depth, they nevertheless demonstrated the ability of the MSDF to cooperate with European naval forces.

The new 2016 EU Global Strategy, published after a two-year process and replacing the 2003 European Security Strategy (ESS), does not specifically mention counter-piracy, but does emphasise the strong desire of the EU to 'develop a more politically rounded approach to Asia, seeking to make greater practical contributions to Asian security' by expanding the 'partnerships, including on security, with Japan, the Republic of Korea, Indonesia and others' (Commission of the European Union, 2016: 38).

Japanese views on EU–Japan piracy cooperation

Since Japan joined the counter-piracy mission off the coast of Somalia, including the related political and military organisational and management infrastructure, this mission has become central to arguments for intensifying Japan's security cooperation on a broader scale. The international community has asked Japan to increase the range of its activities and take over management responsibilities for international counter-piracy operations off Somalia. Japan joined the CGPCS in 2009 and took over the co-chairmanship of some working groups. On 25 June 2013, Japanese Defence Minister Onodera announced that, 'due to various demands being made of the SDF', Japan would assign one destroyer to 'zone defense' operations. The MSDF's destroyer JS *Samidare* would then be allocated to the CTF151 in December 2013.[10] Those demands came in part from the Combined Maritime Forces (CMF) itself as well as from other participating countries, but also from ship owners' associations. This enabled the MSDF to extend its activities from escorting ships in the International Recommended Transit Corridor (IRTC) to actively participating in so-called Zone Defense in the entire area off the coast of Somalia. The climax of Japan's involvement with the CTF-151 was the appointment of MSDF Rear Admiral Hiroshi Ito as CTF-151 commander in May 2015, the first time since World War II that a member of the Japanese armed forces had become the commander of a multi-national military mission. At the 36th SHADE conference on 22 June 2015 in Bahrain, Rear Admiral Ito said that 'by working with other task forces and regional partners [...] we are able to deliver the most effective deterrent and capitalize on the efficient use of our resources. Working together in this way optimizes counter piracy efforts through international cooperation by globally engaged nations and partners' (Combined Maritime Forces, 2015). While more than

30 countries participated in the CMF, this was a good opportunity for the MSDF to closely coordinate with EU forces. Only a month after Ito's inauguration, on 15 June 2015, the EU naval force commander, Rear Admiral Alfonso Gómez Fernández de Córdoba, took over as CTF-151 counter-piracy coordinator. This gave Ito a chance to visit Operation Atalanta's flagship, ESPS *Galicia* (EU NAVFOR, 2015).

In 2014, Japan changed its interpretation of Article 9 of the Japanese constitution, and in September 2015, it passed eleven new or revised security laws. These two changes are going to have a significant effect on future Japanese security practice and policy decisions. How significant has the Japanese experience in counter-piracy operations off the coast of Somalia been in facilitating these changes? For example, could this experience provide a positive case of international cooperation that could be seen as a preparation for future missions of collective defence, and as an example of a mission that involved the SDF but was not a PKO, humanitarian and reconstructions, or rear-area support mission (e.g. the MSDF refuelling mission in the Indian Ocean from 2001 to 2010), as others have been in the past?

Japan, despite its strong anti-militarist values and severe constitutional constraints (see earlier), has not only contributed its experience in the ReCAAP Information Sharing Centre (ISC) and, through exceptionally active contributions, to the military mission and decisions in the CGPCS, but has also experienced a 'boomerang effect' (Keck and Sikkink, 1998). Hence, Japan's involvement in counter-piracy has, in turn, affected Japanese policymaking. The successful mission was at least one reason why the Abe administration was able to further 'normalise' its international role and military contributions to global and regional challenges, such as maritime piracy. In a press conference in February 2014, Donna Hopkins (coordinator for Counter Piracy and Maritime Security, US Department of State) stressed that 'Japan changed its laws and created for the first time since World War II a counter-piracy based out of its own immediate regional sphere. [...] piracy is a great uniter because it's a common enemy. Everybody hates pirates' (US Department of State, 2014).

Therefore, Japan can be seen as an example of a country where the CGPCS participation has not only helped to legitimise the eight-year mission (by 2017) more than 9,000 km away from home (involving the continued deployment of two destroyers and two planes and the setting up of the first out-of-area (semi-permanent military) base since 1945, in Djibouti), but has also facilitated a domestic debate and a series of new laws and regulations that will lead to more active engagement in out-of-area missions in the future. This growth in military engagement can be seen in the establishment of a new National Security Council (December 2013), a new force doctrine with a Dynamic Joint Defense Force, an increase of defence spending in 2014 and 2015, and the increasingly force-focused and assertive defence policy announced in the National Defense

Program Guidelines for 2014 and beyond and the Five-year Defense Program for 2014 through 2018, both decided in December 2013. The June 2014 cabinet decision to reinterpret the Japanese constitution to allow the exercise of the right of collective self-defence can also be seen in this light (see earlier).

The National Security Strategy (NSS), which came into force in December 2013 and lists the future principles of Japan's security policy, specifically mentions the importance of maritime security and the positive example of the counter-piracy missions. It emphasizes that Japan will 'play a leading role, through close cooperation with other countries, in maintaining and developing "Open and Stable Seas"' and that Japan will 'take necessary measures [...] including anti-piracy operations to ensure safe maritime transport and promote maritime security cooperation with other countries'. In other words, it will 'enhance the frequency and the quality of bilateral and multilateral cooperation on maritime security such as joint exercises [...] and in particular, sea lanes of communication, stretching from the Persian Gulf, the Strait of Hormuz, the Red Sea and the Gulf of Aden', which are 'critical to Japan due to its dependence on the maritime transport of natural and energy resources from the Middle East' (NSS 2013).

The National Defense Program Guidelines for FY 2014 and beyond, which also came into force in December 2013, mentioned under 'Priorities in strengthening architecture of the Self Defense Forces' that the 'SDF will work on enhancing transport and deployment capability, information communication capability with a view to long term activities in Africa and other remote locations, and strengthening logistic and medical service structure for smooth and continuous operation' and that 'Japan will consider measures for making more effective use of the SDF Operational Facility for Deployed Air Force for Anti-Piracy Operation in Djibouti' (Government of Japan, 2013).

While the International Peace Support Bill, which was part of the security legislation package passed in 2015 and enabled support activities to 'armed forces of foreign countries collectively addressing the situation which threatens the international peace and security', does not specifically mention the experience of the counter-piracy mission, it results from the necessity for deeper and broader military and security cooperation by the Japanese government and the SDF not only with governments and military forces of partner countries such as the EU, but, currently more importantly, with Australia and India, and with Asian countries other than China with claims in the South China Sea. While the bill was opposed by most Japanese opposition parties and many citizens, who demonstrated in front of the Diet building for weeks in the summer of 2015, the EU Commission and some national European governments (e.g. the UK) embraced and supported Japan's so-called 'proactive contribution to peace' policy and the willingness of Japan to become a more prominent actor in times of crisis.

Conclusion

Through political, military, logistical and governing cooperation in the counter-piracy missions off the coast of Somalia on the ground, at sea, in the air and through institutional structures, Japanese government representatives and SDF personnel have learned new ways to deal with the complexities of multilateral security coordination. The meetings of CGPCS, CMF and SHADE, which are multi-stakeholder organisations, purely solution oriented and non-political, and apply informal decision-making processes, provided a learning experience for Japanese government bureaucrats and military officers.

The counter-piracy missions also provided an opportunity to cooperate with European forces, although in practice military-to-military cooperation occurred to a far smaller degree than one might have expected. Nonetheless, frequent visits of EU NAVFOR and MSDF senior military officers to each other's vessels or the Japanese base in Djibouti, and opportunities to talk with each other during and after meetings of the governing bodies, have certainly been an important opportunity for both sides to exchange ideas and to deepen trust and understanding.

Since April 2013, the EU and Japan have been negotiating a SPA in parallel with the Economic Partnership Agreement (EPA). The SPA is supposed to be a 'binding agreement, covering political, global and other sectoral cooperation in a comprehensive manner, (...) underpinned by their shared commitment to fundamental values and principles' (Council of the European Union, 2011). This will constitute the most fundamental change in the relationship between the EU and Japan since 2001 and will most likely lead to closer cooperation in the areas of international law, intelligence exchange, joint development of weapons systems, weapons trade, counter-terrorism, cyber-security, space, ocean policy, disarmament and regional security.[11] In EU–Japan negotiations and MOFA of Japan statements, the counter-piracy mission is frequently mentioned as a prime example of successful EU–Japan security cooperation.

In essence, the EU–Japan SPA is intended to intensify the way the EU and Japan cooperate in out-of-area security challenges. It will strengthen each side's security by intensifying cooperation in the areas of cyber-security, intelligence exchange and the joint development and trade of military hardware and software, and it might make it easier to coordinate economic and trade sanctions against common adversaries such as Russia or China. In the end, the SPA will make the role of the US somewhat less central and give Japan more options in the event that it cannot support certain US policy positions or decisions. However, neither the EU nor any of its current member states, including the UK, has any intention of extending direct military support in the case of Japan being attacked, and nor has Japan indicated any intention to protect the European mainland in the case of an attack. Closer EU–Japan security cooperation and a security partnership might strengthen Japan's deterrent power, because it will make an attack on its soil or elsewhere in East Asia costlier for the potential aggressor (e.g. sanctions). Closer security cooperation might also further improve cooperation between the EU and Japan in international organisations and weaken the negotiation positions of countries like China and Russia. However, differing threat perceptions of China and Russia in Japan and many EU member states might make coordinated action difficult, a problem that is also evident in Japan's security cooperation with Australia.

We have seen that EU–Japan cooperation in the counter-piracy mission off the coast of Somalia and the Gulf of Aden has frequently been cited in government documents on both sides as an example of successful military-to-military cooperation; however, is this an indication for closer security cooperation in other areas to somewhat balance the strong reliance on the US?

Given the current phase of uncertainty about US security policy and alliance commitments under President Donald J. Trump, Europe and Japan might both consider it advantageous to work more closely together if uncertain US leadership leads to (1) a structural shift in the international order or (2) changes in bilateral alliance dynamics, that is, the US–Japan Security Alliance or NATO. Alternatively, or additionally, (3) the effectiveness of EU foreign and security policy towards its partners outside of the EU might be affected as a result of the UK leaving the EU. The UK was the strongest proponent of stricter economic sanctions against Russia. Without the UK, this position could gradually soften and change EU–Russia relations, a policy that is also in the interest of the Abe administration. While both the EU and Japan share preferences for anti-militarism and diplomatic solutions, there is also growing pressure to increase military spending (i.e. to at least 2 per cent of gross domestic product (GDP)) and develop military capacities that make them somewhat less reliant on the US. In addition, public opinion in some European countries, such as the UK and France, favours a more resilient defence posture.

NOTES

1. The central Japanese law in 2009 refers to 'crimes relating to acts of piracy' and a response to an 'increase in international and organized crimes' (Government of Japan, 2009).
2. Neither the Japanese government nor the ship owner confirmed at the time that a ransom had been paid.
3. Specifically, United Nations Convention on the Law of the Sea (UNCLOS) (1982): Articles 100 and 101.
4. Important earlier studies that analysed the first years of Japan's involvement into the counter-piracy missions off the coast of Somalia and the Gulf of Aden include Black, (2014), Ohn and Richey, (2014), Oh, (2013), Black and Hwang, (2012), Midford, (2012), Black, (2012), Bateman, (2012), Inamoto, (2011) and Christoffersen, (2009).
5. Such as Government of Japan (1948), *Law concerning the Execution of Duties of Police Officials*, Article 7; and Government of Japan (2009), *Law on Punishment of and Measures against Acts of Piracy*, 2009.

6 The phrase 'take measures against acts of piracy' does not mean using weapons against suspected pirates, but assisting the international community in their efforts. The use of weapons was only permitted for the Japanese Coast Guard.
7 As for the two surface vessels, this meant that six vessels were constantly involved in the counter-piracy missions. Two were actually used off the coast of Somalia, two were either on the way to the missions or on the way back to Japan, and two were used for training in waters around Japan.
8 This budget does not include personnel cost, but only the extra budget reserved for this mission (Kantei (The Prime Minister of Japan and His Cabinet), 2015).
9 See chapters by Fukushima and Berkovsky in this volume.
10 Defence Minister Onodera repeated this position at his daily press conference on 25 July 2013.
11 According to some experts, the EU-Japan SPA might include similar areas of cooperation to the EU-Canada SPA, which was signed in August 2016. If this is the case, then we can expect it to include, among other things, a 'more effective multilateralism' on issues such as weapons of mass destruction, small arms and light weapons, the International Criminal Court, cooperation in combating terrorism, promoting international peace and stability, and regional and global forums and organizations such as the Organisation for Economic Co-operation and Development (OECD) and possibly NATO. Other possible areas include law enforcement cooperation to combat illicit drugs, organized crime and corruption, money laundering and the financing of terrorism, cyber-crime, migration and border management, and the protection of personal data.

REFERENCES

Bateman, S., 2012. 'Piracy and Maritime Security: Japan's Strategic Challenges', in Struett, M. J., Carlson, J. D. and Nance, M. T. (eds), *Maritime Piracy and the Construction of Global Governance* (Abingdon: Routledge), pp. 201–216.

Black, L. 2012. 'Debating Japan's Intervention to Tackle Piracy in the Gulf of Aden: Beyond Mainstream Paradigms', *International Relations of the Asia-Pacific*, 12(2): 259–285, doi:10.1093/lrap/lcs004.

Black, L., 2014. *Japan's Maritime Security Strategy: The Japan Coast Guard and Maritime Outlaws* (Houndmills: Palgrave Macmillan).

Black, L. and Hwang, Y., 2012. 'China and Japan's Quest for Great Power Status: Norm Entrepreneurship in Anti-Piracy Responses', *International Relations*, 26(4): 431–451, doi:10.1177/0047117812452441.

Christoffersen, G., 2009. 'Japan and the East Asian Maritime Security Order: Prospects for Trilateral and Multilateral Cooperation', *Asian Perspective*, 33(3): 107–149.

Combined Maritime Forces, 2015. 'International Maritime Community Works Together to Counter Piracy at SHADE', 22 June, at: combinedmaritimeforces.com/2015/06/22/international-maritime-community-works-together-to-counter-piracy-at-shade (accessed 1 March 2018).

Commission of the European Union, Government of Japan, 2009. 18th EU-Japan Summit (Prague: Commission of the European Union.

Commission of the European Union, Government of Japan, 2013. 21st Japan-EU Summit, Tokyo, 19 November, Joint Press Statement, Tokyo, at: www.mofa.go.jp/mofaj/files/000019937.pdf (accessed 1 March 2018).

Commission of the European Union, Government of Japan, 2014. 22nd EU-Japan Summit Brussels, 7 May, Joint Press Statement, Brussels.

Commission of the European Union, Government of Japan, 2015. 23rd Japan-EU Summit, Tokyo, 29 May, Joint Press Statement, EU Commission.

Commission of the European Union, 2016. Shared Vision, Common Action: A Stronger Europe. European Union, at: www.eeas.europa.eu/archives/docs/top_stories/pdf/eugs_review_web.pdf (accessed 2 November 2017).

Council of the European Union, 2010. 19th EU-Japan Summit, Tokyo, 28 April, Joint Press Statement.

Council of the European Union, 2011. *20th EU-Japan Summit Brussels* (Brussels: Council of the European Union).

EU NAVFOR, 2015. 'Operation Atalanta Force Headquarters Assumes Counter-Piracy Coordination Role from CTF 151, 22 July', at: eunavfor.eu/operation-atalanta-force-headquarters-assumes-counter-piracy-coordination-role-from-ctf-151 (accessed 1 March 2018).

European Parliament, 2014. 'Draft Report Containing the European Parliament's Recommendation to the Council, Commission and the European External Action Service on the Negotiations for an EU-Japan Strategic Partnership Agreement', Brussels: European Parliament.

Germond, B. and Smith, M. E., 2009. 'Re-Thinking European Security Interests and the ESDP: Explaining the EU's Anti-Piracy Operation', *Contemporary Security Policy*, 30(3): 573–593, doi:10.1080/13523260903327741.

Gilson, J., 2016. 'The Strategic Partnership Agreement between the EU and Japan: The Pitfalls of Path Dependency?', *Journal of European Integration*, 38(7): 791–806, doi:10.1080/07036337.2016.1176027.

Government of Japan, 2009. *Law on Punishment of and Measures against Acts of Piracy* (Tokyo).

Government of Japan, 2013. *National Defense Program Guidelines for FY 2014 and Beyond* (Tokyo).

Inamoto, M., 2011. 'Somaria Oki Kaizokumondai to Kaizoku Taisho O Mekuru – Kōsatsu' [A Study on the Piracy Problem off the Coast of Somalia and the Anti-Piracy Measures against It], *Journal of the Tokyo University of Marine Science and Technology*, 7(January): 17–29.

Japan Times, 2016. 'ASDF, Royal Air Force to Conduct First-Ever Joint Drills in Japan amid Strengthening Security Ties', 16 October.

Japanese Ministry of Defense, 2009a. 'Press Releases: Issuance of Order for Operation of the Self-Defense Forces concerning Maritime Security Operations', 13 March, at: www.mod.go.jp/e/press/release/2009/03/13a.html (accessed 1 March 2018).

Japanese Ministry of Defense, 2009b. 'Press Releases: Departure of the Dispatched Maritime Force for Response to Piracy', 13 March, at: www.mod.go.jp/e/press/release/2009/03/13b.html (accessed 1 March 2018).

Japanese Ministry of Defense, 2009c. 'Press Releases: Field Investigation in Countries around the Gulf of Aden', 5 February, at: www.mod.go.jp/e/press/release/2009/02/05.html (accessed 1 March 2018).

Kantei (The Prime Minister of Japan and His Cabinet), 2015. 'Heisei 27-nendo kaiyō kanren yosan seifu' [Maritime Related Budget for 2015], Tokyo. Data for: 'Somaria oki Aden-wan ni okeru kaizoku taisaku (Gaimushō kokudo Kōtsūshō bōei-shō)' [Measures against Piracy off Somalia and in the Gulf of Aden (Ministry of Foreign Affairs, Ministry of Land, Infrastructure and Transport, Ministry of Defense)], at: www.kantei.go.jp/jp/singi/kaiyou/sisaku/gaiyou_h27.pdf (accessed 1 March 2018).

Keck, M. and Sikkink, K., 1998. *Activists beyond Borders* (Ithaca and London: Cornell University Press).

Midford, P., 2012. 'By Land and by Sea: the Potential of EU-Japan Security Cooperation', *Japan Forum*, 24(3): 289–316, doi:10.1080/09555803.2012.699454.

Oh, Y.-D., 2013. 'The Escort Mission against Somali Piracy in the Gulf of Aden and Possible Trilateral Naval Cooperation among South Korea, China, and Japan', *The Korean Journal of Security Affairs*, 18(1): 22–42.

Ohn, D. and Richey, M., 2014. 'Cooperation on Counter-Piracy in the Gulf of Aden among China, Korea, and Japan: Implications for Trilateral Security Cooperation in Northeast Asia', *The Korean Journal of Defense Analysis*, 26(1): 81–95.

Reiterer, M., 2014. 'The EU's Comprehensive Approach to Security in Asia', *European Foreign Affairs Review*, 19(1): 1–22.

Riddervold, M., 2011. 'Finally Flexing Its Muscles? Atalanta – the European Union's Naval Military Operation against Piracy', *European Security*, 20(3): 385–404, doi:10.1080/09662839.2011.592979.

Simón, L. and Klose, S., 2015. 'European Perspectives towards the Rise of Asia: Contextualising the Debate', *Asia Europe Journal*, November: 1–22, doi:10.1007/s10308-015-0440-z.

Tardy, T., 2015. 'Operation Sophia', European Union Institute for Security Studies. Brief Issue.

US Department of State, 2014. *Counter-Piracy Update:* Donna Hopkins, Coordinator for Counter Piracy and Maritime Security, US Department of State; and Francois Rivasseau, Deputy Head of the European Union Delegation to the United States, Washington, DC, 20 February, at: https://2009-2017-fpc.state.gov/221827.htm (accessed 1 March 2018).

Conclusion

Wilhelm Vosse and Paul Midford

THE 12 CHAPTERS in this volume set out to analyse the recent emergence and current state of Japan's most significant bilateral cooperative security partnerships, other than its hitherto exclusively central security relationship with the US. How are these new security partnerships discussed and perceived in both Japan and the partner countries? The central questions each chapter asked were about the core rationale for the Japanese and the partner side to engage and intensify the partnership, whether the two sides' rationales are converging or diverging, and whether these partnerships have relevance above and beyond the bilateral partnership itself, for regional security. The Introduction set out three hypotheses, namely that (1) increasingly closer diplomatic dialogue and military-to-military exchange will increase trust and mutual understanding of the partners' security concerns, that (2) cooperation on non-traditional security issues can potentially lead to closer cooperation on traditional security issues, and that (3) these security partnerships give these countries more leverage in security negotiations with the US and encourage a more independent foreign and security policy.

The first two hypotheses refer to diplomatic and military cooperation between governments and their respective military forces. The case studies presented in this volume demonstrated that over the last decade security cooperation between Japan and its security partners has deepened from mere diplomatic exchange between government officials drafting broad, but often unspecific and 'soft', bilateral statements on the future of their cooperation, towards 'hard cooperation' with specific targets, including military-to-military cooperation featuring military exercises, joint development, and acquisition or sale of defence equipment. These case studies find that this evolution has deepened mutual understanding and trust.

The third hypothesis refers to the strategic objective, or consequence, of deepening these security partnerships. Why has Japan, and why have its partner countries, chosen to intensify their security ties? There seem to be two main factors influencing these choices, namely, (1) the current and future role of the US in the East Asia order, as well as in the global order, and (2) the current and future position of China in this order.

Conclusion

The role of the US

The US is an important common denominator in all the partnerships analysed in this volume, because it is a security or alliance partner for Japan and virtually all of its security partners, is the central player in the security and diplomatic trilaterals between Japan and its partners, and is a strong proponent of these partnerships, because it believes they encourage greater and more efficient burden-sharing and facilitate the role of US forces in the Indo-Pacific region. This is, for example, the core understanding of Australia. As Thomas S. Wilkins writes in this volume, for Australia, the 'alignment with Japan is an enhancement of direct security ties with a longer-term partner, which yields multiple benefits', and is thus 'reinforcing its alliance relationship with the US, and the "hub-and-spoke" system as a whole' (Wilkins).

However, alliance theory teaches us that alliance partners always need to take into account the security dilemma of abandonment and entrapment (Snyder, 1984, 2007). We argue that the fear of abandonment as well as the fear of entrapment would make the deepening of security ties with allies of the US a sensible reaction. Closer security cooperation with Australia, the EU and NATO could give Japan more influence when these partners have to decide whether to go along with the US, because they might also consider Japanese concerns. When these partners have closer ties with each other, they also potentially have greater opportunities to, in effect, coordinate their lobbying of Washington to avoid decisions that lead to either entrapment or abandonment. The combination of bilateral, trilateral and multilateral security arrangements in the Asia-Pacific, and to a lesser degree with the EU, could make the allies that build these arrangements more significant for the US and, therefore, less likely to be abandoned. The middle ground between developing a fully-fledged security architecture in the Asia-Pacific, which would weaken the role of the US, and sole reliance on the US, could potentially be a middle power concert, whereby Japan, Australia, India, the EU and other middle powers might be able to dissuade the US from decisions that could run counter to some of the interests of these middle powers. Recent examples include Trump administration debates about ending the nuclear agreement with Iran, or unilateral military action against North Korea. This might also be the view in Australia, where the 'strategic partnership may serve as the nucleus of a wider coalition/concert of medium powers as a "hedge" against future scenarios involving US strategic withdrawal, Chinese hegemony, or "G2" power-sharing' (Wilkins).

In his analysis of Japan's security multilateralism towards ASEAN and other East Asian states, Midford reminds us that Cronin and Green argued already in the mid-1990s that Japan's new focus on security multilateralism might be a possible 'hedge' against 'possible US withdrawal or fatigue'. As Japan's fears of either abandonment or entrapment have alternatively waxed and waned, Tokyo has used

Table C.1 Trade dependency with Japan (2015–2016)

	Rank	Exports (percentage)	Rank	Imports (percentage)
Australia	2	16	3	8
India	15	2	11	3
Philippines	2	13	2	10
Vietnam	3	8	3	8
EU	6	3	6	4
ASEAN	4	13	2	15

Data from http://atlas.media.mit.edu/ (Rounded figures).

regional security multilateralism as a tool for avoiding entrapment or abandonment. Similarly, Nagy explains in his chapter that the behaviour of Southeast Asian states is a form of hedging with the intention of keeping the US in the region.

The China factor

The growing security and economic influence of China in the broader region is a significant factor explaining the development of bilateral security ties for Japan as well as for its partners. On the one hand, China's military expansion into the South China Sea casts a significant military shadow over Southeast Asian nations, and this, plus China's increasing defence spending, can be seen as an important underlying factor explaining the willingness of Southeast Asian nations and Japan to enter into security partnerships. On the other hand, over the last 20 years China has become the most or second most important trading partner for Japan and all of its security partners (see Table C.2; the one partial exception is India, from whom China is only its third most important market). This fact, which is emphasised by all authors in this volume, is a major constraining factor for many of the security partners, and to a lesser degree also for Japan, in that it makes it difficult for them to openly balance against China, or to openly name China as a potential adversary.

From the Japanese perspective, the Japan–Australia partnership is also a response to increasing concerns over 'China's challenges to the rules-based order and the US role in the Asia-Pacific'. However, as Ishihara argues in his chapter, Japan has realised that there is a 'China gap' in perceptions of China between itself, Canberra and Washington, which may impact the ways the Japan–Australia bilateral and Japan–Australia–US trilateral cooperation might develop in the future. Moreover, as Wilkins emphasises in his chapter, Australia has a far more nuanced view as far as the relationship with China is concerned. It does not primarily see the partnership with Japan as a way of balancing against China, a view that is also affected by its strong trade dependency on China (23 per cent of Australian two-way trade is with China).

Table C.2 Trade dependency with China (2015–2016)

	Rank	Exports (percentage)	Rank	Imports (percentage)
Japan	2	17	1	26
Australia	1	33	1	23
India	3	4	1	16
Philippines	1	21	1	20
Vietnam	2	10	1	29
EU	2	10	1	20
ASEAN	1	15	1	24

Data from http://atlas.media.mit.edu/ (Rounded figures).

Chinese military expansionism in the East and South China Seas and the Indian Ocean is one of the central reasons behind the intensifying security partnership between Japan and India. As Ghosh argues in her chapter, India sees China's military expansion into the Indian Ocean and the adjacent South China Sea as an infringement of its economic and strategic interests, and as undermining maritime security in the region. Beijing's 'string of pearls' strategy, which entails setting up military and naval facilities in India's immediate neighbourhood, has alarmed the Modi administration and accelerated the modernisation of New Delhi's naval forces, for which India is seeking cooperation from the US and Japan. India's major aim is to balance Chinese advances in the Indo-Pacific region. Ghosh argues that since India assumes that Japan shares these Indian concerns and has an interest in maintaining the power equilibrium in Asia, it is an ideal partner for India. While Chinese expansionism into the Indian Ocean is a concern for India, Japan sees India as an important partner to deter China's assertiveness and to maintain a military balance in the region. Nevertheless, as Nagao argues in his chapter, Japan's main concerns are in the East China Sea and the South China Sea, where it hopes it can receive more Indian support in reciprocity when Tokyo supports India in regards to the Sino-Indian border dispute, and by sharing the burden in maintaining maritime security in the Indian Ocean. The India–Japan security partnership can thus be seen as a system of dual hedging or soft balancing.[1] Similarly, from a Philippine perspective, DeCastro argues in his chapter that the security partnership with Japan for Manila effectively a 'classic diplomatic gambit of equi-balancing' by 'pitting one great power against another'.

As explained earlier, dependence on the Chinese economy is a central factor in explaining reluctance by some Southeast Asian countries to deepen security ties with Japan. In the future, if the Chinese move away from an export-led, manufacturing-based economy and towards a service-based economy, Indonesia,

Thailand, the Philippines, Myanmar and Vietnam might have a decreasing economic interest in China. Nagy argues in his chapter that this decline in economic dependency might lead to an intensification of bilateral security ties with Japan, as well as with Australia and India.

For Vietnam and Japan, Chinese military expansionism in the East and South China Seas is where Japanese and Vietnamese strategic interests converge. However, Vietnam recognises that Japan is currently more concerned about its interests in the East China Sea, which limits Japan's military engagement in the South China Sea. This is why Vietnam sees the need to further diversify its own security partnerships beyond Japan. On the other hand, close geographic proximity to China and high economic dependence require Vietnam to avoid hostile relations with China. As Koh argues in his chapter, Vietnam maintains some 'geopolitical buoyancy' for itself. However, as Grønning notes in his chapter, Japan does not want to provoke China even further by extending its influence into the South China Sea, because the Japan Coast Guard is already under immense pressure in the East China Sea. Therefore, a preferable option for Japan is to strengthen the capacity of Vietnam to resist Chinese coercion. At the same time this also boosts Japan's defence industry and economy.

For Europe, China is widely seen as an economic opportunity for its own investment, or as an economic challenge, such as when Chinese investment and business practices in Europe are seen as unfair and China is accused of dumping prices. Far less often, especially in comparison with Japan in recent years, do Europeans see China as posing a military threat. In part, this is due to the geographic distance separating Europe and China. Moreover, for Western European countries, with the notable exception of the UK and perhaps France, the lack of a long history of conflict and animosity, certainly in comparison with Sino-Japanese relations, facilitates the relationship. Chinese investment in Europe, on the other hand, has raised concerns about issues such as intellectual property rights and complaints that the Chinese market remains more difficult to penetrate for European companies than is the case for Chinese companies in Europe.

One often-mentioned example that illustrates the gap between European and Japanese threat perceptions towards China stems from the early 2000s, when the EU considered ending the weapons embargo it had imposed on China in 1989. Japan reacted by initiating regular exchanges through the framework of its dialogue with the EU in 2004 to put political pressure on Brussels not to lift the weapons embargo. Fukushima, in her chapter, argues that Japan sees the security relationship with the EU not predominantly in military terms, but as a flexible and dynamic process, whereby both sides can contribute to 'preventing conflicts and building peace', which Fukushima calls a 'hybrid peace'. In the end, the central reason why Japan wants to intensify its security ties with the EU is that it wants to build a more robust international order.

Conclusion

Europe has often been described (Whitman, 2011; Whitman and Wolff, 2012), and is predominantly seen by Japan, as a normative power. Given the lack of any concrete EU–Japanese policies directed at countering Beijing's unilateral territorial expansionism, Berkofsky, in his chapter concludes that Brussels will 'most probably continue to remain (very) reluctant to get involved in Asian territorial disputes beyond issuing statements urging all involved parties to solve disputes peacefully'. However, given Japanese fears of a future G-2 world order where power is shared between the US and China, or of a G-Zero world order (as proposed by Ian Bremmer (Bremmer, 2012; Bremmer and Roubini, 2011)), where no single superpower dominates world order, building closer ties with the other, or third, global powerhouse, the EU, does make sense for Japan.

While strategic cooperation in the Asia-Pacific region might not materialise any time soon, the fact that the EU and Japan have successfully engaged in practical cooperation through the counter-piracy mission off the coast of Somalia since 2009 has provided a valuable opportunity for both sides to exchange ideas, and to deepen trust and understanding. One indicator of the future significance of this military-to-military cooperation is that both sides have frequently mentioned the success of this mission during the EU–Japan Strategic Partnership Agreement (SPA) negotiations as an example for future EU–Japan collaboration towards other out-of-area security challenges and non-traditional security issues, including cyber-security, intelligence exchange, and the joint development and trade of military hardware and software. Given the withdrawal of the US from the Trans-Pacific Partnership under President Donald Trump, the successful conclusion of the EU–Japan Economic Partnership Agreement and SPA in 2017 has taken on even greater significance, and might in the long term weaken the centrality of the US for Japan.

Relevance and future trajectory of Japan's security partnerships

In conclusion, Japan's post-Cold War security partnerships do not constitute competing security structures to the US–Japan alliance, and do not directly serve to balance against Chinese military power in East Asia. These new alignments are flexible, and some may strengthen or weaken over time in reaction to moves by the US and China, or in reaction to the increase or decrease of security threats from countries such as North Korea or Russia, or emanating from regions such as the Middle East. Nonetheless, these security partnerships represent the cornerstone of Japan's new policy of seeking a structural diversification of its security relations and the omnidirectional development of security cooperation. They represent structural diversification because previously the US had been Japan's sole security partner. They represent omnidirectional development because they have implications for all forms of security, non-traditional as well as traditional.

Overall, these new security partnerships, by representing a departure from Japan's Cold War policy of focusing on the US as its sole security partner, offer Japan more options in its security policy to either indirectly strengthen the US–Japan alliance and the US military position in the Indo-Pacific region, which has been largely the way Tokyo has used these new security partnerships so far, or to hedge against the weakening of the alliance and the US will to maintain its regional military presence, or even as a means for pursuing a more independent security policy. The latter two options of hedging or pursuing a more independent security policy have so far not been conspicuously present in Japan's new partnerships. Nonetheless, given the increasing uncertainty and unpredictability of US leadership, as signalled by the launch of the Trump administration, hedging and greater security independence might become more prominent aspects of Japan's security partnerships in the years to come.

Increasing non-traditional security threats are a second factor that has spawned and strengthened these security partnerships over the last two decades, and will most likely continue to do so in the future. The terrorist attacks of 9/11 led to closer cooperation in combatting terrorism, not only between Japan and the US, but in similar ways also between Japan and other US-aligned actors. At about the same time, the increase of maritime piracy, first in Southeast Asia, led to the development of mechanisms for information exchange (i.e. ReCAAP's Information Sharing Centre) under Japanese leadership, an innovation just after the turn of the century that deepened confidence and trust between the countries involved, and later facilitated cooperation in other areas. The same could be said about Japan's involvement in the counter-piracy mission off the coast of Somalia, which has become one of the cornerstones of security practice between Japan and the EU, Australia and India. Cyber-attacks, emergency and disaster management, and emergencies or financial crimes are just some of the non-traditional security threats for which security partnerships are the ideal framework for cooperation, because they are flexible, are based on trust built from long-term cooperation in other areas, and do not openly balance against a specific adversary. However, long-term cooperation in countering traditional and non-traditional security threats offers numerous and multi-faceted opportunities for exchange, not just of government leaders, but also of government officials and bureaucrats, military personnel, businesses, private actors, and non-governmental organisations in multi-stakeholder or public–private forums. Fully utilising these opportunities will increase trust and understanding of the partner countries and their views, not just about the issue at hand, but also about more wide-ranging positions.

Conclusion

NOTE

1 Dual hedging is when a state hedges between two states simultaneously. The fact that Japan's and India's relative military capabilities, as well as their threat perceptions towards China, are high can explain increased hard hedging. Heginbotham and Samuels (2002) argued that Japan under Prime Minister Koizumi was using a dual hedge strategy towards the US after 9/11 out of fear of complicating its relationship with China. For the foundations of the debate on hedging in East Asia, see Evelyn Goh (2005 : xiii), who defines hedging as 'a set of strategies aimed at avoiding (or planning for contingencies in) a situation in which states cannot decide upon more straightforward alternatives such as balancing, bandwagoning, or neutrality. Instead they cultivate a middle position that forestalls or avoids having to choose one side at the obvious expense of another'. For a more recent assessment of hedging in East Asia, see Goh (2016); Lim and Cooper (2015); and Vidal and Pelegrín (2017).

REFERENCES

Bremmer, I., 2012. *Every Nation for Itself: Winners and Losers in a G-Zero World* (London: Portfolio/Penguin).

Bremmer, I. and Roubini, N., 2011. 'G-Zero World', *Foreign Affairs*, 90(2), at: www.foreignaffairs.com/articles/2011–01–31/g-zero-world (accessed 15 February 2018).

Goh, E., 2005. *Meeting the China Challenge: The U.S. in Southeast Asian Regional Security Strategies*, Policy Studies 16 (Washington: East-West Center Washington), at: www.eastwestcenter.org/publications/meeting-china-challenge-us-southeast-asian-regional-security-strategies.

Goh, E., 2016. 'Southeast Asian Strategies toward the Great Powers: Still Hedging after All These Years?', *Theasanforum.org*, 22 February, at: www.theasanforum.org/southeast-asian-strategies-toward-the-great-powers-still-hedging-after-all-these-years.

Heginbotham, E. and Samuels, R. J., 2002. 'Japan's Dual Hedge', *Foreign Affairs*, 81: 110–121.

Lim, D. J. and Cooper, Z., 2015. 'Reassessing Hedging: The Logic of Alignment in East Asia', *Security Studies*, 24(4): 696–727, doi:10.1080/09636412.2015.1103130.

Snyder, G. H., 1984. 'The Security Dilemma in Alliance Politics', *World Politics*, 36(4): 461–495, doi:10.2307/2010183.

Snyder, G. H., 2007. *Alliance Politics*, Cornell Studies in Security Affairs (Ithaca, NY: Cornell University Press).

Vidal, L. L. and Pelegrín, A., 2017. 'Hedging against China: Japanese Strategy towards a Rising Power', *Asian Security*, 0(0): 1–19, doi:10.1080/14799855.2017.1333983.

Whitman, R. G. (ed.), 2011. *Normative Power Europe* (Basingstoke: Palgrave Macmillan), doi:10.1057/9780230305601.

Whitman, R. G. and Wolff, S., 2012. 'The EU as a Global Conflict Manager: Reflections on the Past, Perspectives for the Future', in Whitman, R. G. and Wolff, S. (eds), *The European Union as a Global Conflict Manager* (New York: Routledge), pp. 211–220.

Appendix: List of important multilateral and bilateral security-related agreements

I. Japan–Australia

2006	Trilateral Strategic Dialogue Joint Statement Australia–Japan–United States
2007	Japan–Australia Joint Foreign and Defence Ministerial Consultations Joint Statement (June 2007)
2007	Japan–Australia Joint Declaration on Security Cooperation (September 2007)
2008	Memorandum on Defence Cooperation between JMOD and DoD Australia (December 2008)
2009	Action Plan to implement the Japan–Australia Joint Declaration on Security Cooperation (December 2009)
2010	Japan–Australia Acquisition and Cross-Servicing Agreement (May 2010) (Extended in January 2017)
2012	Japan–Australia Information Security Agreement (ISA) (May 2012)
2014	Agreement: Transfer of Defense Equipment and Technology (March 2014)
2014	Japan–Australia Economic Partnership Agreement (July 2014)

II. Japan–India

2008	Joint Declaration on Security Cooperation between Japan and India (22 October 2008)
2009	Action Plan to Advance Security Cooperation based on the Joint Declaration on Security Cooperation between Japan and India (29 December 2009)
2011	Comprehensive Economic Partnership Agreement between Japan and the Republic of India (February 2011)
2014	Tokyo Declaration for Japan–India Special Strategic and Global Partnership (September 2014)

III. Japan–East Asia

2008	ASEAN–Japan Comprehensive Economic Partnership Agreement (April 2008)
2009	Japan–Philippines Economic Partnership Agreement (December 2009)
2009	Agreement between Japan and the Socialist Republic of Viet Nam for an Economic Partnership (October 2009)

Appendix

2014	The ASEAN–Japan Joint Declaration for Cooperation to Combat Terrorism and Transnational Crime (November 2014)
2015	Japan–Philippines Joint Declaration: A Strengthened Strategic Partnership for Advancing the Shared Principles and Goals of Peace, Security, and Growth in the Region and Beyond (June 2015)

IV. Japan–Europe and NATO

1991	Joint Declaration on Relations between the European Community and its Member States and Japan (July 1991)
2001	Japan–EU Action Plan (2001–2010)
2010	Agreement between the Government of Japan and the NATO on the Security of Information and Material (June 2010)
2013	Japan–France Joint Statement: An 'exceptional partnership' for promoting security, growth, innovation and culture (June 2013)
2013	Japan–EU Strategic Partnership Agreement (beginning of negotiations)
2014	UK–Japan Joint Statement: A Dynamic Strategic Partnership for the 21st Century (May 2014)
2015	Japan–France Foreign and Defense Minister's Meeting Joint Communique (March 2015)
2016	Second Japan–UK Foreign and Defence Ministerial Meeting Joint Statement (January 2016)
2017	Japan–France Foreign and Defense Ministers' Meeting Joint Communique (January 2017)
2017	EU-Japan Economic Partnership Agreement (EPA) finalized (December).

INDEX

abandonment 1, 11, 89, 96, 98, 100, 101, 106, 237
Abe, Shinzō (Japanese prime minister) 9, 20, 24, 27, 36, 41, 60–1, 68–70, 75, 82, 112, 122–3, 130, 136–9, 142–4, 149, 176–9, 192–3, 206, 209–10
Acquisition and Cross-Servicing Agreement 6, 210
Act East policy 65–6
Afghanistan 1, 75, 84, 192–5, 197, 226
Asian Infrastructure Investment Bank 30, 48
Asian Regional Forum (ARF) 2, 22, 47, 89, 96
Aso, Taro 190, 226
Australia National Security Committee 41

China
  military modernization 28, 76–7, 113, 164, 174, 178, 239, 240–1
  China gap 9, 28, 36, 37, 46, 48, 49, 50, 238
Churchill, Winston (British prime minister) 41
collective self-defence 2, 22, 25, 45, 180–1, 196, 210, 230
confidence-building measures 2, 4, 208
constitution of Japan 2, 180, 229–30
  reinterpretation of 5, 99
counter-piracy 6, 13, 63, 75–6, 82, 103–5, 157–60, 178, 219–35, 241–2
cybersecurity 3

diplomatic dialogue 5, 236
Djibouti 221, 223, 226–31

Duterte, Rodrigo (Philippine president) 122

East China Sea 38–40, 47, 67–8, 74–8, 80, 85, 132–5, 155, 174–81, 213–14, 239–40
Economic Partnership Agreement 21, 25, 188, 203, 231, 241
entrapment 1, 96, 106, 237–8
EU Commission 4, 204–5, 230
EU Mission Atalanta 208, 222–6, 229
Exclusive Economic Zone 122, 136, 150

Fukuda Doctrine 90–4

Hashimoto Doctrine 11, 89, 97–9
hedging 5, 11, 30, 32, 89, 95, 106, 114–26, 131, 237–9, 242

Indo-Pacific 42, 63–5, 68–9, 75, 85, 149, 237–9, 242
International Peace Support Bill 4, 230
isolationism 1, 89, 90, 92, 105–6

Japanese Coast Guard 105, 133, 158
Japanese nationalism 173, 179–81
John Kerry 65

Koizumi, Junichiro (Japan prime minister) 59–61, 104

Malabar exercise 47, 57, 65–6
military-to-military 5, 104, 219, 226–8, 236
Modi, Narendra (Indian prime minister) 60, 64–70
multilateralism 39, 105, 89–95, 102–6, 237–8

Index

National Defense Program Guidelines (NDPG) 2–3, 136, 176, 230
National Security Strategy (NSS) 2–3, 175, 187, 230
North Atlantic Treaty Organization (NATO) 3, 187
North Korea (DPRK) 6, 62, 66–7, 97, 101–2, 112, 237, 241

Obama, Barrack (US president) 39, 62, 65, 178

Philippines 2, 6, 8, 10–12, 23, 43–5, 68, 75, 82, 113–45, 150, 164, 239–40

Regional Cooperation Agreement on Combating Piracy and Armed Robbery against Ships in Asia (ReCAAP) 2, 105, 225, 229, 242
Republic of Korea 3, 6, 8, 23–4, 31, 91, 99–102, 137, 188, 228
rule of law 3, 21–3, 31, 113, 137, 154–6, 176–7, 187, 190, 222
Russia 1, 6, 8, 26, 59, 93–4, 98–100, 197–8, 214, 231–2, 241

security alignment 5, 9, 20, 23–4, 29–32, 117, 145, 177–8, 241
security architecture 9, 22, 31, 39, 57, 237
security diplomacy 13, 37–40, 42, 173
security legislation 2, 4, 12, 159, 180, 230
Self-Defense Forces (SDF)
  Air Self-Defense Force 37
  deployment 9, 44, 59, 77, 93, 140, 144–5, 159–60, 189, 211, 220–1, 226, 229, 230
  Ground-Self-Defense Force 9, 25, 139
  joint exercises 25, 46, 48, 84, 140, 144, 194, 208, 230
  Maritime Self-Defense Force (MSDF) 1, 12, 43–5, 92, 105, 130, 137, 158, 178–80, 193, 208, 219–20, 225
Senkaku Islands 37, 39, 47, 68, 120, 133, 135–6, 145, 156, 162, 174
South China Sea 65, 175, 178
South Korea (ROK) 1, 8, 31, 91, 99–102, 131, 137, 188, 206, 225

territorial conflict 1, 8, 12, 22, 28, 37, 68, 74, 115–38, 143–4, 162, 174–7, 180, 206–15, 241
terrorism 62, 67, 75, 103–4, 143, 160, 192, 198, 209, 210, 221, 231, 242
trilateral security cooperation 6, 27, 29, 32, 215
Trump, D. (US president) 232, 237, 241–2
Turnbull, Malcolm 27, 29, 41, 42
two-plus-two 6, 8, 39, 41, 47, 65, 210, 225

United Nations Convention on the Law of the Sea (UNCLOS) 38, 68, 118, 199, 220, 222
United Nations Peace Keeping Operations (UNPKO) 43, 83, 140, 220

weapons of mass destruction 23, 66, 188, 205, 211

EU authorised representative for GPSR:
Easy Access System Europe, Mustamäe tee 50,
10621 Tallinn, Estonia
gpsr.requests@easproject.com

www.ingramcontent.com/pod-product-compliance
Lightning Source LLC
Chambersburg PA
CBHW070237240426
43673CB00044B/1821